BANK REGULATION, RISK MANAGEMENT, AND COMPLIANCE

Bank Regulation, Risk Management, and Compliance is a concise yet comprehensive treatment of the primary areas of US banking regulation – micro-prudential, macro-prudential, financial consumer protection, and AML/CFT regulation – and their associated risk management and compliance systems. The book's focus is the US, but its prolific use of standards published by the Basel Committee on Banking Supervision and frequent comparisons with UK and EU versions of US regulation offer a broad perspective on global bank regulation and expectations for internal governance.

The book establishes a conceptual framework that helps readers to understand bank regulators' expectations for the risk management and compliance functions. Informed by the author's experience at a major credit rating agency in helping to design and implement a ratings compliance system, it explains how the banking business model, through credit extension and credit intermediation, creates the principal risks that regulation is designed to mitigate: credit, interest rate, market, and operational risk, and, more broadly, systemic risk. The book covers, in a single volume, the four areas of bank regulation and supervision and the associated regulatory expectations and firms' governance systems. Readers desiring to study the subject in a unified manner have needed to separately consult specialized treatments of their areas of interest, resulting in a fragmented grasp of the subject matter. Banking regulation has a cohesive unity due in large part to national authorities' agreement to follow global standards and to the homogenizing effects of the integrated global financial markets.

The book is designed for legal, risk, and compliance banking professionals; students in law, business, and other finance-related graduate programs; and finance professionals generally who want a reference book on bank regulation, risk management, and compliance. It can serve both as a primer for entry-level finance professionals and as a reference guide for seasoned risk and compliance officials, senior management, and regulators and other policymakers. Although the book's focus is bank regulation, its coverage of corporate governance, risk management, compliance, and management of conflicts of interest in financial institutions has broad application in other financial services sectors.

Alexander Dill is Lecturer in the Financial Mathematics Program at the University of Chicago and Lecturer in Law at the UCLA School of Law. He is a recognized expert on the financial markets and the regulatory, risk management, and compliance frameworks that apply to them. He worked in the finance industry for nearly 30 years, first in private corporate law practice and subsequently at the US Securities and Exchange Commission and Moody's Investors Service.

PRACTICAL FINANCE AND BANKING GUIDES

Consumer Credit: Law and Practice
Second edition
Alexander Hill-Smith

Bank Regulation, Risk Management, and Compliance
Theory, Practice, and Key Problem Areas
Alexander Dill

For more information about this series, please visit:
www.routledge.com/law/series/PFBG

BANK REGULATION, RISK MANAGEMENT, AND COMPLIANCE

THEORY, PRACTICE, AND KEY PROBLEM AREAS

ALEXANDER DILL

informa law
from Routledge

First published 2020
by Informa Law from Routledge
2 Park Square, Milton Park, Abingdon, Oxon OX14 4RN

and by Informa Law from Routledge
52 Vanderbilt Avenue, New York, NY 10017

Informa Law from Routledge is an imprint of the Taylor & Francis Group, an informa business

British Library Cataloguing-in-Publication Data
A catalogue record for this book is available from the British Library

Library of Congress Cataloging-in-Publication Data
A catalog record for this book has been requested

ISBN: 978-0-367-36749-7 (hbk)
ISBN: 978-0-429-35116-7 (ebk)

Typeset in Times New Roman
by Apex CoVantage, LLC

To Jessica,
my life's North Star

CONTENTS

LIST OF FIGURES

LIST OF TABLES

LIST OF ABBREVIATIONS

3LOD	three lines of defense
ABCP	asset-backed commercial paper
ABS	asset-backed securities
AIG	American International Group
A-IRB	advanced internal ratings-based approach
ALLL	allowance for loan and lease losses
ALM	asset liability management
AML	anti-money laundering
AML/CFT	anti-money laundering and combatting the financing of terrorism
ARCH	assessment of risk of consumer harm
ATM	automated teller machine
BCBS	Basel Committee on Banking Supervision
BCBS 239	BCBS guidance on data aggregation and risk reporting
BHC	bank holding company
BIS	Bank for International Settlements
BoE	Bank of England
BRRD	Bank Recovery and Resolution Directive
BSA	Bank Secrecy Act
BUCO	business unit compliance officer
CAE	chief audit executive
CAMELS	Capital Adequacy, Asset Quality, Management, Earnings, Liquidity, Sensitivity to Market Risk
CCAR	Comprehensive Capital Analysis and Review
CCF	credit conversion factor
CCO	chief compliance officer
CCP	central counterparty
CCPA	Consumer Credit Protection Act
CCR	counterparty credit risk
CCyB	countercyclical capital buffer
CDD	customer due diligence
CDO	collateralized debt obligation
CDS	credit default swap
CEO	chief executive officer
CET1	common equity tier 1 capital

CFPB	Consumer Financial Protection Bureau
CFR	Code of Federal Regulations
CFTC	Commodity Futures Trading Commission
CIP	customer identification program
CLA	Consumer Leasing Act
CLAR	Comprehensive Liquidity Analysis and Review
CMP	civil monetary penalty
CMS	compliance management system
COI	conflict of interest
COPPA	Children's Online Privacy Protection Act
COSO	Committee of Sponsoring Organizations of the Treadway Commission
CRA	Community Reinvestment Act
CRC	country risk classification
CRM	comprehensive risk measure
CRO	chief risk officer
CTR	Currency Transaction Report
CVA	credit value adjustment
DFAST	Dodd-Frank Annual Stress Testing
DLT	distributed ledger technology
DOJ	Department of Justice
DPA	deferred prosecution agreement
EAD	exposure at default
ECB	European Central Bank
ECOA	Equal Credit Opportunity Act
EFA	Expedited Funds Availability Act
EFTA	Electronic Fund Transfer Act
EPS	enhanced prudential standards
ERM	enterprise risk management
ES	espected shortfall
eSLR	enhanced supplementary leverage ratio
EU	European Union
FASB	Financial Accounting Standards Board
FATF	Financial Action Task Force
FBO	Foreign Banking Organization
FCA	Financial Conduct Authority
FCRA	Fair Credit Reporting Act
FDIC	Federal Deposit Insurance Corporation
FDICIA	FDIC Improvement Act
FFIEC	Federal Financial Institutions Examination Council
FHA	Fair Housing Act
FHC	financial holding company
FinCEN	Financial Crimes Enforcement Network
FMI	financial market infrastructure
FMU	Financial Market Utility

FOMC	Federal Open Market Committee
FPC	Financial Policy Committee
FR	Federal Register
FRB	Federal Reserve Board
FRBNY	Federal Reserve Board of New York
FRTB	Fundamental Review of Trading Book
FSA	Financial Services Authority
FSB	Financial Stability Board
FSOC	Financial Stability Oversight Council
FT	financing of terrorism
G20	Group of Twenty
GAAP	Generally Accepted Accounting Principles
GFC	Global Financial Crisis
GSE	government-sponsored enterprise
G-SIB	global systemically important bank
HMDA	Home Mortgage Disclosure Act
HPA	Homeowners Protection Act
HQLA	high-quality liquid assets
HVCRE	high-volatility commercial real estate
IC	internal control
ICB	independent commission on banking
IHC	intermediate holding company
IIA	Institute of Internal Auditors
IMA	internal models approach
IMCR	Individual Minimum Capital Ratio
IRC	incremental risk charge
IRM	independent risk management
ISO	International Organization for Standardization
IT	information technology
KYC	know your customer
LCR	liquidity coverage ratio
LFI	large financial institution
LGD	loss given default
LIBOR	London Interbank Offered Rate
LISCC	Large Institution Supervision Coordinating Committee
LLC	limited liability company
LTD	long-term debt
M&A	mergers and acquisitions
MBS	mortgage-backed securities
MIS	management information system
ML	money laundering
MLO	mortgage loan originator
MPOE	multiple points of entry
MRA	Matter Requiring Attention
MRIA	Matter Requiring Immediate Attention

MRM	model risk management
NCA	national competent authority
NCUA	National Credit Union Administration
NII	net interest income
NPA	non-prosecution agreement
NSFR	net stable funding ratio
NYSE	New York Stock Exchange
OCC	Office of the Comptroller of the Currency
OECD	Organization for Economic Co-operation and Development
OFAC	Office of Foreign Assets Control
OLA	Orderly Liquidation Authority
OTC	over-the-counter
P&Ps	policies and procedures
PCA	Prompt Corrective Action
PD	probability of default
PEP	politically exposed person
PMI	private mortgage insurance
PRA	Prudential Regulation Authority
QCCP	central counterparty
RAF	risk appetite framework
RAROC	risk-adjusted return on capital
RAS	risk appetite statement
RENTD	reasonably expected near term demand
RESPA	Real Estate Settlement Procedures Act
RFPA	Right to Financial Privacy Act
ROE	report of examination
RWA	risk-weighted assets
S&L	savings and loan association
SAFE Act	Secure and Fair Enforcement for Mortgage Licensing Act
SAR	Suspicious Activity Report
SCAP	Supervisory Capital Assessment Program
SEC	Securities and Exchange Commission
SEF	Swap Execution Facility
SFA	supervisory formula approach
SIFI	systemically important financial institution
SIV	structured investment vehicle
SLR	supplementary leverage ratio
SPOE	single point of entry
SRM	Single Resolution Mechanism
SRO	self-regulatory organization
SRP	Supervisory Assessment of Recovery and Resolution Preparedness
SSFA	simplified supervisory formula approach
SSG	Senior Supervisors Group
SSM	Single Supervisory Mechanism
SVaR	stressed Value-at-Risk

TBTF	too big to fail
TILA	Truth in Lending Act
TISA	Truth in Savings Act
TLAC	total loss-absorbing capacity
UDAAP	unfair, deceptive, or abusive acts or practice
UDAP	unfair or deceptive acts or practice
UK	United Kingdom
US	United States
USC	United States Code
USSG	United States Sentencing Guidelines
VaR	Value-at-Risk
WWR	wrong-way risk

TABLE OF LEGAL SOURCES

Note: Statutes, regulations, agency guidance, and international standards are listed below. Certain official publications, including officials' speeches, are not considered official guidance and are listed as References.

INTERNATIONAL

Guidance and Standards

UNITED KINGDOM

Statutory

Guidance

EUROPEAN UNION

Statutory

Guidance

UNITED STATES

Statutory Law - Federal

Regulatory Actions and Judicial Decisions

Guidance - Examination and Enforcement Manuals

Guidance - Other

Statistical Data

NOTE ABOUT THE AUTHOR

Alexander Dill has worked in the finance industry since 1986. He is Lecturer in the University of Chicago's Financial Mathematics Program and Lecturer in Law at the UCLA School of Law. Before joining UCLA in 2019, he was Senior Research Fellow in the Institute for Compliance in Financial Markets at the Chicago-Kent College of Law. He spent most of his career at Moody's Investors Service, from 1996 to 2015. At Moody's, he was Head of Global Covenant Research, which publishes reports on legal protections in corporate high-yield bond and leveraged loan transactions, and previous to that was Global Ratings Compliance Officer for Structured Finance. He also was a Senior Credit Officer in Moody's Structured Finance Group, where he rated a wide variety of traditional and esoteric asset classes and bank-supported liquidity structures. Prior to Moody's, he was a Branch Chief in Trading Practices in the Division of Trading and Markets at the US Securities and Exchange Commission in Washington, DC. He began his law career in New York, specializing in secured lending, bankruptcy issues, and bank regulatory matters. He holds an AB from Harvard University, an MA from Columbia University, and a JD from Emory University School of Law, where he was Executive Articles Editor of the *Emory Law Journal*.

ACKNOWLEDGMENTS

Many people have helped me bring this book to fruition. My debts lie in the intellectual impetus that I have received and the support and institutional resources permitting me to conceive of the ideas underlying the book, develop and deepen my understanding of the subject matter, and ultimately complete the book for publication.

The kernel for a book on the regulation of financial firms and their internal governance was a seed planted by Todd Henderson of the University of Chicago Law School. His advice and intellectual nous in the law of financial services set me on the path to eventually write the book in its present form. Todd also provided invaluable practical guidance on writing a book that has a dual use as a practitioners' guide and as a student textbook. I also am thankful for the insights of Charles Senatore of Fidelity, a widely known industry expert on financial institution compliance. Todd, Charles, and I had stimulating discussions on the most effective pedagogical approach to conveying the basic precepts of financial institution compliance.

Several institutions provided the stimulus and intellectual environment that was critical for developing my knowledge of the subject matter and the theses that underlie this book. First and foremost, I owe thanks to the people who run the Financial Mathematics Program of the University of Chicago. The course material I developed for the program, on model risk management; capital adequacy regulation for credit, market, and operational risk; the resolution regime under Basel III and the Dodd-Frank Act; corporate governance issues unique to financial institutions; and the associated areas of risk management and compliance, forms the book's substantive core. Moreover, teaching this course and conveying a complex subject to quantitatively oriented students in an accessible format compelled me to continually test my own understanding of the subject. I owe thanks to Kevin Corlette, director of the program at the time of my hiring, who marshalled me through the curriculum approval process. I also owe thanks to Roger Lee, the current director, and to Mark Hendricks, associate director, who have provided me resources and support as a course instructor. I also thank Lisheng Su, my teaching assistant, who was a sounding board on the practical aspects of model risk management and the Federal Reserve examination process for stress testing.

ACKNOWLEDGMENTS

I am grateful to the Chicago-Kent College of Law, and to Harold Krent, the school's dean, and to Felice Batlan, director of its Institute for Compliance in Financial Markets, who gave me the opportunity to teach core doctrinal law courses on securities regulation and business organizations, and ultimately the capstone compliance course in the Compliance Institute. In these courses, I was able to develop my argument that understanding a firm's business model – the basis for its revenue generation – and its associated risks is essential in meeting regulatory expectations in the design of a risk management and compliance system. Finally, I thank Elijah Brewer, chair of the Finance Department at Driehaus College of Business at DePaul University, for giving me the opportunity to teach money and banking to DePaul's undergraduate finance majors. Preparing for and teaching this course has helped me to develop my understanding of the economics of banking and the banking business model.

As I researched and began writing the book, numerous people helped me to deepen my thinking through conversations or comments on the manuscript. I owe special thanks to Anil Kashyap, professor of economics and finance at the University of Chicago's Booth School of Business, who helped direct me toward productive avenues of research and away from unproductive ones, and who gave me a more nuanced understanding of the regulation of systemic risk. Conversations with Ingo Walter, professor of economics at New York University's Stern School, helped develop my understanding of conduct risk from an economist's perspective. The book employs his taxonomy of conflicts in financial institutions. Special thanks are owed to Shohini Kundu, a PhD graduate student at Booth who read the manuscript with a specific focus on my formulation of the economics of financial markets and institutions. Victor Hong, a former senior risk management executive, gave me an insider's insights into the practical problems facing professionals in the control functions at financial conglomerates and how Dodd-Frank has transformed risk management, for better and for worse.

I am in special debt to two scholars in fields with which the book is concerned. Sean Griffith, chair in Business Law and director of the Fordham Corporate Law Center, at the Fordham University School of Law, read the entire manuscript and provided invaluable comments on the corporate governance aspects of risk management and compliance and the impact of federal prosecutorial policy on the compliance function. He helped me to refine the book's thesis on the interaction of external government mandates and firms' internal governance. Sean is a leading proponent of one of the two dominant theories of compliance that figure in the book. I also owe special thanks to Jeremy Kress of the University of Michigan's Ross School of Business. Jeremy's deep understanding of Federal Reserve Board rulemaking and guidance on risk management provided invaluable insights that significantly improved the book, in both its technical and substantive aspects.

I am especially grateful to the editorial staff at Routledge, in particular Law Editor Amy Jones, who provided wise counsel on how to bring the manuscript to the light of day, and to Caroline Church, senior editorial assistant, and Naomi Hill, editorial assistant. They were incredibly patient and understanding about my travails in ultimately delivering the manuscript.

ACKNOWLEDGMENTS

My greatest gratitude is to my family, and to my wife, Jessica, most of all, for her constant support and advice in writing the book. Having been in the academic world much longer than I have, her sense of protocol in succeeding in this world has guided me unswervingly in the right direction. Lastly, I owe thanks to my children, Anthea and James, for being so patient with their father as I labored away for so many long hours on the manuscript at home and at school.

Introduction

A transformation of governing assumptions

The global financial crisis of 2007–09 (GFC) forced policymakers, economists, financial commentators, and other market participants to rethink their governing assumptions on how the financial markets operate. Prior to the crisis, a market-based ethos had informed regulators' approach to banks and other financial institutions. Firms were self-regulating and markets were self-correcting. Financial firms knew their risks best and how to manage them. A colloquy between a Federal Reserve Board (FRB) governor and a University of Chicago economist in a 2005 conference of global policymakers reflected the dominant philosophy. In a rejoinder to Raghuram Rajan's warning about the buildup of systemic risk and instability in the financial markets, Governor Donald Kohn expressed the opinion of the vast majority of attendees: 'By allowing institutions to diversify risk, to choose their risk profiles more precisely, and to improve the management of the risks they do take on, they have made institutions more robust'.[1] This confidence in the financial markets' ability to self-regulate was evidenced in the US's bipartisan-backed deregulation of OTC derivatives in 2000,[2] the UK's 'light-touch' philosophy of supervision, and many other areas of financial regulation.

The GFC transformed the prevailing consensus about financial institutions and markets and how best to regulate them. Global policymakers' searing experience in the liquidity and credit crisis in 2008 and the Great Recession converted them into severe skeptics regarding firms' incentives and ability to prudently manage their own risks. The change in ethos deeply affected the regulatory framework and systems of supervisory oversight. The global standard setter for banking regulation, the Basel Committee on Banking Supervision (BCBS), refocused its priorities squarely on the problem of systemic risk in finalizing the Basel III standards. The US Congress in 2010 passed the Dodd-Frank Wall Street Reform and Consumer Protection Act (Dodd-Frank),[3] the most far-reaching financial regulation

---

1 Donald Kohn, 'Commentary: has financial development made the world riskier?', Federal Reserve Bank of Kansas City (2005).
2 Commodity Futures Modernization Act of 2000, Pub. L. No. 106–554, 114 Stat. 2763 (2000).
3 Pub. L. No. 111–203, 124 Stat. 1376 (2010).

since the 1930s. The EU centralized oversight of financial services and resolution of 'too big to fail' (TBTF) firms. The transformation was most evident in the UK, which undertook a root-and-branch overhaul of its financial supervisory structure.

Showing their hard-won sense of distrust, global policymakers adopted a more prescriptive regulatory framework and a more invasive supervisory approach to firms' internal governance practices. The changeover to a Republican administration has not fundamentally altered the basic assumptions underlying the new approach. The FRB recently issued detailed guidance on board effectiveness,[4] the role and accountability of senior and line management, and even technical elements of an effective risk management framework.[5]

Themes in bank regulation and banks' internal governance

Three major themes run throughout this book.

1 Cooptation of corporate governance

First, even before the crisis, policymakers had been increasingly incorporating key components of firms' corporate governance systems into their regulatory expectations. This continued a trend from a 'regulatory' to a 'supervisory' regime that had begun with the emergence of the multiservice financial conglomerate in the 1980s.[6] In addition, regulators increasingly imposed legal obligations on financial holding companies such as guarantees of regulated subsidiaries' obligations in order to 'transfer front-line supervisory responsibility from governmental agencies to the holding companies'.[7] The growing reliance on firms' corporate governance to control their risks was international in dimension.[8] However, the post-crisis assumptions concerning banks' corporate governance differ in essential ways. Only in the post-crisis period did policymakers fully realize the extent to which boards' and senior management's preoccupation with maximizing shareholder value could undermine their duty to maintain franchise value through risk controls and other governance safeguards. Regulators now needed to more affirmatively address core elements of banks' systems of internal corporate governance so that business strategy did not outpace risk management capabilities.

4 Proposed Guidance on Supervisory Expectations for Boards of Directors, 82 Federal Register 37219 (9 August 2017).

5 Proposed Supervisory Guidance, 83 Federal Register 1351 (11 January 2018).

6 A shift has occurred from a bank regulatory system resting principally on generally applicable rules toward a 'supervisory approach' emphasizing particularized review of a specific bank. Daniel Tarullo, *Banking on Basel: The Future of International Financial Regulation* (Peterson Institute: 2008) 15.

7 Howell Jackson, 'The expanding obligations of financial holding companies' (1994), 107 *Harvard Law Review* 507, 513.

8 See, e.g., Basel Committee on Banking Supervision, 'Enhancing corporate governance for banking organizations' (1999); Organization for Economic Co-operation and Development, 'OECD principles of corporate governance' (1999); Basel Committee on Banking Supervision, 'Framework for internal control systems for banking organizations' (1998).

Dodd-Frank codified the new approach in several ways. This includes mandating risk committees and chief risk officers (CROs) in the large bank holding companies with firm-wide scope of authority, independence, and credibility; rigorous forward-looking stress testing, which had so successfully pulled the credit markets out of their deep malaise in spring 2009; and resolution plans, or 'living wills', that require banking firms to reconfigure corporate operations to ensure their orderly wind down. These reforms, and subsequent FRB guidance on effective corporate governance and risk management, were designed to compel boards and management to think programmatically in building an effective risk management infrastructure on an enterprise-wide basis. Enforcement actions also reflect the new post-crisis approach to corporate governance. In 2018, the FRB took the unprecedented action of publicly chastising the former CEO and board chair of a global systemically important bank (G-SIB) for putting sales quotas ahead of risk controls and halting the firm's growth until its risk management capabilities catch up to its risk appetite.[9]

2 Tensions between banks' business models and regulatory mandates

The second theme, related to the first, concerns the challenges firms face in meeting the banking agencies' expectations when these expectations interfere directly with business models and strategy. The imperatives of banks' models of revenue generation are often in a state of tension with the constraints placed on them by many bank regulations. This is to be expected. However, in some cases, regulations place significant limits on business drivers due to the high level of compliance risk the underlying activity creates. These tensions are distinct from conflicts of interest (COIs) between agents, such as senior managers, and their principals, the shareholders, that are pervasive in financial institutions. Risk managers and compliance professionals need to factor in these tensions and understand their origins in designing, implementing, and enforcing internal controls (ICs) and compliance processes, policies, and procedures.

The book cites many instances where the tension is at its sharpest. Capital regulation is the most obvious case in point. Post-GFC capital requirements, particularly for the large banking organizations, significantly exceed the amount of 'economic capital' that firms' risk-return analysis deems optimal. Firms seek to minimize the amount of capital on their balance sheet to meet their target return on equity. Capital arbitrage, which seeks to bring regulatory capital in line with a firm's estimate of economic capital, is within risk management's and compliance's remit in a for-profit business. In fact, the structure of Basel III/Dodd-Frank's risk-based methodology allows and even incentivizes banks to minimize regulatory capital by optimizing portfolio allocation. Another example is Basel III/Dodd-Frank's liquidity regulation. The liquidity rule constrains banks' ability to generate net interest income – a key indicator of bank profitability – by

---

9 Federal Reserve Board, 'Accountability as chair of Wells Fargo & company board of directors', Letter to John Stumpf (2 February 2018).

requiring a specific amount of highly liquid assets, which limits the amount they can invest in high-yielding assets. Still another example is anti-money laundering and combatting the financing of terrorism (AML/CFT) law. Banks need to make a risk-return trade-off between the high costs of an AML/CFT risk management and compliance program and the revenue-rich business lines involving foreign correspondent banking relationships. However, unlike capital regulation, banks have little leeway in arbitraging AML/CFT regulation.

Such decision making, including arbitraging for a 'least cost' solution to capital requirements, occurs within a standard risk management practice in large banking firms. A firm assesses whether a given business strategy is within its 'risk appetite', a board-determined level of risk a firm is willing to accept in the pursuit of shareholder wealth maximization and in theory consistent with shareholder risk preferences. The firm will invest in risk controls until the level of inherent risk, the risk before accounting for ICs, reaches a level of 'residual risk' consistent with this risk appetite. Inherent compliance risk is particularly high in consumer financial products, which include account services, implicating both consumer protection and AML/CFT regulation. FRB guidance that firms' business strategies should not exceed their risk management capabilities implicitly acknowledges firms' risk-return optimization analysis.

3 Flexibility and broad variety of means in conveying regulatory expectations

Third, regulators employ a broad array of means to convey regulatory expectations, both for the industry and for each banking organization individually. In the US, the system of regulation and supervision is adaptable, flexible, and generally effective despite its balkanized supervisory structure. A 'pyramid of regulatory expectations' in Chapter 2 (see subsection 2.7.3) illustrates how expectations increase in granularity and adaptability as one travels from the apex, which contains relatively fixed statutory law and regulation, toward the pyramid's base, where supervisory guidance allows firms to more effectively quantify their compliance cost and compliance risk and more confidently construct internal governance systems. At the base, agencies also have a panoply of flexible means to address emerging trends, such as cyber risk, initially through industry alerts, speeches, and strategically selected enforcement actions based on existing, broadly framed principles before lawmakers eventually address such risks.

Dodd-Frank grants only limited authority to the agencies to explicitly regulate risk management. The mandate for risk committees and CROs is the exception. This congressional forbearance is hard to justify given the role risk management failures played in the crisis.[10] Nonetheless, as noted, in their supervisory capacity the agencies have issued specific guidance on the substantive operational aspects

---

10 Stephen Bainbridge, *Corporate Governance after the Financial Crisis* (OUP: 2012) 176. However, this reticence, including the SEC's limited rulemaking on risk management, may be justified due to the close relationship between risk-taking and boards' business judgment and the evolving state of the risk management profession. Ibid. 177.

of this function, and more general guidance on other aspects of bank holding company (BHC) corporate governance. The agencies have developed a sophisticated supervisory apparatus as financial institutions have grown in size and become more organizationally complex. The FRB created the Large Institution Supervision Coordinating Committee (LISCC) in 2010 to tap internal expertise across the Federal Reserve System in order to effectively oversee the largest financial institutions in the core areas of regulatory concern.[11]

To be sure, each area of bank regulation has a unique framework and oversight mechanism designed to achieve a specific regulatory objective. Prudential regulation has a largely principles-based framework with broad supervisory powers. Consumer protection and AML/CFT regulation is generally rules-based. This difference arises largely from the nature of the underlying business and corresponding regulatory objective – safety and soundness and fair and transparent business conduct, respectively. Client-facing businesses involve recurring types of conduct that detailed, prescriptive rules are well suited to regulate. In contrast, oversight of the financial condition of banks' franchise and management of credit, liquidity, market, and operational risk calls for a high degree of discretion under the safety and soundness standard.

Nevertheless, when appropriate, the principles- and rules-based approaches are frequently combined to achieve a regulatory objective. Broadly, the safety and soundness rationale preserves prudential action in consumer protection and AML/CFT laws as it does in all areas of bank regulation. Similarly, the prescriptive compliance provisions of the Volcker rule prohibiting proprietary trading include an 'anti-evasion' prudential backstop.

Another aspect of regulators' creative approach in formulating and communicating expectations is their strategic use of non-transparency. They have learned when to hold their cards close to their vest. Hewed to a fine art by central bankers, such a strategy has played an important role in post-crisis rulemaking and banking supervision. Making too much information available on loss projections and advance publishing of the FRB's stress testing models could enable firms to reverse engineer the stress tests. The banks need to learn how to manage their risks, but they will not if regulators give them the answers to the test.[12] In its stress tests the FRB can reject banks' capital plans on either quantitative grounds, if projected losses erode capital below the regulatory minimum, or qualitative grounds, including risk management weaknesses. It has frequently done so for the latter reason despite the fact that a bank's capital in severely adverse scenarios was well in excess of the regulatory minimum. A similar dynamic is at play in

---

11 LISCC's broad remit includes supervision of systemically important firms' capital, liquidity, resolution planning, and the effectiveness of their corporate governance system in managing risk. The current LISCC firms are all bank holding companies.

12 Nellie Liang, a former FRB official who played a key role in creating the stress test process after the GFC, cautioned that disclosing too much information to banks could turn the tests into an ineffective 'take-home exam'. Alan Rappeport and Binyamin Appelbaum, 'A tale of two Washingtons awaits Wall Street banks', *New York Times* (9 November 2018).

the agencies' carefully controlled feedback on resolution plans.[13] Such a communications strategy did not typically characterize regulators' pre-crisis interaction with the industry.

However, what might be effective from a policymaker's standpoint is not necessarily optimal for banks' risk-return analysis of compliance costs and risks. The industry has successfully pushed back in some instances against broad discretion and strategic lack of transparency. The first major amendment to Dodd-Frank,[14] enacted in 2018, includes six statutory criteria designed to constrain the FRB's discretion in differentiating between banking firms.[15] The pushback against agency opacity is also evident in a September 2018 interagency statement that the agencies will not take enforcement action for non-compliance with supervisory guidance. Instead, guidance involves iterative feedback in conveying best practices for safe and sound conduct.[16]

Contribution to the literature and intended readership

The book makes two contributions to the literature on bank regulation and banks' systems of internal governance. First, it establishes a conceptual framework that enables students and practitioners to understand the structure and rationale of bank regulation and their implications for the control functions. It does this by elucidating the elements of the banking business model and the risks it generates in credit extension and intermediation and by examining the tensions between regulation and firms' revenue-generating strategies. Understanding these risks and tensions helps prepare readers to address regulatory expectations for their firms and design risk controls and compliance policies and procedures (P&Ps) accordingly. The book provides a roadmap in this respect by explicitly tying a regulatory area to its corresponding regulatory expectations for corporate governance and the control functions.

Second, the book covers, in a single volume, the banking business, the unique features of banks' corporate governance and COIs, and the primary areas of bank regulation and the associated supervisory expectations for risk management and compliance. These primary areas are micro- and macro-prudential regulation, financial consumer protection regulation, and AML/CFT regulation. Readers who want to study the subject in a unified manner have needed to separately consult specialized treatments of their areas of interest. This can result in a fragmented grasp of the subject matter. Banking regulation has a cohesive unity due in large part to national authorities' agreement to follow the global standards of

---

13 Peter Eavis, 'How regulators mess with bankers' minds, and why that's good', *New York Times* (14 April 2016).

14 The Economic Growth, Regulatory Relief and Consumer Protection Act of 2018, Pub. L. No. 115–174 (2018) [Bipartisan Banking Act].

15 These criteria are capital structure, riskiness, complexity, financial activities, and size. Bipartisan Banking Act, Section 401(b).

16 The Federal Reserve Board and others, 'Interagency statement clarifying the role of supervisory guidance' (11 September 2018).

the BCBS and to the homogenizing effects of the integrated global financial markets. The subject's many subspecialties are closely interrelated. In this regard, the books' headings and subheadings, with cross-references throughout the text, allow readers to use the book to understand these interrelationships, and additionally to use it as a reference guide. The book also has a strong international dimension. Its primary focus is US bank regulation but its comprehensive use of BCBS publications and comparisons with UK and EU versions of US regulation offer a broad perspective on global bank regulation and internal governance.

Given its conceptual framework for analyzing risk management and compliance combined with its comprehensive coverage of bank regulation and governance, the book has a dual use for industry practitioners and for the classroom. It can serve as a primer for entry-level finance professionals and as a reference for seasoned risk and compliance officials, senior management, and regulators and other policymakers. The book has a strong practical side, informed by the author's interviews of current and former bank risk managers and his work experience at a major credit rating agency as a structured finance analyst and in helping to design and implement a new ratings compliance system. Although the book's focus is bank regulation, its analysis of corporate governance, risk management and compliance, and COIs has broad application in other financial services sectors. In the academy, the book is suitable for graduate and certificate programs in business and law schools, and in programs specializing in financial institution risk management and compliance.

While comprehensive in coverage, the book does not purport to cover all of the minute intricacies of each area of regulation and the related expectations for risk management and compliance. Each of these would be a book in itself. For specialists who need a deeper knowledge of a given area, the book includes abundant footnotes throughout the text from a wide array of sources, including industry client publications on technical areas; white papers and client memos of accounting, consulting, and law firms; research by financial economists; publications of bank and capital market trade associations; and articles and blogs by risk management and compliance experts. In addition, a list of references includes relevant statutory and regulatory provisions, agencies' rulemaking releases,[17] supervisory letters and examination manuals, and court cases and enforcement actions.

Book overview

The book is in two parts. Part I, Chapters 1 through 3, is foundational to understanding the subject matter of Part II. Part I provides the concepts and tools necessary for readers to engage fully with Part II's chapters on the substantive areas of bank regulation and the related mandates and guidance for corporate governance, risk management, and compliance systems.

---

17 Multiple agencies often issue the same rule. As a default, the book references FRB regulations and guidance. Nonetheless, as necessary, it also includes regulations and guidance of other banking agencies.

Part I

Chapter 1 introduces readers to the banking business model, the risks created by the extreme maturity mismatch of banks' balance sheet, and the factors underlying the rise of the BHC structure and financial conglomerates. It describes banks' central role in the economy – in extending credit, intermediating between savers and borrowers, and operating the payments system – which makes them such a highly regulated industry. The federal government's deposit insurance program and broader safety net exacerbate the risks of the banking business by introducing moral hazard, reducing investor scrutiny of bank management and increasing its incentive to take on excessive risk. The chapter links each of the economic roles of banks and related risks to their corresponding areas of bank regulation. A section on securitization and its role in disintermediating banks' business of liquidity transformation is key to understanding the credit and liquidity crisis of the GFC covered in Chapter 6.

Chapter 2 covers the statutory and regulatory framework, regulatory objectives, the supervisory structures of oversight, agency jurisdiction, the formation of regulatory expectations, and the myriad ways by which regulators convey these expectations. The primary objectives of financial regulation are financial stability, safety and soundness of individual financial institutions, and fair and transparent business conduct. The GFC made the first the foremost objective in global policymaking. The chapter explores how the inefficiencies or obsolescence of a given supervisory structure – such as the US's highly fragmented, entity-based system – can impose significant compliance costs and compliance risks on firms due to a lack of clarity in expectations or unpredictability of supervisory actions. These factors complicate firms' risk-return optimization analysis. Also relevant are the attributes of 'regulatory design' and the choice of a rules- or principles-based approach or a mixture of both, which play a role in communicating regulatory expectations. These attributes also can affect the compliance cost and risk variables. Cross-border comparisons in the areas covered by the chapter are made to the UK and EU.

Chapter 3 begins with a primer on corporate governance, the principal-agent relationship, and COIs in a corporation. This prepares the ground to examine the unique features of banks' corporate governance and the pervasive nature of conflicts in financial institutions. These firms enjoy an informational advantage and the incentives to exploit it. The chapter includes a typology of COIs that is useful in identifying, assessing, and mitigating COIs in the retail and institutional customer domains. Another problem are the potentially conflicting obligations of the boards of parent BHCs and those of their wholly owned bank subsidiaries, which must also consider safety and soundness concerns in addition to shareholders' interests. The FRB's 'source of strength' doctrine, explicitly affirmed by Dodd-Frank, helps to resolve this conflict. Separate sections examine the control functions.

Given the central focus on risk management in post-crisis rulemaking and guidance, the risk management function warrants an extended treatment of its role, status, and structure in banks' systems of corporate governance. This includes the role of a risk appetite, the risk appetite statement and risk appetite framework, risk committees, the importance of making risk measurement independent of its management, and the board's ultimate responsibility for the effectiveness of all of these components. Separate sections of Chapter 3 cover FRB guidance on the challenges in firm-wide monitoring of 'compliance risk' due to lack of effective quantitative metrics. Finally, it gives an overview of the technical components of risk management, which also have become a focus of recent FRB guidance. These include the advantages and disadvantages of using Value-at-Risk as a quantitative risk measurement tool; the process of risk identification, assessment, and mitigation; and issues involving assessment of 'known' and 'unknown' risks.

Chapter 3 also discusses the impact that state corporate law, federal prosecu-torial policies, and US sentencing guidelines have had in incentivizing firms to build meaningful corporate compliance programs. The chapter includes sections on the 'three lines of defense', or 3LOD, model, which seeks to make financial institutions' business lines more accountable for controlling the risks they create, and the two primary third-party enterprise risk management systems.[18] The chap-ter closes with a section on the role of corporate culture and the challenges firms face in establishing a 'culture of compliance' in financial institutions.

Part II

Part II covers the four primary areas of bank regulation and their associated regu-latory expectations for internal governance. It adopts the Basel 'Pillar I' and 'Pil-lar II' concepts to organize its treatment of micro-prudential and macro-prudential capital regulation. Pillar I concerns the minimum regulatory capital requirements applicable to all banks or a subset of banks, and Pillar II, the supervisory assess-ment of individual banks' unique risk profile in determining a bank's need for additional capital.[19] More broadly, micro-prudential regulation is concerned with the safety and soundness of individual banks, and macro-prudential regulation, with the stability of the financial system as a whole. The book concludes with a chapter on the likely pathway of the banking business model as non-bank Fin-Tech firms make inroads into banks' role in credit intermediation and payment services and predicts the future trajectory of bank regulation.

Chapters 4 and 5, respectively, cover Pillar I micro-prudential regulatory cap-ital requirements and the Pillar II supervisory programs. Chapter 4 first explains the concepts of bank capital, leverage, and economic and regulatory capital. Understanding management's incentive to minimize equity on the balance sheet to achieve a target return on capital is helpful in understanding banks' motive for

---

18 The Committee of Sponsoring Organizations of the Treadway Commission (COSO) and the International Organization for Standardization (ISO) developed the COSO and ISO 31000 systems, respectively.

19 'Pillar III', the role of disclosure and market discipline, does not figure prominently in this book.

capital arbitrage. The chapter then turns to the loss-absorption and other rationales for capital regulation and an overview of Basel's risk-weighted assets (RWA) methodology. Basel III/Dodd-Frank has two versions of capital rules, a 'standardized' approach with regulatorily prescribed risk weights and an 'advanced approaches' methodology for large banking firms. The latter firms, subject to regulatory approval, can establish their own risk weights through internal modeling and credit assessments.

Chapter 4 provides a comprehensive overview of the RWA-based capital rules that apply to credit, market, and, for advanced approaches, banks operational risk, and covers the applicable technical requirements for risk management and compliance programs for both groups of banks. Liquidity risk is treated in Chapter 7 with other capital regulation whose primary objective is reducing systemic risk. The market-risk rule seeks to reduce arbitrage by banks that reclassify positions to and from the 'at cost' banking book and 'fair value' trading book, a common practice before the crisis. Leverage ratio capital rules, a backstop to risk-based capital regulation, and portfolio diversity restrictions provide additional safety and soundness protection.

Chapter 5 begins with an overview of the objectives of bank examinations. To highlight their unique features, it contrasts banking agencies' examinations with those of capital markets regulators. The different objectives of the two groups of regulators go far in explaining the differences in their examination processes. Bank examinations are a more intensive, ongoing process focused on business fundamentals. In addition, bank supervision does not have an intermediate layer of oversight by self-regulatory organizations. The chapter then describes the two key components of US Pillar II supervision: the Capital Adequacy, Asset Quality, Management, Earnings, Liquidity, Sensitivity to Market Risk, or the CAMELS bank rating system, and Prompt Corrective Action program, which requires progressively harsher supervisory actions as a bank's financial condition deteriorates.

Chapters 6 establishes a framework for three areas of macro-prudential regulation: risk management (Chapter 6), capital regulation (Chapter 7), and structural regulation (Chapter 8). Chapter 6 lays the groundwork for the three chapters by describing key concepts, such as, and the two competing theories of systemic risk causation, contagion and interconnectedness. To elucidate Dodd-Frank's regulatory approach to systemic risk, Chapter 6 divides the GFC into three periods: (1) the period leading up to the GFC when firms' deficient risk management practices prepared the conditions that later contributed to its severity; (2) the liquidity and credit crisis; and (3) the Great Recession. It indicates what types of macro-prudential risks emerged in each period and Basel III/Dodd-Frank's specific regulatory responses to mitigate these risks.

Faulty risk management practices during the subprime mortgage bubble prepared the ground for the liquidity and credit crisis that began in late summer 2007. Not all financial conglomerates shared these deficiencies. Certain firms weathered the crisis relatively well. They had several characteristics in common: they typically shared information effectively across business lines, had rigorous internal processes requiring critical business judgment in asset valuation, applied consistent valuations across their firms, did independent credit analysis rather than relying exclusively on credit rating agencies, charged business lines for contingent liquidity exposures, and relied on a wide range of risk measures to gain different perspectives on risk.[20] Chapter 6 details the regulatory response, including FRB guidance for large BHCs on effective board practices, roles and accountability of senior and line management, risk committees, CRO authority and independence, and technical guidelines for a firm-wide risk management framework. The FRB has not yet implemented BCBS guidance on risk data aggregation and reporting, but in substance has done so in its stress testing exercises. Leading up to the crisis, firms' risk management was largely relegated to siloes in support of individual business lines, giving boards and senior management only a fragmented view of overall subprime exposure.

Chapter 7 covers the 'capital approach' to systemic risk: Pillar I's RWA capital buffers, leverage ratios, and liquidity regulation governing advanced approaches banks and G-SIBs, and the Pillar II supervisory stress testing regime. Chapter 7 also covers FRB guidance on model risk management, a central element in stress testing supervision. Defective modeling of financial instruments was another important contributing factor to the financial crisis.

Chapter 8 examines regulators' 'structural approach' to systemic risk. This includes *ex post* regulatory schemes to ensure an orderly wind down of failing financial conglomerates: the 'single point of entry' and 'bail-in' capital requirements, the Orderly Liquidation Authority resolution regime, and living wills. The UK and EU have their own versions of these three components. Chapter 8 then turns to *ex ante* regulation of firms as going concerns designed to limit the impact of risky non-bank activities on depository affiliates. This includes the Volcker rule (US) and the Vickers ringfencing reform (UK). For each regulatory area covered, Chapters 7 and 8 discuss the associated risk management and compliance requirements.

Chapters 9 and 10 cover, respectively, financial consumer protection regulation and AML/CFT regulation. Chapter 9 gives an overview of the unique compliance risks that banks' consumer financial services present due to the sector's highly competitive market, the high volume of frequently amended rules, and the sector's high level of reputational risk. Regulators expect banks to establish a formalized firm-wide compliance management system (CMS) to manage these risks. Chapter 9 explains how the design of CMS P&Ps reduces inherent compliance risk to a level of residual risk that meets regulatory expectations. There are three approaches in the regulation of consumer financial products and services: disclosure, terms-and-conditions, and conduct regulation, each of which has its own risk management and compliance best practices. Having established this

---

20 This summary draws on the findings of the Senior Supervisors Group, financial regulatory heads from the world's major financial centers. Senior Supervisors Group, 'Observations on risk management practices during the recent market turbulence' (6 March 2008), at <www.occ.treas.gov/publications/publications-by-type/other-publications-reports/pub-other-risk-mgt-practices-2008.pdf>. § 6.2.5.5 discusses the SSG report in detail.

foundation, Chapter 9 discusses the four primary areas of financial consumer protection regulation – lending; depository services; unfair, deceptive, or abusive acts or practices; and privacy law – and how state consumer protection law interfaces with federal law. Chapter 10 defines money laundering and terrorist financing and examines the regulatory framework that governs these activities. AML/CFT law imposes a high level of compliance cost and potential criminal liability on banks for law enforcement purposes that only indirectly relate to prudential concerns. The regulation centers around 'know your customer', recordkeeping, and reporting to the federal government in which suspicious activity reports and customer due diligence play key roles.

The book concludes in Chapter 11 with a discussion of the challenges to banks' roles in credit intermediation and payment services posed by FinTech, particularly distributed ledger technology. It argues that although FinTech presents significant risks, it will ultimately not displace banks in these core economic roles. The chapter also highlights the future role of RegTech in enabling banks to establish an effective risk data and reporting infrastructure that will enable their regulators to simultaneously monitor the potential buildup of risk in individual banks and the financial system as a whole. The chapter ends with the argument that bank regulation is highly path dependent due to the international standard-setting authority of the BCBS and the homogenizing effect of the integrated financial markets.

PART I

FOUNDATIONS

CHAPTER 1

The banking business model and rise
of the financial conglomerate

*Banking is now, and has always been, a risky business. The key to success in
operating a bank and in supervising a banking system is management of risk.*[1]

1.1 Introductory overview

Banks[2] play a central role in the world's economies yet have one of the most
fragile of business models. These two factors alone explain why these firms have
been at the center of many financial crises throughout history in the US and
abroad. However, an additional factor is the size and complexity of many banking firms. Policymakers' fear that their potential failure in the global financial
crisis of 2007–09 (GFC) would cause a catastrophic disruption of the financial
system led them to make unprecedented bailouts of several financial conglomerates. These three factors together explain why banking today is one of the
most highly regulated industries in the US.[3] Moreover, they help to explain why
national authorities have looked increasingly to these firms' corporate governance systems and risk management and compliance functions as central to the
effective management of the risks inherent in the banking business.

Managing these risks is the core concern of both bank management and a
bank's regulator, but each comes to it from a very different set of incentives.
Banks will manage the risks of their business model to preserve their franchise
and enhance shareholder value. Regulators across the developed world also consider franchise value important but have the additional mission of mitigating the
moral hazard introduced by the government safety net, which can lead banks to
take excessive risks. Moreover, banks have the additional incentive to grow ever
larger, more complex, and more leveraged to take advantage of the federal safety
net, making them 'TBTF', further undermining financial system stability.

---

1 George Kaufman and others, *Perspectives on Safe & Sound Banking: Past, Present, and Future*
(MIT Press: 1986) xiii.

2 In this chapter the term 'bank' refers to all types of depository institutions: commercial banks,
savings banks, savings and loan associations, and credit unions, unless the context otherwise requires.
In the US, only these entities have legal authority to accept deposits and therefore function as banking
organizations. 'Bank' also refers to bank holding companies, which are separately identified as the
context requires.

3 Banking is the most regulated industry in the US with the possible exception of the companies
that manufacture and use nuclear material. Jonathan Macey and Maureen O'Hara, 'Bank corporate
governance: a proposal for the post-crisis world', *FRBNY Economic Policy Review* (August 2016) 94.

National authorities seek to achieve three fundamental objectives in financial regulation: (1) the safety and soundness of individual financial institutions (micro-prudential regulation); (2) protection of investors and consumers of financial products through fair and transparent conduct of business (conduct regulation); and (3) stability of the financial system (macro-prudential regulation). In pursuit of these objectives, banking agencies have issued a wide array of regulations, exercised supervisory oversight, and provided guidance on their regulatory expectations for effective risk management and compliance systems.

This chapter and the following two chapters provide the foundation for understanding the role of corporate governance and the control functions in the four primary areas of bank regulation covered in this book.[4] This chapter highlights banks' central role in the economy and the key risks of their business that cause banks to be so highly regulated. For each of these economic functions and risks, it indicates the corresponding area of bank regulation. It then turns to the factors contributing to the emergence of large, complex bank holding companies (BHCs) that were at the center of the GFC and are a primary focus of the Dodd-Frank Wall Street Reform and Consumer Protection Act of 2010[5] (Dodd-Frank). Chapter 2 examines the regulatory and supervisory framework and sources of risk management and compliance expectations for banking institutions. Chapter 3 provides an overview of basic corporate governance principles and the unique features of bank and BHC corporate governance, followed by an in-depth discussion of the bank compliance and risk management functions. Where relevant, the discussion places these subjects in an international context, specifically relating to the UK and the EU.

1.2 Factors that cause banks to be so highly regulated

Several factors have caused banking to be one of the most heavily regulated industries worldwide. First, banks globally play a central role in the economy, in extending credit, in linking long-term borrowers with short-term savers through liquidity transformation, and in ensuring a smoothly functioning payments system. Second, risks inherent in the banking business model have caused policymakers to impose intrusive, intensive, and ongoing oversight over banking organizations. These risks make it imperative for regulators to closely monitor banks' financial condition and corporate governance system. Third, and relatedly, banks enjoy a government safety net due to federal insurance of deposit accounts, the liquidity backstop at the Federal Reserve System's[6] (Federal Reserve) discount window, and its role as lender of last resort in safeguarding the stability of the nation's financial system. Finally, the GFC has had a profound impact on the bank regulatory

---

4 These are micro- and macro-prudential, consumer protection, and anti-money laundering and terrorist financing regulation, the subjects of Chapters 4–5, 6–8, 9–10, respectively.

5 Pub. L. No. 111–203, 124 Stat. 1376, 1871 (2010).

6 The Federal Reserve, which consists of 12 Federal Reserve Banks, was established in 1913. The Federal Reserve Board (FRB) supervises the Federal Reserve and issues rules governing the banks subject to its jurisdiction.

framework. Previous financial crises have led to enhanced regulation and supervision, but the scale and scope of the legislation and rulemaking following the GFC, and the resulting changes demanded of firms' corporate governance and control functions, through both private and regulatory initiatives, have been unprecedented. These factors, in turn, have fundamentally shaped banking's risk management and compliance systems.

The following four subsections discuss each of these factors in turn. With minor variations, all four apply to the banking sector globally.[7]

1.2.1 Intensity of regulation a function of banks' central role in the economy

Banks' central role in the economy is perhaps the most critical reason for the scope and intensity of banking regulation and the demands the government places on the risk management and compliance functions. This economic role of the banking industry occurs in three primary areas: (1) extension of credit, (2) acting as intermediary in funneling savers' short-term deposits to borrowers in the form of long-term, illiquid loans, and (3) operating the nation's payments system.

1.2.1.1 Banks' role in the extension of credit

Banks serve as engines of the economy by extending credit to individuals and to businesses, some \$10 trillion annually in the US alone, expanding consumers' access to necessities and providing funds to businesses and governmental agencies for capital investments, purchasing inventory, and hiring workers. Banks are vital to the general health of the overall US economy. In addition, banks' extension of credit is the essential link in the FRB's monetary policy by serving as the main transmission mechanism through which it implements this policy.[8]

Banks' pervasive role in the economy in extending credit implicates several regulatory and compliance concerns treated in subsequent chapters. First, capital adequacy requirements, prudential supervision, and capital planning through stress testing help to ensure the financial soundness of banking firms. A bank's failure affects its current and prospective borrowers.[9] When banks cease to lend, businesses and households have less access to necessary funds for investment and consumption, with negative repercussions for the economy. In addition, bank

---

7 In Europe, the banks play an even more critical role as financiers of businesses. In the US, the capital markets have increasingly provided the primary source of funds for business investment.

8 The FRB conducts monetary policy, whose dual mandate consists of price stability and economic growth, in part by adopting a target short-term interest rate by vote of the Federal Open Market Committee (FOMC). Traditionally, the FRBNY would implement the policy through purchases or sales of Treasury securities through primary dealers that transact directly with banks, increasing or decreasing reserves in banks' Federal Reserve accounts, decreasing and increasing the target rate respectively by affecting demand for reserves, and thus the interest rate. This short-term interest rate affects banks' propensity to lend in the broader economy. This mechanism broke down after the financial crisis due to the enormous amount of excess reserves that resulted from the FRB's quantitative easing policy. Thus, the FOMC, among other things, uses interest rates on repurchase agreements and reserves to achieve the target interest rate.

9 Banks have a high level of private information concerning borrowers, enabling them to offer credit at lower cost. If a bank fails, the economy suffers from this loss of a specialized agent.

examiners review loan quality to ensure that banks are not taking excessive credit risks or leverage that could result in taxpayer-funded resolution. Prudential regulation, supervision, risk management, and compliance are the topics of Chapters 4 and 5.

Second, consumer protection laws seek to ensure that banks treat retail borrowers fairly and provide full disclosure of material lending terms. Consumers' reliance on banks for their most basic credit needs, such as residential mortgages, is a driving force for the vast panoply of consumer laws and regulation administered by the federal and state banking regulators, and the associated governance systems. This is the topic of Chapter 9.

1.2.1.2 Banks' role in intermediating between savers and borrowers

Banks' play a second, crucial economic role by intermediating between savers and borrowers in a process termed liquidity, or maturity, transformation.[10] On the one hand, banks incur short-term debt by accepting deposits withdrawable on demand, safeguarding customers' money while meeting their liquidity needs, and providing a medium of exchange for transactions in goods and services. On the other hand, banks provide a crucial service by investing these funds in illiquid assets in the form of loans and other long-term debt (LTD) instruments. In addition, checking deposits are an important component of the nation's money supply.

Liquidity transformation provides an important social good to the economy by helping to ensure a flow of funds from a large group of savers to a large group of borrowers who otherwise would not act as one another's counterparties. Their financial objectives are in conflict, because the savers want liquidity on demand and the borrowers want long-term financing. Banks resolve this conflict on an economy-wide scale.

Bank regulation seeks to ensure the smooth functioning of credit intermediation. By bolstering depositor confidence in banks' ability to safeguard their money, thus reducing the potential of bank runs, FDIC insurance[11] helps banks maintain a reliable source of funds for lending while helping to ensure the financial viability of individual banks and the banking system as a whole. In turn, the government's provision of FDIC deposit insurance is a powerful rationale for prudential regulation to limit taxpayers' exposure to insolvent banks. Consumer protection laws also protect retail customers in the client-facing business of taking deposits, thus also helping to maintain confidence in the banking system, further ensuring that banks remain liquid with a ready supply of funds.

1.2.1.3 Banks' role in the payments system

A third, critical function of banks in the economy is their role in the national and international payments systems. Banks are the primary agents in this system, operating the

---

10 Liquidity transformation is closely related to banks' role in extending credit but is distinct from the latter. Banks play a unique role in intermediating between two parties with highly conflicting interests in the debt market. The result is to enhance credit extension in the financial markets.

11 See § 1.2.3. The FDIC covers individual accounts amounting up to $250,000.

financial plumbing that is critical to the smooth functioning of the economy. Banks play a key role in three respects: providing institutions and individuals a means to safeguard cash or cash equivalents as deposits, satisfying the demand for liquidity; facilitating the transfer and settlement of monetary transactions for a wide variety of purposes, including securities and derivatives transactions; and playing an important role in monetary policy and credit intermediation through the process of creating and transferring deposit credits that other banks use to make loans.

Several important regulatory and corporate governance implications are associated with banks' role in the payments system. The Federal Reserve has regulatory and supervisory oversight over the US payments system and is a key participant itself in its operation.[12] More relevantly for the risk management and compliance functions, the payments system is widely used for money laundering (ML) and terrorist financing. Congress and the agencies have imposed significant regulatory obligations and internal governance mandates on banks to ensure compliance with the laws against ML and combatting the financing of terrorism (AML/CFT). This is the topic of Chapter 10.

1.2.2 Regulation a function of risks inherent in the banking business model

Banking is inherently a fragile business that requires constant supervisory oversight to ensure its prudent operation, while allowing an appropriate level of risk-taking that helps banks to remain in sound financial condition. Banking in the US is a private, for-profit business whose managers, as in other private businesses, seek to maximize profit on behalf of shareholders.[13] Bank managers' incentive to undertake risky investments to boost shareholder return creates a natural tension with regulatory expectations, which federal deposit insurance only exacerbates. Moreover, the growing complexity of the banking business and the financial markets in which banks operate has dramatically affected the regulatory framework and banks' corresponding risk management and compliance obligations. Nevertheless, the business risks inherent in banking would lead bank boards of directors, in the interest of their shareholders, to establish their own internal risk governance systems. In this respect, banks' boards' incentives align to some extent with regulatory expectations.[14] The following subsections cover the key risks posed by the banking business model to a banking organization.

1.2.2.1 Risks relating to revenue generated in banks' role in liquidity transformation

Banks' role in liquidity transformation carries a high level of risk for banks. One of banks' key business strategies on the liability side of their balance sheet is to

---

12 The Federal Reserve operates Fedwire, through which financial institutions transfer funds to one another. It debits and credits firm's reserve accounts upon receiving requisite wiring instructions.

13 The stakeholder claims are more diverse in Europe. See § 3.2.1.1.

14 This alignment contrasts with the misalignment in AML/CFT regulation, which materially interferes with banks' freedom in deposit-taking, a core element in the business model of obtaining low-cost, short-term financing and for revenue generation. See § 10.4.

build a large interest- and non-interest-bearing deposit base. They seek to attract customers with competitive interest rates and service features as well as through third-party deposit brokers. Banks also have other, uninsured short-term liabilities, such as large-denomination certificates of deposits that they issue to corporations or other banks, interbank loans in the federal funds market, repurchase agreements,[15] and deposits exceeding the FDIC insurance ceiling.

Banks then invest these low-cost funds in long-term, higher yielding assets by lending to retail customers and businesses and by purchasing debt securities. The interest on their loan and bond portfolio generates a large part of their income that arises from the difference between the cost of servicing the liability side and the income from the asset side of their balance sheet, or the net interest income (NII). NII is a primary indicator of bank profitability. Another important source of revenue is non-interest income from servicing deposit accounts and loans and income from other fee-based services.

Bank profitability is a key concern of prudential regulation. The CAMELS[16] rating system, which is the cornerstone of prudential bank supervision in the US, addresses bank profitability. In assigning a CAMELS rating, bank examiners will assess the sustainability of a bank's NII, which is central to the 'Earnings' component of the rating. To do this they assess the future interest rate environment, the bank's competitive position, and management strategy and control of risks relating to this income source, among other things.[17]

1.2.2.2 Liquidity risk

A key risk for banks in liquidity transformation is liquidity risk due to their heavy reliance on short-term funding. Depositors want to remain liquid and may withdraw their cash without warning, whereas borrowers prefer long-term funding. The observations in this subsection apply to non-bank financial institutions as well, which by and large rely on short-term debt financing to fund long-term assets.

In a fractional reserve system, banks are required to maintain a relatively low percentage of cash reserves[18] to repay depositors who withdraw their deposits. Management seeks to maximize NII by keeping the amount of non-income-yielding cash on hand above the required reserve ratio just sufficient to avoid fire sales of long-dated, illiquid assets to meet sudden deposit withdrawals. If depositors begin to doubt a bank's solvency due to concerns about its asset quality, they may seek to withdraw their funds in a run on the bank. Before FDIC insurance, bank runs were a frequent occurrence in US history. However, despite the federal

---

15 Repurchase agreements (repos) are contracts to sell and repurchase highly liquid and high-quality collateral, such as Treasury securities, in return for cash for short periods, often overnight.

16 See § 5.4. CAMELS stands for Capital, Assets, Management, Earnings, Liquidity, and Sensitivity to market risk. The rating system is applied in assigning a rating category from 1 (strong) to 5 (severely undercapitalized). In assigning a CAMELS rating, supervisors determine how well banks are managing these indicators of safety and soundness in a bank's operations.

17 See § 5.4.4.4.

18 The current required reserve ratio of reserves to deposits is 10%.

deposit guarantee, a large amount of depositor withdrawals may potentially spark a bank run by itself due to fear that a bank's assets will be insufficient to pay off depositors, particularly those holding deposits above the FDIC's $250,000 insurance cap for individual depositors.[19]

Banks' high leverage exacerbates their liquidity risk by its potential to raise doubts in depositors' minds if the quality of a bank's assets comes into question. In the GFC this was a key problem for 'shadow banks',[20] whose short-term liabilities are not federally guaranteed, as investors had little knowledge of the amount of these financial institutions' exposure to subprime mortgage-related assets whose credit quality was rapidly declining. Banks generally have a small equity cushion above Basel III's minimum capital requirements.[21] Non-bank financial institutions' capital structure shares this characteristic. Uncertainty involving the solvency of many financial conglomerates generated systemic risk in the GFC. The additional risk imposed by high leverage on the financial system was starkly evident when market participants could not distinguish between solvent banks facing a short-term liquidity crisis and banks that were insolvent.

In response, Dodd-Frank imposed prescriptive liquidity rules on banks.[22] Bank examiners assess liquidity risk in banks under the 'Liquidity' component of the CAMELS rating system. In this assessment, examiners also focus on management quality and asset quality as well. Inquiry will concern how a firm could sell liquid non-cash and cash-equivalent assets to meet unexpected deposit withdrawals. Risk management's ICs in managing liquidity are of obvious interest to the supervisor.[23]

1.2.2.3 Interest rate risk and market risk arising from banks' business model

Another risk arising from liquidity transformation is interest rate risk due to the mismatch between the maturities of short-term liabilities and long-term assets. Interest rate risk can directly imperil a bank's financial viability by undermining revenue generation. A bank's positive NII results from an upward-sloping yield curve: longer-term debt (bank assets) generally has a higher interest rate than shorter-term debt (bank liabilities). A bank's NII is at risk should the yield curve flatten out or even become downward sloping.[24]

---

19 It is for this reason that the FDIC resolves troubled banks over the weekend, either by liquidating them and paying off depositors or by arranging an acquisition by a financially sound bank.

20 Shadow banks are discussed at § 6.2.3.

21 The Basel capital adequacy requirements, established by the Basel Committee on Banking Supervision, are internationally agreed upon standards. 'Basel III' refers to the most recent set of Basel capital requirements. As members of the committee, national authorities agree to implement the requirements in legislation and rulemaking. See § 2.2.1 and §§ 4.3.2–4.3.7 for a discussion of the Basel regime and Basel III capital regulation, respectively.

22 See § 7.3.

23 See § 7.3.2.

24 The post-crisis historically low interest rate environment and low long-term rates, which reduce interest income from banks' assets, hurt banks' profitability. The Federal Reserve began raising the federal funds rate, the key short-term interest rate it controls, in December 2015 but lowered it in July 2019 in light of recent macroeconomic developments and a concern over not attaining its inflation target. The increase in the rate had generally improved banks' NII.

Managing interest rate risk was not a concern when interest rates were stable but became a major issue with interest rate volatility in the late 1970s and early 1980s. It thus can dramatically affect banks' earnings because earnings are largely based on interest income from their assets. Moreover, banks have an incentive to engage in extreme maturity mismatching to bolster profits, increasing both interest rate and liquidity risk. Declining NII is a warning sign of capital inadequacy and potential insolvency.

More generally, interest rate risk is an element of market risk, which is the risk arising from changes in financial market prices, including changes in foreign exchange rates, commodity prices, or equity prices in addition to interest rate changes. Banks that engage in significant trading activities are particularly subject to market risk. Banks' capital markets activities, particularly the derivatives trading operations of large, multiservice banking organizations, were a key source of risk that materialized in disastrous fashion in the GFC.

The national authorities have devoted a significant amount of attention to market risk of financial conglomerates by requiring robust risk management,[25] enhancing market risk capital requirements to better address the risks revealed in the GFC, and by imposing restrictions on trading activities in the Volcker rule.[26]

1.2.2.4 Asset liability management (ALM) of liquidity and interest rate risk

Banks address liquidity and interest rate risk through ALM. ALM is one of the most important risk management tasks in banking organizations. Bank examiners will closely evaluate banks' ALM risk management program to determine how well it mitigates these two risks.[27] A bank's ALM committee, typically chaired by the CEO, is the key senior corporate governance committee in many banking organizations.[28] In addition to constantly reconfiguring their capital structure to manage liquidity and interest rate risk on a daily basis, banks also engage in derivatives transactions to hedge their interest rate risk with options on debt instruments and interest rate swaps. A derivatives portfolio carries its own risks, which in turn banks must manage.

1.2.2.5 Credit risk: banks' comparative advantage in mitigating risks of adverse selection and moral hazard

Credit risk relates to the other side of the coin of banks' role in liquidity transformation. Banks want to issue loans that will pay back in full but understand realistically that a certain percentage will default, estimated as the 'expected loss' after factoring in recoveries. They thus seek to establish a risk return on their capital in

---

25 § 4.3.7.4.

26 The Volcker rule is the subject of § 8.3.1.

27 Under the CAMELS system, these risks pertain to the Liquidity and Sensitivity to market risk components.

28 See generally Moorad Choudhry, *The Principles of Banking* (Wiley: 2012) 351–585.

accord with management's risk appetite[29] by making loans and investing in other assets with an acceptable rate of default and diversification.

Banks, like all creditors, face the risks of adverse selection and moral hazard.[30] Banks have a comparative advantage in credit risk management that mitigates these risks due to their superior informational advantage and economy of scale. They are experienced in filtering out bad credits during origination by eliciting relevant information from borrowers. In addition, banks' long-term relationships with borrowers are especially advantageous, enabling them to effectively monitor a borrower's ability to repay a loan.[31] Table 1.1[32] summarizes the key points about these two risks, which confront banks and their regulators in different ways, together with the key risk measures that firms and regulators take. The table is relevant for the next section concerning the risks of adverse selection and moral hazard facing regulators.

Credit risk historically had been banking supervisors' overriding concern. Long before the emergence of market risk following the demise of the Bretton Woods fixed exchange rate regime in 1971, risky lending led to the demise of many troubled banking organizations. Basel I, the first international capital standard, formulated by the BCBS, was solely concerned with credit risk. The S&L crisis of the 1980s was fundamentally an issue of poor underwriting as well as outright fraud. Credit risk pertains directly to the 'Capital' and 'Asset' components of the CAMELS rating system, and indirectly to most of the other CAMELS components.

1.2.2.6 Operational risk arising from banks' business model

Finally, operational risk, defined as the risk of loss from inadequate or failed internal processes, people, and systems or from external events,[33] has become an increasing concern of both the bank regulators and banks as well. Operational risk, which is inherent in all banking products, activities, processes, and

---

29 The board of directors' determination of risk appetite is a central element of risk management, discussed at § 3.7.1.2.

30 Adverse selection occurs at the time two parties enter a transaction and Party A knows more than Party B, such that Party A can act adversely to Party B's interest. Moral hazard occurs during a transaction when Party A is able or has the incentive to act contrary to Party B's interest.

31 The position that banks have a comparative advantage in loan origination is not without its critics. In fact, the dismantling of the barriers to banks' ability to engage in other financial activities, covered in § 1.3.2, was based on the legislative premise that banks could no longer effectively compete in deposit-taking and loan origination. Jonathan Macey argues that in fact commercial banks continue to have unique advantages vis-à-vis non-bank financial institutions on both sides of their intermediation function. See Jonathan Macey, 'The business of banking: before and after Gramm-Leach-Bliley' (2000), 25 *Journal of Corporation Law* 691. Furthermore, the 'originate-and-distribute' securitization model has not significantly removed large BHCs from the various links in this new form of liquidity transformation. § 1.3.1.1.

32 Table 1.1 in part incorporates some of the highly illuminating concepts concerning adverse selection and moral hazard in Stephen Cecchetti and Kermit Schoenholtz, 'Primers', *Money, Banking, and Financial Markets*, at <www.moneyandbanking.com/primers/>.

33 Basel Committee on Banking Supervision, 'Principles for the sound management of operational risk' (June 2011) 3 n. 5.

Table 1.1 Adverse selection and moral hazard risks faced by banks and bank regulators

Adverse selection	*How it is manifested*	*Measures against adverse selection*
Definition Party A to a transaction knows more about the material issues than its counterparty, Party B. The costlier it is for Party B to find out the material attributes of a product or its counterparty, the greater the degree of adverse selection.	Adverse selection occurs when Party A is able to act adversely to the interests of Party B. Adverse selection occurs at the time the transaction closes. The pool of products or services that are the subject of the transaction will deteriorate in quality as higher quality products and counterparties withdraw from the market ('lemon effect'). The credit freeze in the GFC arose from creditors' inability to detect good and bad assets.	**Banks:** Screening (e.g., through credit scores and long-term relationships); required disclosures; guarantees and other forms of bonding; in mortgages, higher equity requirement. **Regulators:** Chartering process and qualification requirements to exclude opportunistic entrepreneurs; additional bank capital.

Moral hazard	*How it is manifested*	*Measures against moral hazard*
Definition Occurs in principal-agent relationship where an agent, Party A, may act contrary to the interest of the principal, Party B. Also occurs when a party's risk is shifted to a third party so that the original party takes more risks than it would otherwise take (e.g., an insurance contract). In both cases, Party A has more information than Party B or an incentive to take risks at Party B's expense. The higher the costs of obtaining the information, the higher the level of moral hazard.	Exists during life of transaction; occurs due to ability of a party to hide its activities that disadvantage Party B and monitoring costs. **Banks:** The borrower does not use the loan proceeds as expected by the lender and violates covenants or collateral requirements. **Regulators:** Regulated firms' employees engage in wrongful conduct. TBTF firms that incur excessive debt due to implicit or explicit government safety net.	**Banks:** Require deposit of loan proceeds in checking account to monitor use of proceeds; collateral; covenants; guarantees and other bonding devices. **Regulators:** Require compensation clawbacks; embed examiners to closely monitor financial conglomerates; enhanced disclosures; higher capital requirements; living wills and stress tests.

systems,[34] includes fraud and other types of wrongdoing that would result in a loss to the enterprise.

Operational risk is not unique to the banking industry but does have features unique to this sector. Rogue trading is a prime example of operational risk. The large trading losses from rogue trading that first came to prominence with the Barings Bank £830 million loss in 1995 led to an increased focus on operational risk in the late 1990s and the eventual imposition of capital requirements to mitigate this risk. The $6.2 billion JPMorgan London Whale trading loss in 2012 is only one of several more recent examples. In addition, the increasing complexity of financial instruments and reliance on increasingly sophisticated information systems have significantly magnified the risk of operational loss. Banks now put significant effort into managing enterprise-wide operational risk and in relating operational risk to risk capital.[35]

'Compliance risk' has emerged as an important source of operational risk in banking organizations and thus is an important factor in structuring the bank risk management and compliance functions.[36] The BCBS defines compliance risk as the 'risk of legal or regulatory sanctions, material financial loss, or loss to reputation a bank may suffer as a result of its failure to comply with laws, regulations, rules, related SRO standards, and codes of conduct applicable to its banking activities'.[37] Risk of financial loss is significant in the banking industry. The need to incorporate compliance risk within a bank's risk management system is one reason the risk management and compliance functions have similar concerns and often are integrated into a common reporting structure, while keeping each of their roles and responsibilities clearly demarcated.

1.2.3 Risk management and compliance a function of the government safety net

The introduction of federal deposit insurance in 1934 fundamentally changed the role and intensity of federal prudential supervisory oversight. The industry pays premiums to the FDIC deposit fund to cover resolution costs, but ultimately US taxpayers fully backstop the deposit guarantee.[38] Not only did federal deposit insurance increase the need for prudential supervision but it also changed the dynamics of the banking business model, introducing additional risks that Congress and the banking agencies have had to address over the following decades. The deposit guarantee and other government and privately funded backstops are ubiquitous throughout the world's banking systems.[39]

---

34 Ibid.

35 See Michel Crouhy and Dan Galai, *The Essentials of Risk Management* (McGraw-Hill Education: 2014) 499–501.

36 See § 3.7.1.4 for a discussion of this subject and FRB guidance on compliance risk.

37 Basel Committee on Banking Supervision, 'Compliance and the compliance function in banks' (2005) 3.

38 The FDIC was created by the Banking Act of 1933, Pub. L. No. 73–66, 48 Stat. 162 (1933). Deposit insurance was initially set at $2,500 and is now set at $250,000.

39 In the EU, 'deposit guarantee schemes' (DGSs) reimburse depositors of failed banks but are entirely funded by the banks, up to €100,000 per deposit account. All EU banks must belong to a

1.2.3.1 Government safety net's effect on adverse selection and moral hazard[40]
Broadening the concept of the government safety net illuminates the myriad ways that adverse selection and moral hazard manifest themselves in the financial system. In addition to the explicit FDIC guarantee, the government safety net includes implicit types of government support of the banks such as the Federal Reserve's role as lender of last resort through the discount window and potential bailouts of failing financial institutions.

Adverse selection facing regulators occurs because those who will most likely cause a bank failure will enter the banking business to take advantage of the safety net. At worst, criminally minded individuals may be attracted to the banking industry due to deficient monitoring that allows them to more easily defraud a bank, whose assets are highly liquid and fungible. In these instances, a skewed risk-reward equation applies: 'heads I win, tails you (the taxpayer) lose'. This factor helps to explain the intense scrutiny regulators exercise in the bank chartering process, which focuses on funding sources and their sustainability, capital structure, and executives' character and competence.[41]

Government backstops also introduce moral hazard into the banking system in a variety of ways.[42] Deposit insurance creates moral hazard by removing incentives of depositors and other creditors, now protected by an explicit guarantee or implicit backstop, to monitor a bank's creditworthiness and risk-taking on an ongoing basis. Depositors will not necessarily withdraw deposits if there are signs the bank is taking on too much risk. Undisciplined by the market, bank management may take greater risks in their lending and other business lines than they otherwise would have. The government faces additional risk if FDIC insurance is underpriced.

1.2.3.2 TBTF status a source of both adverse selection and moral hazard
Large banks further increase the problems of adverse selection and moral hazard. Government bailouts of banks considered 'TBTF', particularly in the last crisis, reduce *uninsured* creditors' incentive to monitor banks' credit quality, increasing moral hazard, while perversely increasing other banks' incentive to achieve TBTF status in order to reduce the cost of LTD – a distinct form of adverse selection.[43] The TBTF label, now firmly attached to all large financial conglomerates, aptly encapsulates the moral hazard problem of large financial institutions (LFIs) and the social outrage at the government bailouts of 2008. Although widely viewed

DGS. An implicit government backstop in emergency situations is always present. See European Central Bank, 'What is a deposit guarantee scheme?' (11 April 2018), at <www.ecb.europa.eu/explainers/tell-me-more/html/deposit_guarantee.en.html>.

40 See Table 1.1 at § 1.2.2.5.

41 Richard Carnell, Jonathan Macey, and Geoffrey Miller, *Law of Financial Institutions* (Wolters Kluwer: 2013) 72.

42 Moral hazard facing regulators is the risk that a bank will act less prudently in running its business because of the government safety net.

43 Frederic Mishkin, 'Prudential supervision: why is it important and what are the issues?' (September 2000), NBER Working Paper 7925, 7–8.

as unavoidable by many economists and other policymakers, these bailouts have only strengthened adverse selection and moral hazard in the financial system.[44]

1.2.3.3 Role of FDIC insurance in banks' capital structure and risk-taking

Finally, banks' decision to finance operations primarily through debt rather than equity can be linked in part to the enactment of FDIC insurance. This backstop incentivized banks to reduce the already low percentage of equity in their capital structure.[45] Non-financial companies, as a rule, finance considerably more of their source of funds from the equity markets than banks.[46] The relatively small amount of equity in banks' capital structure enhances management's and shareholders' incentive to engage in greater risk-taking since there is little to lose on the downside other than an FDIC takeover or sale. Perhaps more than any other factor, the precipitous decline in equity in banks' capital structure since the 19th century has contributed to the fragility of the banking industry.[47] The lack of sufficient loss-absorbing bank capital contributed to the severity of both the GFC and Great Recession.

1.2.4 GFC's pervasive impact on global banking regulation

The GFC has had a pervasive impact on the regulatory framework governing the banking industry globally and expectations for risk management and compliance, an impact that is still being felt. In particular, the risk management function has emerged from its pre-GFC status as primarily a support function for individual business lines to become a core component of a firm-wide corporate governance system that, together with compliance, has direct access to the boardroom.

1.2.4.1 Rajan-Kohn debate reflected market-based regulatory ethos prior to GFC

Both Dodd-Frank in the US and the BCBS's members globally have undertaken or proposed reforms of the financial markets that have fundamentally revamped prudential regulation and its assumptions concerning market behavior. Against the backdrop of stable macroeconomic and financial market conditions in the US and Europe in the decades leading up to the GFC, systemic risk was largely a secondary concern. Lawmakers and policymakers established a generally permissive, market-based regulatory framework that granted considerable leeway to financial institutions to develop and market their products and services. In a competitive market, it was assumed that firms would adopt best-practice ICs and P&Ps that would achieve socially beneficial outcomes.

---

44 § 6.2.2 discusses the TBTF issue in detail.

45 Figure 4.1 at § 4.2.2.4 shows the secular decline of bank capital over the past century to historical lows.

46 Table 4.1 at § 4.2.1.4 illustrates this by comparing the leverage of two major companies, one in the banking sector (JPMorgan Chase & Co.) and the other in the technology sector (Apple Inc.).

47 § 4.2.2.4 discusses the reasons for this decline.

A famous colloquy in a 2005 conference between Donald Kohn, an FRB governor, and Raghuram Rajan, a University of Chicago economist, on the topic of the risks of financial instability encapsulated the consensus view that dominated central bank and financial policymakers' thinking prior to the crisis. Rajan held that competition, spurred by technological change and deregulation, and asset managers increasingly prone to herding and investing in tail risk in the search for yield, presented significant risks to financial system stability.[48] An overwhelming majority at the conference roundly rejected Rajan's position. In a rebuttal,[49] Kohn presented the 'Greenspan doctrine' that, through private self-regulation, markets were efficient in unbundling and allocating discrete types of risk throughout the financial system and were inherently self-correcting. Firms on their own accord would take measures to establish internal control systems that would make them more robust. Allowing firms the freedom to manage their own risks and giving borrowers access to a greater variety of lenders made the financial system more resilient and flexible.[50]

1.2.4.2 Emergence of financial stability as the primary regulatory objective
The financial crisis has made financial stability the top regulatory objective of global bank policymakers. Considerable debate exists regarding the causes of the GFC, but there is consensus that financial institutions utterly failed to adopt an effective risk management control framework that would help to ensure prudent risk-taking. The FRB now considers firm-wide risk management as crucial in a banking institution's system of corporate governance and as a central means of achieving the financial stability objective. This book devotes three chapters to macro-prudential regulation and oversight of large banking organizations to mitigate systemic risk: internal governance and the control functions (Chapter 6), capital requirements (Chapter 7), and structural approaches (Chapter 8).

1.3 The rise of the global financial conglomerate and BHC structure

Financial conglomerates now dominate the global landscape in financial services. In the US, the emergence of these large, complex multiservice financial institutions is the culmination of an evolutionary process in the financial markets that occurred in tandem with the lifting of restrictions on banks' ability to compete with non-bank financial institutions. Understanding the structure of large BHCs and universal banks more broadly, their size and organizational complexity, and the nature and scope of their business lines, is essential to fully grasp the challenges they pose in meeting regulatory expectations concerning corporate governance, risk management, and compliance, covered in Chapter 3 and in later

48 Raghuram Rajan, 'Has financial development made the world riskier?' Federal Reserve Bank of Kansas City (2005).
49 Donald L. Kohn, 'Commentary: has financial development made the world riskier?' Federal Reserve Bank of Kansas City (2005).
50 Ibid. 372.

chapters. There is evidence that large or complex banks[51] have greater appetite for risk with a greater likelihood of government support and that such banks can exhibit poorer credit performance.[52]

In the early 1980s, the banking industry began to evolve from a traditional commercial banking business model funded with retail deposits, originating and holding loans on the balance sheet, and limited to a regional presence to a transactional model based on a securitization 'originate-and-distribute' system, with multiple lines of business spanning the US and international markets. These developments were not limited to the US but occurred globally.[53] This transformation has occurred in four major respects: through securitization, entry into non-banking businesses, increasing size and complexity, and increasing interconnectedness. An important precondition for these developments was deregulation of the banking industry in the 1980s and 1990s. Chapter 2 discusses how the transformation of the banking industry has rendered the existing regulatory and supervisory structure largely obsolete.[54]

1.3.1 The securitization 'originate-and-distribute' model

The financial system underwent a fundamental transformation in the 1980s as securitization became a widespread funding mechanism for financial institutions. Initially, depository institutions began selling home mortgages to government-sponsored enterprises such as Fannie Mae and Freddie Mac.[55] Banks later securitized non-mortgage assets, such as credit card receivables, automobile loans, commercial real estate loans, and corporate commercial loans, in addition to rated private-label mortgage bonds. Banks were also motivated to securitize assets since they received off–balance sheet accounting treatment, allowing banks to incur significantly reduced capital charges. On the eve of the GFC, securitized assets and assets held by firms that financed themselves mainly by issuing securities exceeded total assets on

---

51 Unless the context otherwise requires, the term 'banks' includes both individual banking entities and BHCs and other depository institutions. See § 1.1 n. 2.

52 See Gara Afonso, João Santos, and James Traina, 'Do "too-big-to-fail" banks take on more risk?' (December 2014), *FRBNY Economic Policy Review* 42. The authors use impaired loans, defined as loans either in default or close to default, as a measure of risk-taking incentives. The study includes data reflecting government interventions during the GFC from over 200 banks in 45 countries and Fitch Ratings' metrics to measure the level of government support.

53 The legal structure of these firms varies across national jurisdictions. In the US, banking financial conglomerates are structured as BHCs, with separate subsidiaries running functionally separate businesses. In the UK and Europe, financial conglomerates have long been structured as 'universal banks' which allow multiple businesses to be run within the same corporate entity. UK and European banks were already engaged in multiple business lines as universal banks by the time financial conglomerates arose in the US.

54 § 2.3.2.

55 Tobias Adrian and Hyun Song Shin, 'The changing nature of financial intermediation and the financial crisis of 2007–09' (April 2010), FRBNY Staff Report No. 439, 1–2 [Adrian and Shin, Changing Nature]. Until the 1980s, banks and savings institutions were the dominant holders of home mortgages. Ibid. 2. By 2009, 'market-based' holdings constituted two-thirds of the $11 trillion of outstanding home mortgages. Ibid.

banks' balance sheets.[56] Securitization epitomized the market-based approach that prevailed before the crisis.

1.3.1.1 Case study of securitization: mortgage-backed securities

Figure 1.1 uses mortgage-backed securities (MBS) to illustrate the originate-and-distribute securitization model and the many intermediaries that participate before the MBS are sold to the ultimate risk holders, the investors. In essence, it is a factory conveyor belt in which many participants help to assemble the final product. The three categories of participants consist of the origination parties, the 'gatekeepers', and the risk holders. The originator or purchaser securitizes the mortgages by 'pooling' them and selling them to a special purpose vehicle, which then issues bonds, the MBS, serviced by the cash flow from the pool of mortgages, to investors, subject to review, approval, and certification by the gate-keepers, which include lawyers, accountants, and bond insurers.[57]

1.3.1.2 Securitization, a form of bank intermediation

In many respects, today's financial conglomerate continues the basic service of channeling savings from investors to borrowers, but via the capital markets. Broadly speaking, the banking industry still intermediates the bulk of credit financing.[58] Unlike traditional bank lending, however, securitization involves an extended chain of intermediaries that channel funds from ultimate lenders to ultimate borrowers. Financial conglomerates often own several links in the securitization chain.[59]

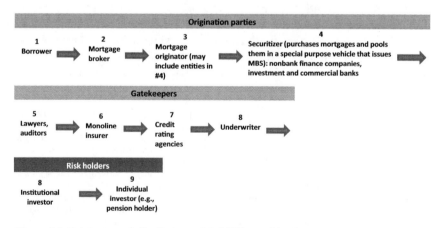

Figure 1.1 Originate-and-distribute model: MBS securitization

---

56 Adrian and Shin, Changing nature 3. Data is of the second quarter of 2007. Ibid.

57 Due to the high profitability of securitizing subprime MBS, each of these parties – including the gatekeepers – were highly incentivized to keep the conveyor belt rolling.

58 Adrian and Shin, Changing nature 1.

59 Ibid. 4.

The economic result is substantively the same as in traditional bank credit intermediation. However, a key difference is a loss of accountability of the asset originators for credit losses of assets they previously held on their books. Such accountability had been a hallmark of the traditional commercial banking model that incentivized prudent risk-taking. Chapter 6 discusses securitization's role in the GFC.[60]

1.3.2 Deregulation and emergence of the BHC structure

The vast majority of US banks are now subsidiaries of BHCs. Today, BHCs range from simple holding companies that own a single banking subsidiary to internationally active banks with trillions of dollars of assets and thousands of subsidiaries engaged in a wide range of businesses across multiple jurisdictions. The Federal Reserve supervises BHCs under its consolidated supervisory authority. It and other agencies are primary regulators of bank and non-bank subsidiaries.[61] BHCs generally must organize non-bank businesses under separate subsidiaries.

1.3.2.1 Unique historical factors prevented concentration in US banking industry

BHCs arose from unique factors in American economic history. Initially, the BHC structure became the favored legal mechanism as a market response to highly restrictive state bank regulation. Populist antagonism toward concentration of power in the finance industry and the success of small, regional banks in thwarting money center banks' expansion efforts resulted in the status quo for two centuries of 'unit' banking in which states largely limited banks to a single location. Even the experience of the Great Depression, in which small, undiversified rural banks constituted the bulk of bank failures, did not dent the political power of regional banks. BHCs could avoid state laws on unit banking by establishing a single bank in a given state under a BHC structure.

1.3.2.2 Competition from non-banks spurred bank deregulation and rise of BHCs

The BHC structure also attained eventual predominance because it allowed banking organizations to expand via separate subsidiaries into non-banking activities, which became increasingly important to banks as competition grew in the 1970s and 1980s on both the liability (deposit-taking) and asset (lending) sides of the balance sheet. The Bank Holding Company BHC Act of 1956 (BCH Act)[62] had limited BHCs from engaging in activities not 'closely related to banking', effectively separating banking

---

60 In the GFC some originators did retain a portion of such assets or invest in them. In such cases incentives to undertake risk management were generally weaker and overly reliant on credit rating agencies. See generally § 6.2.5.

61 See § 2.3.1.1.

62 12 USC § 1841 et seq.

from commerce.[63] The Glass-Steagall Act of 1933[64] (Glass-Steagall) had separated commercial from investment banking. Competition increasingly rendered these restrictions obsolete. Money market mutual funds, with market-based interest rates, became an attractive alternative to deposit accounts, whose interest rates Regulation Q capped.[65] Deposit interest rate restrictions were eventually lifted to allow banks to compete in the high interest rate environment of the 1980s.

On the asset side, banks' lending business lost out to investment banks that serviced large corporate clients' capital needs by underwriting their issuance of commercial paper and in other ways invaded banks' territory. In response, banks sought and won exceptions from the separation of business lines mandated by Glass-Steagall and the BHC Act. The FRB allowed BHCs to engage in an increasing range of non-banking activities 'closely related to banking' under FRB Regulation Y,[66] including brokerage activities and certain securities underwriting. Savings and loan associations in the 1980s were permitted to invest in high-yield bonds and speculative real estate ventures, eventually resulting in the insolvency of more than a thousand of these thrift institutions.[67] Finally, the Riegle-Neal Interstate Banking and Branching Efficiency Act of 1994[68] dismantled the centuries-old restrictions on interstate banking by repealing the restriction on branching across state borders. This allowed BHCs to realize economies of scale from branching to the fullest extent.

1.3.2.3 Gramm-Leach completed deregulation of banking industry

This deregulatory process culminated in Glass-Steagall's repeal by the Gramm-Leach-Bliley Financial Services Modernization Act in 1999[69] (Gramm-Leach), leading to the emergence of all-purpose universal 'megabanks' organized as BHCs, combining commercial, investment, insurance, and banking businesses. As recently as 1994 – five years before Gramm-Leach – the top 50 BHCs were relatively homogeneous, with the vast majority of revenue derived from interest income.[70] Gramm-Leach amended the BHC Act to allow BHCs to register as 'financial holding companies' (FHCs), subject to certain enhanced prudential requirements, allowing BHCs to expand in a broad range financial activities and

---

63 This restriction was designed to prevent self-dealing and monopoly power of holding companies that lent to their non-financial affiliates. It also sought to limit risk-taking of non-bank affiliates that endangered the FDIC insurance fund and potentially eroded the stability of core banking functions such as lending and deposit-taking. Dafna Avraham, Patricia Selvaggi, and James Vickery, 'A structural view of U.S. bank holding companies' (July 2012), *FRBNY Economic Policy Review* 67 [A structural view of US BHCs].

64 Pub. L. No. 73–66, 48 Stat. 162 (1933).

65 The current version of Regulation Q, at 12 CFR § 217, regulates capital requirements.

66 12 CFR § 225.123.

67 The total cost of resolving S&L failures amounted to nearly half a trillion dollars, including more than $130 billion in taxpayer bailouts. Richard Stevenson, 'G.A.O. puts cost of S.&L. bailout at half a trillion dollars', *New York Times* (13 July 1996).

68 Pub. L. No. 103–328, 108 Stat. 2338 (1994).

69 Pub. L. No. 106–102, 113 Stat. 1338 (1999).

70 Adam Copeland, 'Evolution and heterogeneity among larger bank holding companies: 1994 to 2010' (July 2012), *FRBNY Economic Policy Review* 83 [Evolution and heterogeneity]. The smaller BHCs' income generation continues to rely heavily on traditional banking. Ibid. 84.

services, including investment banking, beyond what the BHC Act had previously permitted. Each bank and non-bank subsidiary is subject to 'functional regulation' by separate regulators. Virtually all large BHCs are registered as FHCs.[71]

1.3.3 Increasing complexity, interconnectedness, and size of BHCs

Banks, through BHCs, increased in size and legal and organizational complexity as they developed new business lines and took advantage of a raft of deregulatory measures in their competition for market share. As a result, concentration in the industry increased substantially.

1.3.3.1 Increasing complexity: growth of non-banking business lines in BHCs

The attributes of organizational complexity characterizing this evolution are arguably a natural adaptation of banks to the transformation of financial intermediation from an interest-income model based on deposit-taking and loan-making to a fee-based model centered on asset securitization.[72] As a percentage of total income, non-interest income, a proxy for non-traditional bank business lines, derived from off–balance sheet activities such as trading, rose from an average of 19% over the 1960–80 period to 35% by 1994.[73] In this transformation, under competitive threat from non-banking institutions in the 1980s and 1990s, banks have succeeded in retaining a central role in financial intermediation.[74] Nevertheless, such incremental expansion of the boundaries of the traditional banking firm[75] could not have occurred without regulatory approval.[76] The growing complexity was achieved largely through cross-industry acquisitions of non-bank specialized firms, particularly beginning in the mid-1990s.[77] A typical portfolio of businesses includes non-deposit-taking specialty lenders, asset managers, broker-dealers, insurance companies, and, most recently, FinTech firms.[78]

Banks' derivatives business has become one of the industry's most significant non-banking revenue generators. The largest BHCs and other financial institutions became major dealers in credit default swaps (CDS), which were introduced in the 1990s, reaching approximately $60 trillion in notional amount prior

---

71 A structural view of US BHCs 67. This FHC regulatory structure is covered in more detail at § 2.3.

72 Nicola Cetorelli, James McAndrews, and James Traina, 'Evolution in bank complexity' (December 2014), *FBRNY Economic Policy Review* 87 [Evolution in bank complexity].

73 Franklin Edwards and Frederic Mishkin, 'The decline of traditional banking: implications for financial stability and regulatory policy' (July 1995), *Economic Policy Review* 29 [Decline of traditional banking].

74 Evolution in bank complexity 88.

75 Nicola Cetorelli, Benjamin Mandel, and Lindsay Mollineaux, 'The evolution of banks and financial intermediation: framing the analysis' (July 2012), *FRBNY Economic Policy Review* 9.

76 The FRB, under the BHC Act of 1956, has authority to approve expansion into businesses that are 'closely related to banking'. In 1999, Gramm-expanded the types of businesses BHCs could engage in when they become a 'FHC'. See § 1.3.2.3.

77 Evolution in bank complexity 100. In this case complexity is measured by number of subsidiaries and lines of business. Evolution in bank complexity 86.

78 Evolution in bank complexity 93.

to the GFC. The largest banking firms became the predominate players in the OTC derivatives market. OTC markets pose two significant risks for dealers: counterparty credit risk (CCR), since dealers transact directly with other dealers rather than through an exchange that assumes counterparties' risk of default, and embedded leverage, since a party's position can quickly become out-of-the-money, requiring additional margin to avoid default.[79] A third risk, lack of transparency of OTC trades, negatively impacts both counterparties and regulators.[80] Derivatives are complex financial instruments that pose significant risk, which came to fruition in the GFC. Banks' risk management significantly lagged behind the level of sophistication necessary in light of the explosive growth and complexity of the derivatives markets.

The level of complexity can be quantified by the number of a BHCs' subsidiaries. As of third quarter of 2011, the four most complex firms owned over 2,000 subsidiaries, while only one firm had over 500 subsidiaries in 1991. Each of the seven most internationally active banks controls subsidiaries in at least 40 countries.[81] As of 20 February 2012, of the 2,940 domestic subsidiaries of JPMorgan Chase, only four were domestic commercial banks but held 86% of total assets.[82]

1.3.3.2 Growth of interconnectedness of financial conglomerates

In addition, BHCs and other financial conglomerates have become increasingly interconnected through transactions involving short-term lending and derivatives trades. Over the last three decades, deposits have steadily decreased and replaced by other sources of short-term debt. These include repurchase agreements[83] and other collateralized debt obligations (CDO) as well as unsecured interbank borrowing in the federal funds market.[84] Commercial banks find it necessary to obtain funding in the short-term debt markets since deposits are insufficient to fund their assets.[85] The result has been a high level of linkages between the conglomerates in bilateral OTC trading.

1.3.3.3 Increasing size and complexity of BHCs

Financial consolidation has resulted in larger and increasingly complex financial institutions.[86] As of Q2 2018, the top five and top ten US BHCs held 46.7% and 58.7% in total consolidated assets, respectively. As of Q1 1991, the top five and

---

79 § 4.3.6.3 discusses CCR and the associated capital requirements.

80 OTC transactions are not exchange-traded. The lack of pricing information enhances informational disparities and regulators' ability to monitor the buildup of systemic risk. Dodd-Frank created an elaborate regulatory framework designed to increase transparency in the OTC market, a topic beyond the scope of this book.

81 A structural view of US BHCs 66.

82 Ibid. 70.

83 See § 1.2.2.1.

84 Banks borrow and lend excess reserves held at Federal Reserve Banks overnight in the federal funds market on an unsecured basis.

85 Adrian and Shin, Changing nature 6.

86 See Frederic Mishkin, *The Economics of Money, Banking, and Financial Markets* (Pearson: 2013) 298.

ten BHCs held only 17.3% and 26.3% of total consolidated assets, respectively.[87] Nevertheless, the level of concentration of US banking and complexity should be put in global perspective. At about 6,000,[88] the US has significantly more commercial banks than any other country. In other countries of the developed world, the level of concentration is much higher. Globally, a handful of large banks typically dominate their country's banking industry.

Figure 1.2[89] reflects the significant, continuous growth in bank credit and the increasing role of non-bank business lines (non-bank credit assets) following enactment of Gramm-Leach in 1999, dipping with the onset of the Great Recession in 2009, but continuing their upward trajectories beginning in 2011–12. BHCs have held the vast majority of these assets. Over a 20-year period from 1991 to Q4 2011, US BHCs' total assets grew fivefold.[90]

1.3.3.4 Regulatory and corporate governance implications of conglomerate structure

Significant regulatory and oversight issues and corporate governance challenges are associated with large BHCs' global footprint, multiple business lines, provision of critical banking services, large counterparty exposure and high leverage in derivatives books, off–balance sheet trading assets, and complex legal

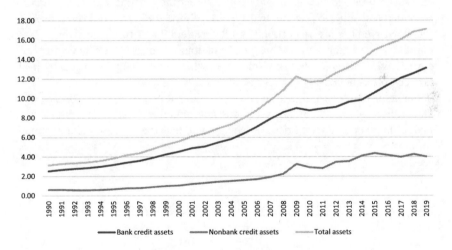

Figure 1.2 Growth in commercial banking assets over time

87 Federal Reserve Bank of New York, 'Quarterly trends for consolidated U.S. banking organizations – second quarter 2018 – data', at <www.newyorkfed.org/medialibrary/media/research/banking_research/quarterlytrends2018q2.pdf?la=en>. The figures include both bank and non-bank subsidiaries' assets.

88 Evolution in bank complexity 85.

89 The data for Figure 1.2 are drawn from Federal Reserve Economic Data, Federal Reserve Bank of St. Louis, at <https://fred.stlouisfed.org/release/tables?rid=22&eid=4828&od=1985-01-01#>.

90 A structural view of US BHCs 65.

structure. These attributes of systemically important BHCs were among the root causes contributing to the severity of the GFC. The following chapters discuss the various ways in which Dodd-Frank and the regulations issued under its authority seek to mitigate the risks that financial conglomerates impose on the financial system.

1.4 Conclusion

Several factors explain the government's concern with the financial well-being of banks and the banking system. Each of the four substantive areas of bank regulation is concerned in some manner with one or more of banks' role in credit intermediation, depository services, and the nation's payments system in their provision of services to borrowers and savers. Taxpayers' exposure to failing banks further heightens the need for close, ongoing regulatory scrutiny.

Later chapters will build upon the current chapter in connecting specific risks in banking to the governing regulatory and supervisory regime. Chapters 4 and 5, respectively, highlight the regulatory and supervisory framework in micro-prudential regulation. Chapters 6 through 8 are devoted to systemic risk regulation and the supervisory expectations for risk management and compliance in financial conglomerates. The GFC dramatically reordered regulatory priorities and severely tested the assumptions underlying the existing regulatory framework that had failed to prevent, in the words of former FRB Chair Ben Bernanke, the worst credit crisis in world history.[91] Chapters 9 and 10, respectively, cover consumer protection and AML/CFT regulation. Chapter 11 concludes that the current Basel III/Dodd-Frank framework will continue largely intact, even as FinTech poses increasing challenges and risks to the banking industry.

For their part, practitioners in risk management and compliance will not be able to translate regulators' expectations into effective IC systems without first understanding the inherent risks of banking and the risks that are unique to their own firms.

---

91 Adam Tooze, *Crashed: How a Decade of Financial Crises Changed the World* (Viking: 2018) 163.

CHAPTER 2

The bank regulatory framework and formation and conveyance of regulatory expectations

2.1 Introductory overview

This chapter takes up where Chapter 1 leaves off. It covers the US bank regulatory framework, with comparisons to the UK and EU, that is designed to address the risks of the banking business and of large, complex BHCs. The three primary objectives of bank regulation worldwide are financial stability, the safety and soundness of individual banks, and fair and transparent business conduct. The uniformity in global bank regulation under the Basel regime is not surprising in view of the increasing integration of the world's financial markets. A primary focus of the current chapter is how policymakers establish and convey regulatory expectations for banks. Like the first chapter and the one that follows, this chapter equips students and practitioners with foundational tools necessary to engage productively with the substantive areas of bank regulation in applying these regulatory expectations.

The chapter first describes the regulatory framework governing US banking institutions and the agencies' jurisdiction and scope of authority, with cross-border comparisons to the UK and EU. It parses the concepts of *regulation, supervision,* and *enforcement* and discusses the four types of supervisory structures: the institutional, twin-peaks, unified, and functional models. It also discusses policymakers' choice of 'regulatory design' along the rules- and principles-based spectrum. The chapter then seeks to identify how the attributes of a supervisory structure and regulatory design affect firms' compliance costs and compliance risks. At bottom, these costs and risks increase when regulatory expectations lack clarity and consistency and regulatory actions are unpredictable. The final section considers the role of the examination process in conveying regulatory expectations to individual banking institutions. The chapter uses a 'pyramid of regulatory expectations' to illustrate how regulators' expectations become increasingly granular, flexible, and multifaceted toward the pyramid's base in addressing rapidly changing conditions such as an individual bank's deteriorating financial well-being or emerging risks in the banking system.

2.2 The regulatory and supervisory structure and its implications for risk management and compliance

A combination of standard setting, legislation and rulemaking, and supervisory oversight ultimately establishes the regulatory obligations and expectations for banking institutions. The BCBS[1] formulates non-binding international standards at the supranational level. The BCBS standards and guidance are a prolific and influential source of regulatory expectations for US and foreign banking organizations' (FBOs) systems of risk management and compliance.

2.2.1 BCBS: history and function

The Basel-based BCBS is part of the Bank for International Settlements (BIS), an organization founded in 1930, headquartered in Basel, Switzerland, and whose members include the world's chief central bankers and finance officials. The drive to establish uniform international standards for banking regulation arose from a handful of dramatic bank failures following the collapse of the Bretton Woods managed exchange rate system in 1973.[2] The creation of the BCBS in 1974 followed shortly thereafter.

Since then, the BCBS has become the world's clearinghouse on best banking practices and a forum for achieving consensus on emerging issues in banking regulation and supervision. The world's banking officials see the critical need for such a forum as the financial markets and banking systems have become increasingly integrated. A financial crisis in one country can quickly have global repercussions, as the currency crisis of the 1990s and the GFC in 2008 graphically showed. The primary focus of the BCBS is mitigation of micro- and macro-prudential risk through capital adequacy requirements, although it regularly provides guidance on the other related areas of banking regulation and compliance.[3]

The Basel I Accord (Basel I) of 1988 concerned mitigation of credit risk through capital adequacy requirements. Since then, the BCBS has expanded capital adequacy standards to cover all key risks in the banking business model. The 2004 Basel II Accord (Basel II) addressed market and operational risk, and the Basel III Accord (Basel III), finalized in 2017, has focused on macro-prudential risk in addition to enhancements of standards for other risks.[4] The BCBS has issued 29 high-level principles that should govern national bank supervision.[5] The next section discusses the world's four primary supervisory structures.

---

1 BCBS members include heads of central banks and bank supervisors from 28 jurisdictions. The BCBS's mandate is the strengthening of the regulation, supervision, and banking practices throughout the world.

2 The initial impetus to create BCBS followed the failure in 1974 of Bankhaus Herstaat after the German government withdrew its license because of its massive foreign exchange exposure. The closure resulted in large losses by banks outside Germany as Herstaat did not make good on its intraday US dollar obligations to these counterparties. Franklin National Bank of New York failed the same year, also due to foreign exchange exposure. See Bank for International Settlements, 'History of the Basel Committee' (April 2018), at <www.bis.org/bcbs/history.htm> [History of the Basel Committee].

3 These include AML/CFT regulation and supervision. See Basel Committee on Banking Supervision, 'Sound management of risks related to money laundering and financing of terrorism' (2017).

4 History of the Basel Committee.

5 Basel Committee on Banking Supervision, 'Core principles for effective banking supervision' (14 September 2012) [BCBS, Core principles for banking supervision]. This guidance updates guidance issued in 1997.

The BCBS considers its regulatory and supervisory standards to be minimum thresholds for bank regulation and supervision and encourages national authorities to impose requirements that go beyond these standards. In fact, the US's implementation of Basel III in the Dodd-Frank Act in some ways surpasses that of European countries' capital adequacy frameworks.[6]

2.2.2 Roles of regulation, supervision, and compliance in achieving the three regulatory objectives

A legislature creates a supervisory structure by designating which agencies will issue rules under the governing statutes, supervise the regulated entities, and enforce the statutory and regulatory provisions. The ultimate goals of these regulatory functions and activities is to achieve one or more of the three primary financial regulatory objectives.

2.2.2.1 The three primary regulatory objectives

Financial regulation has three primary objectives: (1) stability of the financial system, (2) safety and soundness of individual firms,[7] and (3) protection of investors and customers through fair and transparent business conduct of financial institutions. The first goal has priority over the other two goals due to the potential systemic impact of instability of the financial system on the economy as a whole.[8]

2.2.2.2 Role of regulation, supervision, enforcement, and communication of regulatory expectations

It is essential for a sound understanding of bank regulation and its relationship to firms' internal governance to define and distinguish a number of terms widely used in this book. Banking *regulation* consists of the obligations, both affirmative and prohibitive in nature,[9] that banks and their employees must comply with in respect of one or more regulatory objectives.[10] Financial regulation is particularly concerned with influencing or controlling the behavior of participants

---

6 Dodd-Frank introduced several capital-related provisions that are stricter than the Basel III framework. An example is a provision that prevents certain large banks from having capital below the general risk-based capital requirements applicable to all banks. See Shearman & Sterling, 'Basel III framework: US/EU comparison' (17 September 2013), Client Publication.

7 The prudential concept of 'safety and soundness' includes both micro-prudential and macro-prudential regulation. The GFC moved macro-prudential regulation to the forefront, transforming it into an independent policy goal of first importance. In fact, if policies conflict, financial market stability has priority over the other two goals. The policy goal of 'fair and efficient markets' taken alone can be subsumed under the goal of financial stability and conduct-of-business regulation.

8 Charles Goodhart and others, *Financial Regulation: Why, How, and Where Now?* (Routledge: 1998) 189 [Goodhart, *Financial Regulation*].

9 For example, capital adequacy requirements affirmatively require banks to maintain specified levels of capital. The Volcker rule prohibits bank affiliates with a certain level of trading operations from engaging in proprietary trading.

10 '[R]egulation is an instrument or mechanism by which the state (or a state agency) or legislature compels an entity or individual to comply with requirements'. Organization for Economic Co-operation and Development, 'Policy framework for effective and efficient financial regulation:

in the financial system to ensure prudence, safety, integrity, and transparency of the core actors, institutions, systems, and financial markets.[11] Governing statutes establish and grant specified agencies rulemaking authority to issue regulations and to exercise supervisory functions under a *supervisory structure*.[12] The supervisory structure is a country's institutional 'architecture', which allocates the various functions of the governmental bodies that are necessary to achieve regulatory objectives.

Banking *supervision*, carried out through a nation's supervisory structure, entails *monitoring* whether and to what extent banks are complying with regulatory requirements, and enforcing compliance, as necessary. Banking agencies monitor compliance through a wide variety of means, including the review of publicly available information and confidential reports submitted by the banks, and, most importantly, through the examination process.[13] *Enforcement* of these regulatory requirements for non-compliance ranges from requiring banks to provide action plans in reports of examination (ROEs) to remediate deficiencies, ordering replacement of senior executives, and revoking operating licenses to bringing civil and criminal actions. National authorities grant enforcement powers to the supervisory agencies to enforce compliance with regulatory obligations.

Agencies *convey* or *communicate regulatory expectations* through a number of avenues. The principal source of expectations are the governing statutes and regulations issued under their authority. Most directly, bank examiners provide boards and senior executives the results of examinations. Broadly, they convey expectations through interpretive guidance, industry alerts, and speeches, among other avenues. Civil enforcement actions and Department of Justice (DOJ) prosecutions also play a role by creating precedents for the industry. All these sources of regulatory expectations play a crucial role in firms' structuring of the risk management and compliance functions.

Generally, the same federal agency issues rules, supervises regulated entities, conveys regulatory expectations, and enforces statutory and regulatory provisions for non-compliance.

2.2.3 Bank supervisory structures

A variety of factors play a role in determining the degree of effectiveness and efficiency of a supervisory structure. These include the level of development of a country's financial markets, the competence and expertise of its regulators, the independence and accountability of supervisory staff, the degree to which a

---

general guidance and high-level checklist' (29 January 2010), *OECD Journal: Financial Market Trends* 25 [OECD Policy framework].

11 OECD Policy framework 25. For example, capital requirements can affect actors' behavior by increasing the amount of capital required to engage in different types of financial activities. Ibid.

12 The following section, § 2.2.3, discusses supervisory structures in detail.

13 This concept of monitoring differs somewhat from that presented in Goodhart, *Financial Regulation* 189. There, *monitoring* is observing whether the rules are being obeyed, and *supervision*, the more general observation of financial firms' behavior. This book considers monitoring to be one of several aspects of supervision.

supervisory structure is adapted to the structure of the country's own financial services sector, and the resources the national authorities have dedicated to the system.[14]

Until the mid-1990s, regulators and the academy did not consider supervisory structures a worthwhile subject of investigation. This sentiment has changed as the financial services sector increasingly diverged from the regulatory framework originally designed to regulate it. The traditional tripartite regulatory and supervisory framework based on banking, securities, and insurance activities was not well equipped to ensure comprehensive and effective supervision of the financial markets in the 1990s and afterwards[15] with the rise of large, complex bank and non-bank financial conglomerates.

2.2.3.1 Four primary supervisory structures

Supervisory structures can be grouped into four models of financial system supervision: the functional, institutional (or entity-based), unified (or integrated), and 'twin-peaks'[16] models.[17] It is likely no pure form of any of the models exists. A combination of two or more is prevalent.[18] The BCBS adopts a neutral stance on which of the four supervisory structures is most suitable for today's financial markets.[19] Whichever of these structures a national authority selects, the ultimate standard for the wisdom of the choice is its effectiveness and efficiency in achieving the financial regulatory objectives.[20]

---

14 These criteria are an amalgam of criteria suggested by the BCBS and by David Llewellyn and Michael Taylor. See generally David Llewellyn, 'Institutional structure of financial regulation and supervision: the basic issues' (June 2006), Paper presented at World Bank seminar: Aligning Supervisory Structures with Country Needs, 6–7 June 2006 [Llewellyn, Institutional structure] and Michael Taylor, 'Regulatory reform after the financial crisis: Twin Peaks revisited' 12 [Taylor, Regulatory reform] in Robin Huang and Dirk Schoenmaker (eds.), *Institutional Structure of Financial Regulation* (Routledge: 2015) [Huang and Schoenmaker, *Institutional Structure*]. Llewellyn and Taylor highlight other criteria that relate chiefly to achievement of regulatory objectives without obvious implications for the risk management and compliance functions.

15 Taylor, Regulatory reform 13.

16 The twin-peaks model envisions separate supervisory agencies with oversight over business conduct regulation and prudential regulation (often termed 'safety and soundness' regulation). The twin-peaks model can be expanded to a 'three-peaks' version by separating prudential regulation into micro-prudential and macro-prudential regulation. This book applies the term 'twin-peaks' to describe both versions given its prominence in the regulatory literature.

17 Group of Thirty, 'The structure of financial supervision: approaches and challenges in a global marketplace' (2008) [Structure of financial supervision]. These taxonomies of structural design and objectives are broadly accepted. See generally Llewellyn, Institutional structure. The separate monetary policy goal of economic growth and price stability, the key role of a central bank, is relevant to the goal of financial stability. Central banks' role in monetary policy makes them logical candidates for prudential supervision as well, but such a combined role is not without controversy. See § 2.2.3.3.

18 Structure of financial supervision 23.

19 Instead, it provides guidance on the elements of an effective and efficient regulatory regime. The BCBS has established minimum standards for sound prudential regulation and supervision of banks and banking systems. The BCBS emphasizes risk-based supervision that focuses on outcomes beyond 'passive assessment of compliance with rules'. BCBS, Core principles for banking supervision 4.

20 See § 2.2.4 and Table 2.1 for a discussion of 'effectiveness' and 'efficiency' in financial regulation. See also n. 23 for a definition of these terms. It is taken as a given that in constructing

2.2.3.2 Critical need for coordination of agencies in financial crises

The coordination of policy among all agencies at times of crisis is critical. The US, UK, and EU each has a financial stability coordinating authority that acts in this capacity.[21] The need for such coordination poses a challenge for effective bank supervision, particularly in fragmented structures like that of the US.

2.2.3.3 Central bank's combined role in monetary and financial stability

Another issue is whether to delegate the financial stability function to the central bank in addition to its core role of determining and implementing monetary policy. This decision varies from country to country. Commentators vigorously debate the virtues and drawbacks of each of the supervisory structures and whether the central bank should have macro-prudential regulatory and supervisory authority.[22] In the US, UK, and EU, the central bank has this authority in addition to its monetary policy function.

2.2.4 Critiques of the four supervisory structures: lessons of the GFC

Table 2.1 summarizes the core features of the supervisory structures and their efficiency and effectiveness[23] in achieving financial regulatory objectives. The GFC forced governments to reassess the ranking in importance of these objectives and how best to optimize the supervisory structure.

The GFC dramatically showed not only the deficiencies of banking firms' business strategies, risk management, and compliance systems but also the deficiencies of the regulatory and supervisory framework governing systemic risk. Supervisors without exception failed in detecting and preventing the buildup of risks in the banking sector and were slow to comprehend the dimensions of the crisis once it began to unfold. Regulators globally did not fully comprehend the risks associated with the increasing complexity of financial conglomerates' business model; their incentive structure in securitizations; and their legal, operational, and geographical structure as the new millennium approached.[24]

---

its supervisory structure, a national authority is pursuing the public interest. The scholarly debate concerning whether government agencies are pursuing these policy objectives in the interest of the public good, termed 'public interest' regulation, or are pursuing the interests of the industry they are regulating, termed 'public choice' regulation, is beyond the scope of this book.

21 In the US, UK, and EU, these are, respectively, the Financial Stability Oversight Council, the Bank of England, and the European Central Bank. At the supranational level, the Financial Stability Board coordinates policy action by the world's major central banks and supervisors and reviews the work of the BCBS and other standard-setting organizations. §§ 6.2.8.3–6.2.8.4 cover coordination of systemic risk regulation in more detail.

22 See, e.g., Charles Goodhart, 'The organizational structure of banking supervision' (February 2002), 31(2) *Economic Notes: Review of Banking, Finance and Monetary Economics* 1.

23 *Efficient* is defined as 'capable of producing desired results with little or no waste', and *effective* as 'producing a decided, decisive, or desired effect'. Merriam-Webster Dictionary, at <https://www.merriam-webster.com/dictionary>. Peter Drucker famously distinguished effectiveness from efficiency as 'doing the right things and doing things right'. Peter Drucker, 'Managing for business effectiveness' (May 1963) *Harvard Business Review*, at <https://hbr.org/1963/05/managing-for-business-effectiveness>.

24 Goodhart, *Financial Regulation* 39.

Table 2.1 The four supervisory structures of financial regulation: efficiency/effectiveness

Supervisory structure	Structural features	Efficiency/effectiveness
Entity-based (or institutional)	• Oversight based on legal status or charter of the entity (e.g., broker-dealer is regulated by securities regulator). • This regulator supervises all relevant regulatory *objectives*. • Legal status determines scope of permissible activities.	• Becoming obsolete as financial services become more complex and integrated, with blurring of lines between traditional business lines and financial instruments. • Can address drawbacks by coordination among regulators.
Functional	• A separate functional regulator for each type of business activity (e.g., banking or securities transactions). • Each business has its own regulator; potential of several regulators for a single firm.	• Effective if separate regulators coordinate well. • Becoming obsolete; countries moving toward twin-peaks and integrated models.
Unified (or integrated)	• A single 'super-regulator' oversees all aspects of a country's financial services industry. • Combines oversight relating to all regulatory objectives.	• Can be effective and efficient in countries with small financial services sector. • Reduces jurisdictional conflict between agencies and redundancies. • But in large agencies, bureaucratic infighting can still occur. • Agency may be conflicted by favoring one policy goal over others.
Twin peaks (or 'objectives-based)	• Oversight based on regulatory goals, or 'objectives'. • A firm is supervised by separate agencies specializing in each of the three regulatory objectives.	• Supervision by specialized agencies can be effective and efficient. • Eliminates potential conflicts of 'unified' approach. • US Treasury recommended twin peaks in 2008.

Source: Group of Thirty, 'The Structural of Financial Supervision: Approaches and Challenges in a Global Marketplace' (2008).

In the UK, the Financial Services Authority (FSA) focused on business conduct regulation of LFIs with too little regard for their financial stability.

2.2.4.1 Criticism directed at institutional structure

Of the four supervisory structures, the *institutional* approach has generally received the greatest criticism. Under this model, the legal status of a company or what agency it must register with to do business determines which agency acts as the firm's main regulator and supervisor. For example, the Securities and Exchange Commission (SEC) is the primary regulator[25] of firms organized as broker-dealers. They must register with the SEC, whose jurisdiction primarily is limited to the securities industry. Commentators generally consider the institutional model obsolete due to the emergence of large, full-service conglomerate financial institutions dealing in financial instruments that combine features of securities, banking, and insurance.[26] The model may leave significant gaps in financial regulation.[27]

Despite its obvious drawbacks, the institutional model remains largely intact throughout the US's balkanized regulatory framework. In fact, Dodd-Frank extended the model to newly created regulated entities.[28] Moreover, US banking organizations potentially must comply with the laws and expectations of both state and federal regulators; among federal regulators, with those of both banking and capital markets agencies; and among banking agencies, often more than one. Each supervisor's remit is generally defined by the legal status or organizational charter of the regulated entity. Commentators have roundly criticized the regulatory inefficiencies and compliance costs of the US's duplicative, fragmented supervisory system.[29]

2.2.4.2 The functional model

The functional model, like the institutional, relies on neatly confined boundaries of categories of business activity. In today's complex markets, compartmentalized financial activities are more the exception than the rule. Under the functional approach, the type of business activity determines which agency conducts supervisory oversight. Multiple regulators would supervise a single entity that does more than one type of business. For this reason, both the

---

25 Each financial institution under current law is assigned a primary regulator. Other regulators may have more limited authority to examine the firm or rely on the examination results of the primary regulator. Primary regulators are discussed in more detail at § 2.3.1.1.

26 Structure of Financial Supervision 13. An example of such a financial instrument is at § 2.3.2 n. 71.

27 A prime example of a regulatory gap existing before the GFC was American International Group's (AIG) CDS business. A CDS in economic substance is an insurance contract. Under functional regulation a state insurance commission would regulate CDS. AIG assumed the legal status of a savings and loan holding company by registering with the Office of Thrift Supervision, thus becoming subject to its jurisdiction. AIG was thereby able to avoid regulation of its CDS business over which the Office of Thrift Supervision had no jurisdiction.

28 An example includes new intermediaries in the derivatives markets.

29 See generally Saule Omarova, 'One step forward, two steps back?' 137–165 in Huang and Schoenmaker, *Institutional Structure* (Routledge: 2015) [Omarova, One step forward].

functional and institutional models suffer from obsolescence. Furthermore, a functional regulator potentially is responsible for ensuring achievement of more than one regulatory objective, leading to potential conflicts in pursuing multiple objectives.[30]

2.2.4.3 Unified system: a 'super regulator'

A unified system, envisioning a 'super regulator', may be more efficient for supervising the multiservice financial conglomerates. It would be less redundant. It may be particularly important where the conglomerate adopts a centralized approach to risk management and risk-taking, an important goal of the FRB in any case.[31] An apparent advantage of a unified model is lack of jurisdictional conflicts among regulators, while a key disadvantage is that it creates a 'single point of regulatory failure'.[32] The unified approach may be more effectively deployed in countries with smaller financial market sectors.[33] The UK, a leading global financial center, had adopted a unified approach in 1997, creating the FSA, only to eliminate the FSA in 2013 and convert to the current twin-peaks structure.

2.2.4.4 Virtues of twin-peaks model

The virtues of a twin-peaks model are several. It fosters supervisory expertise of examiners in pursuit of a single objective. It can mitigate the conflict between prudential and consumer protection oversight. It reduces the need for interagency coordination. A drawback of the twins-peak approach is the potential of significant compliance obligations, since multiple agencies will potentially supervise the same institution albeit for different purposes.

The twin-peaks approach is becoming the favored choice of banking regulators where revamping supervisory oversight is a feasible option. The GFC caused some countries to push for a twins-peak approach but the path-dependent nature of financial regulation can be an insurmountable roadblock. This was the obvious case in the US, where the Treasury Department recommended a twin-peaks approach and efforts to consolidate supervisory oversight failed.[34] The UK was able to make the switch to the twin-peaks model due to the perceived failure of the FSA in exercising active prudential oversight over Northern Rock and intervening in a timely manner. In addition, London was hit harder by the GFC than other financial centers such as New York and Tokyo. In a nutshell, the changeover was made possible because of the cultural and political shift from the laissez-faire, 'light-touch' ethos seen as highly sensitive to industry concerns prior to the GFC.[35]

---

30 Structure of Financial Supervision 24.
31 Llewellyn, Institutional structure 19.
32 Structure of Financial Supervision 14.
33 Ibid.
34 See § 2.3.2.1.
35 The culture of the system came to 'anything goes, as long as the compliance officer doesn't say no'. Brooke Masters, 'FSA to give way to "twin peaks" system', *Financial Times* (1 April 2013) (Quote of Martin Wheatley, a top FSA official).

2.2.4.5 Potential for regulatory arbitrage

Certain supervisory structures create a potential for regulatory arbitrage, defined as the structuring of activities by financial institutions in a way that reduces the impact of regulation without a corresponding reduction in the underlying risk.[36] Regulatory arbitrage is a risk in institutional supervisory structures. For example, the US has three main banking agencies and two capital market agencies. Financial institutions are motivated to charter under an agency with the weakest regulatory authority and supervisory oversight.

2.2.5 Impact of supervisory structure on firms' risk-return analysis of risk management and compliance functions

The supervisory structure will affect a firm's risk-return optimization analysis in its design, implementation, and enforcement of its risk management and compliance systems. As detailed in Chapter 3,[37] it is assumed that financial institutions in some manner conduct a risk-return analysis of compliance cost and risks whose objective is to maximize shareholder wealth. In this analysis, a firm will try to quantify the *inherent compliance risk* of a given business line and reduce it to a level of residual risk[38] that just falls within its pre-approved risk appetite by incurring the requisite amount of compliance costs.[39] The following benchmark is useful in evaluating a supervisory structure's effect on a firm's compliance cost and inherent compliance risk: *'The overall objective must be to create an institutional structure that reflects the objectives of regulation and that promotes these objectives most effectively and efficiently'*.[40]

2.2.5.1 Supervisory attributes that affect compliance cost and risk analysis

The five categories listed here summarize how a supervisory structure can affect firms' compliance cost and risk calculus. The key variables in this calculus are the degree of clarity of regulatory expectations and variability in inherent compliance risk. This summary draws on the literature on effective and efficient regulatory regimes.[41] The five categories are cross-referenced since they are interrelated and thus cannot be easily compartmentalized. Inadequate funding of regulatory resources (#3) is a problem common to all supervisory structures.

---

36 Danièle Nouy, 'Gaming the rules or ruling the game? – how to deal with regulatory arbitrage' (15 September 2017), European Central Bank, Speech at 33rd SUERF Colloquium, Helsinki.

37 § 3.5.2 provides a fuller description.

38 The concepts of 'inherent risk' and 'residual risk' are adopted from supervisory guidance relating to consumer protection regulation. See generally § 9.3.

39 'Compliance cost' in this context includes the risk management and compliance system designed to mitigate inherent risk. 'Inherent risk' is the risk existing before accounting for the control system. See § 3.5.2 for a full description of risk-return optimization and § 3.7.1.2 for a discussion of risk appetite.

40 Goodhart, *Financial Regulation* 151 (italicized in original text). This statement is primarily from a regulator's perspective.

41 Among other sources, this summary draws on Taylor, Regulatory reform 2.

1 CLARITY IN SUPERVISORS' OWN REGULATORY OBJECTIVES

Firms can more easily assess compliance risk and gauge compliance cost if supervisors have a clarity about their own mission as financial regulators. A high degree of clarity of regulatory mission will translate into clarity of regulatory expectations for the regulated entities, which figures directly in their risk-return analysis. By design, supervisors in a twin-peaks structure have clarity of regulatory mission. Relevant factors are the level of agency competence and resources (#3) that underpin prompt and effective advice that is consistent with the regulatory objective at issue. Under certain circumstances, a unified structure can result in confusion of regulatory objectives and lack of clarity in regulatory expectations. Supervisors who are adept and experienced in assessing financial conglomerates (#2) will also be able to focus regulatory expectations more effectively for such firms.

2 EFFECTIVENESS IN OVERSEEING FINANCIAL CONGLOMERATES

Achieving clarity of regulatory expectations and low variability of inherent compliance risk are particularly challenging in this category. All four other categories are relevant. The developed economies increasingly have a sophisticated financial services sector, dominated by large, complex, and internationally integrated financial institutions boasting multiple business lines, fast-paced innovation in financial instruments, and rapidly changing trading and investment portfolios. As a rule, a supervisory structure should reflect the structure of the industry and markets it regulates.[42] A highly fragmented structure that characterizes the US system can inhibit oversight of increasingly integrated but complex financial institutions, markets, and new financial instruments. A twin-peaks structure can be effective and efficient in regard to these firms' compliance cost and risk analysis.

In any supervisory structure a high level of interagency coordination is necessary to reduce compliance costs and inherent risks for financial conglomerates. This is especially true in institutional and functional supervisory structures.[43] It is also true in a twin-peaks structure, but to a more limited extent.[44] Coordination among division heads with respect to their respective regulatory objectives is also necessary in a unified system.

3 SUPERVISORY RESOURCES

Underfunding, a perennial problem for government agencies, can affect both compliance cost and inherent compliance risk analysis for banking firms. A supervisory structure may be effective on paper but not in practice without

---

42 Richard Abrams and Michael Taylor, 'Issues in the unification of financial sector supervision' (1 December 2000) IMF Working Paper WP/00/213, 3 [Issues in the unification]. The same holds in the supervision of a single industry. For example, the SEC, recognizing the wide diversity of business models and size of broker-dealers, refrains from imposing a 'one-size-fits-all' set of requirements.

43 The US supervisory structure does address the coordination issue. Banking law designates a primary regulator among the bank regulators to examine a depository institution. In addition, the CAMELS system establishes a common platform for rating safety and soundness. Dodd-Frank created the Financial Stability Oversight Council in part to coordinate action among the financial regulators.

44 See Issues in the unification 11.

adequate resources. On the one hand, in the highly dynamic finance industry, lack of experienced supervisory staff can undermine a firm's ability to design the control functions that meet regulatory expectations due to the lack of appropriate supervisory guidance. Lack of sufficient agency funding also can delay launching of innovative financial products, such as the emerging cryptocurrency asset class, due to delay in receiving necessary approvals.[45] On the other hand, lack of funding can *reduce* inherent compliance risk if it results in fewer enforcement actions (#5). In the US, resources are less of an issue in the Federal Reserve due to its self-funding status. However, as a rule, federal agencies must seek annual appropriations from Congress, imposing considerable variability in their budgets from year to year.

4 INDEPENDENCE AND ACCOUNTABILITY

Regulatory agencies that have broadly delegated discretionary powers, coupled with ineffective oversight by the legislative branch, can lead to arbitrary and capricious treatment of their regulated entities due to lack of accountability. This will increase both compliance cost and inherent compliance risk due to the unpredictability or overreaching in supervisory and regulatory actions. Conversely, if an agency also has a weak level of independence from its political master, the result can also be unpredictable, arbitrary, and capricious regulatory and enforcement actions. This category is related to categories 1 and 5.

5 ENFORCEMENT POWERS AND THEIR USE

Governing supervisory statutes typically grant supervisory agencies a wide range of enforcement powers. On the one hand, aggressive enforcement can lead to overreach in a prosecution program, increasing inherent compliance risk. Many commentators have sharply criticized the DOJ's approach in prosecuting organizations as being *ad hoc* and without effective constraints on how much cost the agency imposes on corporate defendants.[46] Rather than using a transparent approach relying on a regulatory process or a process overseen by the judiciary, compliance regulation is generated and enforced through an informal quasi-adjudicative process via privately negotiated deferred prosecution and non-prosecution agreements with little or no judicial intervention.[47] In addition,

---

45 Underfunding in 2018 caused the CFTC to become less flexible involving registration applications, among other things, while also increasing the need for interagency cooperation with the SEC concerning surveillance of cryptocurrency markets. See Gabriel Rubin, 'U.S. markets regulator considers buyouts, extension of hiring freeze', *Wall Street Journal* (8 May 2018). The CFTC's responsibilities for oversight of the derivatives markets have multiplied following the financial crisis. However, Congress has underfunded the agency for years. Its budget has remained unchanged from 2014–17 and was cut in 2018 by $1 million. Ibid.

46 Miriam Baer, 'Governing corporate compliance' (2016) 50 *Boston College Law Review* 949, 952 [Governing corporate compliance]. See also Sean Griffith, 'Corporate governance in an era of compliance' (2016), 57 *William & Mary Law Review* 2075, 2091.

47 Governing corporate compliance 652. 'Regulation-by-adjudication is the government's preferred method of generating compliance.' Ibid. For a comprehensive treatment of the DOJ's use of such agreements, see Brandon Garrett, *Too Big to Jail: How Prosecutors Compromise with Corporations* (Belknap Press: 2014).

multiple authorities may 'pile on' regulatory actions for the same underlying offense, further complicating assessment of compliance risk.[48]

In addition, the federal civil agencies and the DOJ have been criticized for using boilerplate compliance remediation that does not address or give credit to the unique aspects of a company's compliance program.[49] Thus, the unanswered question for firms is, 'How can our risk management and compliance program meet regulatory expectations?' The result is future compliance cost and unexpected compliance risk. Another potential cost is the insertion of bank examiners into a bank's business model if its CAMELS rating is '3' or below, potentially removing senior executives, and requiring costly remediation efforts. Mitigating this risk are the clearly spelled out triggers in the Prompt Corrective Action program, a core component of micro-prudential regulation.[50]

2.3 US regulatory and supervisory framework

The US system of financial regulation exemplifies how history, politics, and culture can play a continuing and determinate role in a regulatory framework.[51] The strong animus throughout US history against concentrated financial and political power and its federated political structure go far in explaining the practical infeasibility of reforming its fragmented institutional supervisory structure. These factors help to explain the US's 'maze of supervisory bodies incomprehensible to those familiar with the supervisory systems of other leading economies'.[52]

2.3.1 Structure of US banking agency regulation and supervisory oversight

The US regulatory regime is divided into several parallel regulatory silos, based largely on the legal status or charter of a financial institution, which includes banks, securities investment advisers and broker-dealers, commodity futures and derivatives intermediaries, and insurance companies.[53]

2.3.1.1 Jurisdiction of banking and capital markets agencies: primary regulators The FRB, Office of the Comptroller of the Currency (OCC), and the Federal Deposit Insurance Corporation (FDIC) are the three major federal bank regulators. In addition, the National Credit Union Administration (NCUA) regulates,

---

48 The DOJ recently announced a policy of coordinating with other federal and state agencies to limit the imposition of multiple fines. See US Department of Justice, 'Deputy Attorney General Rod Rosenstein delivers remarks to the New York City Bar White Collar Crime Institute (9 May 2018), Press Release, at <www.justice.gov/opa/speech/deputy-attorney-general-rod-rosen stein-delivers-remarks-new-york-city-bar-white-collar>.
49 Ethics Resources Center, 'The federal sentencing guidelines for organizations at twenty years' (2013) 87.
50 See § 5.5.1.2.
51 Structure of Financial Supervision 14.
52 Howell Jackson, 'Learning from Eddy: a meditation upon organizational reform of financial supervision in Europe' (9 January 2009) 2, at <http://ssrn.com/abstract=1325510>.
53 Omarova, One step forward 139.

insures, and supervises the nation's credit unions.[54] Each state has a financial regulatory authority that regulates banks and issues charters. Each of the three main federal banking agencies has direct supervisory examining authority, as a 'primary regulator', over a subset of federally insured depository institutions in the US banking system. The FRB is the primary regulator of state-chartered banks that are members of the Federal Reserve and international banking operations in the US organized as intermediate holding companies.

The OCC is the primary regulator of over 1,600 national banks and federal savings associations and about 50 federal branches and agencies of foreign banks, which together account for nearly two-thirds of the assets of the commercial banking system. The FDIC, which is responsible for administering the US's depository insurance fund, is the primary regulator of state-chartered banks that are not members of the Federal Reserve.

The US splits up supervision of capital markets activities between the SEC and the Commodity Futures Trading Commission (CFTC). The SEC and CFTC regulate securities and derivatives instruments, respectively, but a clear division between the two is not feasible, requiring ongoing cooperation by the two agencies.[55] Dodd-Frank does not make these agencies explicitly responsible for regulating systemic risk.[56] However, it grants them oversight authority over entities to mitigate systemic risk.[57] Historically, the SEC and CFTC, staffed largely by lawyers, have been conduct-of-business regulators, with little experience in prudential regulation. There is no federally insured insolvency regime for their regulated entities.[58] Nevertheless, as noted at § 2.3.1.3, the Federal Reserve has consolidated oversight authority with respect to financial stability where the capital markets firms are part of a BHC. The Federal Reserve also has supervisory authority over non-bank institutions designated as systemically important financial institutions, or SIFIs, by the Financial Stability Oversight Council (FSOC).

2.3.1.2 US's dual banking system

In the US's federal system of government, bank regulation exists on both the state and federal level. The OCC charters, regulates, and supervises national banks, and state banking commissions charter, regulate, and supervise banks that choose to obtain banking powers under state law. All state-chartered banks have both a state and one or more federal regulators, another example of duplicative,

---

54 Credit unions are not-for-profit cooperative organizations owned by their depositors. Like the FDIC, the NCUA insures deposits up to $250,000.

55 This is especially the case with swaps instruments that combine features of securities and derivatives. Dodd-Frank created joint jurisdiction by the two agencies over 'mixed swaps' with the expectation that they would closely cooperate in resolving disputes.

56 For example, Title VII of Dodd-Frank grants the two agencies numerous responsibilities regarding regulation of the OTC derivatives markets that only indirectly address systemic risk.

57 For example, the SEC oversees clearing agencies designated as 'Financial Market Utilities' (FMUs) as systemically important. Also, both have some oversight authority over the OTC derivatives marketplace to reduce systemic risk. See 1.3.3.1.

58 The Securities Investor Protection Corporation, a non-governmental agency funded by fees it assesses on its broker-dealer members, insures customers' accounts up to $500,000 per account in the event of a broker-dealer's insolvency. 15 USC § 78aaa et seq.

overlapping regulation and supervision and potential for regulatory arbitrage.[59] With the exception of the First and Second Banks of the United States,[60] banks were chartered exclusively by the states until 1863, when Congress created the OCC. Despite the cost of duplicative regulation and supervision, the competing state-chartering system can offer smaller banks a supervisor that is 'closer to home' and potentially more responsive to the needs of the state banks.

2.3.1.3 Systemic risk regulation: Federal Reserve's consolidated supervisory authority

As part of its remit to ensure financial system stability, the Federal Reserve has consolidated supervisory authority to inspect and monitor all BHCs, savings and loans holding companies, and FSOC-designated SIFIs and their non-bank subsidiaries. The Federal Reserve's supervisory authority includes the large investment banking firms Goldman Sachs and Morgan Stanley, the two remaining large stand-alone investment banking firms that converted to BHCs in 2008. This consolidated supervisory authority is the only other instance of 'objectives'-based, twin-peaks regulation in addition to the Consumer Financial Protection Bureau's (CFPB) conduct-of-business supervisory oversight in the US system.

BHCs can become 'FHCs',[61] a status allowing them to engage in an extremely broad range of financial activities via separate subsidiaries in securities underwriting, merchant banking, and other activities 'incidental' or 'complementary' to financial activities. Each of these activities is 'functionally' regulated by the appropriate regulatory agency. Nearly all large BHCs are now registered as FHCs. There are no longer any 'pure' investment banks that are large financial conglomerates.[62]

The Federal Reserve's consolidated supervision does not entirely address the 'inherent lack of a system-wide focus' on the financial stability objective.[63] Such supervision is essential in light of the emergence of large conglomerate institutions over the last two decades. The FRB does not have supervisory authority over financial institutions with no affiliated banks and that are not designated by FSOC as SIFIs.[64] Dodd-Frank attempted to institutionalize a system-wide focus in creating FSOC as a financial stability overseer whose members are the

---

59 The federal regulator and supervisor is the FDIC or the FRB, or both. See § 2.3.1.1.

60 Congress chartered the First Bank of the United States in 1791. Its 20-year charter expired in 1811. It chartered the Second Bank of the United States in 1816; its charter expired in 1836.

61 To qualify as an FHC, a BHC, among other things, has to be well capitalized and managed and have a satisfactory rating under the CRA. 12 USC § 2901. The CRA requires agencies to rate banks' level of credit-related services to the communities in which they operate and obtain deposits.

62 § 3.3.1 discusses the special issues involving BHC corporate governance, including the risk management and compliance functions. § 1.3.3 discusses the emergence of BHCs and their concentration and complexity. In addition, Gramm-Leach mandates regulation of non-bank subsidiaries. The SEC regulates broker-dealers, the CFTC, commodities future commission merchants, and the state insurance commissioners, insurance subsidiaries.

63 Omarova, One step forward 141.

64 Dodd-Frank by default deems BHCs with over $250 billion in total consolidated assets to be SIFIs and subject to enhanced prudential regulation. FSOC has also designated as SIFIs several

heads of the main US financial market agencies, chaired by the Secretary of the Treasury. However, FSOC is an unwieldly solution to stability oversight and has significant coordination problems and difficulty in achieving consensus. Chairship by a cabinet secretary also injects political considerations into FSOC's deliberations. None of the four financial institutions FSOC originally designated as SIFIs retains this label.[65]

2.3.1.4 Consumer Financial Protection Bureau

Congress in Dodd-Frank did establish some features of the twin-peaks structure in creating the CFPB. The CFPB regulates and oversees consumer protection in financial services[66] provided by both banks and non-bank financial institutions. Before Dodd-Frank, consumer protection was overseen by seven separate federal agencies[67] in addition to state regulators. Nevertheless, Dodd-Frank ensured that some remnant of a fragmented supervisory approach would remain by excluding CFPB authority over depository institutions with total assets under $10 billion. For those institutions, the banking agencies retain full supervisory authority, thus continuing some of the complexity of the previous regime.

2.3.2 Obsolescence of US supervisory structure

Until the 1970s, the institutional approach to banking regulation in the US married form with substance in a very effective manner. Investment banks and other broker-dealers, commercial banks, and insurance companies each carried out lines of business that were easily compartmentalized within these firms' charters. The New Deal's entity-based regulation and supervision made eminent sense for four decades.[68]

However, beginning in the 1970s, several developments in the financial markets called this regulatory architecture into question. Most fundamentally, the transformation in the banking business model and the services and financial instruments that banks provide have evolved beyond the institutional confines of regulation that governs single types of businesses.[69] The financial markets have become much more integrated globally. Commercial banking and capital markets activities have increasingly converged, the prime example being securitization.[70] A new financial product may involve aspects of banking, insurance, derivatives,

---

FMUs, which engage in clearing and settlement of securities and other financial transactions and which pose systemic risk to the financial system.

65 FSOC rescinded the SIFI status of the last financial institution, Prudential Financial, Inc., on 17 October 2018.

66 Consumer protection regulation and its expectations for risk management and compliance are the subjects of Chapter 9.

67 These were the OCC, FRB, FDIC, Office of Thrift Supervision (later folded into the OCC and other agencies), Federal Housing Bank Board, SEC, and CFTC.

68 The most prominent example was the Glass-Steagall Act's separation of banking into investment banking and commercial banking, with separate regulators dedicated to each line of business. For at least 40 years the jurisdictional boundaries were relatively impermeable.

69 § 1.3 covers this transformation.

70 See § 1.3.1 for a detailed description of the securitization process.

and securities activities.[71] Relatedly, the type of business may appear to involve business conduct but can have safety and soundness issues that are not properly overseen.

2.3.2.1 Dodd-Frank retained the institutional structure

Despite the Treasury Department's proposal of a twin-peaks system in the midst of the GFC,[72] the US continued its supervisory structure largely unaltered, organized generally along institutional lines. Entrenched political interests, such as multiple congressional oversight committees, contributed to this path dependency. Moreover, Dodd-Frank replicated the existing entity-based supervisory framework for capital markets intermediaries in creating new swaps intermediaries and derivatives trading and reporting platforms.[73] The path-dependency of US financial regulation and supervision imposes considerable compliance costs and challenges in risk analysis for banking firms and other financial institutions. This costly obsolescence will only increase as financial firms continue to innovate and the financial markets become increasingly integrated. In addition, the US's fragmented system provides a fertile ground for regulatory arbitrage between the state and federal authorities and among the federal regulators as well.

2.3.3 Compliance cost and inherent compliance risk under US structure

The US's complex, fragmented, overlapping entity-based bank supervisory regime imposes significant compliance costs and results in an unduly complicated compliance risk assessment. Regulatory overlap is pervasive. In fact, Dodd-Frank *increased* the number of federal agencies and requires negotiated solutions by FSOC's member agencies for SIFI designations and FSOC's annual reports on emerging systemic risks.[74] Subject to certain restrictions, banks can choose to be supervised by one of several agencies, each of which has unique examination practices, oversight, and oversight priorities.[75] Thus, selection can have important consequences for the compliance risk and cost analysis.

The regime imposes obvious social costs both in terms of public resources and in compliance costs internally for the banking industry. To avoid duplicative and costly bank examinations by multiple agencies with overlapping jurisdictions, Congress in 1979 created the Federal Financial Institutions Examination Council

---

71 Structure of Financial Supervision 20. An example is portfolio insurance, which is effectively an insurance policy that hedges against market risk by combining equities, debt, and derivatives instruments. Specifically, it is hedging a portfolio of stocks against market risk by short-selling stock index futures, with embedded leverage.

72 Treasury Secretary Paulson proposed a three-step process that would eventually result in an objectives-based system of supervision. See Department of the Treasury, 'Blueprint for a modernized financial regulatory structure' (March 2008).

73 See § 1.3.3.1, which discusses the derivatives businesses of multiservice banking firms.

74 While Congress folded the Office of Thrift Supervision, the fifth banking agency, into the OCC, Dodd-Frank created the Office of Financial Research, FSOC, and the Federal Insurance Office, the last of which has a limited remit, with substantive authority remaining with state insurance agencies.

75 I owe this insight to Jeremey Kress.

(FFIEC), to which all the four main banking agencies belong. The FFIEC did reduce compliance costs through the uniform CAMELS system.[76] Neverthe-less, banking firms must host examiners from multiple banking agencies, each with their own set of regulatory objectives and expectations. For regulators, the greatest flaw of the current system under Dodd-Frank is the tension between the increased need for interagency cooperation and structural fragmentation that undermines such cooperation.[77]

2.4 UK regulatory and supervisory framework

The contrast in the evolution in the bank supervisory structure in the UK and the US, both before and following the GFC, is highly instructive. Parliament under-took a root-and-branch transformation of the UK structure to more effectively achieve the three objectives of financial regulation, a change that would have been impossible in the US. Post-GFC, of the US, UK, and EU, the UK has under-taken the most far-reaching and dramatic restructuring of financial supervisory architecture.

2.4.1 Failure of UK's unified structure

Prior to the post-GFC reform, the UK had a unified supervisory structure, with the FSA installed as the 'superagency'. However, the UK's tumultuous experi-ence in the GFC and failure of the FSA to properly exercise effective prudential supervision over Northern Rock, a large bank in Newcastle, and other LFIs led to a decisive break with the model of integrated supervision. The government turned decisively against the 'light-touch' regulatory philosophy that prevailed before the GFC.

2.4.2 Conversion to twin-peaks structure

Parliament adopted the twin-peaks model in the Financial Services Act of 2012.[78] It gave the Bank of England (BoE) responsibility for financial stability and created a new regulatory structure comprised of the BoE's Financial Policy Committee (FPC), operating within the BoE and charged with macro-prudential financial stability; the Prudential Regulation Authority (PRA), a subsidiary of the BoE, charged with prudential supervision with a view to safety and soundness, including minimizing the adverse effect of its regulated entities' failure on the stability of the financial system; and the Financial Conduct Authority (FCA), responsible for conduct-of-business supervision. These names accurately reflect these bodies' objectives-based focus, regardless of the type of financial institution

---

76 See § 5.4 for a discussion of the CAMELS rating system.

77 Omarova, One step forward 164.

78 The organic legislation that governs regulation of banking and financial services in the UK is the Financial Services and Markets Act of 2000.

they oversee. In part, the UK explicitly adopted the twin-peaks model to address a conflict in administering the prudential and conduct-of-business objectives. It was felt that the latter overrode the former in the FSA's supervision leading up to the GFC,[79] an example of how conflicts can undermine the exercise of supervisory oversight.

The PRA and FCA are the lead bank regulators in the UK system and have a duty to coordinate their supervisory activities. The PRA is the principle regulator of banking institutions but, pursuant to the 'twin-peaks' structure, its remit includes the entire range of financial institutions with the safety and soundness objective in mind – depository institutions, insurance companies, credit unions, and financial intermediaries (e.g., hedge funds). The FCA is charged with protecting investors, ensuring fair and orderly markets, and promoting competition. The FCA supervises conduct of the same firms as the PRA, with additional responsibility for brokers, investment advisers, and money managers, among others. The BoE has supervisory authority analogous to that of the US's Federal Reserve in its consolidated supervisory authority over all types of financial institutions.[80] The FPC identifies, monitors, and undertakes action to reduce systemic risks.

2.4.3 Compliance cost and inherent compliance risk under UK structure

The UK's twin-peaks structure has a logical clarity unlike many other supervisory systems. However, it is far from being tested. Critics were concerned that the radical overhaul of the UK's financial supervisory structure and the FSA's disbanding would result in the loss of a considerable number of experienced supervisors. This factor relates to all of the supervisory attributes affecting compliance cost and risk analysis covered in § 2.2.5.1 with the exception of 'independence and accountability'.

2.5 EU regulatory and supervisory framework

By and large, the EU has an institutional supervisory structure, with separate agencies overseeing banking, insurance, and securities intermediaries.[81] The overriding issue in the federated EU structure is harmonization of supervision throughout the eurozone. The BCBS in Basel III provides the framework for

---

79 Parliament sharply criticized the FSA for devoting the bulk of its resources and attention to consumer protection to the detriment of prudential supervision. A converse example is where a supervisor concerned with a bank's safety and soundness may overlook questionable conduct endangering consumer interests because such conduct is generating a steady stream of profits, enhancing its financial viability. This was one rationale in the US for consolidating consumer protection in the CFPB from the several banking agencies whose primary focus is prudential safety and soundness. These agencies had placed consumer protection low in the order of their priorities.

80 The BoE can request information or documents 'reasonably required in connection with the exercise by the Bank of its functions in pursuance of the Financial Stability Objective'. Financial Services Act of 2012, Section 9Y.

81 The EU's European Supervisory Authorities consist of the European Banking Authority, the European Insurance and Occupational Pensions Authority, and the European Securities and Markets Authority.

such harmonization in its standard setting. However, establishing an effective and efficient supervisory system in the EU will be a significant challenge. The EU launched an initiative in 2012 to establish a Europe-wide banking union to promote a stable and integrated financial system. This initiative is yet to be fully realized.[82]

The European Central Bank (ECB) exercises authority over national banking supervision through the Single Supervisory Mechanism (SSM), introduced in 2014, for which it is the lead supervisor.[83] The EU created the SSM based on the premise that national regulation had failed in supervising the highly inter-connected multinational financial conglomerates. The primary objectives of the SSM are to ensure the safety and soundness of the European banking system, to increase financial integration and stability, and to ensure consistent supervi-sion across all member countries. To this end, the SSM promotes the 'single rulebook'[84] approach that aims to ensure coherent and effective supervision throughout the eurozone.[85] In addition, the SSM structure requires separation of monetary from supervisory functions to address conflicts between the ECB's monetary policy objectives and prudential oversight responsibilities.

The EU established the SSM as a coordinating system composed of national competent authorities (NCAs), which are the bank supervisors in participating member states,[86] and the ECB. In the supervisory structure, financial institutions fall into 'significant' and 'less significant' categories.[87] The ECB directly super-vises the former, and the NCAs supervise the latter. The ECB argues that the

---

82 Of the three pillars comprising the banking union, only two, an SSM and an SRM, have been implemented. The third, a European deposit insurance scheme, has not been agreed to. In addition, regulation of banks' sovereign exposures, which played a large role in the eurozone crisis, is still absent. The deposit insurance scheme would shift sovereign default risks to the European level. Isabel Schnabel, 'Europe's banking union lacks the key element of deposit insurance', *Financial Times* (28 August 2018).

83 The European Commission proposes legislation that the European Parliament and EU Coun-cil then approve. Katarzyna Sum, 'The factors influencing the EU banking regulatory framework: impediments for the new regulations' in Katarzyna Sum, *Post-Crisis Banking Regulation in the Euro-pean Union* (Springer: 12 October 2016) 169, 170.

84 The European Banking Authority describes the 'single rulebook' as follows:

The Single Rulebook aims to provide a single set of harmonised prudential rules which insti-tutions throughout the EU must respect. The term Single Rulebook was coined in 2009 by the European Council in order to refer to the aim of a unified regulatory framework for the EU financial sector that would complete the single market in financial services. This will ensure uniform application of Basel III in all Member States. It will close regulatory loopholes and will thus contribute to a more effective functioning of the Single Market.

European Banking Authority, 'The Single Rulebook', at <www.eba.europa.eu/regulation-and-policy/single-rulebook>.

85 EU-level supervision addressed potential cross-border contagion from bank crises. European Council, Council of the European Union, 'Single supervisory mechanism', at <www.consilium.europa.eu/en/policies/banking-union/single-supervisory-mechanism/>.

86 These are member states that are part of the Euro area and other member states entering into close cooperation with the SSM. Ibid.

87 A credit institution is 'significant' if its total assets exceed €30 billion or 20% of national GDP and is one of the three most significant credit institutions in a member state, among other things. Ibid.

SSM combines the strengths of the ECB and of the NCAs. It builds on the ECB's macroeconomic and financial stability expertise and on the NCAs' knowledge and expertise in the supervision of credit institutions within their jurisdictions. The NCAs form the decentralized base of the supervisory pyramid.

2.5.1 Compliance cost and inherent compliance risk under EU regulatory framework

Uncertainty concerning the future of the EU increases both compliance cost and inherent compliance risk. The SSM bank supervisory system is a work in progress that faces several challenges. The success of the system depends on harmonization across the region. However, the EU is encountering strong political headwinds from populist governments that put its harmonization plans in danger.[88] A true banking union is not yet a reality. Nonetheless, the single rulebook promises some degree of cohesion despite the decentralized NCA structure and a saving in compliance costs.

2.6 Conveying regulatory expectations: rules-based and principles-based approaches

Thus far we have considered the effectiveness and efficiency of a supervisory structure in conveying regulatory expectations with respect to compliance cost and compliance risk. To be discussed in this connection is the role of 'regulatory design' – the choice of the format and textual structure – of statutory and regulatory provisions. Regulatory design ranges from highly specific, hard-wired capital adequacy ratios to broadly stated provisions concerning banks' 'safety and soundness' that grant agencies expansive discretionary powers. Choice of regulatory design has critical implications for firms' design and implementation of their risk management and compliance functions.

The choice of regulatory design centers around a dichotomy between a 'rules-based' and 'principles-based' regulatory regime. The rules-principles division has generated considerable debate among policymakers, scholars, and the finance industry. In the UK, the post-crisis backlash against the FSA's principles-based approach helped push the national authorities toward a more prescriptive regime. In the US as well, the finance industry has lobbied to move regulatory design in prudential regulation from a principles-based toward a more rules-based model, with implications for future regulatory change.[89]

---

88 In March 2018 Italy elected a populist government. Hungary and Poland also have populist-oriented governments. *Brexit* also put into question the future of Europe's political union.

89 The GOP introduced bills in the US House and Senate in 2017 with this stated objective in setting monetary policy. See Financial CHOICE Act of 2017, H.R. 10–115th Congress (2017–2018). See Section 1001, inserting Section 2C of the Federal Reserve Act, Subsection (c) includes 'Requirements For A Directive Policy Rule'.

2.6.1 Issues of theory and policy

The debate over the rules-principles dichotomy is far more than an exercise in theoretical line drawing.[90] Classifying this book's four core areas of banking regulation within this framework can help risk management and compliance professionals understand the implications for internal controls and compliance P&Ps.[91] The overriding question is which of the two approaches, or some combination, best accomplishes the banking agencies' regulatory objectives,[92] on the one hand, and enables firms to better assess compliance cost and risk, on the other.

How supervisors administer a regulation on the ground is the result of a complex and dynamic interaction between the governing statutory structure and regulatory framework, the regulatory objectives at issue, and examiners' expertise and supervisory resources. A nation's legal culture also plays a role. *Ex post* enforcement actions play a much larger role in the US's adversarial setting than in the UK, where the focus is more on *ex ante* principles-based supervision.[93] Nevertheless, despite these caveats, an understanding of the theory underlying the division of design approaches is of considerable practical importance.

2.6.1.1 Tradeoffs for regulators and firms

Choosing a rules-based or a principles-based approach involves several tradeoffs for both regulators and firms. The advantages of rules for regulators are as follows. Rules define boundaries of permissible conduct *ex ante* to enforcement actions. The time and resources spent in predefining impermissible conduct reduces the time and resources on proving violations.[94] Rules also can be efficient in defining recurring, homogeneous conduct, such as may occur in providing routine financial consumer services.[95]

However, the disadvantages of prescriptive rules for the government are many. Regulators must spend considerable resources and time in predefining prohibited conduct and responding to public comment during the process. Although rules provide clarity about the compliance process, they can be ambiguous about the regulatory objective and thus undermine its achievement.[96] This lack of clarity can result in regulatory arbitrage. Bright lines and detailed exceptions

---

90 According to a leading scholar on the issue, regulatory enthusiasm for the binary classification is 'misplaced' because it is too crude to guide regulatory design, accounting systems, and corporate law. Invariably, one ends up sorting individual provisions onto a continuum rather than precisely fitting them in the two categories. Regulatory provisions interact within large complex systems and are not isolated from each other. Lawrence Cunningham, 'A prescription to retire the rhetoric of "principles-based systems" in corporate law, securities regulation and accounting' (2007), 60 *Vanderbilt Law Review* 1411, 1413 [A prescription to retire].

91 See § 2.6.2.

92 A prescription to retire 1424.

93 Christie Ford, 'Principles-based securities regulation in the wake of the global financial crisis' (July 2010), 55 *McGill Law Journal* 257, 286 [Principles-based securities regulation].

94 Pascal Frantz and Norvald Instefjord, 'Rules vs principles based financial regulation' (25 November 2014) 1, at <https://ssrn.com/abstract=2561370> [Frantz & Instefjord, Rules vs principles].

95 Dan Awrey, 'Regulating financial innovation: a more principles-based proposal?' (2011), 5 *Brooklyn Journal of Corporate Financial & Commercial Law* 273, 280.

96 Frantz & Instefjord, Rules vs principles 1.

facilitate firms' strategic evasion, allowing artful dodging of a rule's spirit by literal compliance with its technical letter.[97] Bright-line rules can be a 'roadmap for fraud'.[98] Further, bright-line rules can exacerbate informational asymmetries by advantaging an informed, sophisticated party, such as brokers, in dealing with poorly informed retail investors. Finally, in a rapidly changing environment hard-wired rules can become obsolete faster than principles.[99]

Drawbacks for the government of principles-based regulation include the need for a well-funded, competent, and proactive public role in supervision and enforcement to interpret broad precepts and apply them to unique fact patterns. Regulators must have capacity to scrutinize information independently, calling for quantitative expertise and industry experience.[100] In addition, in a principles-based regime a regulator must review and provide guidance on firms' own internal rules, systems, and processes to ensure the achievement of the regulatory objective.[101]

Firms generally prefer prescriptive rules for many of the reasons that the government finds them disadvantageous. Principles-based regulation is generally disadvantageous for firms. Under a principles-based regime, the regulator sets down a clear set of objectives and general principles and leaves it to the firm to demonstrate how it will satisfy the objectives and principles.[102] The firm must decide how to design and implement a compliance system that accords with broad principles of conduct, creating the risk of supervisory rejection. The government sets the boundaries of permissible conduct *ex post*, through enforcement and other supervisory actions. Recently, industry resistance to such *ex post* enforcement may have played a role in the policy 'clarification' that agency guidance will not serve as a basis for enforcement action.[103] Firms prefer a rules-based regime in which costs of ambiguity in regulatory objectives are borne by the government and society rather than the firms.[104]

2.6.1.2 Preference for rules-based regimes

Many market participants in the US generally have viewed rules-based systems as providing greater predictability for regulated entities and individuals, lowering overall compliance risk.[105] A principles-based system can impose interpretive

---

97 A prescription to retire 1423.

98 In the SEC's famous phrase in defending the amorphous, judge-made definition of insider trading law, bright-line rules are a 'roadmap for fraud' for traders seeking a trading advantage.

99 A prescription to retire 1423.

100 Principles-based securities regulation 257, 292. But such experience and competence are called for on the front-end in formulating detailed prescriptive rules.

101 Julia Black, 'The rise, fall and fate of principles based regulation' (14 December 2010), LSE Legal Studies Working Paper No. 17/2010, 8, at http://ssrn.com/abstract=1712862 [The rise, fall and fate].

102 David Llewelyn, 'The economic rationale for financial regulation' (April 1999), FSA Occasional Papers Series 1, 49. Llewelyn terms this arrangement 'contract regulation'. Ibid.

103 Federal Reserve Board and others, 'Interagency statement clarifying the role of supervisory guidance' (12 September 2018) 1.

104 Frantz and Instefjord, Rules vs principles 1.

105 Peter Wallinson, 'Fad or reform: can principles-based regulation work in the United States?' (June 2007), American Enterprise Institute.

risk, which increases compliance risk.[106] Principles require a costly determination of the appropriate compliance system unless it is spelled out in guidance.[107] The need for IC functions, lawyers, and consultants to design the governance infrastructure in a principles-based regime can significantly increase costs.

However, rules-based regulation involving a complex, detailed rulebook[108] may result in excessive compliance costs, in interpretation, seeking guidance and exceptions, and errors in applying rules. Supervisors may not have the competence, experience, or resources to respond effectively to inquiries.[109] A highly prescriptive set of rules will compel firms to expend valuable resources in installing sophisticated IT systems and hiring skilled IT professionals. The Volcker rule is a prime example of a highly complex rule requiring a costly, dedicated risk management and compliance infrastructure.[110]

In the final analysis, a regulatory system will involve a mixture of principles and rules. Prescriptive rules have 'prudential backstops' and savings clauses that give discretion to supervisors to override paper compliance with the rules. General principles require rules to supply guidance on specific situations.

2.6.1.3 Critique of 'principles-based' systems following the GFC

In the postmortem after the crisis, a debate occurred on both sides of the Atlantic at the highest echelons of government concerning the virtues of principles versus rules. In part, differences in regulatory philosophy underlay the two approaches. A principles-based system appeared well suited for the market-based philosophy that prevailed among both US and UK regulators prior to the GFC by allowing firms leeway to design internal governance systems. The GFC illustrates how this approach can slide into bare self-regulation without meaningful regulatory oversight.[111]

As chief FSA executive Hector Sants pithily observed, 'A principles-based approach does not work with individuals who have no principles'.[112] The UK situation is more nuanced than the Sants quote suggests. According to a major postmortem report,[113] the failure in the UK was not due to a principles-based system but due to the deficiencies in the FSA's hands-off, market-based regulatory approach that assumed that markets were self-correcting and that market

---

106 The rise, fall and fate 17.

107 A prescription to retire 1424.

108 Andrew Haldane, the BoE's chief economist, offers a trenchant critique of the Basel III capital rules along these lines. See Andrew Haldane, 'The dog and the frisbee', Speech given at Federal Reserve Bank of Kansas City's 36th Economic Policy Symposium, 'The changing policy landscape' (31 August 2012). There have been several proposals to replace the complex Basel RWA regime with simple, higher capital requirements. See §§ 4.3.3–4.3.7 for a discussion of RWA capital adequacy regulation.

109 § 2.2.5.1.

110 §§ 8.3.1–8.3.2 cover the Volcker rule.

111 Principles-based securities regulation 259.

112 Abigail Townsend, 'Hector Sants says bankers should be 'very frightened' by the FSA', *The Telegraph* (12 March 2009).

113 Financial Services Authority, 'The Turner Review: a regulatory response to the global banking crisis' (March 2009).

discipline to which banks were subject could be trusted to limit risks. The FSA held that the primary responsibility for managing risk resided with senior management, not regulators, since senior management had the information to better assess business model risk. In its view, transparency, not product regulation and intervention, best ensured customer protection.[114]

In the US, a principles-based approach meant devolution to industry coupled with an ideology of self-regulation, contributing to insufficient oversight over the massive expansion of the OTC derivatives market.[115] The same philosophy motivated Congress's repeal of Glass-Steagall in 1999, allowing universal banking. Internationally, a market-based self-regulatory approach, reflected in the 'Pillar III' precepts, characterized certain components of the Basel regime.[116] The large, sophisticated banks[117] were permitted to use internal modeling to establish market-risk capital charges, subject to supervisory approval.[118]

Following the GFC, the US system remains largely 'rule-based' and the UK 'principles-based' with a greater focus on so-called outcomes-based supervision.[119] This generalization only goes so far. Much of US prudential regulation is principles-based, whose discretionary attributes the Trump administration is seeking to reduce as a matter of policy.[120] Nevertheless, despite the different policy solutions to the GFC, both the US and UK share in common a more intensive supervisory approach toward the risk management and compliance functions. Supervisors are much less trusting and skeptical about senior management and paying much more attention to firms' process, policies, and procedures in risk management.[121]

In the EU, principles-based regulation never took hold. National governments and the EU are increasingly relying on prescriptive requirements.[122]

2.6.2 Rules-principles classification of the four areas of banking regulation

Table 2.2 classifies the four areas of banking regulation, risk management, and compliance areas covered in this book as primarily rules-based or principles-based systems and indicates where some overlap occurs. As the literature on the subject

---

114 Ibid. 87.

115 Principles-based securities regulation 280.

116 The 'three pillars' that underpin the Basel capital adequacy regime are minimum bank capital requirements applicable to all banks (Pillar I), additional capital required by supervisors for individual banks (Pillar II), and market discipline based on transparency (Pillar III).

117 Under Basel II, advanced approaches banks could avoid the prescriptive capital ratios under the 'standardized' approach by using internal modeling. Basel III continues this regime, subject to more restrictive conditions.

118 See § 4.3.5.1. Post-GFC, the BCBS has undertaken the 'Fundamental Review of Trading Book' (FRTB) initiative, which places significant restrictions on banks' ability to use internal modeling to calculate capital charges. The FRTB in Europe is scheduled to become effective in 2019. See § 4.3.7.5.

119 Outcomes based on qualitative and behavioral terms, such as to act with 'integrity' or to act 'fairly' in best interests of a client, are hard to game. The rise, fall and fate 7.

120 This is evident in the elimination of the qualitative component of DFAST, the Dodd-Frank stress testing program. See § 7.4.3.

121 The rise, fall and fate 13.

122 Ibid. 19–20.

Table 2.2 Rules-principles classification of core areas of banking regulation

Regulatory area	Regulation	Principles-based or rules-based?
Micro-prudential regulation	Capital adequacy ratios	Rules-based, but large banks can use internal modeling
	Leverage ratio	Rules-based
	CAMELS system: primary safety and soundness regulation	Principles-based
	Prompt Corrective Action program	Combination; increasingly prescriptive as CAMELS rating declines
Macro-prudential regulation	Capital adequacy surcharges for systemically important banks	Rules-based, but with regulatory discretion
	Leverage ratio and liquidity ratios	Rules-based
	CCAR (stress testing)	Principles-based
	Living wills	Principles-based
	SPOE and TLAC	Rules-based
	Volcker rule	Combination; more prescriptive for larger banks
Consumer protection	Equality of access and fair treatment; disclosure; anti-fraud	Rules-based
AML/CFT	Suspicious Activities and Currency Transaction Reports	Combination: risk-based with prescriptive filing requirements
	Customer due diligence (CDD)	Combination
	'Know your customer'	Combination
	Four AML compliance pillars	Principles-based

indicates, all financial regulation necessarily involves a combination of hard-wired rules and supervisory discretion. The balance between prescriptive rules and broad principles has also been subject to significant evolution, which is certain to continue.[123]

Broadly, micro- and macro-prudential regulation is a combination of principles-based and rules-based regulation, and consumer protection and AML/CFT are primarily rules-based.[124] This classification reflects the latter two areas' focus on conduct regulation. A rules-based approach in consumer protection and AML/CTF regulation may be more appropriate for areas involving transactional, client-facing business lines with recurring patterns of conduct. A principles-based

---

123 Frederic Mishkin, a former FRB governor, describes the evolution in the early 1990s from a 'regulatory', rules-based approach to a 'supervisory' approach that focuses on corporate governance and risk management. Frederic Mishkin, 'Prudential supervision: why is it important and what are the issues?' (September 2000), NBER Working Paper 7926, 16, at <www.nber.org/papers/w7926.pdf>. [Mishkin, Prudential supervision].

124 Nevertheless, regulators require firms to adopt an overarching risk-based approach in implementing AML/CFT regulation. See § 10.3 n. 9.

regulatory framework in prudential regulation appears more suited for areas such as governance and risk management, where supervisors seek certain behavioral outcomes, and qualitative, judgmental approaches are needed to assess compliance.[125] The minimum capital adequacy requirements of micro- and macro-prudential regulation fall squarely within a rules-based regime.

2.7 Supervisory tools for conveying regulatory expectations

This chapter concludes with a description of supervisory tools used by regulators to convey regulators' expectations for individual banks' risk management and compliance systems. Up to this point the chapter has described the conveyance of expectations through statutory and regulatory provisions, supervisory structure, and regulatory design, which apply equally to all banks. Examinations are regulators' primary tool to convey expectations that are tailored to individual banks based on their unique risk profile. Enforcement actions are also an important tool, which often arise in connection with examinations.

2.7.1 Bank examinations

Examinations play a unique role in bank regulation and supervision in conveying regulatory expectations. They occur in three stages: pre-planning, the examination itself, and communication of examination findings. This section focuses on the communications stage relating to conveyance of findings. Chapter 5 has a more detailed description of the three stages.[126]

2.7.1.1 Communications stage

The communications stage is a critical component of supervisory oversight. The examination team provides an ROE to the bank's board of directors and senior management. The ROE informs management of the institution's CAMELS ratings and is a compliance examination's principal document of record. Examiners discuss key issues and preliminary findings in order to resolve significant differences concerning findings, conclusions, or recommendations.

At the exit meeting, OCC examiners focus on any significant deficiencies, areas of greatest risk to a bank, and plans for future supervisory activities. OCC examiners seek commitments from management to correct any significant deficiency identified. Management must communicate its commitment to correct deficiencies through action plans that set realistic time frames and benchmarks to measure progress. The plan must indicate how the board and management will monitor the successful implementation and execution of the plan.

---

125 OECD Policy Framework 26. A prudential, principles-based approach may be appropriate in certain areas of securities regulation. A senior official at the SEC has characterized its approach to broker-dealer and investment adviser compliance and risk management structures in prudential supervisory terms. Annette Nazareth, 'Remarks before the SIFMA compliance and legal conference' (26 March 2007), at <www.sec.gov/news/speech/2007/spch032607aln.htm>.

126 § 5.2.3.

The FRB, OCC, and FDIC issue 'Matters Requiring Immediate Attention' (MRIAs) and 'Matters Requiring Attention' (MRAs) to banks following their examinations. MRIAs are supervisory matters of the highest priority and include (1) matters with the potential to pose significant risk to the safety and soundness of the bank, (2) matters representing significant instances of non-compliance with laws or regulations, and (3) repeat criticism that has escalated in importance due to insufficient attention or action by the bank. MRAs, on the other hand, are matters that the agency expects a banking organization to address over time.[127]

2.7.2 Sliding scale of increasing strictness of supervisory actions

Bank supervisors have a range of tools that they typically use in a graduated escalation of enforcement actions to the extent a firm does not meet its expectations. In the enforcement area these include cease and desist orders, civil monetary penalties (CMPs), suspension or termination of FDIC insurance, civil and criminal litigation, and ultimately conservatorship and receivership.[128] The relationship between a banking agency and the firm under its supervision is less adversarial than in the case of the SEC and CFTC. Banking agencies' examinations provide the opportunity for initial feedback and an action plan. Inability or refusal to resolve issues raised in a supervisor's ROE can then lead to more formal enforcement actions such as a cease and desist proceeding, the agencies' primary enforcement tool.[129] In the case of written agreements, the agency has statutory authority to undertake a cease and desist proceeding or impose CMPs based on a breach of provisions in the agreement.[130]

Also important are the wide range of informal actions available to the banking agencies. Informal actions are generally available only for banks with composite CAMELS ratings[131] of 3 or better. A bank's board of directors will often enter into commitments with the aim of ensuring compliance with laws and regulations and to correct deficiencies highlighted in examination reports. The board resolution approving a commitment directs a bank's personnel to take corrective action regarding noted deficiencies. Board commitments are not public documents and thus do not provide indirect guidance to the industry as a whole.

Agencies also employ memoranda of understanding, to which they are parties and that include provisions similar to those in cease and desist orders, when they

127 See Federal Reserve Board, 'SR 13–13: supervisory considerations for the communication of supervisory findings' (17 June 2013).

128 Generally, receivership involves liquidating or winding up a depository institution's affairs and conservatorship involves preserving its going concern value in order to return it to health or ultimately to put it into receivership.

129 To carry its burden of proof, the agency must demonstrate that the bank (1) has engaged, is engaged, or is about to engage in an unsafe and unsound practice or (2) has violated, is violating, or is about to violate a regulation, a condition imposed in writing, or a written agreement. 12 USC § 1818(b).

130 12 USC §§ 1818(b), (e)(i)(2).

131 CAMELS component ratings rank banks' safety and soundness in six areas on a five-point scale ('1' being the highest rating). § 5.4 covers the CAMELS rating system and related compliance issues.

believe a board resolution would not adequately address deficiencies noted during an examination. More formality is attached to 'Individual Minimum Capital Ratios' (IMCRs), a supervisory letter addressed to the board of directors. Agencies give notice to a bank before issuing an IMCR. Failure to comply with an IMCR may be deemed an unsafe or unsound practice.[132]

Supervisory actions that are publicly disclosed impart regulatory expectations for the industry. This is true of settled enforcement actions and DOJ settlements, including deferred and non-prosecution agreements.

2.7.3 Pyramid of regulatory expectations

It is useful to conceive of the range and types of sources of regulatory expectations for the banking industry as consisting of a pyramid, illustrated by Figure 2.1. The diagram summarizes the various sources of regulatory expectations covered in this chapter. Statutory and regulatory obligations reside at the pyramid's apex. They establish requirements with which all or a defined subset of banking institutions must comply and agencies' authorization for rulemaking and enforcement

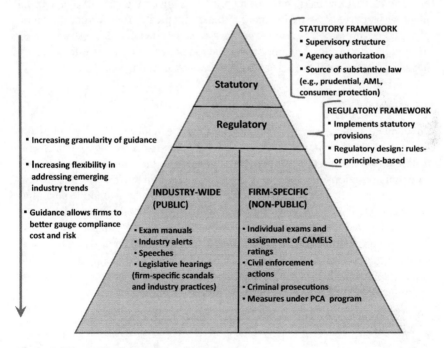

Figure 2.1 Pyramid of regulatory expectations

---

132 Meredith Boylan, 'Overview of federal bank enforcement actions', Venable LLP (15 February 2012), at <www.venable.com/insights/publications/2012/02/overview-of-federal-bank-enforcement-actions>.

authority.[133] They provide the foundation for the sources of expectations in the lower parts of the pyramid. To a limited extent, prescriptive statutory provisions and rules provide sufficient guidance by themselves, such as the capital adequacy requirements under the Basel capital regime.

As one travels toward the pyramid's base, supervisory guidance becomes more granular, allowing firms to some extent to quantify their compliance cost and compliance risk and make qualitative judgments in constructing their risk management and compliance programs. Agencies have a wide range of means with which to convey regulatory expectations. As the diagram indicates, the guidance in the lower half is in two categories: guidance directed to the banking industry as a whole and guidance for individual firms, but which provide, indirectly, guidance for the industry, provided such are publicly disclosed. In sum, the pyramid reflects the large menu of options agencies have to convey regulatory expectations.

Another key aspect of this schematic is the increasing flexibility the agencies have in addressing emerging trends in the banking industry as one approaches the pyramid's base. An example is the rapidly escalating issue of cyber risk, which is initially addressed through industry alerts, speeches, and strategically selected enforcement actions based on existing principles governing business conduct and industry practices. Legislation and rulemaking typically follow after this initial phase unless prompted by a high-profile scandal or other event. These are subject to significant procedural requirements, such as notice and comment for rulemaking and congressional consensus for new laws or amendments.

2.8 Conclusion

Policymakers' success in achieving their primary regulatory objectives ultimately lies in how clearly and effectively they convey their expectations for banks' control functions and systems of corporate governance through their guidance and enforcement actions. Their success in this regard will in turn affect firms' estimation of compliance cost and compliance risk in deciding how to implement regulatory expectations in the optimization of risk-return tradeoffs. Two major factors contributing to policymakers' desired outcome are national authorities' choice of the governing supervisory structure and their choice of regulatory design. A complex interplay exists between the clarity of agencies' own regulatory mission, resources, independence and accountability, enforcement policy and practices, and supervisory expertise in overseeing financial conglomerates.

---

133 Statutory provisions are either self-enforcing or require rulemaking by the federal agencies to implement them.

CHAPTER 3

Managing banks' risks through a corporate governance framework

3.1 Introductory overview

Over the last two decades policymakers have increasingly raised and formalized their expectations for banks' internal governance systems in managing the risks of their various lines of business. They have had little choice. The size, complexity, and opaqueness of financial conglomerates and the risks these firms impose on the financial system have made it virtually impossible for external regulation alone to ensure the *safety and soundness*[1] of individual banks and the banking system.[2] The GFC greatly accelerated the trend in regulatory cooptation of corporate governance and the control functions in minting the new macro-prudential framework, the subject of Chapters 6 through 8.

To explain this evolution in corporate governance, this chapter provides an overview of banks' governance system and of the risk management and compliance functions. This analysis finishes the foundational overview initiated by Chapter 1, regarding the risks created by the banking business model and conglomerate structure, and Chapter 2, which details the statutory and regulatory framework and the formation of regulatory expectations.

The chapter begins with a basic treatment of the role of a corporation's board of directors, their fiduciary duties, and the principal-agent problem that underlies COIs. It considers the corporate governance attributes that are unique to banks, examines the reasons why COIs are pervasive in the financial sector, particularly in the conglomerates, and presents a typology useful for evaluating COIs in the retail and institutional markets. The chapter then turns to the risk management, compliance, and internal audit control functions. It discusses the impact of state corporate law, federal prosecutorial policies, and the US Sentencing Guidelines on corporate compliance. Banks seek to optimize the amount of compliance costs by seeking to reduce inherent compliance risks to a level consistent with the board-approved risk appetite. The chapter treats two other important developments in corporate governance, the 3LOD model and enterprise risk management (ERM). The final section discusses the role of, and challenges in fostering, a culture of compliance in financial institutions.

---

1 'Safety and soundness' is the guiding standard for all prudential bank regulation. See § 5.3.
2 Charles Goodhart and others, *Financial Regulation: Why, How and Where Now?* (Routledge: 1998) 39. '[T]he nature and functions of external regulation must be turned away from generalized rule setting and towards establishing incentives/sanctions to reinforce external control mechanisms'. Ibid. 40.

3.2 A corporate governance primer

This section provides an elementary overview of the corporate governance system of corporations[3] organized in the US.

3.2.1 Core components of a corporate governance system

At its most basic, a corporate governance system is a structure through which the objectives of a company are established and the means of attaining those objectives and monitoring performance are determined.[4] In the modern corporation, in which managers, the agents, have a duty to act on behalf of the interests of owners, the shareholders, a corporate governance system is a system of checks and balances designed to achieve the objective for which it was organized and in doing so protect the owners' (shareholders) and, as necessary, other stakeholders' interests.[5]

3.2.1.1 Objectives of companies organized in the US and elsewhere
The primary objective of US and UK for-profit businesses organized as corporations is maximization of shareholder value. Shareholder wealth maximization is the law and a basic feature of corporate ideology.[6] In the case of banking institutions, the mandate to act in a safe and sound manner as defined by banking regulation and in supervision conditions this corporate governance precept. Elsewhere, particularly in continental Europe and Japan, boards must consider other stakeholders' interests in formulating companies' governing objectives alongside prudential regulatory objectives.[7] Shareholder wealth maximization in the US and UK is coming under increasing scrutiny but remains the reigning paradigm.

3.2.1.2 Managing the principal-agent relationship and conflicts of interest
A principal function of a corporate governance system is to manage the 'principal-agent' relationship to ensure the achievement of a company's objectives.

---

3 Sponsors use a variety of legal structures of which there are four main types: sole proprietorships, general and limited partnerships, limited liability companies, and corporations. Nearly all banks in the US are organized as corporations. Non-US banking organizations also have a corporate, limited liability structure. For these reasons, this section focuses on corporations' corporate governance system. Corporations' governance system has the most extensive set of mandated internal requirements of all four business organizations. Investment banks originally were organized as partnerships but converted to public corporations in the last quarter of the 20th century. The last major investment bank to become a corporation was Goldman Sachs in 1999 when it became a public company.

4 OECD, 'Principles of corporate governance' (2004) 11.

5 Michael Mauboussin and Alfred Rappaport, 'Reclaiming the idea of shareholder value', *Harvard Business Review* (1 July 2016), at <https://hbr.org/2016/07/reclaiming-the-idea-of-shareholder-value> [Reclaiming the idea].

6 Stephen Bainbridge, *Corporation Law and Economics* (Foundation Press: 2002) 417 [Bainbridge, *Corporation Law*]. Directors of US corporations generally define their role as running the company for the benefit of its shareholders. Ibid. 418.

7 To generalize, there are two basic types of market economies: the Anglo-Saxon, 'shareholder' variety and the 'social market', 'stakeholder' variety. David Collison and others, 'Shareholder primacy in UK corporate law', Certified Accountants Educational Trust (2011) 5.

This relationship arises when one party (the agent) agrees to act in the interest of another party (the principal), subject to the principal's control. The agent owes a fiduciary duty to the principal to act in good faith in the best interest of the principal.[8] Principal-agent relationships are ubiquitous in business organizations.

The alignment of an agent with the interest of the principal varies by type of business organization. In a general partnership, the partners are both owners and managers whose interests are thus generally aligned with the partnership's objectives. The unlimited liability of partners for the partnerships' debts reinforces this alignment. The case in corporations is fundamentally different. In a corporation, the owners, the shareholders, depend on agents, the managers, to pursue the company's objectives on their behalf. Both a corporation and its shareholders have limited liability. Figure 3.1 illustrates the principal-agent relationship, how it arises, its basic attributes, and examples of such relationships in a corporation.

3.2.1.3 Genesis of COIs in principal-agent relationships
The separation of ownership by shareholders, as the 'principals', and control by managers, as 'agents', which is an essential attribute of the public corporation,[9] introduces potential conflicts into the actions of corporate management on behalf of shareholders. The interests of an agent and its principal are rarely fully

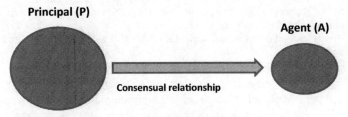

Principal (P)

Agent (A)

Consensual relationship

Attributes of all principal-agent relationships
- A (employee) acts on behalf of P (owner, manager, etc.)
- P has power to hire and fire an A
- P in theory has control (direct or indirect) over A
- A owes a fiduciary duty to P – to act in P's best interests

Examples of principal-agent relationships in a corporation
Shareholder (P) - Board of directors (A)
Board of directors (P) - CEO (A)
Corporation (P) - Employees (A)
Manager (P) - Employees (A)

Figure 3.1 Principal-agent relationship

---

8 § 3.2.1.6 discusses fiduciary duty in greater detail.

9 In this context, a 'public corporation' is a company registered with the SEC and subject to its mandatory disclosure system, which requires it to file quarterly and annual reports, among other

aligned. 'Agency costs' result when an employee, as agent of the company, is able to extract corporate value for her personal benefit instead of for the benefit of the principal, the firm and its owners, the shareholders. Agency costs reflect COIs. A conflict of interest exists when a person or firm has an incentive to serve one interest (theirs or a third party's) at the expense of another interest or obligation (typically that owed to the principal in an agency-principal relationship). The agent may be disloyal through double-dealing or inattentive through slackness on the job. It is the function of a corporation's board of directors, assisted by management and advised by risk management and compliance, to eliminate conflicts or to reduce risks of their exploitation.

The problem of agency costs is acute in the large modern corporation due to thousands of dispersed shareholders who, because of small equity interests, have little incentive or ability to monitor management. Corporations' and thus shareholders' limited liability further exacerbates this lack of incentive to monitor. Similarly, the managers, unlike partners in a partnership, do not have unlimited liability and thus have incentives to engage in risky conduct that can benefit them personally at the cost of the company and its owners.

The SEC, whose expertise lies in conduct-of-business supervision, considers COIs to be at the heart of much wrongdoing:

> [W]e have identified conflicts of interest as a key area for our risk analysis. This is based on the long experience of our exam program that conflicts of interest, when not eliminated or properly mitigated, are a leading indicator of significant regulatory issues for individual firms, and sometimes even systemic risk for the entire financial system.[10]

3.2.1.4 Corporations have principal-agent relationships at many levels
Principal-agency relationships in which conflicts can appear exist at many levels in a corporation. The most important one is between the shareholder-owners, the principals, and the board of directors, their agents. In addition, the employees (including senior executives and directors) are agents of the corporation. The company's CEO is the agent of the board of directors as well as the corporation. Employees are agents of their managers as well as the corporation.

3.2.1.5 Board's broad discretion under the business judgment rule
The corporate law grants broad discretion to management since the widely dispersed owner-shareholders cannot realistically exercise control over corporate

---

filings. See Sections 12 and 15(d) of the Securities Exchange Act of 1934. 15 USC §§ 78l and 78o, respectively.

10 Carlo di Florio, 'Conflicts of interest and risk governance', Speech before National Society of Compliance Professionals (22 October 2012), at <www.sec.gov/news/speech/2012-spch 103112cvdhtm> [di Florio, Conflicts].

strategy.[11] The key decision maker in a corporation is the board of directors. State corporate law[12] recognizes the board's central role in managing the affairs of a corporation.[13]

The *business judgment rule* (BJR) embodies the board's broad discretionary authority. The BJR is the presumption by courts that in making a business decision directors act on an informed basis, in good faith, and in the honest belief that the action was in the best interests of the company. Its underlying premise is that the board of directors needs to have broad protection against personal liability in making decisions in the best interests of the company.

3.2.1.6 Corporate law mechanisms that balance board's authority with accountability

Corporate law and internal corporate mechanisms seek to achieve a balance between the authority of the corporation's managers that is necessary to determine business strategy and their accountability to the shareholder-owners. The most important of these shareholder protections is the *fiduciary duty* that the board, like all agents in a principal-agent relationship, owes to its shareholders. The fiduciary duty is divided into the duty of care and duty of loyalty to protect, respectively, against shirking, incompetence, and inattention, on the one hand, and self-dealing and other forms of disloyal, self-interested transactions, on the other.

Several other features of corporations' corporate governance enhance accountability of agents to shareholders. These include, among other things, shareholders' right to elect directors annually, stock market prices that reflect poor management and managerial competence and loyalty or incompetence and disloyalty, pay incentive schemes that enhance long-term shareholder value, and activist shareholders and other institutional investors who have a substantial holding in the company's stock.[14] Figure 3.2 illustrates these types of controls enjoyed by shareholders.

The corporate governance principles discussed here apply broadly on a global basis.[15]

---

11 Bainbridge, *Corporation Law* 204. Bainbridge considers the board's decision making to be 'largely unreviewable'. Ibid. The case law supports his observation.

12 When discussing the board and its role in corporate governance, this book assumes that Delaware law applies. Thus, 'state corporate law' is shorthand for Delaware law. Nearly 66% of the largest 500 corporations are incorporated in Delaware and are therefore subject to its corporate law. *Delaware Division of Corporations 2015 Annual Report* (2016) 1.

13 'The business and affairs of every corporation organized under this chapter shall be managed by or under the direction of a board of directors, except as may be otherwise provided'. § 141(a), Delaware General Corporation Law.

14 Statutory state corporate law governs the rights and obligations of the board, executives, and shareholders. A corporation is formed by filing a certificate of incorporation while by-laws, its internal 'housekeeping', are more granular in establishing rights of shareholders vis-à-vis the board, and procedures for administering the corporation.

15 See generally Basel Committee on Banking Supervision, 'Corporate governance principles for banks' (8 July 2015) [BCBS, Corporate governance principles].

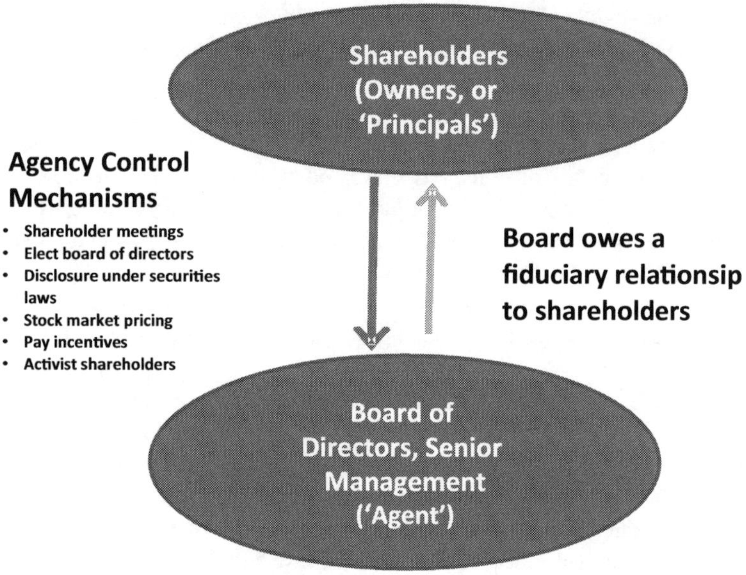

Figure 3.2 Principal-agent relationship in a corporation

3.2.1.7 Role, structure, and composition of boards of directors in US and internationally

The board of directors is legally a company's highest authority and representative of shareholder interests.[16] Within the broad context of pursuing the corporation's wealth-maximizing objective, the directors have several major responsibilities. These include setting the company's overall business strategy that senior executives are charged with implementing; selecting the CEO and other top operational officers; compensating, monitoring and, when necessary, replacing key executives; managing the corporate organization by broad policies and objectives; monitoring and managing potential COIs of management and board members; setting the 'tone at the top' by modeling ethical conduct and compliance; and managing the control functions.

Directors are of two kinds: executive (inside) directors and outside directors. Executive directors are either large shareholders or high-level managers from within the company. Outside directors are not executive employees of the corporation. They are often CEOs from other corporations. Executive directors have direct knowledge of the corporation's business. Outside directors are presumed to provide unbiased and impartial perspectives on issues brought to the board and

---

16 Other governing authorities exist, depending on the business organization. For example, sponsors can contractually appoint a group of managers, including non-equity holders, as the governing authority in a limited liability company (LLC). The default is for all members with voting rights proportionate to their equity share to manage the LLC. The principles stated in this section apply to governing authorities in LLCs and other organizations.

diversity of opinion. Outside directors are generally independent directors, who must meet certain eligibility criteria to be considered 'independent'.[17]

Congress and US financial regulators have increasingly focused on board composition as a means of strengthening boards' oversight responsibilities and in preventing wrongdoing. Certain laws and regulations require boards' audit and compensation committees to have a majority or all of their members to be independent directors. For example, NYSE-listed companies' audit committees must be composed wholly of independent directors.[18] These laws are often the result of major corporate scandals.[19] The theory is that independent directors are less prone to COIs existing in the corporation than executive directors. Among other things, the banking agencies mandate independent director membership in board-level risk committees.[20]

US corporations have a 'one-tier', or single, board of directors, reflecting in part the supremacy of the US board in managing corporate affairs. Some European companies have a 'two-tier' board structure, with a 'supervisory' board directly elected by shareholders, and an executive, management board overseen by the supervisory board. All of the directors of the supervisory board are non-executive outside directors. All of the directors of the executive board are inside directors of the company. Germany is one of the most notable examples of a two-tier board governance system, which is mandated by law.[21]

3.3 Corporate governance issues unique to banks and other financial institutions

Banks present special corporate governance issues for several reasons. Their capital structure, federal safety net, and business of handling 'other people's' money', whether deposited funds or funds for securities transactions, create serious moral hazard and incentive issues. Principal-agent conflicts abound in banks and other financial institutions. When exploited, these conflicts can not only harm customers but imperil the solvency of the firm itself and in rare cases create systemic risk for the entire financial system.

Significant agency problems arise in financial institutions due to heightened incentives to engage in exploitative conduct because the costs of detection are very high. The complexity of financial transactions and the lack of sufficient

---

17 Regulations typically incorporate listing standards of stock exchanges such as the NYSE. The NYSE has criteria for 'independent directors'. NYSE-listed companies are required to have a majority of independent directors. NYSE Listed Company Manual, § 303A.01.

18 Ibid.

19 The Enron, WorldCom, and other accounting scandals of the early 2000s led Congress to enact the Sarbanes-Oxley Act of 2002, Pub. L. No. 107–204, 116 Stat. 745, designed to prevent accounting fraud through reform of the independent auditing profession and disclosure requirements.

20 See § 6.3.4.1.

21 A German supervisory board (*Aufsichtsrat*) that oversees the management board (*Vorstand*) consists of shareholder and labor representatives, reflecting the broader stakeholder interest of continental European governance systems. Other countries that mandate a two-tier structure are Austria and the Netherlands. The two types of board structures coexist in many other European countries.

disclosure create significant informational disparities between customers and other counterparties and banking institutions. The incentive problems appear most severe in the largest financial conglomerates that engage in multiple business lines.[22]

3.3.1 Special governance issues involving boards of BHCs and bank subsidiaries

BHCs present special governance issues due to potentially conflicting obligations of two boards of directors, of the BHC and of its banking subsidiaries, which have overlapping oversight obligations vis-à-vis BHCs' banking businesses. The board of a BHC, like other corporate boards, has a fiduciary duty in the Anglo-American system primarily to maximize shareholder value from its multiple lines of business. BHC boards may be tempted to opportunistically place more risky activities in their bank subsidiaries to take advantage of the FDIC insurance umbrella. In contrast, a subsidiary bank's board has a fiduciary duty not only to its shareholders but is required under prudential regulation to exercise its business judgment in the public interest as well.[23]

BHCs' centralized decision making at the BHC board level strengthens their boards' role in overseeing the banking business.[24] Banks, including the largest ones, such as Citibank, N.A. or JPMorgan Chase N.A., are wholly owned subsidiaries of a BHC. In addition, the typical overlap between the board membership of a BHC and of its banks[25] and holding companies' managerial activities[26] ensures good information flow from subsidiary to parent. Each BHC director thus has a duty to control risk down to the level of the bank subsidiaries. The holding company's wholly owned bank subsidiaries are not the prototypical US corporation, with ownership divorced from control due to widespread shareholding.[27] These factors make centralized decision making at the BHC level a natural outcome.

In view of this centralized control, as part of their policy of corporate governance cooptation, regulators have sought to transfer some supervisory responsibility from agencies to BHCs.[28] This transfer reflects a long historical trend in

---

22 Stephen Cecchetti and Kermit Schoenholtz, 'Conflicts of interest in finance' (12 January 2015), *Money, Banking, and Financial Markets*, at <www.moneyandbanking.com/primers/>.

23 Jonathan Macey and Maureen O'Hara, 'The corporate governance of banks' (April 2003), *FRBNY Economic Policy Review* 101 [Bank corporate governance].

24 Jonathan Macey and Maureen O'Hara, 'Bank corporate governance: a proposal for the post-crisis world' (August 2016), *FRBNY Economic Policy Review* 91 [A proposal for the post-crisis world]. The corporate separateness of BHCs and their wholly owned banks does not release BHC directors from responsibility for the actions of their subsidiary banks. Ibid.

25 A proposal for the post-crisis world 96.

26 Howell Jackson, 'The expanding obligations of financial holding companies' (1994), 107 *Harvard Law Review* 507, 513 [Jackson, Expanding obligations].

27 Bank corporate governance 96.

28 The FRB has recently issued proposed guidance that significantly raises regulatory expectations of boards, senior management, business-line management, and the control functions. See §§ 6.3.1–6.3.4.

Congress's and the agencies' expansion of financial holding company obligations due in part to the need to recover federal insurance fund deficits and losses and in part to the desire to contain risky corporate practices.[29] It is for safety and sound-ness concerns that the Federal Reserve assesses the entire holding company's financial strength and risks. By statute, BHCs must serve as a 'source of strength' to their bank subsidiaries.[30] Moreover, a BHC's board must ensure that a bank is 'well managed' as a condition for engaging in expanded non-bank businesses.[31]

3.3.2 Managing conflicts of interests in financial institutions

Poorly controlled and managed COIs lay at the heart of the GFC, the mis-selling of MBS, and the subsequent scandals such as the London Interbank Offered Rate (LIBOR) and foreign exchange manipulation cases that globally resulted in hundreds of billions of dollars of fines against banking organizations. This section discusses the tool kit available to boards, senior management, and the control functions to address COIs in their firms. To this end it provides a typol-ogy of COIs that is useful in identifying, assessing, and managing or eliminating COIs.[32]

3.3.2.1 Risk management and compliance relating to COIs
COIs in the heavily regulated finance industry are a form of 'compliance risk'. Compliance risk is the risk of legal or regulatory sanctions, material financial loss, or loss to reputation a bank may suffer as a result of its failure to comply with laws, regulations, rules, related SRO standards, and codes of conduct appli-cable to its banking activities.[33] Their regulatory implications aside, COIs can also undermine and even endanger franchise value, perhaps best exemplified by a series of multi-billion dollar rogue trading disasters in the last two decades.[34] A firm's corporate governance system should address the potential exploitation of conflicts by a firm's employees through risk management and compliance, effective ICs, and compliance P&Ps that will enforce those controls.

Management of conflicts generally involves the following three steps: (1) identifying conflicts, (2) assessing the level of compliance risk they pose, and (3) mitigating the compliance risk created by the conflicts. However, the integration

---

29 Jackson, Expanding obligations 559–560.

30 Dodd-Frank expressly requires that BHCs serve as sources of financial strength to their banks. 'The appropriate Federal banking agency for a bank holding company or savings and loan hold-ing company shall require the [holding company] to serve as a source of financial strength for any subsidiary of the bank holding company or savings and loan holding company that is a depository institution'. 12 USC § 1831o–1(a). The legal validity of the 'source of strength' doctrine articulated by the FRB policy had previously been unclear.

31 Bank corporate governance 96.

32 This typology is based on that formulated by Ingo Walter. See §§ 3.3.2.3–3.3.2.5.

33 Basel Committee on Banking Supervision, 'Compliance and the compliance function in banks' (April 2005) 7 [BCBS, Compliance and the compliance function].

34 In one of the most famous trading disasters, the derivatives trader Nick Leeson caused Baring Bank's collapse in 1995 by incurring a $1.3 billion loss.

of the management of conflicts into the compliance function is relatively new.[35] Having a disciplined process is especially important in the highly competitive environment in which financial conglomerates continually develop new products, activities, and trading strategies that create new conflicts.[36]

A broad range of ICs address conflicts in financial institutions. These include conflicts that can be managed through compensation structures, conflicts managed through pre-specified transaction protocols, conflicts that must be controlled by 'walling off' various activities, and conflicts that must be eliminated by more radical means such as by ringfencing in separate subsidiaries.

3.3.2.2 Determining 'root cause' of conflicts in order to establish effective risk controls

To effectively mitigate COIs and compliance risk through corporate governance mechanisms, one should understand the origin of a COI and how it relates to regulatory expectations. This is a form of preventive 'root cause' analysis, a best practice used in internal investigations designed to remediate risk management and compliance failures after the fact. By finding answers to these questions, a firm can design effective risk controls and compliance P&Ps that will reduce the risks posed by a COI. To such end it is helpful to classify COIs into two groups.

(1) *COIs between employees and their firm and its shareholders.* The first group are COIs that exist between a company's employees acting for their personal benefit, on the one hand, and the company and its shareholders, on the other. These COIs are often difficult to identify and assess since they arise in the course of an employee's activities on behalf of the firm. This makes them challenging to address in risk management and compliance systems. Conflicts in this group can directly impact the safety and soundness of a firm. As a consequence, they implicate prudential regulatory expectations in the first instance. Examples abound. In addition to the example of rogue traders, an illustrative example are the S&L executives in the 1980s who underwrote highly risky real estate loans or committed outright fraud against their firms, resulting in their firms' bankruptcy and enormous taxpayer losses.

(2) *COIs involving a firm and its customers and other counterparties.* The second group involves business conduct by a company's employees vis-à-vis third parties, such as depositors and other lenders, borrowers, and investors in transactional lines of business. These situations generally involve more easily identifiable COIs that arise in client-facing units of a financial institution. These COIs typically implicate a bank's safety and soundness indirectly. An example is the poor and often fraudulent subprime mortgage underwriting that contributed to the GFC. Borrowers

---

35 Securities Industry and Financial Markets Association, *The Evolving Role of Compliance* (March 2013) 20.
36 di Florio, Conflicts.

entered into loans they could not pay. These loans also imperiled not only the individual banks that underwrote them but also undermined the stability of the financial system.

Because of the regularity and acuteness of conflicts arising in client-facing businesses (the second category above), regulators mandate compliance systems for certain sensitive business lines more frequently than in employee-company conflicts (the first category above). A prime example are investment advisers, who provide investment advice to customers and belong to a typical line of business of a financial conglomerate. Advisers already have a fiduciary duty to their clients, but Congress and the SEC have gone further by requiring specific ICs and P&Ps designed to manage advisers' conflicts. Among other things, designated employees must report, and the investment adviser review, their personal securities transactions and holdings periodically to ensure they are not violating their fiduciary duty.[37]

3.3.2.3 Two types of COIs in client-facing business lines

Ingo Walter has formulated a useful methodology for analyzing this second category of COIs.[38] He divides business conduct conflicts involving a firm's clients and other counterparties into Type 1 and Type 2 conflicts. Type 1 conflicts involve conflicts between the firm and its clients, while Type 2 conflicts involve conflicts between different clients, often due to the firm favoring the interests of one over another,[39] largely because of the greater revenue potential from the favored customer. A firm's board, management, and control functions can use such sub-classification to more precisely identify, assess, and mitigate or eliminate risks in these business conduct COIs.

3.3.2.4 Retail and institutional domains reflect differing compliance risks

Walter further distinguishes between retail and wholesale, or institutional, markets in his COI methodology. This division provides further granularity in identifying and assessing risks arising from conflicts with clients, and second, designing compliance P&Ps to address these conflicts.

Compliance risk is generally higher for COIs involving the retail domain. The degree of market failure is often the underlying cause of the difference between the domains of retail and wholesale end-users. The retail investor suffers from a much higher degree of information asymmetry and transaction costs vis-à-vis his counterparty than the institutional investor. Measures that help remedy problems in one domain may not be appropriate in the other. For institutional customers, the more level playing field engenders a greater level of competition that helps to reduce transaction costs. They also generally enjoy leverage to demand greater

---

37 SEC Rule 204A-1 under the Investment Advisers Act of 1940. 17 CFR § 275.204A-1.
38 Ingo Walter, 'Conflicts of interest and market discipline among financial services firms' (August 2004), 22(4) *European Management Journal* 362 [Walter, Conflicts of interest].
39 Walter, Conflicts of interest 362.

disclosure. The retail domain generally is subject only to Type 1 conflicts, and the wholesale domain to both Type 1 and Type 2 conflicts.[40]

The Wells Fargo account opening scandal is a Type 1 conflict involving the domain of retail customers. Wrongful conduct toward the bank's depositors was due to an incentive scheme that led employees to engage in fraudulent conduct in order to garner bonuses or to safeguard their jobs. The retail depositors individually were at a severe disadvantage in addressing the fraud. The bank's franchise value has suffered enormously as a consequence of the damage to its reputation.[41] A scenario generating a potential Type 2 conflict in the wholesale domain is a research group in a multiservice financial institution that provides research to institutional investors while its underwriting arm is selling a client-issuer's securities.[42]

3.3.2.5 Financial conglomerates present greatest compliance risk from COIs

Large, complex multiservice financial conglomerates encounter more COI issues than smaller, more simply organized firms. The greater the range of services, the greater the likelihood that the firm will have potential conflicts, the higher the potential costs facing customers, and the more difficult and costly will be the ICs and compliance safeguards that are needed to prevent exploitation of customers.[43] The multi-billion dollar fines against banking firms for their broker-dealer and derivatives divisions' interest rate and foreign exchange rigging and for mis-selling MBS in the wholesale market are cases in point.[44]

3.3.2.6 Best practice risk analysis and compliance procedures for conflicts

Julie Riewe, SEC co-chief, Asset Management Unit of the Enforcement Division in 2015, provided a useful best-practices list for assessing COIs.[45] The guidance relates to asset managers but has broader application.

40 Ibid. 364–365.

41 Wells Fargo's initial fines amounting to $185 million were paltry and raised no direct safety and soundness issues. However, the recurrent and systematic nature of the fraud and the firm's other consumer law violations eventually led the FRB to take unprecedented action against it. It issued a cease-and-desist order finding 'pervasive compliance and conduct failures involving violations of consumer protection laws'. It froze the company's growth until it was satisfied that the firm's corporate governance, risk management, and compliance practices met its expectations. *In the matter of Wells Fargo & Company*, Docket No. 18–007-B-HC (2 February 2018).

42 Walter, Conflicts of interest 8. Walter observes that conflicts involving equity research are among the most intractable conflicts confronting a multiservice firm and that firewalls between the underwriting and research groups are ineffective. 'Researchers cannot serve the interests of both buyers and sellers at the same time … as long as research is not profitable purely on the basis of the buy-side … the conflict can only be constrained but never eliminated as long as sell-side functions are carried out by the same organization'. Ibid. 365.

43 Ibid. 366.

44 Deutsche Bank, with a market capitalization of $18 billion in 2016, faced a potentially crippling $14 billion fine by the DOJ arising from its mis-selling of MBS prior to the GFC. See Frances Coppola, 'Deutsche Bank: a sinking ship?', *Forbes* (2016). The DOJ later reduced the fine to $7 billion in a settlement. Jan-Henrik Foerster and Yalman Onaran, 'Deutsche Bank to settle U.S. mortgage probe for $7.2 billion', *Bloomberg* (23 December 2016).

45 Julie Riewe, 'Conflicts, conflicts everywhere', Remarks to the IA Watch 17th Annual IA Compliance Conference: The Full 360 View (26 February 2015), at <www.sec.gov/news/speech/conflicts-everywhere-full-360-view.html>.

- For each COI identified, can it be eliminated? If not, why not?
- If the adviser cannot, or chooses not to, eliminate the COI, has the firm mitigated it and disclosed it?
- Is there someone – a person, a few individuals, a committee – at the firm responsible for evaluating and deciding how to address COIs? Are such persons or committee sufficiently objective?
- Is the process used to evaluate and address COIs designed to be objective and consistent?
- Does the firm have P&Ps to identify new COIs and monitor and continually re-evaluate ongoing COIs?
- Are the firm's P&Ps reasonably designed to mitigate the identified COIs and are they properly implemented?

3.4 The role of the three control functions in bank corporate governance

The three primary control functions consist of risk management, compliance, and internal audit. Control functions are groups in a bank and other companies that, in varying capacities, are designed to independently and objectively oversee, monitor, and advise senior management and the board on management of business and regulatory risks and thus should not report to revenue-generating business units.[46] This independence is essential to manage the considerable COIs existing among employees in the revenue-generating business lines as well as between the non-revenue-generating groups and control functions themselves. The three groups in banks tend to be more specialized and sophisticated than in non-financial firms given the high level of regulation of financial institutions and pervasiveness of conflicts in financial services.

This section first discusses the reporting lines of the control functions. It then discusses the reporting structure of the control functions and the 3LOD model.

3.4.1 Reporting structure of the three control functions

Risk management, compliance, and internal audit should all report ultimately up to the board of directors through their senior executive head.[47] Even if 'embedded' as business unit compliance officers (BUCOs) in a business line, BUCOs should remain part of the compliance department, report to its managers, and otherwise retain independence of the business units. BUCOs provide benefits in both directions. BUCOs can contribute to business units' understanding of their compliance responsibilities. In turn, BUCOs can learn the technical issues relating to the business of the business unit so that they can better design, implement, and enforce P&Ps for that unit. The same concept of independent reporting

---

46 The BCBS defines control functions as follows: 'Those functions that have a responsibility independent from management to provide objective assessment, reporting and/or assurance'. BCBS, Corporate governance principles iv.

47 Risk management and compliance are discussed in greater detail in §§ 3.5 and 3.7, respectively.

coupled with close interaction with the business units is true of the risk management function as well.

The matter is somewhat different in the case of internal audit. Internal audit's
objectivity and independence historically has been its defining attribute in the
system of corporate governance. More than the other two functions, the internal audit function has had a long-standing independent reporting line to one of
the key committees of the board, the audit committee. Moreover, internal audit
assesses not only the other two functions but also that of a firm's corporate governance system as a whole. It provides assurance on the efficiency and effectiveness of each of these components.[48]

3.4.2 The 3LOD model

Bank regulators have endorsed the 3LOD model, which the industry had developed shortly after the GFC to more systematically manage operational risk[49]
in financial institutions. Considered a best-practice standard by the BCBS,[50]
3LOD has global application.[51] A primary rationale for the 3LOD is to imbue
the business side of financial institutions with a full awareness of the dimensions
of the risks they are taking in their daily operations, making it accountable for
the downside as well as upside of risk-taking. The GFC graphically illustrated
how one-sided senior management's risk-taking could be, focusing on the upside
while showing little appreciation of its downside. However, the model has caused
financial institutions no small degree of confusion[52] while calling for considerable investment in developing a 3LOD in line with regulatory expectations, in
some cases inserting compliance programs in each line of business.[53]

The 3LOD model formally divides the management of risk among three
corporate groups, assigning each well-defined responsibilities. The first line is
comprised of the businesses that generate revenue. They must 'own' the risks

48 Basel Committee on Banking Supervision, 'The internal audit function in banks' (28
June 2012), Principle 13, 3.
49 See § 1.2.2.6 for a discussion of operational risk arising from the banking business model and
§§ 4.3.6.5–4.3.6.6 for a discussion of its regulation.
50 The BCBS has provided guidance on the 3LOD. Basel Committee on Banking Supervision,
'Review of the principles for the sound management of operational risk' (4 October 2014) [BCBS,
Sound management of operational risk].
51 Ibid. 1. In light of the GFC and continuing scandals, the Financial Stability Council (FSB),
jointly created by the BIS and BCBS, formulated the concept of the 'four lines of defense' to account for
the specific governance features of banks and insurance companies. The bank supervisors and external
auditors are the 'fourth line'. The FSB considers them to have a specific role in the organizational structure of the internal control system. See Financial Stability Board, 'The "four lines of defense model" for
financial institutions' (December 2015), Occasional Paper No. 11 [FSB, Four lines of defense]. Industry
commentators have also developed the 'fourth line' concept. See Sisi Liang and Joseph Breeden, 'Keys
to Success in Model Risk Management for CCAR & DFAST' (2013) 11–12, at <https://prescientmod
els.com/articles/Best-Practices-in-Model-Risk-Management.pdf>.
52 Some commentators find 3LOD to blur distinctions between the first and second lines, between
those who take risk and those who control risk. See Simon Boughey, 'The three lines of defense – a
Sisyphean labor?', Risk.net (31 October 2017).
53 Lyn Farrell, 'Making "Three Lines of Defense" work: Coordination, cooperation, and communication, for a start', Banking Exchange (11 June 2015).

that they create through their activities, acknowledging and managing them.[54] The second line is comprised of the control functions that oversee and control risk, including risk management, compliance, and the finance function.[55] The third line is internal audit, which provides independent assurance of the integrity and effectiveness of risk controls.[56] In a perfect world, only the first line of defense would suffice for effective risk management.[57] Regulators' adoption of the 3LOD model reflects the considerable agency costs in financial institutions imposed by the short-term 'risk-taking', revenue-generating operations side.

The 3LOD model as formulated by the BCBS has effectively become a regulatory expectation despite its lack of codification in agency rulemaking. While the FRB has not formally adopted 3LOD, it has proposed principles that align with it.[58] Furthermore, the Institute of Internal Auditors (IIA) published a position paper[59] endorsing it as a best practice and, together with the Committee of Sponsoring Organizations of the Treadway Commission (COSO), published a white paper on how to modify ICs by relating the COSO ICs framework to the 3LOD model.[60]

3.4.2.1 First line of defense: revenue-generating business lines
Under 3LOD, business line management can no longer off-load risk management to the control functions. Operational management[61] has primary responsibility for maintaining effective ICs and executing risk and control procedures.[62] They identify, assess, and report risk exposures, taking into account the bank's risk appetite.[63] First-line operational staff are involved in these processes on a daily basis and are familiar with the workflow and possible control weaknesses.[64] The rationale is that it is easier for the first line to implement controls that target more granular processes and detect weaknesses early, provide immediate notification internally, and ensure timely implementation of necessary measures.[65]

---

54 BCBS Corporate governance principles 5.

55 The corporate finance function is responsible for accurately capturing and reporting business performance and profit and loss results to the board and management who will use such information as a key input in business decisions. Ibid. 11.

56 Institute of Internal Auditors, 'The Three Lines of Defense in Effective Risk Management and Control' (January 2013) 3 [IIA, 3LOD].

57 IIA, 3LOD 4.

58 Proposed Supervisory Guidance, 83 Federal Register 1351 (2018) [FR, Proposed Supervisory Guidance]. § 6.3.3 discusses this guidance in greater detail.

59 IIA, 3LOD.

60 Institute of Internal Auditors, 'Leveraging COSO across the three lines of defense' (July 2015). § 3.7.3.2 discusses COSO's enterprise risk management guidelines.

61 The FRB defines a business line as a unit or function of a financial institution, including associated operations and support, that provides products or services to meet the firm's business needs and those of its customers. These units would include corporate treasury and IT support. This broad definition has led to significant criticism by firms for expanding the scope of the guidance beyond revenue-generating businesses. FR, Proposed Supervisory Guidance 1354.

62 IIA, 3LOD 3.

63 BCBS Corporate governance principles 11.

64 FSB, Four lines of defense 5.

65 Ibid.

Criticism focuses on the fact that although the first line is acknowledged to be the most important of the 'defenses',[66] its new risk management responsibility conflicts with the objective of risk-takers as profit generators. Attempting to promote a stronger risk culture and embedding risk and controls in the first line blurs the distinction between the risk and business functions.[67] Management historically has emphasized and set compensation based on achieving financial objectives rather than control-based objectives.[68] In the US, banks are resisting the FRB's effort to hold business lines accountable for risk management.[69]

3.4.2.2 Second line of defense: risk management and compliance

The second line establishes *detect, prevent,* and *remediate* control requirements and embeds these requirements in the ICs and P&Ps that the first line follows.[70] Critics of the 3LOD model's second line argue that it compromises the organizational independence of the control functions. The risk management and compliance functions may report to the board of directors, but the daily dotted-line reporting lines[71] and communication channels are likely to be to senior managers. Second-line staff are often embedded as BUCOs in the business lines through engagement and exchange of communication. Moreover, they may lack the necessary expertise to do independent analysis and to effectively challenge practices and controls, a problem highly specific to the finance industry. The highly quantitative prerequisites for MRM are a case in point.[72] In addition, remuneration and experience is considerably higher in the first than in the second-line functions, making attracting suitable talent challenging.[73]

3.4.2.3 Third line of defense: internal audit

Internal audit provides independent assurance to the board and senior management concerning a wide range of items. These include the efficiency and effectiveness of business operations; security of assets; reliability and integrity of reporting processes; the effectiveness of governance, risk management, and ICs; and the effectiveness of the first and second lines of defense. Internal audit generally performs an annual risk assessment of a company to identify business units or processes that exhibit a high level of residual risk.[74] The risk assessment identifies risk areas that require more frequent audits[75] and forms the basis for

---

66 Ibid. 7.

67 Steve Marlin, 'Fed's risk proposal puts banks on the defensive: new supervisory guidance will make business heads responsible for risk management', *Risk.net* (2 April 2018) [Marlin, Fed's risk proposal].

68 FSB, Four lines of defense 7.

69 Marlin, Fed's risk proposal.

70 FSB, Four lines of defense 6.

71 The control group formally reports to the board but has a secondary reporting relationship to management. In theory, the formal reporting structure determines the performance evaluation.

72 See § 7.5 for a discussion of model risk management in the context of stress testing.

73 FSB, Four lines of defense 8.

74 Residual risk is the risk remaining after implementing risk controls and compliance P&Ps to reduce inherent risk. See § 9.3.3.

75 FSB, Four lines of defense 8.

the audit plan. Due to limited substantive expertise, the third line generally can only ensure a periodic risk-based assessment rather than a granular and ongoing monitoring that is typical of the first line of defense.[76]

The third line's effectiveness depends critically on the highest level of independence and objectivity and thus requires unalloyed organizational independence. This consists of a direct reporting line of the chief audit executive (CAE) to the board's audit committee and unrestricted access to senior management and the board.[77]

3.5 The bank compliance function

Today's bank compliance function in financial conglomerates, and to a lesser extent in many smaller banking organizations, is highly specialized and integrated into banks' risk management and corporate governance systems. It plays an important role in banks' risk-return strategies that assess compliance risk. This section discusses these aspects of this core control function. It also discusses the emergence of 'compliance risk', which calls for a close working relationship between the compliance and risk management functions.

3.5.1 Role of compliance in addressing the principal-agent problem

Simply put, compliance has always been about ensuring the adherence by a company and its employees to applicable legal and regulatory obligations and to a company's internal policies and norms. Such an objective has been implicit from the very beginning of modern business organizations. As long as ownership and control were synonymous, the manager-owners, the 'first line of defense' in compliance terminology, were the *only* line of defense against legal action by the government and private litigants. In the early history of financial institutions, partnerships were the predominant form of business organization, assuring attention by manager-owners, who had unlimited liability, to legal and regulatory requirements. This internal governance framework changed with the rise of the modern corporation in the 20th century that introduced limited shareholder liability. This development eventually transformed companies' governing internal authorities of companies into manager-agents.[78]

Modern internal governance and the purpose and role of compliance within this system reflect the same objective of ensuring adherence to law and norms but must do so by tackling the principal-agent problem inherent in the corporate form of business organization. In the latter part of the 20th century, the government

---

76 Ibid. 6. Due to the highly quantitative nature of risk analysis and the widespread use of modeling in banks' business lines, internal audit may not have the necessary skill set to craft an audit plan reflecting a sound understanding of a firm's risk profile. Ibid.

77 Institute of Internal Auditors, 'Attribute Standards 1100, Independence and Objectivity' (2017).

78 The process lasted longer for the major investment banks. In 1999, Goldman Sachs was the last to convert from a partnership to the corporate form.

began to raise regulatory expectations of, and precepts for, corporate governance and compliance. By the 2000s the modern principles governing corporate compliance were firmly established. These were that compliance must be independent of the business lines whose compliance it is overseeing; its compensation cannot depend on the performance of these business lines; compliance must have sufficient resources to reasonably carry out its function; compliance reports up to, and has access to, the board of directors through a non-business line head; and the board and senior management ensure its stature and credibility throughout the organization by setting an appropriate 'tone at the top'.

3.5.1.1 Specialization and professionalization of the bank compliance function
The myriad and varied risks associated with the banking business model and substantial body of law and regulatory obligations that apply to banks have contributed to the structure and responsibilities of the bank compliance function. In broad outline, it shares much in common with corporate compliance in other industries. The compliance function comprises the following four areas of responsibility:

(1) Assessing regulatory obligations to determine their application to a firm's business;
(2) Designing and implementing P&Ps to prevent and detect wrongdoing;
(3) Monitoring and testing compliance by employees with the P&Ps; and
(4) Training, education, and guidance.

Compliance works closely with risk management in the first two areas. Among other things, compliance designs P&Ps for the ICs that risk management, in consultation with compliance, determines are necessary to address a firm's material risks. Moreover, implicit in these four tasks is compliance's obligation to keep the board and senior management apprised of material developments related to compliance for which they have ultimate responsibility.

Today's bank compliance function has endeavored to keep up with a rapidly changing industry and an evolving legislative-regulatory framework. In the process, the function has become increasingly specialized and professionalized. This is evident in two ways. First, each of the four primary areas of banking regulation covered by this book – micro-prudential, macro-prudential, consumer protection, and AML/CFT regulation – has a unique regulatory framework, regulatory design, and set of regulatory expectations. The demands on and skills demanded of the compliance professional in each of these areas differ accordingly.[79]

Second, this specialization is reflected in the substantive banking expertise demanded of compliance professionals in order to act competently in each area. Compliance officers must have the necessary level of technical skills to adequately exercise independent and objective assessment of compliance by a given

---

79 §§ 3.5 and 3.7 of this chapter and Chapter 6 detail how the agencies have increasingly created substantive and procedural expectations of both the risk management and compliance functions.

business line. The banking agencies have clearly stated their expectation that each compliance group is staffed with competent, skilled, and experienced professionals in their respective disciplines.

3.5.1.2 Two theories of compliance in the system of corporate governance

Broadly, there are two dominant theories of compliance and its role in corporate governance. The first one views the compliance function and the internal governance mechanisms that apply to it as a result of externally imposed government mandates. The government's demands often exhibit an arbitrary nature, offering little ability to senior management to gauge future compliance costs and risks. In this respect, banking compliance is the prime example of the government's invasive reach into the internal mechanics of a firm's corporate governance, co-opting them for regulatory purposes.[80]

The second theory holds that a compliance function is less a direct effect of regulatory and supervisory mandates and more a rational response to the government's external demands. A firm is a free agent interacting with cost structure constraints imposed by regulation and other external factors. The firm seeks an equilibrium that minimizes compliance risk at least cost in funding risk management and compliance. To be sure, great uncertainty applies in the risk analysis in forecasting compliance risk from government prosecutions.

This book adopts the second theory to explain the internal decision making by firms regarding investment in governance structures. However, the two theories are not incompatible. The first theory provides a realistic description of the unpredictability that often characterizes financial regulatory action and policymakers' use of compliance for regulatory objectives. It helps a board to gauge the level of compliance risk and cost constraints under which it operates. Moreover, the design of the compliance function increasingly hews to mandates established by the bank regulators. The following subsection explicates the second theory in greater detail.

3.5.2 Compliance risk-return optimization

Investment in the risk management and compliance systems can be viewed through the lens of shareholder wealth maximization realized through risk-return optimization of compliance cost and risk.[81] A board's approach to the control functions does not differ fundamentally from its approach to generating profit for

---

80 Sean Griffith is one of the chief proponents of this model of the compliance function. Through compliance, the government dictates how firms comply with regulation, imposing specific governance structures expressly designed to change how a firm conducts its business. Sean Griffith, 'Corporate governance in an era of compliance' (2016) 57 *William and Mary Law Review* 2075, 2078 [Griffith, Corporate governance].

81 Risk-return optimization is now the standard practice of many large, sophisticated financial institutions. See Brian Nocco and Rene Stulz, 'Enterprise risk management: theory and practice' (Fall 2006) 18 *Journal of Applied Corporate Finance* 8 [Nocco and Stulz, ERM]. In this context, 'compliance cost' includes expenditures relating to all related governance infrastructure, including risk management, in the optimization process. See also Geoffrey Miller, 'An economic analysis of

its shareholders generally. In this analysis, a banking institution first quantifies the amount of *inherent compliance risk*[82] in a particular business line. It next determines what risk management and compliance expenditures, or *compliance cost*, will result in a level of residual risk[83] that just falls within the firm's predefined risk appetite.[84] The decision to mitigate risk by spending on a risk control and compliance system both incurs compliance costs in the present but also reduces future costs arising from potential liability in enforcement actions.[85] Firms seek to maximize profit by incurring the optimal amount of compliance cost.

The concept of risk-return optimization is intended to capture a firm's decision-making process regarding expenditures and revenue projections related to the control functions. The concept is an idealized depiction of what firms' boards and senior management presumably do on a daily basis, either through an *ad hoc* or a more formalized process.

3.5.2.1 Difficulty in assessing residual compliance risk

Achieving the appropriate amount of residual risk associated with a particular business line or initiative is exceedingly difficult because of the uncertainty involving the level of acceptable, residual compliance risk.[86] There is no universally acceptable definition of an effective compliance program.[87] This is in part due to the wide variety of types of financial institutions and, within those firms, a broad range of risk profiles and business models. Regulators regularly propound the maxim that no one size of a compliance or risk management program fits a particular banking organization. Boards thus face a difficult balancing act. Over-investment in compliance that only marginally decreases compliance risk would not satisfy a board of director's duty to maximize shareholder value.

Also problematic is the challenge of measuring the effectiveness of risk controls and P&Ps comprising a compliance program in achieving compliance's three main objectives: to prevent misconduct, detect misconduct, and align corporate activities with regulation.[88] Many firms track a wide variety of metrics, only some of which truly measure a program's substantive effectiveness rather

---

effective compliance programs' (December 2014), New York University Law and Economics Working Papers 396 [Miller, Economic analysis].

82 Compliance risk is defined in § 3.3.2.1. § 9.3 discusses inherent and residual risk in greater detail in connection with consumer protection regulation.

83 Residual risk is the risk remaining after accounting for all risk mitigation measures.

84 See § 3.7.1.2 for a discussion of risk appetite within the general risk management framework. The term 'compliance cost' in this context includes the risk management and compliance systems designed and implemented to mitigate the inherent risk.

85 The firm performs a present value discount analysis of the future savings and costs in its optimization analysis.

86 Avoidance of compliance risk and reputational harm are difficult to quantify against the hard dollar outlay for people, systems, and processes. Ben Heineman, 'Too big to manage: JP Morgan and the mega banks', *Harvard Business Review* (3 October 2013), at <https://hbr.org/2013/10/too-big-to-manage-jp-morgan-and-the-mega-banks>.

87 Miller, Economic analysis 8. Miller highlights several sources of compliance requirements and best practices. Ibid. 3–8.

88 Eugene Soltes, 'Evaluating the effectiveness of corporate compliance programs: establishing a model for prosecutors, courts, and firms' (Summer 2018), *Journal of Law & Business* 965, 974.

than its degree of 'paper compliance'.[89] Without the ability to effectively measure this effectiveness, gauging residual compliance risk will not be feasible.

3.5.2.2 Limiting assumptions in compliance risk-return optimization

A crucial limiting assumption in addition to the lack of standards on effective compliance is that compliance costs imposed by regulation are firm-specific. Otherwise, costs become non-quantifiable. The upshot is that risk-return optimization for compliance cost and risk may be most germane to micro-prudential regulation and, to a limited extent, consumer regulation. Current and prospective regulation of systemic risk cannot be effectively incorporated into the individual firm's compliance risk and cost analysis. This is due to the objective of macro-prudential regulation to internalize the unmeasurable amount of social costs created by financial conglomerates. Regulators and economists have only begun to try to quantify systemic risk. A similar argument applies to AML/CFT regulation, which also endeavors to reduce the significant social costs of the underlying criminal activities.[90]

In addition, a timing problem makes this risk-return analysis especially challenging. Projecting compliance cost involves long-term analysis while analyzing and quantifying inherent compliance risk is more short-term in nature, involving an ongoing, dynamic analysis of issues that will vary from one board meeting to next, and even on a daily basis during firm-specific and market crises. Compliance costs are relatively long-lived capital expenditures. This timing disjuncture can result in a compliance spend that does not correspond to a firm's analysis of its current compliance risk. Such may be the case in the current deregulatory environment that implies a lower level of compliance risk and cost. US firms have largely finished implementing a Dodd-Frank-compliant infrastructure and are unlikely to significantly eliminate it even in the reduced compliance risk environment of the Trump administration.

3.5.3 Interrelationship between risk management and compliance

The risk management and compliance functions have distinct roles in a financial institution's corporate governance framework. Nevertheless, these functions are interrelated in certain important ways. Managing risk has become a regulated area itself, particularly since the GFC. Thus, regulatory requirements regarding risk management have led to the need to create compliance P&Ps governing risk management practices, a role for which compliance is uniquely qualified.[91]

---

89 Ibid. 985. In its evaluation of compliance programs, in one query the DOJ asks how companies measure the effectiveness of training. In a survey by *Compliance Week*, of the firms responding, 50% used completion rates to measure training's effectiveness, although no causal link exists between the former and latter. Ibid. 988. Metrics should be designed to assess progress and diagnose and rectify problems through remediation. Measures of effectiveness need to closely track the desired outcome, i.e., a compliance objective such as preventing misconduct. Ibid. 985. Soltes proposes an analytical framework that would measure substantive compliance effectiveness.

90 §§ 10.2.2.2 and 10.4.1.

91 'Time to merge risk management and compliance?', *Reuters* (5 April 2012).

Moreover, the compliance function can overlap significantly with risk management since conduct that violates social norms can also lead to significant losses.[92]

More generally, risk of non-compliance, or compliance risk, is now a separate risk category. Many of the multibillion-dollar fines in conduct-related violations such as have occurred in AML/CFT involved compliance failures. Like other risks, risk management must identify, assess, and advise management in the control of compliance risk. To adequately perform this role, it must consult with compliance. In addition, the risk analysis involving business initiatives in new regions or in developing new products inevitably have legal compliance issues, requiring a compliance framework to manage the risk.[93] In sum, the compliance function has the background and expertise to assist risk management in assessing these legal and regulatory risks.

3.6 Formative impact of state law and federal prosecutorial policy on compliance

Developments in state corporate law and federal prosecutorial policy have had a formative influence on the compliance function. This influence has consisted primarily in providing incentives for companies to establish meaningful compliance systems rather than in specifying the content of these systems. Later chapters develop in greater detail how financial regulation affects the content of compliance obligations.

3.6.1 Role of Delaware judiciary in incentivizing firms to establish compliance programs

The Delaware judiciary has emphasized the importance of boards' oversight role and of a compliance system in fulfilling this role. Its decisions have incentivized boards to establish compliance systems. Decisions by the state's judiciary have an outsized impact on corporate America since most of the largest US corporations are incorporated in Delaware. However, the actual legal significance of the decisions regarding compliance is quite limited. The Delaware standard for director liability is extremely high. Moreover, as a post-GFC decision makes clear, directors cannot be held liable for poor management of business risk, only for poor management of compliance risk. Business risk is the risk that a business strategy, such as an investment portfolio, will yield less than the expected rate of return, including a net loss on the investment.

3.6.1.1 Board's duty to monitor compliance with laws and regulation under Delaware law

Two Delaware decisions established the importance of a compliance system in ensuring directors were not in violation of their fiduciary duties. In *In re Caremark*

---

92 Griffith, Corporate governance 2081.
93 A-J Secrist, 'The link between risk management and compliance', *Lexology* (30 October 2013).

International Inc. Derivative Litigation,[94] shareholder plaintiffs sued to hold the company's directors liable for the damages resulting from alleged violations of various federal and state healthcare laws.[95] They argued that the defendant directors violated their fiduciary duty of care to monitor and prevent violation of applicable laws and regulations. The issue before the court was whether to approve the company's settlement agreement with the plaintiffs, blunting the legal impact of the decision. Nevertheless, the lesson for boardrooms was the importance of establishing a compliance system that would ensure that the board receives information to adequately monitor compliance risk and more broadly to satisfy their supervisory and monitoring role under Delaware law.[96] According to the court, boards could not satisfy their obligation to be reasonably informed

> without assuring themselves that information and reporting systems exist in the organization that are reasonably designed to provide to senior management and to the board itself timely, accurate information sufficient to allow management and the board, each within its scope, to reach informed judgments concerning both the corporation's compliance with law and its business performance.[97]

Despite its limited legal import, the *Caremark* decision caused corporations to design and implement compliance systems to monitor for signs of corporate malfeasance.

The *Caremark* articulation of the importance of compliance monitoring was affirmed and fleshed out ten years later in *Stone v Ritter,*[98] which nonetheless placed significant conditions on director liability[99] in holding that courts would not inquire into the objective adequacy of a firm's monitoring and oversight mechanisms.[100] The court ruled against the plaintiffs who alleged that a bank's directors had failed to ensure the existence of a reasonable AML compliance and reporting system. Despite the extremely high hurdle for shareholder plaintiffs, the Delaware decisions have continued to exercise a significant influence on corporate compliance programs.

The *Stone* case also provides an interesting view of the factors a court will consider in determining whether board oversight of a company's compliance systems is adequate to withstand challenge. The court based its decision primarily on the

---

94 698 A.2d 959 (Del. 25 September 1996).

95 These violations resulted in some $250 million of fines by state and federal authorities.

96 698 A.2d 959, 970. The statute reads: 'The business and affairs of every corporation organized under this chapter shall be managed by or under the direction of a board of directors'. Delaware General Corporation Law, § 141(a).

97 698 A.2d 959, 970.

98 911 A.2d 362 (Del. 6 November 2006).

99 The court converted the *Caremark* fiduciary duty to monitor from one of care to loyalty but set a high hurdle for director liability in monitoring cases. It found that *scienter*, or intent, is an element of bad faith. Eric Pan, 'The duty to monitor under Delaware law: from Caremark to Citigroup', The Conference Board (February 2010) 3 [Pan, Duty to monitor]. The court held that directors are liable only if they 'utterly failed to implement any reporting or information system or controls; or having implemented such a system or controls, consciously failed to monitor or oversee its operations'. 911 A.2d 370.

100 Griffith, Corporate governance 2111.

structure of oversight of the compliance systems at the bank. These included the position of a compliance officer specializing in AML/CFT matters, a corporate security department responsible for detecting and reporting suspicious activity, and the role of the board's suspicious activity oversight committee. The court also pointed to the staff designated to implement the program, training and policies, and monitoring systems.[101]

3.6.1.2 *In re Citigroup*: business risk decisions are unreviewable

In early 2005, Citigroup's board decided on a business strategy that the firm should undertake higher-yielding investment, including mortgage-related assets. In November 2008, it disclosed losses of over $65 billion. The question in some investors' minds was whether the board violated a duty to monitor its risks, specifically the firm's investment strategy. A Delaware court in *In re Citigroup Inc. Shareholder Derivative Litigation*[102] dismissed a suit to hold Citigroup's board liable for the company's losses on this theory. The court relied on *Caremark* and *Stone* in holding that Citigroup's board did not breach any of its fiduciary obligations. The end result is that directors do not have a duty to shareholders to monitor risk that can harm a company's business.[103] The Delaware court's policy of deferring to directors' business judgment strongly contrasts with federal bank regulators' mandate to boards to engage actively in risk management.[104]

3.6.2 Role of USSG and prosecutorial policy in creating compliance obligations

The increasing volume of federal criminal and civil prosecution of business organizations in the latter part of the 20th century has had an enormous impact on corporate compliance throughout the US and abroad as applied to foreign firms with a US presence. Companies have expended considerable resources to create compliance systems that will help detect and prevent employee wrongdoing. Most importantly, the DOJ has issued extensive guidance on effective compliance programs and how they can mitigate corporate criminal liability. This section covers one of the most important of these sources, the US Sentencing Guidelines (USSG) for business organizations.[105] The topic is of considerable importance to banking institutions. From 2008 to 2017, by one account, banks globally had paid $321 billion in fines.[106]

---

101 Rebecca Walker, 'Board oversight of a compliance program, the implications of *Stone v. Ritter*', at <www.corporatecompliance.org/Portals/1/731_1_stone-v-ritter_walker.pdf>.
102 964 A.2d 106 (Del. Ch. 2009).
103 Pan, Duty to monitor 3.
104 Ibid.
105 United States Sentencing Commission, Organizational Guidelines (USSG), § 8B2.1: Effective Compliance and Ethics Program.
106 Boston Consulting Group, 'Global risk 2017: staying the course in banking' (March 2017) 4–5, at <http://image-src.bcg.com/BCG_COM/BCG-Staying-the-Course-in-Banking-Mar-2017_tcm9-146794.pdf>.

3.6.2.1 Multiple roles of compliance in dealing with prosecutions

Compliance programs have emerged as a critical component in government prosecutorial policy and companies' strategies involving potential criminal and civil liability. Financial institution compliance has two roles relating to potential government prosecution of wrongdoing. First, an effective compliance program plays a *preventive* role in minimizing the occurrence of wrongdoing in the first instance and thus government investigation and prosecution. Second, when serious wrongdoing has occurred, the compliance function plays several roles in developing a strategic role in *minimizing* the compliance risks relating to potential and existing government investigations and prosecutions. Compliance is a key player in managing internal investigations concerning the wrongdoing. The ideal timing is for the internal investigation to precede a government investigation, if any, with self-reporting to the government on the investigation.

Compliance's role involving actual government prosecution, in turn, has two aspects. If a company has established an effective compliance system in the first place, the firm will likely gain credit under the USSG and under DOJ and SEC enforcement policies. In addition, compliance plays a critical role in crafting a remediation program that may help to further mitigate criminal or civil penalties and prevent future wrongdoing. Government investigations and prosecutions typically result in a deferred or NPA.[107]

3.6.2.2 Premises underlying USSG for business organizations

The USSG for business organizations have had a far-reaching, formative effect on firms' corporate compliance programs since their issuance in 1991. Remarkably, given corporations' pervasive social and economic importance, only in the 1980s did the federal authorities begin to systematically analyze organizational sentencing practices.

The underlying premise of the guidelines is that incentives to reduce penalties by taking preventive action will cause firms to reform their corporate culture and create robust compliance programs. In fact, though not mandatory, the USSG have led boards to institute meaningfully robust compliance programs throughout corporate America. This is not only true in the US but internationally as well, since many multinational companies operate within the US. The historic $1.6 billion settlement with Siemens AG in 2008 is a case in point. In the consent agreement, Siemens agreed to a comprehensive restructuring of its global operations and implementation of a sophisticated compliance program.[108]

Corporations and other business organizations are 'legal persons', capable of suing and being sued and committing crimes. These entities cannot themselves act but do so only through human agents, who are a firm's directors, officers, and employees. These agents' actions, pursuant to the doctrine of *respondeat superior*, can create civil liability for their employer as the principal in a transaction.

---

107 § 3.6.2.4 covers these agreements.
108 Cary O'Reilly and Karen Matussek, 'Siemens to pay $1.6 billion to settle bribery cases', *Washington Post* (16 December 2008).

The doctrine applies even when an employee acted against company policy and instructions or managerial direction, provided he was acting within the scope of employment. The entire organization, despite its best efforts to prevent wrongdoing, can be held strictly liable under this doctrine for employees' wrongful acts.

3.6.2.3 Relevant provisions of USSG

The USSG provide credit to a company that can reduce a sentence, fines, and probation if it has an 'effective compliance and ethics program'.[109] The USSG's main relevance is in settlement negotiations, as the vast majority of investigations end in settlements rather than court litigation. The USSG authors' motivation for granting credits was to alleviate the draconian consequences of the *respondeat superior* doctrine in addition to incentivizing firms to establish meaningful compliance programs. Section 8B2.1, 'Effective Compliance and Ethics Program', reflects this motivation:

> Such compliance and ethics program shall be reasonably designed, implemented, and enforced so that the program is generally effective in preventing and detecting criminal conduct. The failure to prevent or detect the instant offense does not necessarily mean that the program is not generally effective in preventing and detecting criminal conduct.[110]

Thus, prosecutors in applying the guidelines might still award credit even if wrongdoing has occurred. In this sense, a compliance program satisfying the USSG conditions can be an important element of compliance risk analysis in the compliance risk-return calculus that can reduce inherent risk.

However, to gain credit two conditions are necessary. First, the organization must have exercised due diligence to prevent and detect criminal conduct. Second, it must promote a culture of compliance.[111] Seven minimum requirements under the USSG satisfy the requirements of due diligence and a compliance culture.

(1) Standards and procedures to prevent and detect criminal conduct.
(2) The board is knowledgeable about and oversees the program.
(3) Reasonable efforts to exclude senior executives who the firm knew or should have known engaged in conduct not consistent with an effective program.
(4) Communication of standards and procedures through training.
(5) The firm monitors and audits to detect criminal conduct, evaluates the program periodically, and has and publicizes a whistleblowing program.

---

109 Credits are formalized in USSG § 8C2.5(f) (Culpability Score) and USSG § 8D1.4(b)(1) (Recommended Conditions of Probation – Organizations).

110 USSG, § 8B2.1.

111 In the words of the USSG, 'the organization shall … otherwise promote an organizational culture that encourages ethical conduct and a commitment to compliance with the law'. USSG, § 8B2.1.

(6) The firm promotes and consistently enforces the program through incentives and discipline for conduct consistent with the program.

(7) After detecting criminal conduct, the firm takes reasonable steps to respond appropriately and prevent further similar conduct.

3.6.2.4 DOJ's guidance on effective compliance programs

In 2017, the Fraud Section of the DOJ issued guidance on the factors that contribute to an effective compliance program and updated the guidance in 2019.[112] This guidance is the most comprehensive and clearest statement of the Fraud Section's areas of focus. It significantly elaborates the guidance in USSG § 8B2.1 by providing a roadmap of the elements that constitute an effective compliance and ethics program. The 2019 update summarizes DOJ evaluation of compliance programs by asking three overarching questions. The following highlights the key points of the 2019 update under each of these three questions.

- *First, is the program well-designed?* Prosecutors should ask whether the program is adequately designed for maximum effectiveness in preventing and detecting wrongdoing by employees and whether corporate management is enforcing the program or is tacitly encouraging or pressuring employees to engage in misconduct. The program should be comprehensive in ensuring that there is not only a clear message that misconduct is not tolerated, but also that P&Ps, including appropriate assignments of responsibility, training programs, systems of incentives and discipline, ensure that the compliance program is well integrated into the company's operations and workforce. The company should tailor its compliance program in line with its risk assessment.[113]

- *Second, is the program effectively implemented?* Prosecutors should determine whether a compliance program is a 'paper program' or one effectively implemented, reviewed, and revised; whether the corporation has provided sufficient staff to audit, document, analyze, and use the results of the corporation's compliance efforts; and whether the corporation's employees are adequately informed about the compliance program and are convinced of the corporation's commitment to it.[114]

- *Third, does the compliance program actually work in practice?* One of prosecutors' most difficult questions in evaluating a compliance program is whether the program was working effectively at the time of the offense, especially where the misconduct was not immediately detected. Did the program evolve over time to address existing and changing compliance risks? Prosecutors should also consider whether the company undertook an adequate and honest root cause analysis

---

112 US Department of Justice, 'Evaluation of corporate compliance programs', Criminal Division (April 2019), at <https://www.justice.gov/criminal-fraud/page/file/937501/download>.
113 Ibid. 2.
114 Ibid. 9.

to understand what contributed to the misconduct and the degree of remediation necessary to prevent similar events in the future. Did the corporation make significant investments in, and improvements to, its compliance program and IC systems? Did it test the program and ICs to demonstrate their effectiveness in the future?[115]

3.6.2.5 DPAs and NPAs

Financial conglomerates have had a large share of mandated compliance elements imposed through settlement agreements that include significant fines and agreements to enhance compliance systems and an independent monitor who charts the progress in compliance remediation. Companies and the DOJ agree to such terms in deferred prosecution agreements (DPAs) and non-prosecution agreements (NPAs). Both types are subject to probationary periods. If a company violates the terms of an agreement, in DPAs the DOJ has the right to file charges, and in NPAs, to initiate a prosecution. In entering these agreements, both parties are seeking a low-cost resolution that allows each to proclaim a 'win': generally, no criminal prosecution for the companies' senior executives and preservation of scarce resources and a press release touting the fine for the DOJ.

3.6.2.6 Coercive and arbitrary nature of DPAs and NPAs can nullify firms' risk-return optimization analysis

DPA and NPA settlements are examples of *compliance-by-prosecution*.[116] In proposing settlement terms, prosecutors generally do not follow a set of guidelines. Compliance-by-prosecution is often *ad hoc*, coercive, and arbitrary in the obligations imposed on firms.[117] This has been controversial due to the lack of transparency, oversight by the judiciary, and lack of consistency in application.[118] Thus, the precedential value of DPAs and NPAs is quite limited. Nevertheless in the case of DPAs, the DOJ makes the fine amounts, the elements of the compliance program, and the settlement agreements publicly available. They can provide guidance to other firms regarding the type of compliance systems that the DOJ finds acceptable in formulating its prosecution strategy.

However, the most serious drawback of these agreements lies in their negative impact on the defendants' systems of corporate governance. They can effectively render fruitless a firm's assessment of compliance cost and risk in its risk-return optimization analysis. Contrary to the objective of the USSG in incentivizing compliance measures through sentencing 'credits' and the DOJ's own compliance program evaluation guidelines,[119] the agreements may have little relevance to the specific attributes of a firm's given compliance program. Without such

115 Ibid. 13–14.

116 See generally the discussion of DPAs and NPAs at § 2.2.5.1, 5 Enforcement powers and their use.

117 Miriam Baer, 'Governing corporate compliance' (2016) 50 *Boston College Law Review* 949, 952 [Governing corporate compliance]. See also Griffith, Corporate governance 2091.

118 Ethics Resource Center, *The Federal Sentencing Guidelines for Organizations at Twenty Years* (2012), Ethics Resource Center's Independent Advisory Group 4.

119 See 3.6.2.4.

linkage, firms are unable to determine the effectiveness of their program in a risk-return analysis.

3.7 The bank risk management function

This section discusses the best practices of risk management in banking organizations and provides an overview of the two dominant ERM systems. Chapter 6 details the FRB's formal risk management expectations for the largest BHCs, from a macro-prudential standpoint. In regulating and overseeing risk management, the banking agencies must combat human nature. Risk management is 'not a natural act for humans to perform'.[120] Psychological and sociological biases in organizations cause people to overlook important risks and systematically underestimate those they do identify.[121]

3.7.1 Corporate governance framework for risk management

The banking agencies expect a banking institution to establish a comprehensive risk management framework fully integrated into its corporate governance system to identify, assess, measure, monitor, report, and mitigate or eliminate all material risks on a timely basis. The BCBS and the US banking agencies expect, and for the large BHCs require, that a bank's risk management function has the independence, resources, and stature and credibility to be effective agents in these firms' achievement of these objectives. This contrasts with the risk management function as originally established, which was concerned chiefly with financial risk, such as the interest rate exposure of a bank's portfolio, and typically operated separately within silos defined by business line.

3.7.1.1 Basic corporate governance framework of risk management function
The board of directors is ultimately responsible for ensuring that a banking organization has in place an effective risk management system. On an ongoing basis the board should be well informed of the material risks in each line of business. The communication of these risks to the board is the remit of risk management. In addition, the banking agencies expect a bank's board to approve and oversee communication of corporate culture and values involving management of risk within a robust internal control environment.[122] All three groups of the 3LOD play a role in achieving these objectives.

The risk management function, together with business line management, identifies material risks, formulates the parameters of a firm's risk appetite, and

---

120 Quote from NASA systems engineer Gentry Lee, cited in Robert Kaplan and Anette Mikes, 'Risk management – the revealing hand' (Winter 2016) 28 *Journal of Applied Corporate Finance* 8.

121 Ibid. For example, individuals tend to put too much weight on recent events and experiences when forecasting the future, leading them to grossly underestimate the range and adverse consequences of potential outcomes. Ibid. 10.

122 Basel Committee on Banking Supervision, 'Core principles for effective bank supervision' (September 2012) 40 [BCBS, Core Principles for bank supervision].

develops a firm-wide risk governance framework, all subject to board approval. Risk management measures identified risks on an ongoing basis and develops controls in conjunction with business line management and compliance. Internal audit validates the effectiveness of the IC environment.[123] Although Basel III's and Dodd-Frank's focus is principally financial and operational risk, they encourage firms to establish an enterprise-wide risk management framework that incorporates all risk categories.[124]

Like compliance, its sister function, risk management should be independent of the business lines and thus report ultimately up to the board. A bank's organic documents should clearly articulate its responsibilities and reporting lines.[125]

3.7.1.2 Risk appetite

The *risk appetite* reflects the level of aggregate risk that the board is willing to assume and manage in pursuit of the bank's business objectives. It includes both quantitative and qualitative elements encompassing a wide range of metrics and measures.[126] Senior managers reflect the risk appetite in the control limit structure of their respective lines of business.

Determining risk appetite, or tolerance,[127] is inherently a subjective, judgmental process in which quantitative analysis plays an important but subsidiary role. In economic terms, the outcomes, or payouts, of risk-taking are uncertain. The *distribution* of outcomes is 'objective' in the sense that it can be quantitatively ascertained. In contrast, the *utility* of outcomes depends on individual preferences, which in turn are the preferences of the ultimate owner, the shareholder.[128] It is the function of the board, as the shareholders' agent, to establish the parameters of the firm's risk appetite.

3.7.1.3 Risk appetite framework and risk appetite statement

Regulators expect financial institutions to develop a holistic, firm-wide board-approved 'risk appetite framework'[129] (RAF). The RAF establishes and documents a firm's risk profile[130] in relation to its risk capacity. Specifically, the RAF should align with the firm's business plan, strategy, capital planning,

---

123 Basel Committee on Banking Supervision, 'Framework for internal control systems in banking organizations' (1998) Principle 1, 2 [BCBS, Framework for internal control systems].

124 'Financial institution risk management issues', Advisen Insurance Intelligence, White Paper (January 2014) 3.

125 BCBS, Corporate governance principles 11.

126 BCBS, Core principles for bank supervision 40 n. 51.

127 The BCBS, and this book also, consider 'risk appetite' and 'risk tolerance' to have equivalent meanings.

128 Thomas Coleman, *A Practical Guide to Risk Management* (Research Foundation of CFA Institute: 8 July 2011) 58 [Coleman, *Practical Guide*].

129 See Financial Stability Board, 'Principles for an effective risk appetite statement' (18 November 2013) [RAS Principles]. The FSB defines a RAF as the overall approach, including policies, processes, controls, and systems, through which risk appetite is established, communicated, and monitored. It includes a risk appetite statement, risk limits, and an outline of the roles and responsibilities of those overseeing the implementation and monitoring of the RAF. Ibid. 2.

130 A firm's risk profile is a point-in-time assessment of a bank's risk exposures, either on a gross or net basis after accounting for risk mitigants.

and compensation schemes, explicitly setting the boundaries within which management may operate. RAFs are most effective when incorporated into the decision-making process of the firm-wide risk management framework and communicated firm-wide.[131]

An important component of an RAF is a 'risk appetite statement'[132] (RAS), which translates the board's risk appetite for the firm as a whole and enables lower level management to implement the risk appetite in its risk limits structure.[133] RASs clearly articulate the firm's risk appetite for all levels of management, can be implemented across an enterprise, and must relate to the pursuit of strategic business objectives, from the C-suite to the desk and loan officer level. In sum, the RAS must be a clear, accessible statement of risk appetite yet with sufficient detail since it is a key device for communicating the risk appetite and guiding action across a firm.[134]

3.7.1.4 Unique issues involving 'compliance risk': necessity of firm-wide compliance program

Compliance risk, defined as the risk of legal or regulatory sanctions, material financial loss, or loss to reputation a bank may suffer as a result of its failure to comply with laws, regulations, rules, and codes of conduct,[135] is of particular concern to regulators. Firms must address it through other means than those relevant for market and credit risk. A strong system of ICs is particularly essential in reducing compliance risk.[136]

The FRB devoted an entire SR letter[137] to this risk, the substance of which this subsection summarizes.[138] Management and oversight of compliance risk present unique challenges. Compliance and risk management requirements relating to this risk are challenging for large, complex banks since compliance risks transcend business lines, legal entities, and jurisdictions. Unlike market and credit risk, a firm cannot establish the board's risk appetite for compliance risk in each business line and monitor it through independent units. Compliance risk metrics are often less meaningful for aggregation and trend analysis.[139]

---

131 RAS Principles 3.

132 The RAS is the written articulation of the aggregate level and types of risk that a bank will accept, or avoid, in order to achieve its business objectives. The statement includes quantitative measures relating to earnings, capital, liquidity, and other relevant quantitative measures of risk and qualitative statements to address reputation and conduct risks, money laundering, and unethical practices. BCBS, Corporate governance principles 2.

133 Ibid. 26.

134 Committee of Sponsoring Organizations of the Treadway Commission, 'Enterprise risk management: understanding and communicating risk appetite' (January 2012) 6.

135 Federal Reserve Board, 'SR 08–8: Compliance risk management programs and oversight at large banking organizations with complex compliance profiles' (16 October 2008) n. 1 [FRB, Compliance risk].

136 BCBS, Framework for internal control systems 1.

137 'SR letter' refers to 'Supervision and Regulation letter'. SR letters address significant policy and procedural matters related to the Federal Reserve's supervisory responsibilities.

138 FRB, Compliance risk. The FRB's guidance is largely consistent with that provided by the Basel Committee. See BCBS, Compliance and the compliance function.

139 FRB, Compliance risk.

These attributes of compliance risk underscore the need for a firm-wide, integrated approach to compliance risk exposure and management. A firm-wide compliance program establishes a framework for identifying, assessing, controlling, measuring, monitoring, reporting, and providing training with respect to compliance risks across the company. The need for a firm-wide compliance function is clearly evident in areas such as AML/CFT, privacy, affiliate transactions, COIs, and consumer fair lending laws, where legal and regulatory requirements may apply to a firm's multiple business lines or legal entities.[140]

3.7.1.5 Risk committees

A risk committee formalizes the operation of the risk management process and procedures outlined in the previous subsections. Risk committees advise and support management in supervising and monitoring a BHC's overall actual and future risk appetite and strategy. US and Basel regulatory expectations regarding risk committees vary depending on a BHC's size.[141] For smaller firms, they play a key role in overseeing implementation of strategies for capital and liquidity management in addition to managing market, credit, operational, and compliance risk. Risk committees assess the adequacy of these risk management strategies against the firm's approved risk appetite. Risk committees also oversee the alignment between all material financial products and services offered to clients and the firm's business model and risk strategy.[142]

For larger BHCs, a board risk committee advises the board on the bank's overall current and future risk appetite, oversees senior management's implementation of the RAS, reports on the state of risk culture in the bank, and interacts with and oversees the chief risk officer (CRO).[143] Chapter 6 discusses board risk committees of large BHCs in greater detail.[144]

3.7.1.6 Risk measurement is not risk management and should be independent

Risk *measurement* and risk *management* are two very different concepts. Risk measurement is a prerequisite for the management of risk. Risk measurement is the specialized task of quantifying and communicating risk for the business lines that manage their specific business risk. It entered the modern era in 1973 with the breakdown of Bretton Woods, initiating freely floating, and volatile, exchange rates and publication of the Black-Scholes option pricing formula that provided its tools.[145] In the finance industry, risk measurement has evolved into

---

140 Ibid.

141 Prior to the GFC, many banks delegated risk oversight to audit committees or divided the function among other board committees. When they did exist, risk committees were focused on specific legal entities and risks, rather than risks on a firm-wide basis. Dan Ryan, 'Board governance: Higher expectations, but better practices?', PwC (January 2016) 2 [Ryan, Board governance].

142 European Banking Authority, 'Final report on guidelines on internal governance' (26 September 2017) 25–26.

143 BCBS, Corporate governance principles 17

144 § 6.3.4.

145 Thomas Linsmeier and Neil Pearson, 'Risk measurement: an introduction to value at risk' (July 1996) 1 [Introduction to VaR], Working paper 96-04, available at SSRN: <https://ssrn.com/abstract=7875>.

a specialized quantitative discipline. However, one risk management expert has cautioned that the industry has focused too much on quantitative measurement, while neglecting the old-fashioned approach to managing risk based on experience and intuition in addition to quantitative analysis and measurement.[146]

A corporate governance structure should clearly distinguish, and separate, through independent reporting lines, the performance of risk management and risk measurement.[147] The business lines, from the board and CEO down to individual business units, perform the former activity and a separate control group within the risk management function should perform the latter function.[148]

3.7.1.7 Role of ICs in risk management

The risk management function, together with other control functions that include the treasury, finance, compliance, and legal groups, establishes a firm's ICs for each identified material risk. Internal controls help to ensure process integrity, compliance, and effectiveness.[149] Compliance, in collaboration with risk management and the business lines, creates P&Ps for monitoring and enforcing the ICs. These P&Ps formalize the firm's risk limits.

Financial firms originally introduced ICs to reduce fraud, misappropriation, and operational errors, but their status has been significantly upgraded. In addition to controls required for regulatory compliance, controls are now critical to meeting a firm's strategic goals such as long-term profitability targets and its maintenance of reliable financial and managerial reporting, and more generally maintaining financial viability.[150] The board of directors bears ultimate responsibility for establishing and maintaining effective ICs.

Effective ICs have a policy, process, or other procedure attached to each key risk. Compliance with a control system depends critically on a well-documented organizational structure that clearly shows lines of reporting responsibility and authority and provides for effective communication throughout the organization.[151]

3.7.2 Technical components of risk management

Risk management in financial institutions demands a set of highly quantitative skills combined with qualitative judgment in assessing tail risk. Risk managers need to be able to translate modeling assumptions and other aspects of risk for lay senior management. Too often, risk management breaks down in the process of communicating material risks to non-quantitatively minded executives. This

---

146 Coleman, *Practical Guide* 57. An apparent paradox exists in dealing with both avalanches and financial accidents. Better measurement and management of risk can actually increase risk exposure. As skiers acquire more skill and tools to manage avalanche risk, they often take on more objective exposure. Coleman, *Practical Guide* 83.
147 Coleman, *Practical Guide* 1.
148 Coleman, *Practical Guide* 57.
149 BCBS, Corporate governance principles 27.
150 BCBS, Framework for Internal Control Systems 10.
151 Ibid. 12

section discusses the use of Value-at-Risk (VaR) and other financial technology and concepts used in risk management. Senior management places significant reliance on VaR in managing risk.

3.7.2.1 Risk assessment: identification and evaluation of key material risks

Risk assessment is the first step in the development of a risk management framework. Risk assessment is the process of identifying and evaluating internal and external material risks that could adversely affect or advance a firm's achievement of its objectives. Once identified, firms analyze the risks, considering likelihood and impact, as a basis for determining how to manage them. Firms assess risks on an inherent and a residual basis.[152]

More generally, risk identification establishes the firm's exposure to risk and uncertainty and requires an intimate knowledge of the firm; its markets; and the legal, social, political, and cultural environment in which it exists, in the context of its strategic and operational objectives. Management can use the assessment to produce a risk profile of the firm and then map risks to relevant business units.[153]

3.7.2.2 Assessing 'known' and 'unknown' risk

At bottom, risk management engages with two categories of risk, 'known' and 'unknown' risks. *Known* risks are risks that a firm can identify, measure, and understand with study and analysis based on similar risks experienced in the past. This experience and analysis with known risks make them easy to compare in an effective and transparent reporting system. In this respect, VaR is the most widely used tool in risk management due to its ability to compare and report risk exposure at all levels of a firm.[154]

The greatest challenge to modern risk management is to uncover, understand, and measure *unknown*, or unanticipated, risks.[155] The art of risk management is in building a culture and organization that can respond to and withstand these unanticipated events.[156] In the context of events leading to financial crises, quantitative risk measurement tools may not forewarn managers of unanticipated market events that most endanger an individual firm. An example of an unknown risk is CCR. One does not know one's counterparties' counterparties, or more broadly, the entire network's topology.[157]

3.7.2.3 VaR and other measurement tools

VaR is defined as the probability that losses in normal market conditions will exceed a VaR loss amount, estimated with a very low probability (e.g., 99%

---

152 Committee of Sponsoring Organizations of the Treadway Commission, 'Enterprise Risk Management – An Integrated Framework: Executive Summary' (September 2004) 4 [COSO, ERM].
153 Institute of Risk Management, 'A Risk Management Standard' (2002) 8, at <www.theirm.org/media/886059/ARMS_2002_IRM.pdf>.
154 Coleman, *Practical Guide* 2.
155 Ibid. 2–3.
156 Ibid. 80.
157 Philippe Jorion, 'Risk management lessons from the credit crisis' (2009) 11, at <https://merage.uci.edu/~jorion/papers/RiskMgtCreditCrisis.pdf> [Jorion, Risk management].

confidence interval). Important variables are the holding period of losses (typically one day for internal reporting purposes) and the time period for collecting data on market factors to calculate the VaR.[158] Viewing everything through the lens of variability of profits and losses (P&L) provides a unifying framework across asset classes and across a firm, from the trading desk up to the board.[159] In essence, quantitative risk measurement is all about understanding the P&L distribution.[160]

There are both benefits and drawbacks to VaR. The benefits of VaR are several. First, VaR can be calculated at each level of a firm's hierarchy, from trading desk up to the parent level, in the boardroom. The volume, constant trading, and complexity of financial instruments of financial conglomerates require a firm-level assessment of risk through aggregating unit-level VaRs. Conversely, VaR can reveal where risk is concentrated in a firm.[161] VaR can also be used to calculate regulatory capital requirements. However, there are some significant drawbacks to using VaR. The value of VaR is much less indicative of portfolio risk in times of market turmoil since VaR is based on past market data and assumes normal market movements. In addition, VaR is useful only when markets do not become illiquid as they did in the GFC. It is thus essential to supplement quantitative risk measures with other risk measures such as stress testing and scenario analysis.[162]

Another risk measure used by trading desks to gauge market risk are 'the Greeks', named after letters in the Greek alphabet.[163] The Greeks are measures of the sensitivity of a derivative's value to a change in underlying parameters such as the price of the underlying asset or a volatility rate.[164] However, each Greek is only a partial measure of the risk of a trading position. The Greeks also cannot be aggregated to produce an overall measure of the position's risk.[165]

3.7.2.4 Internal controls based on limits

Limits are an important category of ICs and are a critical tool in risk management. They are a key means of anchoring risk-taking strategies to the firm's predetermined risk appetite at the business unit level such as the trading desk. Moreover, by being translated into limits, risk appetite compels senior managers to carefully consider the scale and scope of a new business because they must do so in terms of the limits and the risk areas for which limits must be granted.[166]

---

158 In constructing VaR, the modeler must select market factors, such as an exchange rate, that affect the price of the financial instrument.

159 Coleman, *Practical Guide* 4.

160 Ibid. 128.

161 Michel Crouhy and Dan Galai, *The Essentials of Risk Management* (McGraw-Hill Education: 2014) 243 [*Essentials of Risk Management*].

162 Ibid. 263.

163 For example, delta is the rate of price change of an option based on a small change in the underlying stock.

164 Introduction to VaR 5.

165 *Essentials of Risk Management* 238.

166 Ibid. 78.

3.7.3 Enterprise risk management: COSO and ISO

Over the last two decades, private industry has undertaken several efforts to establish a systematic, rigorous framework for firm-wide risk management, also known as ERM. Although financial regulators have not officially endorsed any standard setter's ERM system, the GFC has focused financial institutions and regulators on the premises underlying ERM.

The crisis underscored the critical importance of a holistic understanding and approach to managing risks in a financial institution. In several instances, boards of financial conglomerates had little or no grasp of the firm-wide exposure to MBS assets.[167] More broadly, an enterprise-level, integrated approach to the several risks to which financial institutions are exposed has become a core regulatory expectation. At the time of the GFC, ERM standard setting was in its initial stages of development. Thus, a combination of business need and regulatory mandates has led all LFIs to adopt some version of integrated, firm-wide risk management. ERM appears to be an off-the-shelf solution to the need for an overarching, integrated approach mandated by the banking agencies.

3.7.3.1 Overview of ERM
ERM is a comprehensive, integrated process encompassing all categories of risk, ranging from market risk, credit risk, operational risk, and business risk to reputation risk, that can impact the achievement of a firm's objectives. ERM provides a particularly apposite set of guidelines for large, complex BHCs. ERM provides a structure for management to identify risks and to determine the appropriate risk responses, which consist of risk avoidance, reduction, sharing, and acceptance. ERM has been defined as:

> a process, effected by an entity's board of directors, management and other personnel, applied in strategy setting and across the enterprise, designed to identify potential events that may affect the entity, and manage risk to be within its risk appetite, to provide reasonable assurance regarding the achievement of entity objectives.[168]

The creators of ERM systems and the consulting firms that generate considerable revenue from ERM implementation tout ERM as turning 'good risk management into a competitive advantage by optimizing the potential of meeting strategic objectives.[169] In fact, the Basel policymakers and US banking agencies emphasize the same virtues to incentivize banks to move in the same direction as advertised by the ERM standard setters. More generally, ERM creates value

---

167 See Senior Supervisors Group, 'Observations on risk management practices during the recent market turbulence' (6 March 2008), at <www.occ.treas.gov/publications/publications-by-type/other-publications-reports/pub-other-risk-mgt-practices-2008.pdf>; UBS, 'Shareholder report on UBS's write-downs' (18 April 2008), at <http://maths-fi.com/ubs-shareholder-report.pdf>. 'Risks were siloed within the risk functions, without presenting a holistic picture of the risk situation of a particular business'. Ibid. 39.

168 COSO, ERM 2.

169 According to COSO, '[u]ncertainty presents both risk and opportunity, with the potential to erode or enhance value'. COSO, ERM 1.

by giving tools to senior managers to quantify and manage the optimization of the risk-return trade-off.[170] ERM also provides a framework for risk-return optimization.[171]

Two approaches to ERM have achieved widespread acceptance, one from the accounting industry and the other from the international standard-setting body, the International Standard Organization (ISO).

3.7.3.2 COSO

The COSO, a private-industry organization, published its ERM initiative in 2004. COSO's ERM framework is the predominant corporate ERM system, particularly in the US. Founded in 1985, COSO initially focused on fraudulent corporate financial reporting by public companies[172] and published an IC framework in 1992.[173] COSO's IC framework became the US benchmark for companies' ICs.[174]

COSO bases its ERM framework on its ICs framework since many companies had already invested heavily in this system. Its ERM framework has eight basic components:[175]

- *Internal environment* (the risk culture and tone of the firm);
- *Objective setting* (objectives must be established so that management can identify potential events affecting their achievement);
- *Event identification* (internal and external events that might affect such achievement, distinguishing between risks and opportunities);
- *Risk assessment* (risks are assessed considering likelihood and impact on an inherent and residual basis);
- *Risk response* (actions to align risks with risk appetite: avoidance, reduction, sharing, and acceptance);
- *Control activities* (P&Ps ensuring that risk responses are carried out);
- *Information and communication* (identify, capture, and communicate relevant information in a form and time frame so people can carry out their responsibilities); and
- *Monitoring* (firm monitors entirety of ERM and modifies as necessary).

COSO's system lists four categories of business objectives for a firm: (1) strategic (high-level goals aligned with and supporting its mission), (2) operational (effective and efficient use of its resources), (3) reporting (reliability of reporting), and (4) compliance (compliance with laws and regulations).[176] A firm

---

170 Nocco and Stulz, ERM 8.

171 § 3.5.2.

172 Robert Charette, 'Chapter 15: Enterprise risk management – supplemental material' 2, in Phil Simon (ed.), *The Next Wave of Technologies: Opportunities in Chaos* (2010) [Charette, ERM].

173 COSO, 'Internal control – integrated framework' (1992).

174 The Sarbanes-Oxley Act of 2002 cited it as an acceptable standard for demonstrating adequate financial controls. Charette, ERM 3.

175 COSO, ERM 4. See also Charette, ERM 3.

176 COSO, ERM 3.

needs the eight components to be functioning effectively in order to achieve these objectives.[177] These eight ERM components are applied in the firm's primary organizational divisions (entity level, division, business unit, and subsidiary). A precondition is that the firm's risk appetite captures all material weaknesses or material risks.[178] ERM is a multidirectional and iterative process in which components influence one another.[179]

3.7.3.3 ISO
The ISO, the world's largest developer and publisher of international standards, published its ERM framework, ISO 31000, in 2009.[180] ISO 31000's objective is to provide a system that any public or private organization or group can implement. Its ERM framework can be adapted to the specific context and information needs of an organization's decision makers.[181] Very simply, ISO defines risk as the 'effect of uncertainty on objectives'. It defines risk management as 'coordinated activities to direct and control an organization with regard to risk'.[182]

3.7.3.4 Comparison of COSO's and ISO's ERM frameworks
Both ERM frameworks have several goals in common. First, they are both based on the idea that organizations should use a common process of accessing and managing risk, from the senior management down to the operational level. Second, both recognize that different contexts and perspectives must be supported. Third, they embrace the notion that ERM must support a risk-taking ethic.[183] More generally, ERM provides a means to change organizational behavior from being reactive to being proactive in the face of changing situations.[184]

There are also distinct differences. ISO 31000 is more generic and less detailed than the COSO framework. COSO's ERM framework is more top-down than ISO 31000 due to COSO's origins as a US accountancy-based organization. COSO's ERM perspective is chiefly that of the CEO and CFO and the risks that he or she believes are essential to address. These are the executives most on the legal hot seat, especially relating to corporate compliance risks.[185] ISO 31000 supports both a top-down and bottom-up approach to ERM. Information flow of risk information from the bottom to the top is essential. Any enterprise-level risk analysis and management results are only as good as the information received from the ground level.[186]

---

177 Ibid. 4.
178 Ibid. 5.
179 Ibid. 4.
180 ISO, 'International Standard 31000: Risk management – principles and guidelines' (2009) [ISO 31000].
181 Charette, ERM 5.
182 ISO 31000 10.
183 Charette, ERM 6.
184 Ibid. 6–7.
185 Ibid. ERM 6.
186 Ibid.

3.8 Role of corporate culture in bank risk management and compliance

The role of corporate culture and ethics in fostering or constraining wrongdoing is a much discussed topic.[187] The USSG credits require an 'effective compliance and ethics program'.[188] Compliance culture has become a supervisory concern in client-facing lines that involve conduct-of-business regulation, where ethical lapses and misconduct are most likely to occur. Client-facing business lines are laden with COIs and information asymmetry. The enormous multi-billion dollar fines over the last decade have occurred in wrongful conduct cases involving AML/CFT, LIBOR rate and foreign exchange-rate market manipulation, fraudulent underwriting and selling of MBS bonds, and mortgage foreclosure fraud. These fines, often for repeat offenders, also present safety and soundness issues.

3.8.1 Historical trends and other explanatory factors in financial firms' culture

Long-term trends in the financial markets may have reduced firms' incentive to monitor and penalize employee wrongdoing. A decline in relationship banking and a movement toward a more transactional model exemplified by 'originate-and-distribute' securitization have undermined a sense of obligation and trust between banks and their clients.[189] More controversial is the argument that firms are not as constrained by risk of reputational loss in their interaction with clients, leading to a decline in counterparty trust.[190] Many recent examples reflect the continuing need for management of reputational risk for financial institutions.[191]

3.8.1.1 Regulation of ethical behavior
Financial market regulators have not attempted to prescribe detailed rules of ethical conduct, nor could they do so feasibly. Regulators understand that ethical codes will not by themselves instill an ethical culture. The firms that have incurred billions of dollars of fines all had codes of conduct. In some sectors, most notably in the investment adviser industry and derivatives markets, Congress and the agencies have required codes of ethics and appointment of chief

---

187 See di Florio, Role of compliance.

188 § 3.6.2.3.

189 The aspirational statements in the *Salz Review* may no longer be achievable. See Anthony Salz and Russell Collins, 'Salz review: an independent review of Barclays' business practices' (April 2013). 'A bank's licence to operate is built on the trust of customers and of other stakeholders.... Trust is built from experience of reasonable expectations being fulfilled – a confidence that an organisation will behave fairly.... [T]rust in banks has been "decimated and needs to be rebuilt"'. Ibid. 4.

190 See Jonathan Macey, 'The demise of the reputational model in capital markets: the problem of the 'last period parasites' (2010) 60 *Syracuse Law Review* 427. 'Where a company has no reputation for integrity and honesty in the first place (or where it has such a reputation but does not rely on it to attract and retain business), then the company cannot rationally be trusted.' Ibid. 432.

191 The most recent examples are Wells Fargo's multiple consumer law violations and Goldman Sachs' 1MDB money laundering scandal involving allegedly embezzled proceeds from a multi-billion dollar Malaysian investment fund bond offering. Shamim Adam, Yudith Ho and Cedric Sam, 'How the 1MDB scandal led to Goldman's first criminal charges', *Bloomberg* (21 December 2018).

compliance officers (CCOs).[192] Other structural approaches in corporate governance have included specific guidelines on the roles and responsibilities with respect to board oversight and compensation structures that impose downside risk on employees through clawbacks and other devices.

3.8.1.2 Role of unethical conduct in increasing compliance risk

Creating the *impression* that ethical behavior is not important to a firm increases its compliance risk simply because bank examiners will more closely scrutinize a firm's overall corporate governance and controls. A senior SEC official observed that how regulators perceive a firm's culture of compliance and ethics informs his or her overall perception of the risks posed by a particular entity.[193] Supervisory actions may become more invasive and aggressive if an examiner believes that a firm tolerates a nonchalant attitude toward compliance, ethics, and risk management. Moreover, ethical values can broadly reflect a firm's overall approach to risk management:

> The effectiveness of enterprise risk management cannot rise above the integrity and ethical values of the people who create, administer, and monitor entity activities. Integrity and ethical values are essential elements of an entity's internal environment, affecting the design, administration, and monitoring of other enterprise risk management components.[194]

These observations should figure in firms' analysis of compliance cost and compliance risk. Regulators expect the board and senior management to establish the value system of an entire firm in terms of 'tone at the top'.[195] Compliance has a sound foundation where a corporate culture emphasizes standards of honesty and integrity and in which the board of directors and senior management lead by example and promote the values of honesty and integrity throughout the firm.[196] Every level of a bank should view compliance as integral to the bank's business activities.[197]

3.8.1.3 Prudential issues arising from unethical conduct

Unethical conduct raises safety and soundness issues. This is the view of former Federal Reserve of New York President Dudley.[198] Although the linkage is not immediately apparent, he points to the critical importance of banks' intermediation

---

192 In addition to requiring appointment of CCOs for swap execution facilities (SEFs) who are required to resolve COIs, Dodd-Frank requires SEFs to have codes of ethics. 17 CFR § 37.1501(c), (d). SEFs enhance transparency in the OTC derivatives markets by providing bid-offer quotes and a trading platform.

193 The agency official will factor his or her perception into the overall assessment concerning which firms to examine, what issues to focus on, and how deeply to go in executing the examinations. di Florio, Role of compliance.

194 COSO, ERM 29–30.

195 BCBS, Corporate governance principles 20.

196 BCBS, Compliance and the compliance function 9.

197 Ibid. 7.

198 William Dudley, 'Opening remarks at reforming culture and behavior in the financial services industry: expanding the dialogue' (20 Oct. 2016) [Dudley, Reforming culture].

role in the economy. He observes that wrongful conduct has eroded the banking industry's trustworthiness, thereby impeding the ability to serve as the intermediary between savers and borrowers and in helping customers manage financial risks. Internal audit verification of internal or external controls is an expensive substitute for trustworthiness.[199]

3.8.1.4 Is ethical conduct a matter of macroeconomic cycles?

A leading compliance scholar voices a cautionary note regarding the effectiveness of corporate governance measures in instilling ethical behavior. He opines that corporate culture is largely a function of economic cycles. In his view, macroeconomic conditions, such as loose monetary policy that causes rapidly escalating asset prices and likely a contributing factor to the GFC, are the principal force shaping corporate conduct in the banking industry.[200] A former rogue trader responsible for a more than $2 billion loss at his bank provides testimony supporting this view.[201]

3.9 Conclusion

This chapter concludes the foundational overview that prepares students and practitioners to fully engage productively with the issues of micro- and macroprudential regulation, consumer protection, and AML/CFT regulation and their associated risk management and compliance systems. These topics are covered in the remaining chapters. Readers should now have a rudimentary understanding of banks' system of corporate governance, the principal-agent relationship in financial institutions that fosters COIs, the basic components of the control functions and a risk management system, and the formative influences on the evolution of the compliance function. This extended treatment reflects the special role that banks' internal governance systems play in bank regulation.

---

199 Ibid.

200 Geoffrey Miller, 'Banking's cultural revolution', NYU Compliance and Enforcement Blog (8 June 2016), at <https://wp.nyu.edu/compliance_enforcement/2016/06/08/bankings-cultural-revolution/>.

201 Kweku Adoboli, 'How to stop finance companies succumbing to cultural failure', *Financial Times* (12 March 2017). 'In the heat of the crisis, under extreme pressure to minimize costs and maximize profits, that sense of community [a shared purpose and collaborative problem solving] was lost in a climate of fear and insecurity'.

PART II

PRIMARY AREAS OF BANK REGULATION AND INTERNAL GOVERNANCE

CHAPTER 4

The role of risk management and compliance in micro-prudential capital regulation

4.1 Introductory overview

Micro-prudential regulation is the regulation and supervision of individual banks to ensure that they are managing their risks in a safe and sound manner, contributing to the stability of the financial system as a whole.[1] It is the oldest of the four regulatory areas covered in this book and the foundation of all subsequent banking regulation. Capital requirements form the cornerstone of prudential regulation. The banking business model, detailed in Chapter 1, provides a key means of understanding the structure of bank capital regulation. Banks' role in liquidity transformation creates liquidity risk, interest rate risk, credit risk, and operational risk. Each of these risks has an applicable regulatory capital requirement.

An organizing principle for understanding capital regulation are the Basel concepts of 'Pillar I' and 'Pillar II'.[2] Pillar I refers to the set of hard-wired, generic capital adequacy requirements with which all banks must comply, and which is the subject of this chapter. Pillar II refers to the discretionary, principles-based approach in micro-prudential supervision in which examiners review a bank's internal governance, risk management, compliance, management capabilities, and unique risk profile to determine whether to require additional capital. Put another way, Pillar I is the regulatory side and Pillar II the supervisory side of capital regulation.[3]

The chapter first explains the concepts of bank capital, leverage, and economic and regulatory capital and discusses bank management's incentive to minimize equity as a percentage of total assets. It then turns to the rationales for regulatory capital requirements and an overview of Basel's RWA methodology, which is the core component of Basel III/Dodd-Frank's approach to capital regulation.

---

1 Micro-prudential regulation is a necessary, but not sufficient, condition for financial system stability. Systemic risk can develop within a financial system even if each of its individual units is financially sound. For example, this would occur if each firm followed a rational policy of portfolio diversification but collectively all firms' portfolios were comprised of the same asset classes. It is an example of the fallacy of composition: what is good for the individual is not necessarily good for the whole. A key lesson of the GFC was the need to assess the financial system in its entirety: hence, macro-prudential regulation.

2 The 'Pillar' concepts were introduced in Basel II. 'Pillar III' concerns the use of disclosure to exert market discipline on banks' risk-taking and operations. This book employs Pillar I and Pillar II as an organizing principle but not Pillar III.

3 A shift has occurred post-GFC away from a bank regulatory system resting principally on generally applicable rules (Pillar I) toward a 'supervisory approach' emphasizing particularized review of a specific bank (Pillar II). Daniel Tarullo, *Banking on Basel: The Future of International Financial Regulation* (Peterson Institute: 2008) 15 [*Banking on Basel*].

It then covers in detail the RWA-based capital rules that apply to credit, market, and operational risk. It next turns to the new leverage ratio capital rules and non-capital portfolio restrictions. In most of these cases, more rigorous capital requirements apply to the largest, 'advanced' approaches banks. As necessary, the chapter summarizes the risk management and compliance requirements associated with a capital rule.

4.2 Overview of bank capital, leverage, and capital adequacy requirements

Bank capital regulation is a complex subject. To prepare readers to better understand it, this section covers certain key concepts involving bank capital.

4.2.1 Economic capital, regulatory capital, and leverage

The economics of capital and leverage in the banking industry are a key to understanding capital regulation. This involves an accounting definition, and the concept of economic capital, regulatory capital, and leverage.

4.2.1.1 Accounting definition: net worth
In accounting, a company's capital is defined as 'net worth', or assets minus liabilities.[4] A company is insolvent when it has no net worth or negative net worth. In the GFC, many LFIs approached insolvency or became insolvent as their MBS-related assets declined in value. Non-bank financial companies that are insolvent can be put into bankruptcy, and banking firms into receivership by the FDIC. Lehman Brothers filed for bankruptcy protection because its net worth was negative.

4.2.1.2 Role of economic capital in bank risk management
To gain a satisfactory understanding of bank risk management and compliance issues relating to capital, it is essential to understand the difference between *economic* capital and *regulatory* capital, also known as risk capital. Economic capital is the amount of capital that bank management reserves for a specific category of risk of the company as a going concern. Companies with sophisticated risk management systems generally apply the concept of economic capital. Economic capital functions as a disciplining device in corporate management. Management provisions capital for business lines in order to achieve a target risk-adjusted return on capital (RAROC). Those business lines with higher return will receive a higher amount of capital. The concept of RAROC is widely used in risk management, as discussed in subsequent sections.

4.2.1.3 Regulatory capital
The banking law and implementing regulations define what constitutes capital for capital adequacy purposes and the minimum amount of capital that banks

---

4 The following equation applies: assets − liabilities = net worth.

must maintain to be in compliance with capital regulation. Regulatory capital may be a subset of economic capital. However, when the former is more than the latter, a firm's compliance with capital adequacy requirements may become problematic. Banks' incentive is to reduce the amount of regulatory capital to equate it to economic capital, typically through regulatory arbitrage.

4.2.1.4 Calculating bank leverage

Leverage is calculated in two different ways. Accounting leverage is widely used in the finance industry. It is defined by total assets divided by shareholders' equity.[5] This is the arithmetical inverse of regulatory capital, which is equity divided by assets.

Comparing the regulatory capital ratio of a banking institution and a non-financial institution with similar ratings is highly instructive. Table 4.1 compares the ratio of JPMorgan Chase & Co., the BHC, and Apple Inc., whose credit ratings are high investment-grade.[6] Ratios are calculated by dividing capital by total consolidated assets. Even considering the significant debt incurred by Apple over the last several years, Apple's regulatory capital ratio is more than three times that of JPMorgan's. In general, the equity percentage of total assets of both bank and non-bank financial institutions is abnormally small when compared to that of firms in non-financial sectors. This reflects the business strategy of many financial institutions toward capital and management priorities, discussed in the next section, both of which depend on a high amount of leverage.

4.2.2 Factors contributing to the amount of capital on banks' balance sheet

Several factors, both external and internal, explain management's decisions regarding a bank's capital structure. These factors have important risk management and compliance implications.

Table 4.1 Regulatory capital ratios of JPMorgan Chase & Co. and Apple Inc.*

	JPMorgan Chase & Co. (rated A2)	Apple Inc. (rated Aa1)
Total liabilities	$2,332.6 billion	$234.3 billion
Total shareholders' equity	$257.5 billion	$115.0 billion
Total assets (on and off BS)	$2,590.1 billion	$349.2 billion
Regulatory capital ratio	9.9%	32.9%
Accounting leverage	10.1:1	3.0:1

* Balance sheet figures are as of 30 June 2018, and Moody's ratings are as of 12 March 2019.

5 Accounting leverage ratios were quoted widely in the financial press leading up to the financial crisis. On the eve of its bankruptcy filing, Lehman Brothers' accounting leverage ratio was reported to be 31:1. Lehman Brothers 2007 Annual Report 1.

6 JPMorgan's rating is one category below that of Apple, reflecting the generally lower ratings of financial institutions.

4.2.2.1 Importance of return on equity in banks' capital structure and risk-taking

Of all the factors that influence a banking firm's capital structure the incentive of management to attain a high return on equity is one of the most important. Bank management targets a high return on equity because its compensation is typically partly a function of this metric on the theory that it promotes shareholder wealth maximization. This compensation structure helps to explain several aspects relating to management's approach to a firm's capital structure and risk-taking.

First, other things being equal, a smaller amount of capital generates a higher return on equity,[7] resulting in an incentive to optimize a capital structure with a low percentage of capital. In this connection, risk management can *reduce* the amount of economic capital by using it more effectively in managing risk and generating a return.[8] A second effect of the return on equity target is the incentive to engage in regulatory arbitrage. Banks can achieve higher return on equity by optimizing their compliance with an existing regulation or finding a more advantageous capital regime with lower capital requirements. Third, a high return on equity target incentivizes management to disguise risky bets with long tail risk,[9] a predilection that regulators seek to counter through Pillar III disclosure of risk management practices.

Finally, and relatedly, FDIC insurance contributes to the incentive to reduce capital as a proportion of total liabilities. Management can take greater risks when supported by a government backstop. Also, the government backstop gives less incentive to creditors and shareholders to monitor management's risk-taking, enabling management to reduce the capital cushion without pressuring the market prices of a bank's securities.

4.2.2.2 Negative implications of 'signaling' by equity sales

Banks also seek to avoid equity issuance because it may serve to signal weakness to the market. Two of the primary components of regulatory capital are equity provided by shareholders and retained earnings. If banks have to raise capital by issuing equity because retained earnings are low, investors may view the issuance as a sign of financial weakness. Moreover, equity investors disfavor equity sales because they dilute existing shareholders' claims.[10]

4.2.2.3 Importance of a high amount of short-term liabilities in banks' capital structure

As discussed in Chapter 1,[11] the banking business model includes deposit-taking as a key source of low-cost, short-term funding. The logic of the

---

7 Return on equity is calculated by dividing the amount of after-tax profit by the amount of equity in a capital structure. Holding profit constant, the lower the amount of equity, the higher the return on equity.

8 '[R]isk management can be viewed as a substitute for equity capital'. Brian Nocco and René Stulz, 'Enterprise risk management: theory and practice' (2006), 18 *Journal of Applied Corporate Finance* 11.

9 In such instance a bank's management will disclose a high return on equity based on an artificially low amount of risk.

10 Viral Acharya and Matthew Richardson, 'Causes of the financial crisis' (2010), 21 *Critical Review* 198.

11 § 1.2.2.1.

banking business model is to ensure a high proportion of these liabilities in order to generate NII and fee income from deposit account services. This aspect of banks' business reinforces the tendency to have a highly leveraged capital structure.

4.2.2.4 Historical evolution of bank leverage

Figure 4.1 puts banks' capital structure in historical perspective. It underscores the steady decline of banks' economic capital over the last century in the US. This decline reflects in part the increased efficiency in bank operations and development of the US financial system.[12] The decline in capital is precipitous following the creation of the Federal Reserve in 1913[13] and the creation of the FDIC in 1933. The first reduced risk of bank failure by providing liquidity during periods of market stress,[14] and the second reduced depositors' risk of bank failure through deposit insurance. These abrupt declines thus reflect banks' estimation of the amount of necessary economic capital given the government backstops as there were no explicit capital requirements until the 1980s. The high level of capital in the early period reflects in part banks' need to protect against the perennial bank runs and uninsured depositors' concern about bank solvency.

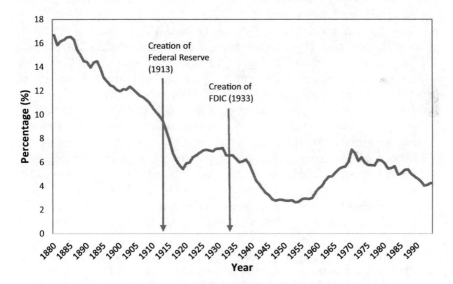

Figure 4.1 Evolution of bank capital ratio in the US

12 Allen Berger, Richard Herring, and Giorgio Szegö, 'The role of capital in financial institutions' (1995), 19 *Journal of Banking & Finance* 393, 401 [Berger, Role of capital].

13 One of the key reasons for creation of the Federal Reserve was the need for a federal lender of last resort.

14 Berger, Role of capital 401.

4.2.3 Rationales for capital adequacy regulation

All types of bank capital regulation seek to mitigate the risks of the banking business model and moral hazard fostered by FDIC insurance. This regulation seeks to counter the factors that have led to secularly declining levels of bank capital and managements' incentive to minimize equity capital in the capital structure.

Regulation and supervision is not costless, either for individual firms or for society as a whole. A trade-off exists between regulation and supervisory oversight intended to enhance safety and soundness, on the one hand, and ensuring a reasonable availability of credit for business investment and consumer purchases through banks' intermediation, on the other.[15] Capital regulation directly affects this economic trade-off.

Regulators promote the importance of capital in three ways.[16] First, a mandated minimum level of capital acts as a buffer against losses and, in extreme circumstances, contagion in the financial system. As insurer of bank deposits, the federal government is potentially a bank's largest creditor. Deposit insurance attaches automatically to all new deposits. Insurance premiums also do not accurately track banks' riskiness. These factors underscore the importance of banking agencies' policy of regulating individual banks' safety and soundness on an ongoing basis.[17] Further strengthening this rationale, the central bank's lender-of-last-resort function in conditions of market turmoil provides an implicit guarantee of a bank's obligations.[18]

Second, minimum capital requirements can internalize negative externalities imposed by banks on society by preventing their failure or mitigating the impact of their failure on the financial system. This is particularly the case with systemic risk because of interconnectedness among large banks in the interbank funding market and the payments system.[19] The GFC is the most obvious example of the costs to society of contagion. In addition, an individual bank's specialized knowledge of its borrowers is lost when it becomes insolvent, introducing costs into a country's intermediation function and making it less efficient.

Third, capital buffers can discourage opportunistic behavior by management by limiting undue risk-taking by bank managers. Banks and other debtors have an incentive to leverage their firms to generate high profits with a thin capital base.[20] Shareholders have more to lose if higher capital is required. In addition, opportunistic behavior is a particular problem in financial institutions whose

---

15 Banking on Basel 26. Minimum capital requirements should not be confused with optimal capital levels. Setting the amount of capital is a much more difficult challenge for regulators. Ibid. 27.

16 The following discussion draws substantially from the excellent summary on the rationales for capital regulation by Daniel Tarullo. Banking on Basel 29.

17 Ibid. 20–21.

18 Ibid. 19–20. The federal safety net creates moral hazard among banks' creditors, who demand less than optimum capital to protect them against losses. In effect, capital requirements compensate for this effect of moral hazard. Ibid. 21.

19 Ibid. 21–22. Before the GFC this rationale has not generally been officially cited by bank regulators. Ibid. 22. Since then, however, the BCBS and national authorities have imposed capital surcharges on systemically important banks in order to internalize their 'systemic footprint'. See § 7.2.2.

20 The earlier discussion is at § 4.2.2.1.

assets are generally difficult to value by creditors and shareholders. Moreover, the complexity of financial conglomerates exacerbates the information asymmetry between insiders and outsiders.

4.3 Prescriptive micro-prudential regulation and compliance

This section discusses capital adequacy requirements, liquidity regulation, and portfolio restrictions, which comprise the prescriptive components of micro-prudential regulation.

4.3.1 Historical evolution of prudential regulation

Broadly speaking, micro-prudential regulation evolved in three distinct phases: the period preceding the enactment of federal deposit insurance in 1934, the period from that point to the 1980s, and the adoption of the Basel regime of bank regulation in 1988 to the present. Capital regulation as an established and preferred mode of bank regulation only occurred in the third period.

4.3.1.1 Period 1: pre-FDIC insurance

Since the early 1800s bank supervision became necessary because the early banks supplied the nation's money supply in the form of banknotes. State and federal laws required banks to hold specie and bonds against banknotes, assets that could be easily stolen.[21] Examiners would visit individual banks to check on their reserves and quality of assets with a view to reducing risk of losses to depositors caused by bank failures.

Supervisory oversight was overhauled with the creation of the OCC in 1863. Congress imposed diversification, cash reserve, capital, dividend, real estate ownership, and reporting requirements on national banks. State-chartered banks, however, generally had less stringent requirements. The system preceding the 1930s reforms was even more balkanized than at present. Two separate systems, one operated by the federal government and the other by individual state governments, competed with one another with very different regulatory frameworks. There was no overarching federal framework although the two short-lived Banks of the United States did have branches.[22]

4.3.1.2 Period 2: FDIC insurance

The second period began with the introduction of federal deposit insurance in 1934, which exacerbated the moral hazard that already existed in the banking industry, fundamentally changing the intensity and dynamic of prudential supervisory oversight.[23] Nevertheless, US regulators prior to the 1980s did not impose

---

21 George Kaufman and others, *Perspectives on Safe & Sound Banking: Past, Present, and Future* (MIT Press: 1986) 247.

22 § 2.3.1.2 n. 60.

23 The broader topic of the federal safety net is treated in detail in § 1.2.3.

explicit minimum capital requirements.[24] Instead of capital ratios, supervisors applied informal and subjective measures by focusing on management and loan quality of individual banks.

4.3.1.3 Period 3: Basel regime

The adoption of the Basel regime of capital regulation, spurred by financial market disruptions and high-profile defaults in the 1970s and early 1980s, marked the final chapter in the evolution of bank regulation. Basel III, implemented by Dodd-Frank and the US financial regulatory agencies, introduced a uniform, formalized model of regulation, based primarily on capital adequacy requirements but structural features as well.

4.3.1.4 Evolution internationally

Prudential regulation abroad varied widely until the developments following the Basel Accord in 1988. By 1992, not only had all G-10 Basel member countries signed on to the Accord but more than 100 non-Basel member countries had done so as well.[25] All jurisdictions with internationally active banks now adhere to the Basel regime.

4.3.2 Overarching objectives of Basel capital regulation and regulatory philosophy

Despite the criticism of the Basel regime for being poorly prepared for the GFC and for the increasing complexity of its system of capital regulation, it stands for a remarkable achievement in ensuring that all internationally active banks adhere to the same system of regulation. It established a durable framework for capital regulation and an internally consistent philosophy of financial regulation.

4.3.2.1 Two interrelated objectives

Basel's capital regime is designed to achieve the two overriding objectives of the Basel Accord:[26] to strengthen the international banking system and to introduce a uniform system of banking regulation that would prevent a 'race to the bottom' through regulatory arbitrage. These two goals are inextricably interconnected. Without a uniform framework, global prudential regulation would deteriorate as jurisdictions compete for banking businesses by offering bank-friendly regulation and supervision. Such a competitive dynamic would make a uniform approach to bank regulation impossible.

4.3.2.2 Resilience of Basel regime's methodological approach

Two elements present at the creation of the Basel regime have continued to characterize it to the present day. First, the architects of the Basel Accord of

---

24 Banking on Basel 29.
25 Banking on Basel 65–66.
26 The events leading up to the Basel Accord of 1988 are covered at § 2.2.1.

1988 developed a risk-weighted assets methodology that grouped assets with levels of risk that were assumed to be similar into risk categories and assigned weights to each category, at first covering only credit risk. Second, the Basel authorities have progressively refined this methodology and expanded it to different types of risks in an effort to keep up with market developments. The increasing complexity of Basel capital regulation, which has become controversial among policymakers, financial institutions, and other market participants, can be ascribed to these two basic attributes of the Basel capital regime. For better or worse, the RWA framework has proved highly durable.

4.3.2.3 Basel's Three Pillars of capital regulation and supervision

The BCBS's 'Three Pillars' framework of bank capital regulation is a distillation of the Basel authorities' distinct regulatory philosophy. Although not widely used in US regulation, the Three Pillars framework nevertheless has global relevance in framing a uniform approach to prudential regulation and supervision and accompanying risk management and compliance expectations. In short, Pillar I consists of the minimum regulatory capital requirements applicable to all banks; Pillar II, of supervisors' determination of additional capital required of individual banks, generally arising from findings in a bank's examination; and Pillar III, of market discipline facilitated through disclosure of banks' capital ratios, capital quality, and capital planning.

For purposes of risk management and compliance, the first two pillars embody the most relevant concepts. Pillar I entails prescriptive regulation applicable to all banks and covers credit, market, and operational risk. It is the foundation for supervisory requirements under Pillar II, following the pyramid of regulatory expectations.[27]

One of the key goals of capital adequacy requirements is to internalize the social costs of troubled banks and bank failures. The capital adequacy regulations under Basel III and Dodd-Frank (Pillar I) are the foundation and starting point in this effort. Capital add-ons required through bank supervision (Pillar II) seek to ensure full internalization of costs of individual banks based on their unique risk profiles. Through filed disclosures of publicly traded BHCs and through CALL reports[28] required of all banks, banking agencies can make a preliminary assessment of banks' compliance with the hard-wired requirements of Basel III. Under Pillar III, banks' disclosures facilitate market discipline by requiring institutions to disclose details on the amount of bank capital, risk exposures, and risk management. If market participants understand a bank's internal risk management's capital planning, they can more easily distinguish between the various banking firms. The market disciplines individual banks through the stock market's pricing mechanism.

---

27 § 2.7.3.
28 Call reports, 'Reports of Condition and Income', are regulated by the FFIEC.

4.3.2.4 Risk-return optimization involving RWA

At first glance, the Pillar I prescriptive requirements would appear to involve little involvement by the risk management and compliance functions: a bank meets the mandated capital ratio or it does not. This, however, is not the case. The largest banks are permitted to calculate their own capital levels for certain risk categories. They seek to optimize their portfolio asset composition subject to the constraints imposed by regulatory requirements. The accounting and IT system to manage the RWA calculation can be extremely costly. Nevertheless, in pursuing risk-return optimization banks expend significant resources in managing their RWA to achieve the lowest amount of equity as possible in pursuit of their business strategy.[29]

4.3.3 Overview of Basel III's risk-weighted capital adequacy methodology

The basic concept underlying the RWA methodology is relatively straightforward. Basel capital regulation establishes a minimum ratio of regulatory capital to RWA of 8%, which has remained the minimum capital requirement to the present day, subject to Basel III's add-ons.[30]

4.3.3.1 Precursors and foundation of Basel III: Basel I and Basel II

National authorities implemented Basel I throughout the world wherever there were internationally active banks. The Basel I regime established five risk categories of varying weights. The face amount of an asset is multiplied by its assigned risk weight. Corporate debt, whether its credit rating was speculative grade or high grade, had a 100% risk weight. Residential mortgages had a 50% risk weight. These adjusted amounts were then added up to equal the total RWAs in the denominator. Bank capital in the numerator consisted of 'tiers' of decreasing quality based on their loss-absorbing capacity.

Table 4.2 illustrates the calculation of regulatory capital necessary for a sample bank portfolio of assets under the Basel I RWA methodology.[31] Of the portfolio of $10,000 of total assets, the final amount of minimum regulatory capital required is $360, which is 8% of the calculated RWA amount of $4,500. Note that sovereign debt, including Greek government bonds, had a risk weighting of 0%, requiring no regulatory capital. The inaccuracy and implications of the risk weighting of government debt became painfully evident during the eurozone crisis of 2011–13.

In 1996, reflecting the enormous growth of large banks' derivatives and capital markets activities, the Basel authorities introduced market risk capital rules, which were formalized in Basel II in 2004 and carried over and further refined in Basel III. Banks had to have the 8% minimum against capital against risks

---

29 The calculation of the leverage ratio is more straightforward § 4.3.8.

30 Basel I generally did not require capital for off–balance sheet assets. But Basel II required capital against certain off–balance sheet items.

31 This is a simplified model based on Basel I regulation.

Table 4.2 RWA sample calculation

Assets	Total $ amount on balance sheet	Basel I risk weights			
		0%	20%	50%	100%
Cash and cash equivalents	$2,000	$0			
Corporate bonds	$2,000				$2,000
Residential mortgages	$5,000			$2,500	
Greek sovereign debt	$1,000	$0			
Total balance sheet assets	$10,000				
Total amount of RWA	$4,500	$0		$2,500	$2,000
Regulatory capital	$360 ($4,500 × 8%)				

arising from volatility in stock prices, interest rates, foreign exchange rates, and commodity prices. The US, which never adopted Basel II, was subject to Basel I on the eve of the GFC. Dodd-Frank implemented Basel III.

Basel II's market-risk rules illustrate the Basel authorities' efforts to continuously update their framework to reflect the changing banking business model.

4.3.4 Basel III's RWA framework: regulatory capital (numerator)

> Basel III is essentially a bold new layer built over the old Basel II architecture, in much the same way that early versions of Windows were layered on top of DOS. And just as early versions of Windows shared some of the weaknesses of DOS, so has Basel III inherited some of the problems of Basel II.[32]

The financial crisis revealed significant deficiencies in Basel capital regulation relating to both the numerator and the denominator. The need for an overhaul was patently obvious as all systemically important BHCs were in compliance with the applicable Basel requirements on the eve of the GFC. We begin with the Basel III requirements for the numerator.

4.3.4.1 Basel III's 'going concern' and 'gone concern' loss absorption rationales

Regulatory capital's loss absorption capacity is a primary focus of the BCBS. Enhancing the capital requirement after the crisis required both a purer form of capital and an increase in the amount of capital in the form of add-ons to the 8% floor. The BCBS enunciated two controlling principles.[33] First, capital must enhance a bank's ability to continue its basic role in credit intermediation in an economic downturn through lending as a *going* concern.[34] Second, a bank must

---

32 Felix Salmon, 'The biggest weakness of Basel III', *Reuters* (15 September 2010). According to Salmon, although Basel II took a decade to launch, Basel III was much more of a 'rush job'. Ibid.

33 The requirements for the capital numerator are located at 12 CFR § 217, Subpart A-C.

34 Losses in an economic downturn will lower capital. If this becomes serious, banks will no longer have the capacity to lend because they do not have capital to support the increase in

have adequate *gone* concern capital to bolster its ability to make full restitution to depositors without taxpayer exposure in the event that it fails.

These two principles underlie the rationale for Basel III's three categories of capital. Common equity tier 1 capital (CET1), shareholders' interest, is the purest form of capital. It consists mainly of common equity and retained earnings on the bank's balance sheet, is perpetual,[35] has no dividend rights, and is paid after all other claims. The second category, 'additional tier 1 capital', cannot have a maturity date or issuer incentive to redeem. The issuer can redeem shares only after five years, with regulatory approval. The third category, 'tier 2 capital', includes cumulative preferred stock and subordinated debt, with at least a five-year maturity date. Together, CET1, additional tier 1, and tier 2 are 'total capital'. Tier 1 and tier 2 capital are intended to be 'going concern' and 'gone concern' capital, respectively.

4.3.4.2 Amount required of each tier of capital

The next issue involves the *amount* of required regulatory capital in each of the three categories. Banks must have the following minimum amounts of capital as a percentage of RWA: 4.5% of CET1, 6% of tier 1 capital (comprised of CET1 and additional tier 1 capital), and tier 2 capital comprising the remaining 2%, totaling the same Basel 8% minimum. This equity capital structure is a waterfall in which losses first erode tier 2 capital, followed by additional tier 1 capital, and finally by CET1 capital.

4.3.4.3 Capital conservation buffer

Basel III does not stop with the 8% floor, unlike Basel I and II. An additional 'capital conservation buffer' of 2.5% of CET1 results in a total CET1 ratio requirement to 7% and a total capital ratio of 10.5%. The purpose of this buffer is to maintain sufficient capital above the 8% floor to withstand economic downturns and more serious episodes of financial distress. Again, the GFC provided important lessons to regulators. During the crisis, banks paid out dividends and large bonuses despite their weakening condition. This industry-wide practice weakened the banking sector as a whole as the crisis reached its peak stage.

The buffer is designed to act counter-cyclically with regard to all types of equity distributions. As capital falls below the buffer, the banking organization is subject to decreasing maximum allowed dividends, share buy-backs, and bonuses.[36] The regulators have supervisory discretion to impose additional restrictions based on a bank's risk profile. Critics of the buffer argue that a decrease in payouts can act as a market signal of a bank's weakness. Additional capital charges apply to the largest BHCs, which are covered in Chapter 7.

---

assets resulting from additional loans. However, they may also be unwilling to lend due to risk aversion.

35 'Perpetual' means that the claimholder has no right of redemption from the issuer. It is 'unrunnable'.

36 The payout ratios as a percentage of eligible retained income corresponding to the amount of a banking organization's buffer are as follows: > 2.5%: no limit; > 1.875%–2.500%: 60%; > 1.250%–1.875%: 40%; >0.625%–1.250%: 20%; < 0.625%: 0%.

4.3.4.4 Risk management and compliance relating to regulatory capital numerator

Point-in-time compliance with the RWA-based capital formulas is relatively straightforward but still requires a set of ICs and compliance P&Ps. It is the role of a bank's finance department to ensure that the various types of capital on the balance sheet meet the Dodd-Frank definitions for CET1, additional tier 1 capital, and tier 2, an arithmetic accounting issue. However, accounting practices and FASB rules[37] may not align with regulatory capital categories (CET1, tier 1, tier 2) consisting of a variety of types of equity instruments. Moreover, the rule has detailed provisions on what accounting items cannot be included and the deductions required from capital, such as minority interests.[38]

To the extent there is leeway under the capital definitions, risk management will assist in optimizing the bank's capital structure, as a bank will rationally seek to minimize regulatory capital requirements that exceed economic capital. Thus, management must ensure that robust ICs exist for such calculations that track these regulatory capital categories over time. Firms must publicly disclose the various capital ratios, raising the bar on accuracy under the federal securities laws.

Much more demanding of risk management and compliance are the forward-looking capital planning exercises under Dodd-Frank Annual Stress Testing (DFAST) and CCAR. A BHC will not pass these stress tests if it has a capital deficiency under the Federal Reserve's stress test macro scenarios. This is the subject of Chapter 7.[39]

4.3.5 Overview of Basel III's risk-based framework: RWA (denominator)

The denominator is the total amount of a bank's 'risk-weighted' on– and off–balance sheet assets. Following Basel I and II, Basel III assigns each asset category a risk weighting that, when applied to the asset's face amount, determines the dollar amount of RWA. Calculating RWA is a complex process due a combination of Basel III's highly granular approach to calculating risk-weighted capital charges and the complexity of some of the financial instruments in banks' portfolios. The Basel regime's risk-based methodologies reflect its estimate of the asset's average probability of default (PD) and loss given default (LGD).

A comprehensive description of the myriad categories of risk weights and their determination is beyond the scope of this book.[40] The primary purpose of the following sections is, first, to explain the mechanics and rationale of the rules for each type of risk and, second, to describe the key risk management and compliance implications and requirements associated with the rules.

---

37 The Financial Accounting Standards Board in the US issues accounting standards known as 'Generally Accepted Accounting Principles' (GAAP) applicable to public companies.

38 These numerator deductions, which are highly detailed and complex, are beyond the scope of this book. See Definition of Capital, 12 CFR § 217.20 et seq., Subpart C.

39 § 7.4.

40 Footnotes reference relevant provisions of the regulatory capital rules.

4.3.5.1 Separate methodologies for 'standardized' and 'advanced' approaches banks

Basel III's capital framework divides banking organizations into two groups, reflecting its enhanced prudential regulation of financial conglomerates. 'Advanced' approaches banking organizations have $250 billion or more in total consolidated assets or $10 billion or more of on–balance sheet foreign exposure and include their depository subsidiaries. These firms are required to use 'advanced' approach RWA methodologies for capital charges, based on internal modeling and internal ratings-based methodologies to estimate PD and LGD for various specified asset classes.

All other banks are 'standardized' approach banks, subject to a separate set of RWA methodologies prescribed by regulators.[41] Advanced approaches banks also must comply with 'standardized' approach requirements, which in certain cases serve as a floor for regulatory capital.

In addition, the market risk capital rules apply to a separate category of banking organizations ('market-risk banks'), which may include both advanced and standardized approaches banks. Market-risk banks[42] are banking organizations whose gross trading assets and liabilities equal at least 10% of total consolidated assets or at least $1 billion of such assets. RWA rules treat market risk capital charges separately from credit risk charges. In addition, advanced approaches banks have a CCR requirement and an operational risk capital requirement, while standardized approach banks do not.

For standardized approach banks, the formula for aggregating all RWAs is as follows: total RWA = credit risk RWA + market risk RWA (if bank is a market risk bank). For advanced approaches banks, the RWA formula is: RWA = credit risk RWA + market risk RWA (if bank is a market risk bank) + operational RWA.

The compliance burden is significant for an advanced approaches banking organization. Supervisory approval of internal modeling is contingent on a written implementation plan and completion of a satisfactory four-calendar quarter parallel run of the modeling, with continuous compliance with the qualification requirements and otherwise adequate processes and risk management to ensure ongoing compliance.[43] The burden is not especially heavy for standardized approach banks unless they also must apply the market-risk capital rule.

4.3.6 Credit risk RWA capital requirements

The rules governing credit risk capital charges are highly complex. For advanced approaches banks they specify detailed risk management and compliance requirements. Advanced approaches banks must make substantial investments in their risk management, compliance, and IT infrastructure in order to receive approval

---

41 A BHC subsidiary of a foreign banking organization may, with prior written FRB approval, elect not to comply with the advanced approaches rule. It must then comply with the standardized risk-based capital rules. See 12 CFR § 217.30 et seq., Subpart D.

42 The market risk rules are at § 4.3.7.

43 The qualification process is located at 12 CFR § 217.121.

by their primary regulator before using internal modeling for calculating capital charges.

4.3.6.1 Standardized approach RWA methodologies for credit risk

The standardized approach rules treat credit risk under several categories of assets:[44] on–balance sheet exposures (other than cleared and unsettled transactions, default fund contributions to central counterparties (CCPs), securitization exposures, and equity exposures, all of which are separately treated), and OTC derivative contracts and various other off–balance sheet exposures.

General risk weights for on–balance sheet exposures. The rule specifies general risk weights for certain on–balance sheet exposures,[45] ranging from 0% for US government debt and certain other sovereign exposures to 600% for certain equity exposures;[46] Basel III bases risk weights for sovereign exposures on the Organization for Economic Co-operation and Development's (OECD's) country risk classifications (CRCs).[47] The rule also specifies risk weights for depository institutions,[48] residential mortgages,[49] high-volatility commercial real estate (HVCRE),[50] public sector entities,[51] and government-sponsored entities (GSEs),[52]

---

44 12 CFR §§ 217.31–38, .41–.45, .51–.53.

45 Other than cleared and unsettled transactions, default fund contributions to CCPs, securitization exposures, and equity exposures.

46 To arrive at a Basel III minimum capital charge, the risk weight (e.g., 600%) is multiplied by 8%. Risk weights over 100% indicate that the RWA percentage applied to an exposure exceeds the 8% minimum. For example, a bank holding $100 of assets with a risk weight of 600% would need to provision $48 of capital against it (8% × 600% = 48%). The rule permits banks to reduce the risk weight according to certain specified conditions.

47 The OECD's CRC risk categories range from 0 to 7, with corresponding risk weights as shown in Table 4.3 (the resulting Basel III capital charge percentage is indicated):

Table 4.3 Risk weights for sovereign exposures
(Table 1 to 12 CFR § 217.32)

CRC of sovereign	Risk weight (in %)
0–1	0
2	20
3	50
4–6	100
7	150
OECD member with no CRC	0
Non-OECD member with no CRC	100
Default by sovereign	150

48 The rule assigns a 20% risk weight for US-based institutions and otherwise a weight correlated with the OECD's CRC rating.

49 The rule assigns a 50% risk weight for first-lien mortgages that meet certain other criteria and a 100% risk weight for others.

50 The rule assigns a 150% risk weight to HVCRE assets.

51 The rule defines such an entity as a state, local authority, or other governmental division below a sovereign entity. General obligations have a risk weight of 20% and revenue obligations, a risk weight of 50%.

52 GSEs have a 20% risk weight for non-equity exposures and a 100% risk weight for preferred stock issued by a GSE.

among other institutional categories. Corporate exposures (e.g., loans and bonds) have a risk weight of 100%.[53] A separate category of credit risk mitigants consisting of guarantees, credit derivatives, and financial collateral can substitute for credit exposures, subject to specified conditions.[54]

Risk weights for off–balance sheet exposures. For off–balance sheet exposures, to arrive at the RWA amount, a bank must multiply the exposure amount (usually the contractual amount) by a credit conversion factor (CCF). Off–balance sheet exposures include guarantees, financial standby letters of credit, forward agreements, and warranties, among others.[55] OTC derivative contracts are separately treated. To arrive at RWAs, banks determine the exposure amount[56] for the contract and multiply it by a risk weight based on the applicable CCR.[57] The rule separately treats single OTC derivative contracts and multiple contracts under qualifying master netting agreements.

Cleared transactions.[58] An important intermediary in the financial markets is a CCP that assumes credit risk between two counterparties, ensuring future performance under their contracts, while also providing clearing and settlement services.[59] A special category of 'qualifying central counterparties' (QCCPs) play a crucial role under Dodd-Frank in addressing systemic risk associated with the derivative markets. Bank members of QCCPs and clients transacting with QCCPs have significantly reduced capital requirements for cleared transactions under the capital rule, with risk weights applied to trade exposures equaling either 2% or 4%.[60] This presumably reduces systemic risk by incentivizing counterparties to migrate to QCCPs. Banks transacting with non-qualifying CCPs must apply the rule's general on–balance sheet risk weights.[61] CCP members must make default fund contributions to their CCPs, which are capital contributions designed to mitigate the latter's counterparty risk. The rule specifies how to calculate RWAs for such contributions to QCCPs and non-qualifying CCPs.[62]

Unsettled transactions.[63] The standard approaches provisions for calculating RWAs for unsettled transactions specify risk weights depending on the status of a

---

53 Dodd-Frank prohibits the use of credit ratings in regulations.

54 12 CFR § 217.36 (guarantees and credit derivatives) and 12 CFR § 217.37 (financial collateral).

55 For example, financial standby letters of credit, forward agreements, and guarantees have a CCF of 100%, and unused portions of commitments that are unconditionally cancelable have a CCF of 0%. 12 CFR § 217.33(b).

56 The exposure amount is equal to the sum of the current exposure, which is the greater of fair value or zero and the potential future credit exposure, which is calculated by multiplying the contract's notional principle amount by a conversion factor set forth in a table.

57 12 CFR § 217.34(c) (credit derivatives) and 34(d) (equity derivatives). Risk weights of counterparties are at 12 CFR § 217.32.

58 Cleared transactions are transactions in which two counterparties transact with a clearing organization rather than bilaterally with themselves.

59 An example of a CCP is the Options Clearing Corporation.

60 Four percent applies if conditions involving margin collateral and legal due diligence are not satisfied. 12 CFR § 217.35(b)(3)(A)–(B).

61 12 CFR § 217.32.

62 12 CFR § 217.35(d).

63 Unsettled transactions involve securities, foreign exchange instruments, and commodities that have a risk of delayed settlement or delivery. 12 CFR § 217.38(b).

transaction as 'delivery versus payment' or 'payment versus payment' or whether the transaction falls outside these categories.[64]

Securitization exposures.[65] Poorly performing securitizations of residential mortgages played a central role in the GFC. As a consequence, the capital rule imposes several conditions on banks that want to receive favorable off–balance sheet capital treatment for securitizations.[66] For traditional securitizations, if a bank fails to meet specified conditions it must hold capital against transferred assets as if the assets had not been securitized and deduct from CET1 any gain-on-sale from the transfer. Among several other conditions, the exposure cannot be reported on a bank's consolidated balance sheet under Generally Accepted Accounting Principles (GAAP), and the exposure's credit risk must be transferred to one or more third parties.[67] Banks *not* subject to the market risk rule may use the simplified supervisory formula approach (SSFA) to calculate risk weights[68] and, if not applied, a 'gross-up' rule. A 1,250% risk weight applies to all securitization exposures for which a bank does not use either of these formulas.[69] This punitive risk weight also applies if the bank does not meet certain due diligence requirements.[70]

Equity exposures. Banks must use a simple risk-weight approach (SRWA) for equity exposures that are not exposures to investment funds and a look-through approach if the latter is the case.[71] Under the SRWA, risk weights are based on the counterparty's credit risk.[72] Equity risk weights range from 0% to 600%.[73]

4.3.6.2 Compliance issues under standardized RWA methodology for credit risk
Compliance steps under the standardized approach are twofold. A bank must first determine its on– and off–balance sheet exposure amounts. It then must multiply these exposure amounts by the risk weights for the various exposure types or counterparty, eligible guarantor, or financial collateral as prescribed by the rule to arrive at the RWAs for the capital ratio denominator. By and large, banks' existing operational systems will enable them to achieve compliance under the standardized approach. This is not true under the advanced approaches RWA methodologies, which the following subsection covers.

4.3.6.3 Advanced approaches A-IRB RWA methodologies for credit risk
The advanced approaches rule requires banks to use an advanced internal ratings-based approach (A-IRB) and certain other methodologies to calculate

---

64 12 CFR § 217.138. Total RWA is the sum of RWAs for all such transactions. Ibid.
65 12 CFR § 217.41. For an explanation of securitizations, see § 1.3.1.
66 12 CFR § 217.41–.45.
67 12 CFR § 217.41(a)(1)–(4). Separate conditions apply to synthetic securitizations. 12 CFR § 217.41(b).
68 12 CFR § 217.43(a)–(d). Banks must have sufficient data for five input parameters in the SSFA approach. 12 CFR § 217.43.
69 This equates to a 100% capital charge (1,250% × .08 = 100%).
70 12 CFR § 217.41(c).
71 12 CFR § 217.53.
72 12 CFR § 217.52.
73 12 CFR § 217.52.

risk-based capital requirements for credit risk. The A-IRB approach requires banks to estimate several internal risk components: the PD, LGD, exposure at default (EAD) for wholesale and retail credits, and maturity (for wholesale exposures) instead of prescribed regulatory inputs. The advanced approaches rules categorize credit risk in three separate groups: general credit risk,[74] securitization exposures, and equity exposures, with an additional category of operational risk.[75] The rule also separately treats CCR, a risk that contributed significantly to the GFC. The credit value adjustment (CVA) is the market value of CCR. During the GFC, roughly two-thirds of losses attributed to CCR arose from CVA losses and only about one-third from actual defaults, which the rule governs separately.[76]

Unlike the standardized approach rules, the advanced approaches rules require an extensive risk management and compliance infrastructure.[77]

Wholesale and retail exposures. An important concept underlying A-IRB analytics for general credit risk is the advantage of classifying exposures as either wholesale or retail in addition to securitization and equity exposures. This is effective in establishing PD, LGD, and EAD inputs for banks' credit models for these first two asset classes. Retail and wholesale exposures each have several further subcategories.[78] A bank is required to calculate its total wholesale and retail RWA amount in four phases:[79] (1) categorizing exposures; (2) assigning wholesale obligors and exposures to rating grades and segmenting retail exposures;[80] (3) assigning risk parameters to wholesale exposures and segments of retail exposures;[81] and (4) calculating RWA amounts pursuant to the formula in Table 1 of section 131 of the rule.[82]

Cleared transactions. For cleared transactions,[83] clearing members must use specified methodologies to calculate RWAs. For cleared transactions with a

---

74 General credit risk under the advanced approaches methodology pertains to CCR of repo-style transactions, eligible margin loans, and OTC derivative contracts; cleared transactions; guarantees and credit derivatives; and unsettled transactions.

75 Operational risk is separate from credit risk but is included in the credit risk rules.

76 Basel Committee on Banking Supervision, 'Basel Committee finalises capital treatment for bilateral counterparty credit risk' (1 June 2011), Press Release, at <www.bis.org/press/p110601.pdf>.

77 These qualifying criteria are at 12 CFR §§ 217.100–.101, .121–.124. These criteria are discussed at § 4.3.6.4.

78 Retail exposures are subdivided into residential mortgages, qualified revolving exposure, and other retail exposure. Wholesale exposure is subdivided into corporate exposures, HVCRE exposures, sovereign exposures, OTC derivatives contracts, repo-style transactions, eligible margin loans, eligible purchased wholesale exposures, cleared transactions, default fund contributions, unsettled transactions, and eligible guarantees or eligible credit derivatives.

79 12 CFR § 217.131(a)–(e).

80 In phase 2 a bank must segment the retail exposures into segments with homogeneous risk characteristics.

81 This involves assigning PDs, LGDs, EADs, and effective maturities (M) to each wholesale grade, or in some cases, exposure, and PDs, LGDs, and EADs to each retail exposure segment. Special rules apply to certain subcategories of general credit risk.

82 Table 1 in 12 CFR § 217.131 provides capital formulas for non-defaulted wholesale and retail exposures. The outputs are multiplied by the exposure's or segment's EAD.

83 12 CFR § 217.133.

QCCP, 2% of the collateral posted by the bank applies or the member is subject to another arrangement specified in the rule preventing loss to the clearing member, and the member's client has conducted legal due diligence. If these requirements are not met, 4% of posted collateral applies. For transactions with non-qualifying CCPs, clearing members must calculate their risk weights according to the general risk weights under the standardized approach.[84] For default fund contributions, the rule requires a 1,250% risk weight or as otherwise determined by the agency for contributions to non-qualifying CCP funds. For contributions to QCCP funds, the rule specifies two methods for calculating default-fund contributions to non-qualifying QCCPs.[85]

Guarantees and credit derivatives. Banks frequently use guarantees and credit derivatives such as CDS to reduce their credit exposures. The rule permits banks to reflect these risk mitigants in reduced RWAs but imposes several conditions on their use. If these instruments fully cover wholesale exposures or partially cover them on a pro rata basis a bank may elect to use a PD substitution approach and LGD adjustment approach[86] using Table 1 of section 131 of the rule. If applicable, a bank can use 'double default treatment'[87] in using a guarantee or credit derivative.

Calculation of CCR and CVA capital charges.[88] A bank's CCR consists of the replacement cost of a defaulting counterparty and risk of potential future exposure to the counterparty when the bank is 'in the money'. CCR involves daily mark-to-market risk. CCR has separate capital charges for credit risk (default and credit migration) and market risk. The CVA measures CCR's market value. For repo-style transactions, eligible margin loans, and OTC derivative contracts, the banks use an internal model methodology to determine counterparty exposures and the associated CVA capital charge. The rule mandates banks to calculate risk weights for OTC derivatives according to the standardized approach. However, subject to prior agency approval, banks can use the advanced CVA approach based on its VaR model to calculate a CVA RWA amount.[89] Dodd-Frank also addresses 'wrong-way risk' (WWR) for which it requires banks to assess a capital charge.[90]

---

84 See 12 CFR § 217.32.

85 12 CFR § 217.133(d)(3)(i) (Method 1) and (d)(3)(iv) (Method 2).

86 12 CFR § 217.134(a)–(e). A bank may substitute a guarantee or credit derivative in full for a credit exposure by using Table 1 of section 131 of the rule or partially if the instrument covers only a pro rata amount of the credit exposure. In such cases, the PD and LGD risk parameters are substituted and adjusted, respectively, in accordance with section 134 and Table 1.

87 12 CFR § 217.135. 'Double default treatment' refers to use of guarantees or credit derivatives. The guarantor or issuer of the credit derivative must be an eligible guarantor as defined in 12 CFR § 217.100 ('eligible double default guarantor'). The RWA capital requirement is calculated pursuant to the formula in 135(e).

88 The rule includes CCR and CVA under general credit risk. However, it is separately discussed here since it has a unique, complex set of requirements.

89 See 12 CFR § 217.132(e)(5) (standardized or 'simple' approach) and (e)(6) (advanced approach).

90 WWR relates to credit risk involving a counterparty, a component of specific market risk. Banks have specific WWR if their future exposure to a given counterparty is positively correlated

Unsettled transactions.[91] The advanced approaches provisions specifying calculation of RWAs for unsettled transactions are substantially the same as for the standardized approach.[92]

Securitization exposures. The A-IRB rule imposes substantially the same conditions as the standardized approach rule on banks that want to receive favorable off–balance sheet capital treatment for securitizations. The rule requires banks to apply a 1,250% risk weight to securitization exposures that are non-A-IRB exposures[93] if certain conditions are not satisfied. The rule also requires banks to use the supervisory formula approach[94] (SFA) if it can calculate certain parameter inputs for the SFA on an ongoing basis. However, banks may use the SSFA if they have sufficient data for the parameter inputs specified for the SSFA by the rule.[95] The SFA is generally more risk sensitive than the SSFA. Both formulas calculate risk weights based on underlying assets and the relative position of the exposure in the capital structure.[96]

Equity exposures. The requirements for the RWA calculation by advanced approaches banks are substantially the same as under the standardized approach.[97]

4.3.6.4 Compliance and risk management for general credit risk under A-IRB approach

Credit risk other than CCR. The rule deals extensively with the qualification process and requirements for advanced approaches banks[98] for A-IRB credit risk analysis.[99] The bank must conduct a 'parallel run' during which it complies at all times with the rule's qualification requirements for four consecutive calendar quarters. The rule's requirements for banks' credit risk analytics and processes are relatively prescriptive. Among other things, the bank must be able to integrate the prescribed A-IRB systems and processes into its existing internal risk management processes and management information reporting systems. These systems must accurately and reliably differentiate among degrees of credit risk for its wholesale and retail exposures and accurately and reliably assign each wholesale obligor to a rating grade reflecting its PD. The bank must either assign LGD estimates to individual wholesale exposures or have an internal rating system for assigning loss severity rating grades. Retail exposures must be grouped into separate segments with homogeneous risk characteristics.

---

with the counterparty's PD. The correlation between the credit exposure to a counterparty and an underling asset can rapidly amplify portfolio deterioration.

91 Unsettled transactions involve securities, foreign exchange instruments, and commodities that have a risk of delayed settlement or delivery. 12 CFR § 217.38(b).

92 12 CFR § 217.136.

93 A-IRB securitization exposures comprise wholesale, retail, securitization, and equity exposures.

94 12 CFR § 217.143.

95 12 CFR § 217.144.

96 PwC, 'A closer look: US Basel III regulatory capital regime and market risk final rule' (July 2012) 17.

97 12 CFR § 217.151–.155.

98 A bank may also elect to qualify for the A-IRB approach.

99 12 CFR § 217.121 (qualification process) and 122 (qualification requirements). A-IRB banks must adopt an A-IRB implementation plan that sets a start date of no more than 36 months after it qualifies as such a bank.

The risk parameter quantification process must be comprehensive and capable of producing accurate, timely, and reliable estimates of the risk parameters for wholesale and retail exposures. Firms must review the process at least annually. PD, LGD, and EAD estimates require data quality and relevance to actual exposures and be based on extended periods ranging from five to seven years and either include periods of economic downturn or compensate for lack of such data.[100]

CCR and CVA capital charge. The agencies' CCR rule requires banks to establish and maintain a CCR management framework consisting of policies, processes, and systems to ensure the identification, measurement, management, approval, and internal reporting of CCR and procedures for ensuring compliance with these policies, processes, and systems. Firms must inventory the set of risk factors of their entire trading portfolio. The rule requires initial and ongoing validation of CCR exposure models with a view to the levels of risk factors and a pricing model and CCR exposure model. For WWR, banks must have procedures in place to identify, monitor, and control cases of specific WWR, beginning at the inception of a trade and continuing through the life of the trade.

4.3.6.5 Requirements for advanced approaches banks in calculating operational risk RWA[101]

Only advanced approaches banks have a capital requirement for operational risk. Operational risk is defined as risk of loss resulting from inadequate or failed internal processes, people, and systems or from external events, including legal risk.[102] Regulators expect banks to use past operational losses in their operational exposure models unless they can show that these losses are no longer relevant.[103] As with internal modeling generally, regulators are concerned with gaming of their rules for estimating operational risk exposure and resulting RWA risk-weighted capital. Scenario estimates are subjective. Banks have incentives to underestimate exposure to correspondingly limit capital requirements.

Banks are required to use the advanced measurement approach[104] using the 99.9th percentile of their one-year operational loss exposure to establish their operational risk capital. In this calculation, banks are required to consider four types of data: past internal losses; past losses of other banks; scenario analysis; and business, environment, and control factors.

The rule permits banks to use certain risk mitigants to reduce the capital requirements for operational risk, subject to several conditions. To adjust

---

100 12 CFR § 217.121.

101 Operational risk, which the rule includes under general credit risk, has a separate set of requirements for calculating RWA and is thus treated separately here.

102 Basel Committee on Banking Supervision, 'Principles for the sound management of operational risk' (June 2011) 3 n. 5.

103 Marco Migueis, 'Is operational risk regulation forward-looking and sensitive to current risks?' (21 May 2018), FEDS Notes, at <https://doi.org/10.17016/2380-7172.2198> [Is operational risk regulation forward-looking?].

104 12 CFR § 217 Subpart E.

operational risk exposure[105] in order to reflect mitigating factors, a bank must have an 'operational risk quantification system'[106] for estimating such exposure. Eligible risk mitigants include insurance provided by an unaffiliated company or mitigants that have agency approval.[107] The rule specifies two avenues depending on eligibility of risk mitigants for calculating the dollar risk-based capital requirement.[108] The resulting capital requirement is then multiplied by 12.5 to arrive at the RWA amount for operational risk. It also is important to note that the FRB's models in the CCAR stress test for operational risk can result in additional Pillar II charges.[109]

4.3.6.6 Risk management and compliance for operational risk

The rule requires banks to have an operational risk management function that is independent of business-line management and is responsible for designing, implementing, and overseeing operational data and assessment and operational risk quantification systems. Risk management must also have and document a process to identify, measure, monitor, and control operational risk in the bank's products, activities, processes, and systems. It should also ensure that relevant operational risk information is reported to business units, senior management, and the board.[110] A bank's operational data and assessment systems must be capable of being integrated into its existing risk management system.[111]

---

105 Operational risk exposure is defined as the amount in the 99.9th percentile of the distribution of potential aggregate operational losses generated by a bank's operational risk quantification system over a one-year horizon, not adjusted for eligible offsets or qualifying mitigants.

106 Among other requirements, the system must generate the bank's operational risk exposure using its operational risk data and assessment systems; not combine business activities or loss events with demonstrably different risk profiles within the same loss distribution; and use a 'credible, transparent, systematic, and verifiable' approach for weighting four specified elements that must be incorporated into its operational risk data and assessment systems. 12 CFR § 217.122(g)(3).

107 Approval is based in part on whether the mitigant covers potential operational losses in a manner equivalent to holding total capital. If the bank uses insurance to mitigate operational risk it must have a methodology that discounts the amount of mitigation through various insurance terms and conditions set forth in the rule.

108 If a bank is not eligible to use such qualifying risk mitigants for operational risk, the dollar risk-based capital requirement is equal to the bank's 'operational risk exposure' *minus* its 'eligible operational risk offsets'. Eligible operational risk offsets are amounts that are (1) generated by internal business practices to absorb highly predictable and reasonably stable operational losses, including reserves calculated consistent with GAAP; and (2) available to cover expected operational losses with a high degree of certainty over a one-year horizon. If the bank is eligible to use operational risk mitigants, the dollar risk-based capital requirement equals the greater of (1) the operational risk exposure adjusted for qualifying risk mitigants *minus* eligible operational risk offsets or (2) 0.8 times the difference between operational risk exposure and eligible operational risk offsets. 12 CFR § 217.162.

109 Operational risk is included in projections of 'Pre-Provisions Net Revenue' (PPNR), which are part of the buffer the FRB requires banks to hold to face stress test losses.

110 These requirements of the operational risk management function are listed at 12 CFR § 217.122(g)(1)(i)–(iii).

111 The operational data and assessment systems must be structured so that they are consistent with the bank's current business activities, risk profile, and technological and risk management processes. 12 CFR § 217.122(g)(2)(i).

4.3.7 Market risk RWA capital requirements

Market risk first became a policy concern for bank regulators in the 1990s as banks' trading operations grew exponentially amidst periodic episodes of market turmoil. Market risk is the risk of loss arising from movements in market prices,[112] which fair value accounting mandates be reflected in reported income.[113] A bank can measure its exposure to market risk by assessing the effect of changing rates and prices on the earnings or economic value of a financial instrument, portfolio, or the entire institution. For most banks, the most significant market risk is interest rate risk.[114] The impetus to incorporate market risk began in the mid-1990s, eventually resulting in the 2006 Basel amendment.[115] The GFC greatly accelerated rulemaking regarding market risk. During the crisis, write-downs of trading assets without counterparty default accounted for two-thirds of losses incurred by financial institutions.

4.3.7.1 Regulatory distinction between 'banking book' and 'trading book'
The focal point of market risk regulation is the classification of a bank's assets in either its 'trading book' or 'banking book'. Broadly speaking, capital requirements for the banking book, which is valued 'at cost', protect against credit loss, and those for the trading book, which is valued at 'fair value', protect against market loss.[116] Capital charges differ for each, resulting in potential regulatory arbitrage as banks seek to classify assets in a way that minimizes their overall capital requirements.

Since the GFC, bank regulators have sought to tighten restrictions on asset reclassification between the banking and trading books to prevent regulatory arbitrage. Leading up to the GFC, banks' leverage steadily accreted, especially in

---

112 Risks subject to market risk include default risk, interest rate risk, credit spread risk, equity risk, foreign exchange risk, and commodities risk for trading book instruments and foreign exchange risk and commodities risk for banking book instruments. BCBS, 'Minimum capital requirements for market risk' (2017) 5 [BCBS, Minimum capital requirements for market risk]. See § 1.2.2.3 for a discussion of market risk in the context of the banking business model.

113 These losses are realized due to fair value accounting. In fair value accounting, banks subject to US reporting requirements must report revalued trading book assets on a quarterly basis. Basel III requires banks to mark to market these assets on a daily basis.

114 Federal Reserve Board, Bank Holding Company Supervision Manual – Supervisory Policy Statement on Investment Securities and End-User Derivatives Activities, 2126.1.1.1 (January 2013).

115 Basel Committee on Banking Supervision, 'Amendment to the capital accord to incorporate market risk' (January 2006). The 1996 amendment allowed banks to use their VaR models to calculate capital charges for market risk.

116 'Banking book' positions are accounted for at amortized cost, fair value, or under the equity method, are subject to credit risk capital rules (thus potentially providing arbitrage opportunities vis-à-vis the trading book), and are held to maturity. Firms are not forced to write down banking book assets due to a decline in their market value. Banking book assets are not generally held for the purpose of short-term resale or with the intent of benefiting from actual or expected short-term price movements or to lock in arbitrage profits. 'Trading book' positions are accounted for at fair value and are generally used in firms' market-making and underwriting businesses. They are held 'for the purpose of short-term resale'.

the trading book, due in part to the Basel II's deficient capital standard for certain key risks.[117]

4.3.7.2 Evolution of market risk rulemaking

Post-crisis market risk rulemaking has occurred in two stages. During the first phase, regulators revised but did not fundamentally alter the Basel II framework. The rules made capital charges more granular, in harmony with Basel III's over-all regulatory philosophy. With minor revisions,[118] Dodd-Frank followed suit. The three US banking agencies issued a final market risk capital rule in 2012.

In the second stage, known as the 'fundamental review of trading book' (FRTB), the Basel policymakers significantly altered the market risk framework. Implementation of the FRTB rulebook in its current form[119] is far from assured in the US.[120] In Europe, the Basel policymakers encountered considerable industry resistance but issued the final standard in January 2019.[121] The reasons in both cases generally are the substantial increase in capital charges the FRTB will cause and the substantial infrastructure necessary for compliance by advanced approaches banks. Additionally, European banks are concerned with avoiding a competitive disadvantage should other jurisdictions not adopt the FRTB.

4.3.7.3 US market risk rule

The US market risk rule provisions apply to all banking organizations with aggregate trading assets and liabilities of at least 10% of total assets or $1 billion or as required by their primary regulator ('market risk banks'). Provisions apply separately to standard approaches and advanced approaches banks. The rule terms trading book assets and all foreign exchange and commodity positions 'covered positions' to which market risk rules apply.[122]

The rule reflects regulators' intention to reduce regulatory arbitrage. It reduces the types of assets previously eligible for the trading book and the advantages of such classification.[123] Market risk banks must assess securitization assets under

---

117 Basel Committee on Banking Supervision, 'Revisions to the Basel II market risk framework' (2011) 1. The Basel II framework by and large used an unstressed VaR framework.

118 Most notably, Dodd-Frank prohibits use of credit ratings in financial regulation. Financial regulators used credit ratings widely in capital requirements for various asset categories. Outside of the US, Basel III regulation continues to use credit ratings.

119 The BCBS has scheduled its final implementation in 2022.

120 The US Treasury Department has recommended postponing implementation of FRTB until the FRTB can be 'appropriately calibrated'. Department of the Treasury, 'A financial system that creates economic opportunities: banks and credit unions' (June 2017) 13.

121 EU lawmakers will remove capital charges for market risk from the rule and only require reporting initially, potentially postponing full implementation beyond the BCBS 2022 deadline. The rule will result in an average increase of about 22% in total market risk capital requirements, which is nearly one-half of the increase as originally structured. Huw Jones, 'Basel eases capital hit from new trading book rules for banks' (2019) Reuters.

122 The bank must also have an intent to benefit from short-term price fluctuations, among other things. The rule expressly excludes several types of instruments, such as positions held for securitization or any direct real estate holding. The market risk rule is at 12 CFR § 201 et seq., Subpart F.

123 'Final Market Risk Capital Rule', Practical Law, Article No. 8–522–3223 (2012) 2. This article is an accessible resource on the US market risk rule.

the standardized approach, with few exceptions.[124] Several procedures serve to disincentivize advanced approaches banks from using the advanced approaches rule, which allows internal modeling. Furthermore, the agencies have supervisory discretion to rescind approval of a model at any time and impose a capital charge for a covered position. Advanced approaches banks must calculate RWA for covered positions under both the credit risk capital rules and the advanced approaches methodology and apply the higher of the two.

Basel III's more granular approach to market risk assessments reflect lessons gleaned from the GFC. To a large extent, these additional risk metrics supplement the industry's VaR modeling, which relies on normal market conditions. To arrive at market-risk RWAs, a bank must multiply the standardized or advanced approach measure, as applicable, for market risk by 12.5. The rule distinguishes between securitized and non-securitized credit instruments. The total market risk RWA amount is the sum of six individual components based on model outputs:

VaR. VaR measures potential loss in value of a risky asset or portfolio over a ten-day period for a given confidence interval.[125]

Stressed VaR (SVaR). SVaR uses inputs based on historical data from a continuous 12-month period of significant market stress. SVaR uses the same VaR methodology but with data representing a continuous 12-month period of stress. This long horizon is designed in part to address procyclicality of the non-stressed VaR metric, potentially based on extended benign periods. Also, it reflects the importance of banks' capital capacity to continue providing market liquidity despite trading losses, consistent with regulators' 'going concern' policy.[126]

Incremental risk charge (IRC). The IRC is a regulatory capital charge that protects against migration and default risk for an extended period (one year). The IRC addresses the fact that the GFC triggered enormous losses in trading books with exposure to unsecuritized products, such as loans, bonds, and CDS, due to ratings and credit migration, combined with a widening of credit spreads and loss of liquidity. A bank's VaR-based risk measure did not reflect these risks.[127]

Comprehensive risk measure (CRM). Like SVaR, the CRM is structured to address periods of market stress. The CRM imposes capital charges for banks' 'correlation trading' positions that they buy and sell as credit protection for clients based on specific tranches of credit portfolio

---

124 A 1,250% risk-weight applies to securitization exposures for which banks do not meet required due diligence obligations. Re-securitizations require additional capital.

125 The formula is as follows: max [99% 10-day $VaR_{prior\ day}$, 99% 10-day $VaR_{60\text{-}day\ avg}$ × (3–4)].

126 Basel Committee on Banking Supervision, 'Guidelines for computing capital for incremental risk in the trading book' (2009) 3 n. 3 [Computing incremental risk].

127 See Basel Committee on Banking Supervision, 'Revisions to the Basel II market risk framework' (February 2011) 1. Non-stressed VaR does not capture infrequent losses or the potential for large cumulative price movements over extended periods of time. Moreover, capital charges for default risk do not cover this risk, which does not arise from *actual* defaults.

indices.[128] The GFC showed that correlations between securities can be highly volatile, particularly if hedging strategies use proxy indices that do not perfectly match the underlying exposures. Thus, the CRM incorporates basis risk, or the risk that a hedge becomes less effective, and the potential costs of resetting the hedge after a change in the underlying position.[129] The standard VaR does not fully capture this risk. The CRM uses the same stress variables as in the IRC.[130] The CRM is subject to a floor of at least 8% of the capital charge under the standardized approach.

Add-ons. Two additional categories address specific risk and de minimis exposures. These are the default risk charge[131] and the residual risk[132] add-ons.

More broadly, these six risk metrics are designed to measure two broad risk categories: *general* market risk and *specific* market risk.[133] VaR and SVaR, IRC, and CRM capture general market risk. The two add-ons address specific market risk.

4.3.7.4 Risk management and compliance requirements under US market risk rule

Supervisors will approve advanced approaches banks' internal market risk models based on four minimum criteria.[134] Risk management controls and compliance systems must be built around the unit of the 'trading desk',[135] defined by the bank but subject to supervisory approval. Design of regulatory and internal risk models should use similar valuation models. In addition, the bank must have a routine

---

128 Correlation trading is a structured credit trading strategy offered by banks in their market-making capacity to their clients.

129 JPMorgan Chase's $6.2 billion 'London Whale' loss arose out of efforts to reduce RWAs that increased under the CRM capital charge.

130 This is a one-year confidence interval and liquidity horizon.

131 The default risk charge captures jump-to-default-risk, which is the risk of sudden price changes relating to an instrument whose value depends on one or more entities' credit quality if one of these entities unexpectedly defaults. See BCBS, Minimum capital requirements for market risk 18–19.

132 This add-on is calculated for instruments that bear residual risk in addition to other capital requirements under the standardized approach. Ibid. 19–20.

133 General market risk is risk of loss arising from broad market movements, such as changes in the general level of interest rates, credit spreads, equity prices, foreign exchange rates, or commodity prices. Specific market risk is risk of loss arising from factors specific to the issuer or counterparty, or idiosyncratic risk such as an event of default. Risk-Based Capital Guidelines: Market Risk, 77 Federal Register 53060, 53070 (30 August 2012) [FR, Market Risk Capital]. Idiosyncratic risk is risk of loss in the value of a position arising from changes in risk factors unique to that position.

134 These criteria are as follows. (1) The supervisor is satisfied that the bank's risk management system is conceptually sound and implemented with integrity. (2) The bank has sufficient staffing skilled in sophisticated models not only in the trading area but also in risk control, audit, and if necessary, the back office. (3) The bank's models have a proven track record of reasonable accuracy in measuring risk. (4) The bank regularly conducts stress tests in accordance with previously stated supervisory guidance. Ibid. 53067–68.

135 The BCBS defines 'trading desk' as a group of traders or trading accounts that implements a well-defined business strategy operating within a clear risk management structure. BCBS, Minimum capital requirements for market risk' (4 January 2016) 9. The Volcker rule's focal point for risk management and compliance is also the trading desk. See § 8.3.2.3.

stress testing program to supplement the output of the bank's risk measurement model that senior management reviews at least monthly.

Banks must demonstrate a comprehensive understanding of each securitization exposure. Analysis must be updated at least quarterly. If not, a 1,250% risk weight applies. A bank may use the SSFA methodology only if it cannot calculate all of the required SFA parameters and the bank has current data (no more than 91 days old) necessary to determine the SSFA inputs. The bank must assign a 1,250% risk weight to all other securitization exposures.[136]

The rule requires a bank to have clearly defined P&Ps that determine what positions are 'trading positions' and correlation trading positions. A bank must have clearly defined trading and hedging strategies, including the expected holding period and associated market risk, which receive senior management approval. The trading strategy must articulate for each portfolio the level of market risk the bank is willing to accept and detail the instruments, techniques, and strategies the bank will use to hedge the risk. Banks must have clearly defined P&Ps for actively managing all covered positions.[137] The agencies expect re-designations of positions to be rare.

4.3.7.5 FRTB

Broadly, the FRTB seeks to enhance Basel III's effort to prevent gaming by banks in their classifications between the banking and trading books. Several FRTB provisions strongly discourage banks from using the internal models approach (IMA) approach. The FRTB replaces the SVaR methodology with the expected shortfall (ES) approach.[138] The ES approach imposes significant infrastructure costs on banks through extensive data requirements and operational complexities in order to measure ES.[139] The FRTB also introduces a new 'non-modellable risk factors' approach that imposes a capital charge for risk factors that cannot be modelled under the IMA, further discouraging resort to the IMA. The default risk charge replaces the IRC.[140] Furthermore, the standardized approach acts as a 'floor', a minimum capital charge under the IMA. This would require advanced approaches banks that use IMA to ensure compliance under the standardized approach as well.

---

136 This equates to capital equaling 100% of amount of the securitization exposure.

137 The P&Ps must, at a minimum, require (1) daily marking positions to market or model; (2) daily assessing the bank's ability to hedge positions and portfolio risks and the extent of market liquidity; (3) establishing and daily monitoring of limits on positions by a risk control unit independent of the trading business unit; (4) daily monitoring of (1)–(3) by senior management; (5) senior management's reassessing at least annually position limits; and (6) at least annually, qualified personnel's assessing of the quality of market inputs to the valuation process, the soundness of key assumptions, the reliability of parameter estimation in pricing models, and the stability and accuracy of model calibration under alternative market scenarios. FR, Market Risk Capital 53067.

138 The ES measures tail risk by averaging tail losses, accounts for market liquidity through specified liquidity horizons, and recognizes stressed correlations through restraints on diversification benefits.

139 It requires for all 'trading book' positions model approval at the trading desk level and imposes a punitive multiplier that increases capital requirements for inaccurate model results.

140 See § 4.3.7.3.

4.3.8 Leverage ratio requirements

The Basel authorities and Congress in Dodd-Frank established a leverage ratio requirement based on non-risk weighted assets as a backstop to Basel's RWA-based capital regulation to limit arbitrage under the RWA regime and to prevent buildup of excessive leverage. Bailed-out banks had capital in excess of the Basel minimum requirements before the crisis. Citigroup Inc. received the most US bailouts, amounting to $476 billion, but was one of the most well-capitalized large BHCs under the Basel regime.

A leverage ratio based on on–balance sheet total consolidated assets applies to all banks. Separate leverage ratios based on both on– and off–balance sheet assets apply to advanced approaches banks and G-SIBs. Policymakers designed an absolute floor to prevent wide fluctuations in bank capital in business cycles. In fact, a leverage ratio based on total assets was a reversion to the first form of bank capital regulation that preceded the Basel regime.

4.3.8.1 4% leverage ratio applicable to all banks

Dodd-Frank requires all banks to meet a 4% leverage ratio of tier 1 capital to non-risk weighted total consolidated on–balance sheet assets. The leverage ratio incorporates the more rigorous capital requirements for the numerator. The amount of tier 1 capital must equal or exceed 4%, and the amount of CET1 must equal or exceed 3%. More broadly, US banks must maintain a 5% leverage ratio to be considered 'well-capitalized' in Pillar II supervision.[141] The US framework imposes two supplementary leverage ratios (SLRs) on larger banking organizations, one for advanced approaches banks and one for G-SIBs. These requirements apply to both on– and off–balance sheet assets. Chapter 7 discusses the leverage ratios for advanced approaches banks and G-SIBs in greater detail.[142]

4.3.9 Non-capital adequacy-based restrictions

An important set of prescriptive statutory and regulatory prudential safeguards are limitations on banks' lending activities. These involve diversification and other measures designed to reduce banks' risky activities to a prudential level of risk-taking. The following are among the most important of these restrictions. Under Pillar II, supervisors may impose additional restrictions in addition to capital requirements based on safety and soundness considerations.[143]

4.3.9.1 Single borrower limit

The single borrower limit is one of the oldest of prudential safeguards.[144] Nationally chartered banks cannot make an unsecured loan to any one borrower in excess

---

141 The Prompt Corrective Action program specifies this leverage ratio. See § 5.5.

142 § 7.2.3.

143 Loans made by national banks must also be 'consistent with safe and sound banking practices'. 12 CFR § 32.3(a).

144 Richard Carnell, Jonathan Macey, and Geoffrey Miller, *The Law of Financial Institutions* (Wolters Kluwer: 2013) 258 [*The Law of Financial Institutions*].

of 15% of total capital, and additionally to the same person not in excess of an additional 10% of total capital if such loan is secured, resulting in a total cap of 25% of total capital.[145] State laws impose similar, albeit typically less rigorous, limits on state-chartered banks.[146] The regulatory rationale of the single borrower limit is that restricting lending to a single borrower reduces the risk to a bank's solvency.[147] Dodd-Frank and its associated rulemaking amended the lending limits to include credit exposures arising from derivative transactions, repo agreements, reverse repo agreements, securities lending transactions, and securities borrowing transactions.[148]

4.3.9.2 Limits on exposures to other financial institutions

Another important restriction limits a bank's exposure to other financial institutions, reflecting Dodd-Frank's concern with interconnectedness. A bank with a high capital ratio may still fail if it experiences significant losses on large exposures in the event of a sudden failure of a counterparty or a group of connected counterparties.[149] The rationale for the restriction is to make the banking system more resilient and avoid 'TBTF' treatment.[150] The FRB limits a bank's credit exposure to other banks ('correspondent banks') to 25% of its capital.[151] For G-SIBs, the FRB limits credit exposure to another SIFI to 15% of the G-SIB's tier 1 capital.[152]

4.3.9.3 Other non-capital-based restrictions

Other important restrictions include limits on asset investment and activities, such as a prohibition on holding common stock; risk-based deposit premiums, based on the amount of a bank's capital and supervisory rating;[153] and bank chartering, which enables regulators to determine who operates a bank, thus reducing adverse selection.[154]

4.3.9.4 Risk management and compliance: non-capital adequacy-based restrictions

Risk assessment ICs are relatively straightforward for loan restrictions. For traditional cash-based assets, management of BHCs can use their existing

---

145 12 USC § 84.

146 *The Law of Financial Institutions* 258.

147 Ibid.

148 12 CFR § 32.9.

149 Bank for International Settlements, 'The treatment of large exposures in the Basel capital standards – executive summary' (30 April 2018) 1.

150 The Law of Financial Institutions 265. Banks lend excess reserves held by the Federal Reserve to other banks needing reserves or funds for lending in the federal funds market.

151 12 CFR § 206.4(a)(1). A bank can lend in excess of this limit if it can demonstrate that the other bank meets the 'adequately capitalized' standard or better under 12 CFR § 206.5(a). *The Law of Financial Institutions* 265.

152 12 CFR § 252.72(b). Section 165(e) of Dodd-Frank requires the FRB to establish single-counterparty credit limits for large US and foreign BHCs and non-bank financial companies to limit the risks that the failure of any individual firm could pose to them.

153 The Prompt Corrective Action program, introduced in 1992, discussed at § 5.5, introduced a three-tier premium structure based on a bank's level of capitalization and CAMELS rating.

154 Frederic Mishkin, 'Prudential supervision: why is it important and what are the issues?' (September 2000), 28 NBER Working Paper No. 7926, 9–16.

infrastructure of accounting and SEC reporting. More challenging are the off–balance sheet derivatives and securities financing transactions, whose accounting treatment is more complex. Nevertheless, the ICs for market risk valuation can be used for purposes of compliance with the credit exposure restrictions.

4.4 Conclusion

Dodd-Frank revised but did not fundamentally revamp the Basel risk-weighted capital regulatory framework while introducing important innovations spurred by the lessons of the financial crisis. Basel III/Dodd-Frank significantly strengthens regulatory capital's loss-absorption capabilities, a preeminent concern of policymakers. Furthermore, national authorities introduced leverage ratios as backstops to RWA.

The revised and enhanced framework has imposed significantly higher risk management and compliance requirements. The risk-based capital rules have become ever more complex with each new rollout of capital regulation. Advanced approaches banks bear the most significant costs. CCR requires complex quantitative analyses. Modeling RWA can involve millions of separate calculations, as a BoE official has noted.[155] This, in turn, creates model risk that in turn must be managed. In part, these developments arise from policymakers' attempt to keep up with the innovations of the banking business and financial conglomerates' expanding risk profile. They are also due to Basel authorities' understandable desire to create risk sensitivity commensurate with the risks in the banking and trading books.

However, as with many other areas of bank regulation, a tension exists between bank management's incentive to minimize capital and the mandates of capital regulation. This tension only increases the more regulatory capital exceeds the amount of economic capital estimated by the firm to be optimal from a risk-return perspective.[156] Moreover, this tension introduces conflicts into the control functions by tasking them with regulatory arbitrage, which plays out visibly in RWA optimization. That such arbitrage can have unfortunate consequences was realized dramatically in the 2012 London Whale debacle in which an internal asset management office incurred a $6.2 billion trading loss. The loss resulted in part from top management's directive to reduce the new Basel III capital requirements for market risk.

---

155 For large, complex banks, the number of risk categories has 'exploded' from around seven under Basel I to 200,000 under Basel II, requiring hundreds of millions of calculations to calculate regulatory capital. Andrew Haldane, 'Capital discipline', Speech to American Economic Association (9 January 2011) 2–3, at <www.bis.org/review/r110325a.pdf>.

156 In addition to meeting regulatory expectations, risk management has the task of using equity more effectively in managing risk and generating a return. Brian Nocco and René Stulz, 'Enterprise risk management: theory and practice' (Fall 2006) 18(4) *Journal of Applied Corporate Finance* 8, 11.

CHAPTER 5

The role of risk management and compliance in micro-prudential oversight

5.1 Introductory overview

This chapter covers the supervisory framework governing Pillar II micro-prudential regulation.[1] The hard-wired, prescriptive framework of Pillar I, covered in Chapter 4, remains a foundational source of compliance expectations under Pillar II. Although a key objective of bank examiners is to review banks' compliance with prescribed capital ratios, a more critical goal is to determine whether firms have a risk management and capital assessment and capital planning system that correspond to their particular risk profile. Banks' ability to control risk through sound management practices has become increasingly the focus of bank supervision rather than compliance with specific regulatory requirements.[2] For banks with weak business management and risk management and compliance practices, supervisors will demand capital materially in excess of the regulatory minimum. Pillar II supervisory oversight of banks' safety and soundness has come to dominate regulatory attention and resources.

The chapter proceeds as follows. It first discusses the rationale and objectives of the bank examination process and the features that distinguish bank examinations from those by capital markets regulators. It then describes the two key features of US Pillar II supervision: the CAMELS bank rating system[3] and the PCA program. Prudential banking regulation worldwide shares a great deal of commonality.

5.2 General overview of Pillar II bank supervision

The overarching objective of micro-prudential regulation and supervision is the safety and soundness of individual banks. Supervisory oversight of banks

---

1 Chapter 4 describes the Basel Pillar components of bank regulation and supervision. See § 4.1.

2 A shift has occurred away from a bank regulatory system resting principally on generally applicable rules toward a 'supervisory approach' emphasizing particularized, ongoing review of a specific bank. Daniel Tarullo, *Banking on Basel: The Future of International Financial Regulation* (Peterson Institute: 2008) 15. Today, financial innovation produces new markets and instruments that make it easy for banks to make huge bets easily and quickly, which can rapidly undermine their financial condition. Frederic Mishkin, 'Prudential supervision: why is it important and what are the issues?' (September 2000), NBER Working Paper 7926, 16 [Mishkin, Prudential supervision].

3 Discussed at § 5.4, CAMELS stands for 'Capital adequacy, Assets Management capability, Earnings, Liquidity, and Sensitivity to market risk.

includes a wide range of activities, ranging from bank chartering,[4] off-site oversight such as review of Call Reports[5] and public SEC filings, the examination process, and a wide range of enforcement actions. Various types of enforcement actions, often arising from examinations, have become increasingly important due to the proliferation of laws in consumer protection and AML/CFT regulation, among many other areas.

Before turning to the statutory and regulatory framework of safety and soundness in § 5.3, this chapter discusses the rationale for bank supervision, the focus and nature of supervisory activities, and the focus of examinations and the examination process.

5.2.1 Rationales for bank supervision

Chapter 1 detailed as the chief reasons for bank regulation and supervision banks' central role in the economy, the inherent risks of their business model, and the existence of a federal backstop.[6] To recap, banks have highly leveraged balance sheets due to their role in liquidity transformation, which relies on short-term debt in the form of deposits, and management's incentive to minimize equity in their capital structure.[7] The relatively small amount of equity enhances management's incentive to engage in greater risk-taking with little downside but significant upside.

In addition, all governments provide an implicit or explicit safety net[8] for their banking system. Though well intentioned, this backstop increases the inherent risks of the banking business model by exacerbating the risk of adverse selection and moral hazard. Protected by an explicit or implicit guarantee, depositors and other creditors have little incentive to monitor a bank's creditworthiness and risk-taking. Lack of market discipline can also lead those most likely to cause a bank failure to seek a banking license in order to exploit the safety net.

For all of these reasons, banks require ongoing and intensive supervisory oversight.[9]

5.2.2 Capital: focus of supervisory review for all banks

Modern bank regulation views capital as the cornerstone of bank safety and soundness. A bank's CAMELS rating is largely a function of the amount and quality of capital it has in relation to its risk profile as determined through examination. As a consequence, internal capital assessment and planning is a key focus

---

4 Chartering allows supervisors to mitigate adverse selection created by the government safety net. Mishkin, Prudential supervision 14–15.

5 These are the quarterly consolidated reports of condition and income that depository institutions must file with their regulators. 12 CFR §§ 324, 1817, 161, 1464.

6 § 1.2.3.

7 See § 4.2.2.

8 In addition to FDIC deposit insurance, the safety net includes the Federal Reserve as lender of last resort and the availability to depository institutions of the Federal Reserve's discount window in case of need for liquidity.

9 Chapter 1, § 1.2.

of supervisory review for all banks.[10] Moreover, analysis of a bank's current and future capital requirements in relation to its strategic objectives, beyond regulatory minimum capital requirements, is central to capital planning and setting capital levels commensurate with a bank's risk profile.[11] This review is in addition to the stress testing programs[12] and other enhanced prudential standards (EPS) applicable to BHCs with at least $250 billion in total consolidated assets.

5.2.2.1 Assessment of firms' risk management and ICs relating to capital

In addition to capital assessment, supervisors review the capacity of bank management to develop, apply, and improve ICs and strengthen levels of provisions and reserves.[13] Banks should have a rigorous process for assessing overall capital adequacy in relation to their risk profile and a strategy for maintaining their capital levels in relation to the current stage of the business cycle.[14] The CAMELS rating system formalizes these objectives in a systematic, uniform framework of bank supervision.

5.2.3 Scope and nature of bank supervision through examinations

Prudential oversight through the examination process plays a central role in conveying regulatory expectations.[15] A comparison of banking agencies' supervisory oversight through examinations with that of the capital markets agencies highlights the distinguishing features of bank examinations. Bank examinations occur in three main stages: planning, examination, and communications of findings to a bank's board and senior management. The three main banking agencies share a common approach to their examinations.

5.2.3.1 Key features distinguishing bank from capital market agencies' examinations

Examinations play a key role for both the banking and capital markets agencies, the SEC and CFTC. For both types of regulators, examinations are the key

---

10 Since the GFC, financial stability has become the foremost concern of bank regulators. Supervisory review and minimum capital requirements for SIFI BHCs are the subject of Chapter 7.

11 Basel Committee on Banking Supervision, 'International convergence of capital measurement and capital standards' (June 2006) 206 [International convergence]. In this, the board is responsible for setting the bank's risk tolerance. Ibid.

12 The DFAST and CCAR stress test programs form the cornerstone of the agencies' supervisory oversight of large banks' capital planning. See § 7.4.

13 International convergence 204.

14 The BCBS identifies five features of a rigorous capital assessment process: (1) board and management oversight to ensure sound risk management as the foundation of capital assessment; (2) sound capital assessment in terms of P&Ps designed to ensure the bank identifies, measures, and reports all material risks; (3) comprehensive assessment of all material risks; (4) an adequate system for monitoring and reporting risk exposures and assessing how a changing risk profile affects the need for capital; and (5) effective controls of the capital assessment process. International convergence 205–209.

15 § 2.7.1.1 covers the final communications stage of examinations. The summaries in this section are based on examination manuals of all three banking agencies and reflect the approach that is common to all of their examination procedures.

means of monitoring firms' compliance with regulatory obligations and in conveying regulatory expectations for individual firms. In both cases, examinations have the potential to result in enforcement actions. However, a comparison of the agencies' approaches highlights the distinctive differences between each groups' examination practices.

First, bank examinations are a more intensive, ongoing, and in-depth review of the fundamentals of a company's franchise and financial condition. Banking agencies make a determination of a banks' safety and soundness, while the SEC and CFTC focus on conduct and practices that affect market fairness, transparency, and market efficiency. Banks provide extremely detailed periodic financial data and other information to their agencies. The Federal Reserve's continuous monitoring program for the large, complex BHCs illustrates the ongoing nature of banking agency oversight.[16] Although the capital market regulators regularly visit securities and futures and derivatives firms, the banking agencies are unique in 'embedding' examiners in the largest banks,[17] which become their daily workplace.

Second, banking agencies generally take a more gradual approach to issues that they want firms to remediate. The process is generally less adversarial than that of the capital markets agencies,[18] with gradually increasing formality and seriousness in potential outcomes. Third, the banking agencies take a more aggressive approach to a firm's corporate governance practices largely due to the prudential aspect of bank regulation, which focuses on management of risk. Fourth, capital market SROs, an intermediate layer of quasi-governmental regulators, do not exist in the bank regulatory framework. SROs supervise regulated entities through examinations and other means of oversight. In contrast, the banking agencies exercise exclusive, direct, and comprehensive regulation and supervision over their regulated entities.

5.2.3.2 Types of examinations

The OCC conducts three types of examination. The full-scope, on-site examination[19] is a regularly scheduled examination performed during the supervisory

---

16 In continuous monitoring, the Federal Reserve assigns examiners and risk specialists to the task of monitoring daily operations in order to understand a bank's strategic business developments and changes in its risk profile.

17 At the time of the $6.2 billion London Whale loss approximately 40 examiners from the FRBNY and 70 staff from the OCC reported daily to JPMorgan Chase, although they reported to their managers at their agencies. Jessica Silver-Greenberg and Benn Protess, 'Bank regulators under scrutiny in JPMorgan loss', *New York Times* (25 May 2012).

18 Annette Nazareth, an SEC Commissioner at the time, contrasted the 'rules-based', prescriptive and aggressive 'name and shame' enforcement program of the SEC with the prudential approach of bank regulators. She noted, however, that the SEC has moved toward a more prudential approach to effectively address the increasingly complex business lines of broker-dealers for which an institution-based supervisory structure is no longer appropriate. A prudential approach is more effective with respect to businesses where risk management is essential, such as portfolio margining in which firms use modeling to manage credit risk, but not with respect to sales practices where investor protection concerns may require a more rules-based approach. Annette Nazareth, 'Remarks before the SIFMA compliance and legal conference' (26 March 2007), at <www.sec.gov/news/speech/2007/spch032607aln.htm>.

19 This examination is required by regulation. 12 CFR §§ 4.6 and 4.7.

cycle that, among other things, is sufficient in scope to assign or confirm a bank's CAMELS rating and concludes with an ROE following the OCC's 'supervisory framework'.[20] Targeted examinations generally focus on a particular product (e.g., credit cards), a function (e.g., audit), or risk (e.g., credit risk), or may cover specialty areas.[21] These include specific regulatory areas such as AML/CFT and consumer protection regulation by examiners with relevant expertise, either as part of the full-scope examination or as required by statute or interagency commitments.[22]

For large banks, the Federal Reserve conducts continuous monitoring, as already noted.[23] It also conducts 'horizontal reviews' of large banks, focusing on specific areas of risk.[24] It conducts 'inspections' rather than examinations of BHCs in its capacity as a consolidated supervisor, relying to some extent on examination reports of the BHC subsidiaries' primary regulators.[25]

5.2.3.3 Preparation or planning stage for examinations

Pre-examination planning plays a significant role in the overall examination process. The OCC, FDIC, and Federal Reserve assign an 'Examiner in Charge' (EIC), who is familiar with a bank's portfolio, to oversee examinations. OCC examiners develop a supervisory strategy for each bank in a strategy document that describes the objectives of the examination, discusses any planned supervisory activities, and outlines how the examiner plans to conduct these supervisory activities. The FDIC follows a similar, but more formalized, path. FDIC staff draft a preliminary risk profile of the targeted institution, request current information relevant to the examination, and receive certain electronic data downloads through a 'Compliance Information and Document Request' (CIDR).[26]

5.2.3.4 Examination stage: review of risk management and compliance systems

FDIC examiners[27] review where risks intersect with weaknesses in the CMS[28]; the commitment of the board, management, and staff to compliance; the qualifications of the compliance officer; the scope and effectiveness of compliance P&Ps;

---

20 The 'supervisory framework' consists of three components that enable examiners to tailor examinations to the level of risk within a specific area. 'Core knowledge' provides a foundation for risk assessment by capturing elements of a bank's culture, risk tolerance, and products and services. 'Core assessment' establishes minimum conclusions for assessing risks and assigning uniform ratings. 'Expanded procedures' relate to areas in which risks are higher or for complex activities. Comptroller of the Currency, *Comptroller's Handbook: Bank Supervision Process* (September 2007) 23 [*Comptroller's Handbook*].

21 *Comptroller's Handbook* (18 June 2018) 15.

22 Ibid.

23 § 5.2.3.1.

24 These reviews are done under the LISCC program. See § 6.3.7.1.

25 George Kaufman and others, *Perspectives on Safety and Soundness – Banking: Past, Present, and Future* 249 (MIT Press: 1986).

26 See generally FDIC, 'Compliance examinations – pre-examination planning', II-4.1–4.4 (September 2017).

27 The following summary of the FDIC's scope of examination relates primarily to examination of compliance with consumer protection regulation. Ibid. II-1.2–1.3.

28 See § 9.3.2.1 for a discussion of CMS.

the effectiveness of training; the thoroughness of monitoring and any internal/external reviews or audits; and the board's and management's responsiveness to findings of internal and external reviews and previous examination findings.

5.2.3.5 Focus in examination stage in prudential oversight

The core of prudential oversight consists of examination of a bank's balance sheet, including its loan portfolio and other fixed-income assets, review of collateral for secured loans, and P&Ps relating to underwriting and monitoring of asset quality. Loans are generally the largest source of credit risk, but other sources exist, particularly market risk, both on- and off-balance sheet. Supervisors classify loans as adversely or non-adversely classified assets.[29] The former further fall into substandard, doubtful, or loss categories. Supervisors also examine banks' allowance for loan and lease losses (ALLL) to determine whether the ALLL is adequate to absorb estimated credit losses. In addition, they review financial information and management practices to detect fraud and insider abuse, key causes of bank failures.[30] Most importantly, supervisors examine management quality in their internal oversight of these activities.

5.2.3.6 Communications stage

Examiners provide a ROE to the bank's board of directors and senior management indicating the bank's CAMELS ratings. They discuss key issues and preliminary findings in order to resolve significant differences concerning findings, conclusions, or recommendations. Examiners focus on any significant deficiencies, areas of greatest risk to a bank, and seek management's commitment to correct significant deficiencies through action plans that state how the board and management will ensure successful execution of the plan. The agencies employ MRIAs and MRAs to formally communicate priorities for remediation.[31]

5.2.4 Graduated escalation of supervisory actions

Regulators possess a broad arsenal of enforcement powers to ensure effective supervisory oversight of banks under their jurisdiction. Both due to the nature of their prudential objectives and statutory requirements under the Prompt Corrective

---

29 Adversely classified loans are considered impaired, meaning their payments of interest and principal are in doubt.

30 FDIC, Risk Management Manual of Examination Practices, 'Bank fraud and insider abuse' (30 July 2018), § 9.1, 1.

31 MRIAs are supervisory matters of the highest priority. MRIAs include (1) matters with the potential to pose significant risk to the safety and soundness of the bank; (2) matters representing significant instances of non-compliance with laws or regulations; and (3) repeat criticism that has escalated in importance due to insufficient attention or action by the bank. MRAs are matters that the agency expects a banking organization to address over time. See Federal Reserve Board, 'SR 13–13: Supervisory considerations for the communication of supervisory findings' (17 June 2013). The FRB has revised its communications procedure to provide MRIAs and MRAs generally only to senior management to allow boards to focus more on corporate strategy and risk management, among other things.

Action program,[32] supervisors generally follow a graduated enforcement program in addressing banks' deficiencies. These typically begin with informal actions, available only for banks with composite CAMELS ratings of 3 or better. Among other measures, these include commitments with banks to correct deficiencies identified during the examination process and memoranda of understanding. If a bank does not follow through or is in danger of failing, agencies can apply for court approval of cease-and-desist orders, the most common type of enforcement action. They may also impose civil monetary penalties, suspend FDIC insurance, and ultimately enter a bank into conservatorship or receivership.[33]

5.3 Statutory and regulatory foundation of safety and soundness oversight

Regulators' remit to assess safety and soundness of individual banks intrudes the government to an extraordinary degree into a banking institution's business operations, its business model, and its system of corporate governance. To this end Congress granted the federal banking agencies broad authority over insured depository institutions. The power to ensure banking institutions' safety and soundness originates in Section 39 of the Federal Deposit Insurance Act.[34]

This section first fleshes out the concept of safety and soundness. It then summarizes the statutory grant of authority to ensure safety and soundness of individual banks and the regulation issued under this authority.

5.3.1 Banks as 'going' and 'gone' concerns

In their examination role, regulators' primary focus is on banking institutions as *going* concerns, in part to ensure that banks can continue lending to businesses and consumers in an economic downturn to forestall a deep recession. Nevertheless, the safety and soundness framework is designed ultimately to ensure preservation of the FDIC insurance fund – when a bank has become a *gone* concern.[35] In the case of failing banks, capital requirements, both the regulatory minimum and the amount required in Pillar II supervision, are designed to provide adequate loss absorption capacity of banks. The 8% floor under Basel III for capital as a percentage of RWA is only a floor. Even well-managed banks will have capital materially in excess of the 8% floor and any applicable capital buffers.

5.3.2 What is 'safety and soundness'?

Given its status as the foundational concept underlying prudential bank regulation, what does 'safety and soundness' mean? Surprisingly, banking agencies'

---

32 The PCA program is covered later in this chapter. See § 5.5.
33 See § 2.7.2 for a discussion of enforcement remedies possessed by federal bank regulators.
34 12 USC § 1831p-1.
35 § 4.2.3 discusses these two rationales.

enormous powers in examining and ordering a bank to modify its business model is ultimately based on a term undefined by statute. Rather, the meaning of the term is fleshed out through the voluminous precedent embedded in supervisory guidance and enforcement actions.

By general acclaim, John E. Horne, a former chair of the Federal Home Loan Bank Board, got at the essence of the concept of safety and soundness over half a century ago:

> The concept of 'unsafe and unsound practices' is one of general application which touches upon the entire field of the operations of a financial institution. For this reason, it would be virtually impossible to attempt to catalog within a single all-inclusive or rigid definition the broad spectrum of activities which are embraced by the term.... Contributing to the difficulty of framing a comprehensive definition is the fact that particular activity not necessarily unsafe or unsound in every instance may be so when considered in the light of all relevant facts.... Like many other generic terms widely used in the law, such as 'fraud', 'negligence', 'probable cause', or 'good faith', the term 'unsafe and unsound practices' embraces any action, or lack of action, which is contrary to generally accepted standards of prudent operation, the possible consequences of which, if continued, would be abnormal risk or loss or damage to an institution, its shareholders, or ... the insurance funds.[36]

Chairman Horne's description of safety and soundness provides context to the statutory provisions on this concept. The agencies, through regulation and supervisory guidance, have implemented a relatively objective and transparent framework for prudential oversight. Broadly speaking, this supervisory framework fleshes out the statutory elements of operational and managerial standards, asset quality and earnings, and compensation standards.

5.3.3 Section 39 of the Federal Deposit Insurance Act

Section 39 provides broad discretion to the banking agencies in their rulemaking and guidance on safety and soundness of banking institutions.[37] At the same time, it mandates that the agencies issue standards in specified areas. Section 39's framework is bare, almost skeletal, in detail. Standards fall into five primary areas of which two are replicated here: operational and management standards and standards relating to asset quality, earnings, and stock valuation, Sections (a) and (b).[38]

12 U.S. Code § 1831p-1 – Standards for safety and soundness

(a) Operational and managerial standards. Each appropriate Federal banking agency shall, for all insured depository institutions, prescribe –

---

36 Financial Institutions Supervisory and Insurance Act of 1966: Hearings on S. 3158 and S. 3695 before the House Comm. on Banking and Currency, 89th Cong., 2d Sess., 49–50 (1966).

37 Section 39, 'Standards for Safety and Soundness'. 12 USC § 1831p-1.

38 There are three other areas. Section (c), concerning compensation, section (d), concerning standards to be prescribed, and section (e), provisions concerning banks' remediation plans in case of failure to meet the standards prescribed in (a) and (b), are not included in the preceding text.

(1) standards relating to – (A) internal controls, information systems, and internal audit systems, in accordance with section 1831m[39] of this title; (B) loan documentation; (C) credit underwriting; (D) interest rate exposure; (E) asset growth; and (F) compensation, fees, and benefits, in accordance with subsection (c); and

(2) such other operational and managerial standards as the agency determines to be appropriate.

(b) Asset quality, earnings, and stock valuation standards. Each appropriate Federal banking agency shall prescribe standards, by regulation or guideline, for all insured depository institutions relating to asset quality, earnings, and stock valuation that the agency determines to be appropriate.

The consequences of a bank's failure to meet the standards issued by an agency depends on whether the agency issued the standard as a 'regulation' or a 'guideline'. If the standards are issued pursuant to a regulation, the agency is mandated to *require* the bank to provide an acceptable plan of remediation; if the standard was issued as a guideline, the agency *may* require the bank to submit such a plan.[40] The statute requires a bank to specify in a plan the steps that it will take to correct the deficiency.[41]

5.3.4 Interagency guidelines under Section 39: Operational and Managerial Standards

The agencies issued standards for safety and soundness under Section 39, Appendix A, as interagency guidelines. The following summarizes the interagency guidelines for 'Operational and Managerial Standards'.[42]

Internal controls and information systems. A bank should have ICs and information systems that provide for an organizational structure that establishes clear lines of authority and responsibility for monitoring adherence to established policies and for effective risk assessment, among other things.[43]

Internal audit system. Among other things, a bank should have an internal audit system that provides for adequate monitoring of the system of ICs through an internal audit function, independence and objectivity, adequate testing and review of information systems, verification and review of management actions to address material weaknesses, and review by the board or audit systems.

---

39 12 USC § 1831m is entitled 'Early identification of needed improvements in financial management'.

40 12 USC § 1831p-1(e)(1)(A).

41 If the institution is undercapitalized, the plan may be part of a capital restoration plan. 12 U.S.C. § 1831p.

42 12 CFR Appendix A to Part 30, II. Operational and Managerial Standards.

43 Other standards include timely and accurate financial, operational and regulatory reports, adequate procedures to safeguard and manage assets, and compliance with applicable laws and regulations. Appendix A to Part 30, II.(2)–(5).

Loan documentation. A bank should maintain practices that, among other things, enable it to make an informed lending decision, identify the purpose of the loan and source of repayment and the borrower's ability to timely repay the loan, ensure the claim's enforceability, and account for the size and complexity of the loan.

Credit underwriting. A bank should establish and maintain prudent underwriting practices that consider the nature of the markets in which loans will be made. It should consider the borrower's overall financial condition and resources and financial responsibility of any guarantor, the nature and value of any underlying collateral, and the borrower's character and willingness to repay the loan.

Interest rate exposure. A bank should provide for periodic reporting to management and the board of directors regarding interest rate risk with adequate information for management and the board of directors to assess the level of risk.

Asset growth. An institution's asset growth should be prudent and consider the source, volatility and use of the funds that support asset growth, any increase in credit risk or interest rate risk as a result of growth, and the effect of growth on the institution's capital.

Asset quality. A bank should establish and maintain a system that identifies problem assets and prevents deterioration in those assets. It should conduct periodic asset quality reviews to identify problem assets, estimate the inherent losses in those assets, establish reserves that are sufficient to absorb estimated losses, compare problem asset totals to capital, and take appropriate corrective action to resolve problem assets.

Earnings. A bank should establish and maintain a system to evaluate and monitor earnings and ensure that earnings are sufficient to maintain adequate capital and reserves. The bank should compare recent earnings trends relative to equity, assets, or other commonly used benchmarks to the institution's historical results and those of its peers. It should also evaluate the adequacy of earnings given the size, complexity, and risk profile of the institution's assets and operations; and assess the source, volatility, and sustainability of earnings.

5.3.4.1 Appendix A's Operational and Managerial Standards: a CAMELS precursor

Although Appendix A's Operational and Managerial Standards do not correspond precisely to the six CAMELS rating components, they nevertheless provide a foundation for examiners' approach to individual banking organizations' risk management and compliance systems in assessing their degree of safety and soundness. CAMELS, introduced in 1979, formalized the process of examining safety and soundness. Notably absent in the standards is the CAMELS Capital component, although 'capital and reserves' and 'ratio of assets to capital' do play a role in the standards' last three components. Capital regulation did not play a central role in bank regulation until the 1980s,[44] when work began on the Basel Accord that resulted in Basel I in 1988.

5.3.5 Safety and soundness finding as prudential backstop for Pillar I rules

The safety and soundness standard provides broad authority for a prudential backstop that supervisors can rely on if they determine that prescriptive rules do not provide sufficient protection. An example is the requirement that banks ensure that borrower concentration does not breach the statutory 10%/15% borrower concentration provision.[45] Compliance should be straightforward in making this calculation. Furthermore, the denominator is total regulatory capital, not RWA.

However, the safety and soundness standard allows examiners who find that the prescriptive provision is not sufficient to challenge the single-borrower loans under agency rules, which provides that 'loans and extensions of credit must be consistent with safe and sound banking practices'.[46] Financial regulators employ prudential backstops widely.[47]

5.3.5.1 Analysis of compliance risk under safety and soundness standard

The discretionary safety and soundness fallback can be a major factor complicating banks' design of an effective compliance system that minimizes compliance risk. For example, analysis of compliance risk under the statutory borrower concentration limit consists of two steps: first, to ensure that the quantitative limits are not breached; and second, to ensure that the loans' underwriting satisfies the safety and soundness standard. The latter involves a more involved discussion between senior management, risk management, and compliance, often as a result of ongoing feedback from the bank's examiner. In the final analysis, risk management and senior management may determine that borrower concentration, or other indicators of portfolio quality, should be materially below the statutory thresholds in order to satisfy potential supervisory concerns.

5.3.5.2 Focus on loan quality

The agencies consider loan quality review one of the most important components of an examination.[48] Much of the focus of the Operational and Managerial

---

44 US regulators had long used bank capital ratios as a supervisory instrument but did not impose explicit minimum capital requirements until the 1980s. In the following decades, policymakers developed capital requirements to reflect the particular risks facing a financial institution. Daniel Tarullo, 'The evolution of capital regulation' (9 November 2011), Clearing House Business Meeting and Conference, at <www.federalreserve.gov/newsevents/speech/files/tarullo20111109a.pdf>.

45 § 4.3.9.1.

46 12 CFR § 32.1(c)(5).

47 See the discussion on the prudential backstop under the Volcker rule at § 8.3.1.4.

48 The FDIC's examination manual calls the examiner's evaluation of the quality of the loan portfolio 'among the most important aspects of the examination process'. Further, 'to a great extent, it is the quality of a bank's loan portfolio that determines the risk to depositors and to the FDIC's insurance fund. Conclusions regarding the bank's condition and the quality of its management are weighted heavily by the examiner's findings with regard to lending practices.' FDIC, 'Risk

Standards of Appendix A is on asset (loan) quality and growth, including a separate section on loan documentation. The considerable supervisory focus on loans also arises from the potential conflict between the need to safeguard the FDIC insurance fund and the fact that loans can be a powerful profit-making engine. To this end:

> [L]oans comprise a major portion of most bank's assets; and ... it is the asset category which ordinarily presents the greatest credit risk and potential loss exposure to banks.... [P]ressure for increased profitability, liquidity considerations, and a vastly more complex society have produced great innovations in credit instruments and approaches to lending. Loans have consequently become much more complex.[49]

Poor loan underwriting standards were a major factor leading to the GFC and Great Recession.

5.4 The CAMELS rating system

The CAMELS bank rating system, adopted by the FFIEC[50] in 1979, has long played a central role in Pillar II micro-prudential regulation. All US examining banking agencies use the CAMELS rating system. The system is an internal supervisory means of evaluating the safety and soundness of banking firms and identifying those institutions needing a heightened supervisory focus. The system considers financial, managerial, and compliance factors that are common to all depository institutions. The system also assists Congress in tracking safety and soundness trends and in assessing the aggregate strength and soundness of the financial industry.[51] The LFI rating system replaced the RFI/C(D) rating system for large BHCs that had applied to all BHCs.[52]

5.4.1 Purpose and mechanics of CAMELS rating system

CAMELS ratings provide regulators with a systematic means of evaluating the strengths and weaknesses in a particular bank's business model and its ICs, risk management, and compliance frameworks. It enables supervisors to rank order banks based on quantitative metrics and qualitative criteria. The system also helps supervisors to identify and categorize banks with deficiencies in particular component areas and give specific feedback to, and substantiate remedial measures requested of, senior management.

Management Manual of Examination Policies' (2016), § 3.2–1, at <www.fdic.gov/regulations/safety/manual> [FDIC Risk Management Manual].

49 FDIC Risk Management Manual § 3.2–1.

50 The FFIEC is discussed at § 2.3.3. Policymakers added the 'S' of the rating system in 1996 to assess market sensitivity.

51 *Comptroller's Handbook* 53.

52 The LFI rule applies to BHCs and non-insurance, non-commercial S&L holding companies with total consolidated assets of at least $100 billion and US intermediate holding companies of FBOs with total consolidated assets of at least $50 billion. 12 CFR Parts 211 and 238.

5.4.1.1 Six components of CAMELS

CAMELS ratings address six areas relating to a bank's business and compliance framework: capital adequacy, asset quality, management, earnings, liquidity, and sensitivity to market risk. Individual CAMELS component ratings are assigned for each of these six areas. Based on a CAMELS evaluation in the examination process, supervisors assign individual component ratings on a numerical scale from 1–5 to every bank, as follows: 1, strong; 2, satisfactory; 3, less than satisfactory; 4, deficient; and 5, critically deficient. Evaluations of the component areas take into consideration the institution's size and sophistication, the nature and complexity of its activities, and its risk profile.

5.4.1.2 Composite CAMELS rating

The agencies also assign a single composite CAMELS rating according to the following standards: 1, sound in every respect; 2, fundamentally sound; 3, some cause for concern; 4, unsafe and unsound; and 5, extremely unsafe and unsound. A composite rating is not an average of component ratings. It is a qualitative evaluation of overall management, operational, and financial performance, with a specific emphasis on management quality. The rating may incorporate any factor that bears significantly on a firm's overall safety and soundness.

5.4.2 Enforcement consequences of a low CAMELS rating

Where a bank is located on the 1–5 CAMELS spectrum of safety and soundness has important supervisory and enforcement consequences, including ultimately the bank's liquidation. As a practical matter, CAMELS ratings are of significant importance to any banking institution as low ratings may result in more frequent and intensive examinations. The lower a bank's CAMELS rating, the more intrusively its primary regulator may intervene in its business operations, strategy, and even business model. A bank with a composite rating of 3, 4, or 5 can expect informal and formal enforcement actions. A CAMELS rating also determines the FDIC insurance premium that a bank must pay for federal deposit insurance.

5.4.3 Importance of management quality in CAMELS rating system

The overarching element in the CAMELS rating system is management quality. The agencies consider the quality of management to be the 'first line of defense' in any compliance system because of its central role in ensuring an institution's safety and soundness. For this reason, the regulators may take steps that, in other regulated industries, may appear draconian and highly invasive. They may oust senior executives and require banks to submit business plans that will return them to profitability if they consider such actions necessary to resolve safety and soundness concerns.

5.4.3.1 Elements of the separate management quality rating

By the 1990s, regulators had formalized their heightened emphasis on corporate governance and management quality, requiring examiners to assign a separate risk management rating from 1 through 5 that contributes to the regular management component rating of CAMELS. This special rating has four elements: (1) quality of oversight by the board of directors and senior management, (2) adequacy of policies and limits on significant risk exposures, (3) quality of risk management and monitoring systems, and (4) adequacy of ICs to prevent fraud or unauthorized activities by employees. Moreover, management's ability to identify, measure, monitor, and control the specific risk in the other CAMELS components is also a critical attribute for each of those components.[53]

5.4.4 Elements of each CAMELS ratings component

The following subsections discuss the key elements of each of the CAMELs component ratings.[54]

5.4.4.1 Capital adequacy component

Apart from the Basel III ratios, banks first need to ensure that they have adequate capital corresponding to their unique risk profile. Among other things, this includes management's ability to address future needs for additional capital by identifying and measuring risks. Management must assess balance sheet composition, risk exposure from off–balance sheet activities, quality and strength of earnings, access to the capital markets, and a corporate parent's support.

The *FDIC Risk Management Manual* ascribes several benefits to bank capital. Capital absorbs losses, promotes public confidence, helps restrict excessive asset growth, and protects depositors and the federal deposit fund:

> Capital allows institutions to continue operating as going concerns during periods when operating losses or other adverse financial results are experienced. Capital provides a measure of assurance to the public that an institution will continue to provide financial services even when losses have been incurred, thereby helping to maintain confidence in the banking system and minimize liquidity concerns. Capital, along with minimum capital ratio standards, restrains unjustified asset expansion by requiring that asset growth be funded by a commensurate amount of additional capital. Placing owners at significant risk of loss, should the institution fail, helps to minimize the potential for moral hazard, and promotes safe and sound banking practices.[55]

5.4.4.2 Asset component

Bank assets include, in addition to cash and cash equivalents, commercial and consumer loans, a wide array of government and corporate debt securities, and off–balance sheet items. Important attributes for this component include adequacy of underwriting standards, adequacy of ALLL, credit risk arising from

---

53 See Fredric Mishkin, *Economics of Money, Banking, and Financial Markets* (Pearson: 2013) 303.

54 These descriptions draw mainly from FDIC, '5000 – statements of policy – uniform financial institutions rating system' (1997), at <www.fdic.gov/regulations/laws/rules/5000-900.html> [5000 Statement of policy].

55 FDIC Risk Management Manual § 2.1.

or reduced by off–balance sheet transactions, diversification and quality of loan and investment portfolios, and management's ability to timely identify problem assets.

5.4.4.3 Management component

The management component reflects the governance capability of the board of directors and management in identifying, measuring, monitoring, and controlling the risks of an institution's activities and in ensuring a bank's safe, sound, and efficient operation in compliance with applicable laws and regulations.[56] The ability of management to respond to the risks arising from changing business conditions or from launching new products or services is an important factor in a bank's overall risk profile and the level of supervisory attention that is warranted. Regulators' focus on management and corporate governance reflects an evolution in the prudential supervisory process since point-in-time balance sheet analysis several decades ago.

5.4.4.4 Earnings component

The earnings rating reflects the quantity and trends of earnings and other factors that may affect the sustainability or quality of earnings. Excessive or inadequately managed credit risk can affect earnings quantity and quality. The agencies are concerned with both the amount and sustainability of earnings, as well as management' ability to estimate future earnings. The quality of certain other CAMELS components can positively or adversely affect earnings.

The agencies' approach to the earnings component reflects the level of intensity of supervisory involvement in the banking business. The *FDIC Risk Management Manual* provides:

> From a bank regulator's standpoint, the essential purpose of bank earnings, both current and accumulated, is to absorb losses and augment capital. Earnings is the initial safeguard against the risks of engaging in the banking business, and represents the first line of defense against capital depletion resulting from shrinkage in asset value.... The analysis of earnings includes all bank operations and activities. When evaluating earnings, examiners should develop an understanding of the bank's core business activities.[57]

5.4.4.5 Liquidity component

Important attributes in this component include a bank's ability to meet liquidity needs without adversely affecting its operations or condition; availability of assets readily convertible to cash without undue loss; access to money markets and other funding sources; diversification of on– and off–balance sheet funding sources; reliance on short-term and volatile funding sources; and management's ability to identify, measure, monitor, and control the institution's liquidity position.

---

56 Tom Hinkel, 'CAMELS ratings and financial regulatory reform: the (m)anagement element', *Safe Systems Newsletter* (12 August 2010).
57 FDIC Risk Management Manual § 5.1.

5.4.4.6 Market sensitivity component

Sensitivity to market risk includes, in addition to changes in interest rates, changes in foreign exchange rates, commodity prices, or equity prices since these also can adversely affect bank earnings and capital. The market risk CAMELS component rating is based upon, but not limited to, an assessment of the following factors:

- The sensitivity of the financial institution's earnings or the economic value of its capital to adverse changes in interest rates, foreign exchange rates, commodity prices, or equity prices.
- The ability of management to identify, measure, monitor, and control exposure to market risk given the institution's size, complexity, and risk profile.
- The nature and complexity of interest rate risk exposure arising from non-trading positions.

5.5 Prompt Corrective Action program

The FDIC Improvement Act of 1991 (FDICIA) established the PCA program. Congress introduced highly formalized procedures and dramatically increased mandatory administrative tools in a quest to eliminate agencies' supervisory discretion as much as possible. The primary objective of the PCA program is to safeguard the FDIC insurance fund. Congress determined that a more rules-based approach to safety and soundness issues was necessary. Supervisory forbearance in the S&L crisis of the 1980s had resulted in hundreds of billions of dollars in losses. Moral hazard incentivized owners and bank managers to engage in risky activities.

5.5.1 PCA program's 'tripwire' approach

To reign in regulatory discretion the PCA program adopts a 'tripwire' approach.[58] The FDICIA requires FDIC-insured institutions and regulators to take 'prompt corrective action' to resolve capital deficiencies, based on the level of capital adequacy on a five-point scale ranging from 'well-capitalized' to 'critically under-capitalized', as set forth in Table 5.1. Table 5.1 indicates the PCA categories mapped against their required RWA, leverage, and SLRs.

5.5.1.1 PCA program's three-prong approach

The PCA program takes a three-pronged approach in pursuit of the overall objective of safeguarding the FDIC insurance fund. First, it institutes a regime of predetermined regulatory actions tied to capitalization thresholds as set forth in Table 5.1.

---

58 Lawrence Baxter, 'Administrative and judicial review of prompt corrective action decisions by the federal banking regulators' (1993), 7 *Administrative Law Journal* 505, 516 [Baxter, Administrative and judicial review].

Table 5.1 PCA levels for all insured depository institutions

PCA category	Total risk-based capital (RBC) measure (ratio %)	Tier 1 RBC measure (ratio %)	CET 1 RBC measure (ratio %)	Leverage ratio (%)	Supplementary leverage ratio (%)
Well capitalized	≥10	≥8	≥6.5	≥5	Not applicable
Adequately capitalized	≥8	≥6	≥4.5	≥4	>3.0
Undercapitalized	<8	<6	<4.5	<4	<3.0
Significantly undercapitalized	<6	<4	<3	<3	Not applicable
Critically undercapitalized	Tangible equity (defined as Tier 1 capital plus non-Tier 1 perpetual preferred stock) to total assets ≤2				Not applicable

Source: Regulatory Capital Rules, Subpart H, § 324.401, Final Rule, FDIC (Sept. 2013). Note: leverage ratios are based on total assets; all others are based on RWA.

Second, it establishes risk-based FDIC insurance premiums based on a bank's capital level and composite CAMELS rating. The rationale is to reduce the moral hazard incentive of owners and managers by increasing the premium as a bank takes on more risk. A bank cannot make a capital distribution if it would render it undercapitalized. Third, the FDIC must adopt a least-cost resolution approach toward a troubled bank. To enforce this requirement, the FDIC's inspector general must issue a report in the event of a loss in the FDIC fund, thus facilitating congressional oversight and incentivizing supervisors to intervene in a timely manner.[59]

5.5.1.2 Increasingly harsh enforcement actions required as capital ratios decline
The threshold level for requiring capital restoration plans is below 'adequately capitalized'. Under the FDICIA, such banks *must* provide a capital restoration plan acceptable to regulators and are restricted in pursuing strategic business plans such as mergers, among other things. At this point the agencies still have discretion to impose a wide variety of restrictions, such as limiting the rate of asset growth, limiting interest paid on deposits, and requiring election of a new board of directors. Importantly, the agency can take action based on supervisory criteria other than capital adequacy in classifying a bank as 'undercapitalized' due to an unsafe and unsound condition or practice. Agencies also have discretion to use a 'PCA directive',[60] which is a formal enforcement action.

---

59 See Richard Carnell, 'A partial antidote to perverse incentives: the FDICIA Improvement Act of 1991', 12 *Annual Review of Banking Law* 317, 330 (1993).
60 Section 38(f) of the FDI Act grants the agencies authority to issue PCA directives.

If a bank is significantly undercapitalized or fails to submit a restoration plan, the agencies are *mandated* to exercise certain of the aforementioned powers against the bank. Critically undercapitalized banks are automatically prohibited from making payments on subordinated debt and engaging in non-routine business, among other things. Finally, such a bank may be placed in conservatorship or receivership within 90 days under certain circumstances and *must* be put into receivership if it remains critically undercapitalized during the calendar quarter beginning 270 days after it is so classified.[61]

5.6 Conclusion

By design, Congress left the safety and soundness standard undefined, providing only the bare outlines of agencies' authority in Section 39 of the Banking Act. The agencies fill in the interstices through rulemaking, guidance, examinations, and enforcement actions in varying degrees of prescriptive detail. Examinations are the agencies' key means of staying on top of rapidly changing conditions in banks that can quickly threaten a firm's solvency and expose taxpayers to loss. Regulators' broad authority under Section 39 allows the government to intrude to an extraordinary degree into a bank's operations, question the logic of its business strategy, and mandate changes in its system of corporate governance.

Nevertheless, several features of micro-prudential regulation constrain supervisory discretion by requiring justification for regulatory actions according to relatively objective guidelines. These include the PCA program's transparent grid of predetermined inflection points that trigger increasingly stringent enforcement actions. Moreover, the CAMELS rating system is a uniform, relatively objective framework for classifying a bank's level of safety and soundness. Bank supervisors also take a gradualist, iterative approach to safety and soundness issues and seek improvement by bank management before turning to more draconian measures. Examiners provide detailed feedback on deficiencies to which bank management must respond with action plans. Boards and management will know what to expect if they do not meet these remediation targets. These features go far in enabling banks to gauge compliance risk in their business strategies and design effective risk management and compliance systems to meet regulatory expectations.

---

61 Baxter, Administrative and judicial review 520–521.

CHAPTER 6

The role of corporate governance in macro-prudential regulation of systemic risk

6.1 Introductory overview

Global regulators only began to think programmatically about systemic risk when the enormity of the GFC's damage to the financial system became clear. Before then, a handful of systemic events in US financial history after the introduction of FDIC insurance periodically focused attention on the topic. Systemic failures had been a recurring staple of the period prior to the inception of FDIC insurance, leading eventually to the creation of the Federal Reserve System in 1913. The term 'TBTF' originated with the failure of Continental Illinois National Bank in 1984, the largest bank failure until the GFC.[1] However, an extended period of stable economic growth in the US since the 1980s, known as the 'Great Moderation', helped downgrade financial instability to a secondary concern of regulators and other policymakers.

The country's experience in the GFC and Great Recession fundamentally reshaped prudential regulation and bank supervision. Broadly, Basel and US policymakers have chosen three avenues for mitigating the risks of future financial crises. First, the GFC revealed severe deficiencies in risk management, which post-crisis regulation and supervision have sought to remedy. The current chapter covers this aspect of post-crisis reform. Second, policymakers have extended Basel's capital adequacy framework to macro-prudential regulation in an effort to compel financial conglomerates to internalize their systemic footprint. The 'capital approach' is the subject of Chapter 7. Third, policymakers have adopted a 'structural approach' to reduce systemic risk[2] by proscribing or walling off certain activities deemed unduly risky, requiring financial conglomerates to

---

1 The US government bailed out Continental Illinois by extending deposit insurance to all of the bank's depositors and bondholders. The FDIC estimated that nearly 2,300 banks had invested in the bank and that nearly half of these in amounts greater than the FDIC deposit insurance limit. Renee Haltom, 'Failure of Continental Illinois' (22 November 2013), Federal Reserve Bank of Richmond', at <www.federalreservehistory.org/essays/failure_of_continental_illinois>. Such risky behavior reflected the absence of meaningful bank risk management at the time.

2 The use of the term 'structural approach' does not imply that Dodd-Frank's structural regulation is an innovation in regulatory policy, only that the new legislation adopted novel mechanisms to achieve its regulatory objectives. Limitation on bank activities to contain systemic risk, such as activities 'closely related to banking', has a long history beginning from the outset of bank regulation. John Coates, 'The Volcker rule as structural law: implications for cost–benefit analysis and administrative law' (2015), 10(4) *Capital Markets Law Journal* 447, 449. Coates defines a structural law as a law that bans certain otherwise unobjectionable behavior in order to increase desirable behavior or to simplify supervision of risky behavior. Ibid. 448.

prepare 'living wills', and enhancing resolution mechanisms for failing systemically important firms, the subject of Chapter 8.

The chapter proceeds as follows. After discussing key concepts relating to systemic risk such as TBTF, it turns to the GFC. To lay a foundation for understanding Dodd-Frank's approach to tackling systemic risk, it examines three periods: the period preceding the crisis during which firms' deficient risk management practices prepared the ground for the severity of the financial crisis when it occurred; the liquidity and credit crisis; and the Great Recession, which this chapter denotes as Phase I, II, and III, respectively. The chapter indicates the regulatory responses with respect to each phase. It then turns to recent FRB regulatory guidance on the role of large BHCs' boards and senior and line management, risk committee requirements, and the LISCC program whose objective is to improve firm-wide risk management and compliance of the largest BHCs.

6.2 The role of the GFC in the formulation of macro-prudential regulation

This section lays the groundwork for understanding the rationale and structure of macro-prudential regulation, the associated regulatory expectations for risk management and compliance, and the capital and structural approaches to systemic risk in later chapters.

6.2.1 Definitions and concepts

Definitions matter in understanding financial crises. Because of their widespread impact on the general economy, financial crises invariably become politicized and laden with loosely chosen jargon.[3] This is particularly the case with the GFC, one of the most momentous and controversial events in US and global financial history. This section discusses the concepts of *financial crises, banking crises, systemic risk, shadow-banking,* and *TBTF*. Such discussion, in turn, should lead to a sounder understanding of the factors contributing to the GFC that conditioned policymakers' approach to systemic risk in Basel III and Dodd-Frank and their regulatory expectations for risk management and compliance.

6.2.1.1 Banking crises as a subset of financial crises
By definition, this book's focus is on banking crises. In a recent, timely, and comprehensive treatment, Carmen Reinhart and Kenneth Rogoff employ both quantitative and qualitative criteria in their lengthy, empirical taxonomy of financial crises, including banking crises.[4] According to Reinhart and Rogoff, the antecedents and aftermath of banking crises share common patterns of housing

---

3 Depending on one's political persuasion, Dodd-Frank, which was overwhelmingly passed on a partisan basis, is either an 'anti-bailout' law ending 'TBTF' (the Democrats' view), or a bailout law (the Republican view).

4 Carmen Reinhart and Kenneth Rogoff, *This Time Is Different: Eight Centuries of Financial Folly* (Princeton University Press: 2009) 3 [*This Time Is Different*]. Their categories of financial events include sovereign debt default, banking, inflationary, and exchange-rate crises.

and equity prices, unemployment, declining government revenues, and high levels of debt.[5] Financial crises, including banking crises, by their nature last an extended period of time. Among other things, asset market collapses are deep and prolonged, and the aftermath of a financial crisis is associated with profound declines in output and employment and an explosion of government debt.[6] All of these were true of the GFC. Banking crises by definition involve runs on banks due to their fragile business model of liquidity transformation. Banking crises also cannot be adequately understood without first understanding systemic risk.

6.2.1.2 Two theories of the causes of systemic risk

The term 'systemic risk' has import that extends well beyond academic theory. The concept is integral to the regulatory framework established under Basel III and Dodd-Frank. However, an absence of a clear understanding of systemic risk complicates identification of its causes, its measurement, and ultimately its regulation. The measurement of systemic risk is within the remit of the FSOC and FRB, but scholars and policymakers have only recently begun to develop methodologies to gauge this risk. This perhaps reflects the uniqueness of the genesis of each financial crisis. The FRB has endeavored to measure systemic risk as reflected in its rule mandating the G-SIB capital surcharge.[7]

In contrast to the issue of the causes of systemic risk, economists, central bankers, and other policymakers have reached some level of agreement on whether a systemic event or events have occurred by considering the *effects* of disruptions in a financial system. Financial disruptions that do not *cause* significant disruptions in the real economy are not a systemic risk event.[8] This approach focuses on the breakdown of financial intermediation that stops the flow of credit to businesses and consumers, which is the engine of economic growth and output.

Consideration of the *causes* of systemic events have coalesced around two approaches. These are first, a simultaneous shock to the financial system, through contagion, and second, the interconnectedness of financial institutions,[9] which transmits the problems of one or a handful of institutions to their counterparties. As this book will make clear, Dodd-Frank approaches bank regulation from both standpoints but structures its framework primarily based on the concept of

---

5 *This Time Is Different* 223.

6 Ibid. 224.

7 § 7.2.2.

8 Xavier Freixas, Luc Laeven, and José-Luis Peydró, *Systemic Risk, Crises, and Macroprudential Regulation* (MIT Press: 2015) 15 [*Systemic Risk and Macroprudential Regulation*]. The authors contrast such systemic events with the bursting of the mostly equity-financed dot-com bubble in 2000, which did not produce significant adverse effects in the financial system. Ibid.

9 The treatment in this section draws in part on David VanHoose, 'Systemic risks and macroprudential bank regulation: a critical appraisal' (April 2011), Networks Financial Institute, Indiana University, 2011-PB-04 [VanHoose, Systemic risks]. In placing systemic risk into two categories, VanHoose in turn draws on Craig Furfine, 'Interbank exposures: quantifying the risk of contagion' (2003) 35 *Journal of Money, Credit, and Banking* 111–128. See Markus Brunnermeier and others, *The Fundamental Principles of Financial Regulation* (Princeton University Press: 2009) 15–18 [Brunnermeier, *Fundamental Principles*], which also classifies systemic risk in this binary manner.

interconnectedness. Both transmission mechanisms in combination also likely played a role in the GFC.[10] They can be summarized as follows:

(1) *Simultaneous shock to the financial system.* First, there may be an external, unexpected shock to the entire financial system, causing simultaneous adverse effects throughout it, and radically disrupting its normal functioning in the transmission of funds and credit extension. There is a generalized collapse of depositor confidence. Examples are a war in the Middle East that causes a severe disruption in oil supply or a cyberattack on the payments system. This theory has been called the 'panic view', or more specifically 'illiquidity induced by a contagion of fear'.[11] Closely linked but different in approach is the asymmetric theory of a rational, information-based bank run, which ends in the same result – a generalized collapse of the financial system. This generalized collapse approach encompasses a demand-based concept of decisions of individual depositors acting in concert and with correlated asset strategies, known as 'herding' behavior.[12]

(2) *Interconnectedness.* Second, systemic failure may begin with the failure of a single financial institution or small group of institutions, which is then transmitted throughout the system through a chain reaction, commonly called the 'domino effect', or more generally 'interconnectedness'.[13] Moreover, financial institutions trade much more among themselves than firms in other industries, particularly in the interbank lending and derivatives markets.[14] Connectedness occurs on both the liability and asset sides of the balance sheet. In its pure form the theory assumes stable asset prices in the midst of market turmoil.

Critics of the domino effect argue that it unrealistically assumes a model of passive institutions that do nothing as a sequence of defaults unfolds. In practice, firms will take action to protect against unfolding events and liquidity spirals spurred by declining asset prices.[15]

The mechanics of interconnectedness failure vary. They typically include failures of counterparties to the institutions or group of institutions that initially failed. This transmission mechanism relies on closely knit interconnections via,

---

10 The GFC illustrates the two channels of contagion: cross-linkages and common shocks. *This Time Is Different* 242. The authors, however, point primarily to contagion and spillover from the US to foreign markets as the agent of transmission. Ibid.

11 VanHoose, Systemic risks 4.

12 Ibid. at 4–7.

13 The BIS defines this as the risk that 'the failure of a participant to meet its contractual obligations may in turn cause other participants to default with a chain reaction leading to broader financial difficulties'. Bank for International Settlements, *64th Annual Report 177* (1994).

14 Brunnermeier, *Fundamental Principles* 4.

15 Brunnermeier, *Fundamental Principles* 16. In particular, the domino theory assumes stable asset prices whereas prices decline in a liquidity spiral, producing contagious effects on the market as a whole. Ibid. 16.

e.g., payment obligations, between institutions, or between markets. Counterparty failure can disrupt the payments system, the critical plumbing of the financial markets. Certain factors can exacerbate the domino effect, such as high leverage among the financial institutions in the system, making them vulnerable to counterparty failures. The interconnectedness approach emphasizes supply-side channels regulated by central banks, such as interbank clearings, securities exchanges, and foreign currency transfers. A transaction failure between two banks can result in settlement failures in a line of financial institutions.[16]

The interconnectedness theory perhaps has the most relevance on the regulatory side. Regulators' *perception* of counterparty risk in the midst of a crisis may be to assume the importance of interconnectedness without telling evidence. Fear of the domino effect in large part prompted regulators globally to rescue many large, failing institutions in the GFC. Reflecting regulators' perceptions and fear of the domino effect, Dodd-Frank imposes restrictions on exposure of G-SIBs to other SIFIs.[17]

6.2.2 Too big to fail

TBTF is another concept that Basel III/Dodd-Frank seeks to resolve. This amorphous term means different things to different market participants and commentators.[18] Dodd-Frank systematically addresses TBTF without truly defining it. TBTF continues to be a public policy issue because of disagreement over its definition and thus the costs and benefits of resolving TBTF firms.[19] Generally, difference of opinion centers on two issues: (1) which counterparties are partially or fully protected and (2) whether losses in the bailout are funded privately or by the government.[20] The populist furor over taxpayer-funded bailouts in the GFC provided a driving force for many of Dodd-Frank's TBTF provisions.

6.2.2.1 TBTF and moral hazard
A unifying theme throughout the TBTF debate is the moral hazard it generates. According to the economist George Kaufman, it is not the source of funds such as taxpayers that matter in understanding TBTF, but the mere possibility of a creditor bailout, which creates moral hazard. US policymakers have established a policy of constructive ambiguity to create doubt about bailouts to mitigate the

---

16 VanHoose, Systemic risks 7. The Herstatt settlement failure in 1974 was a prime example of interconnectedness that had the potential of a systemic event. See § 2.2.1.

17 A G-SIB's credit exposure to another SIFI is capped at 15% of its tier 1 capital. 12 CFR § 252.72(b).

18 According to the economist George Kaufman, various definitions of TBTF have different policy and regulatory implications. These include too complex to fail, too important to fail, too interconnected to fail, too big to liquidate, or too big to prosecute. Franklin Allen and others, 'Enhancing Prudential Standards in Financial Regulations' (3 December 2014), Harvard Law School Forum on Corporate Governance and Financial Regulation, at <https://corpgov.law.harvard.edu/2015/03/16/enhancing-prudential-standards-in-financial-regulations/> 15 [Enhancing Prudential Standards].

19 George Kaufman, 'Too big to fail in banking: What does it mean?' (2014) 13 *Journal of Financial Stability* 214–223 [Too big to fail in banking].

20 Too big to fail in banking 216.

moral hazard problem, a policy at play in the GFC. However, the inconsistency in the US bailout strategy during the crisis likely contributed to the market turmoil, particularly to the chaos following the Lehman bankruptcy.[21]

6.2.2.2 Types of TBTF resolution

TBTF resolution undoubtedly exists when a firm is insolvent (meaning that net worth is negative and thus shareholders are ordinarily wiped out) but a third party protects shareholders against loss. All creditors are made whole. Such a bailout is one of the least disruptive in financial markets and occurred in the Bear Stearns transaction in March 2008.[22] TBTF more frequently is applied to resolutions in which shareholders are not protected, the firm fails, and its assets are sold or liquidated. Some uninsured depositors and other creditors may be fully or partially paid out.[23] Regulators decide this loss allocation based on their estimated benefits of avoiding financial instability against the moral hazard and other costs of protection.

TBTF and government bailouts in the GFC are intertwined, although, more broadly, bailouts do not always involve TBTF institutions, and TBTF bailouts do not always involve the government.[24] As traditionally understood, bailouts range from nationalization, explicit infusion of cash through equity investment, and government guarantees to purchases of deteriorating assets and shotgun marriages. However, the Federal Reserve, acting as lender of last resort and providing liquidity loans against adequate collateral of solvent financial institutions is *not* a government bailout.

6.2.2.3 TBTF a phenomenon of the financial sector

TBTF status is particularly problematic in the financial sector given the fragile business model of financial institutions, a feature reflected in banks' ineligibility for resolution under the Bankruptcy Code.[25] In addition, TBTF is controversial because by definition bailouts occur outside of the established bankruptcy regime, which statutorily ensures that creditor counterparties receive liquidation proceeds according to their seniority. TBTF resolution may alter the predetermined loss allocation scheme of the Bankruptcy Code.[26]

Large BHCs' and other financial conglomerates' increasing complexity helps to cement their TBTF status. TBTF status gives a bank a competitive edge in debt

---

21 Enhancing Prudential Standards 16. According to David Skeel, the bailout of Bear Stearns in March 2008 set the stage for the turmoil following the Lehman Brothers bankruptcy. David Skeel, *The New Financial Deal* (Wiley: 2010) 31.

22 JPMorgan Chase acquired Bear Stearns as an ongoing entity, paying its shareholders $10 per share.

23 Too big to fail in banking 215.

24 The S&L rescues in the 1980s did not involve TBTF firms. The US government, through the offices of FRB Chairman Greenspan, orchestrated the private funding of the orderly liquidation of the hedge fund Long Term Capital Management, perceived as TBTF, in 1998 to limit systemic risk in the financial markets.

25 11 USC § 109(b), (d). BHC corporate parents are so eligible.

26 The Bankruptcy Code expressly sets forth the priority scheme for claimholders. Secured creditors come first in priority, followed by unsecured creditors, subordinated debt, preferred shareholders, and common stockholders. 11 USC § 507 – *Priorities*.

financing costs as investors, assuming government protection, will buy TBTF bank debt at a discount. The discount and expectation of bailouts further incentivizes banks to take on riskier activities to retain their TBTF status. Smaller banks must compete and follow suit, further worsening the negative impact of TBTF in the financial system.[27] Another negative feature of TBTF bailouts is inefficient allocation of resources, a result that the adversarial, privately negotiated bankruptcy process is better equipped to avoid. There is, however, evidence of a narrowing cost-of-funding advantage following the Dodd-Frank reforms, indicating some success in solving the TBTF problem.[28]

6.2.2.4 GFC's contribution to the TBTF debate

The GFC greatly roiled the controversy involving TBTF and its contribution to systemic risk. The government's vast expansion of the federal safety net in the GFC significantly increased moral hazard in the financial system. The bailouts further incentivized financial institutions to become ever larger and increase leverage in order to fall under the government's protective umbrella.

6.2.3 Shadow banking and bank runs

The GFC was a banking crisis and bank run, using these terms in a broad sense. The run in the GFC was on non-bank financial institutions, or 'shadow banks', that, like commercial banks, use short-term debt financing to fund long-term, illiquid assets but fall outside FDIC insurance protection and prudential regulatory restrictions. In lieu of FDIC-insured deposits shadow banks offer liquid securities as collateral or operate on an unsecured basis in exchange for short-term funding. On the eve of the GFC, wholesale non-deposit taking shadow banks comprised the majority of short-term financing as shadow banks increasingly assumed the liquidity transformation role.[29]

6.2.3.1 Economic equivalence of shadow bank and commercial bank runs

In both bank and non-bank financial sectors, liquidity transformation is a fragile business model. A bank or shadow bank faces, respectively, the risk of short-term creditors withdrawing deposits or ceasing to renew, or roll over, collateralized short-term debt financing. Runs occur due to uncertainty among investors about the composition and quality of both of these types of financial institutions' long-term assets. To meet these cash withdrawals, these institutions are forced to

---

27 Gara Afonso, João Santos, and James Traina, 'Do "too-big-to-fail" banks take on more risk?' (December 2014) *FRBNY Economic Policy Review* 41–42. The authors find evidence of higher levels of impaired loans following an increase in government support.

28 Martin Baily, Douglas Elliott, and Phillip Swagel, 'The big bank theory: breaking down the breakup arguments' (31 October 2014), Brookings Institution, Economic Policy Program 6. Darrell Duffie has found evidence that lenders, by and large, believe the government will cause them to suffer a loss in the failure of a financial conglomerate. Darrell Duffie, 'Prone to fail: the pre-crisis financial system' (8 December 2018), *Journal of Financial Perspectives* [forthcoming] 33–34.

29 Gary Gorton, 'Slapped in the face by the invisible hand: banking and the panic of 2007' (9 May 2009) NBER 3 [Slapped in the face].

liquidate these assets in 'fire sales', driving down prices in these asset classes. At the extreme, a banking panic occurs. In a panic these firms are insolvent because they have insufficient capital to meet short-term creditors' demands for their assets.[30] Cash withdrawal *en masse* results in the insolvency of the financial system and a freezing of the credit markets, which occurred following the Lehman bankruptcy.

Shadow banking arose in part because large creditor institutions have liquidity demands far in excess of the FDIC deposit account threshold.[31] Insured demand deposits are of no use to large firms, other commercial banks, hedge funds, and corporate treasuries that need to deposit large amounts of money in interest bearing accounts for a short period of time. Instead, these creditors 'deposit' their funds in the repo and asset-backed commercial paper (ABCP) markets[32] backed by high-quality collateral consisting of Treasury securities and securitization bonds. The collateral is valued at market prices. Uninsured money market funds and the interbank funding market, in which banks lend reserves on an overnight basis, are also a part of the shadow-banking system.

6.2.4 Regulatory responses to risks revealed in GFC's three phases

In assessing the wide range of regulatory responses to the GFC, it is useful to identify three distinct phases: the periods before, during, and following the liquidity and credit crisis that began in summer 2007. Each phase presents a distinct set of risks that policymakers addressed in the Basel III and Dodd-Frank macro-prudential framework. The first phase (Phase I) involved deficient risk management decisions that contributed to the liquidity and credit crisis, particularly the decision to retain long-term MBS-related assets financed by short-term credit. The second phase (Phase II), from August 2007 to 2009, marked the critical stage of the GFC with the collapse of credit intermediation and runs on shadow banks. The third phase (Phase III) was the Great Recession, which officially extended from December 2007 into 2009 but its negative repercussions extended several years following the crisis. A brief summary of these regulatory responses follows the discussion of each phase.

6.2.5 Phase I: corporate governance and risk management failures reflected in banks' capital structure

The severity of the crisis in the fall of 2008 that required rescues of a broad array of financial conglomerates can be attributed largely to financial institutions'

---

30 Slapped in the face 3.

31 Shadow banking also includes bank deposit accounts with holdings exceeding the FDIC maximum account threshold of $250,000. These accounts are uninsured and unsecured.

32 In the ABCP market, financial institutions sponsor that fund MBS and other asset-backed securities by issuing ABCP, with an average maturity of 90 days, and medium-term notes, secured by these assets. Prior to the GFC, both were sold primarily to money market funds. The market had viewed ABCP as equivalent to insured deposits.

excessively risky capital structure.[33] Firms' system of corporate governance had failed to keep up with changes in the complex, opaque, and globally integrated financial system.[34] Many banks entered the crisis with substantial exposure to long-term subprime assets financed with highly runnable short-term whole-sale debt. Heated competition ensured that firms across the financial landscape shared these two weaknesses in their capital structure. The composition of these firms' balance sheet provided much of the fuel that was ignited in the liquidity and credit crisis,[35] leading to emergency interventions by the Federal Reserve and Treasury Department to rescue failing financial conglomerates. Faulty board decision making that downgraded the risk management and compliance functions and poorly constructed or absent internal controls (ICs) were critical elements in creating the combustible mix of assets and liabilities.

6.2.5.1 Siloed risk management

Many of the large firms had a siloed[36] approach to corporate governance prior to GFC. In many cases, these firms were an amalgamation of different cultures and businesses resulting from a series of mergers and acquisitions (M&A) that left a tangle of cultural conflicts and conflicting IT systems. This fragmentation poses a significant challenge to BHC boards, which need to have relevant information on existing and emerging risks in business units across their firm before acting upon it. In a 2007 survey of banks, only 10% of firms had adopted a holistic approach to risk management.[37] Post-crisis guidance seeks to correct this deficiency by emphasizing an enterprise-wide, integrated approach to risk and, in certain areas, compliance. Basel 239 guidance seeks to remedy the poor risk data aggregation and information flow.[38]

6.2.5.2 Challenges in identifying, communicating, and acting on tail risk

Tail risk, the central risk management issue in the GFC, is a significant challenge for financial conglomerates to incorporate effectively into their business strategy

---

33 See Anil Kashyap, Raghuram Rajan, and Jeremy Stein, 'Rethinking Capital Regulation' (2008) 2008 Economic Symposium, 'Maintaining Stability in a Changing Financial System', Federal Reserve Bank of Kansas City 1–2 [Rethinking Capital Regulation]. As the authors put it, 'the proximate cause of the credit crisis (as distinct from the housing crisis) was the interplay between two *choices* made by banks' – significant exposure to MBS subprime-related assets financed by short-term debt (emphasis added). Ibid. 1.

34 Ben Bernanke, 'The real effects of disrupted credit: evidence from the global financial crisis' (13 September 2018), Brookings Papers on Economic Activity, Brookings Institution 1 [Real effects of disrupted credit].

35 Rethinking Capital Regulation 1. The financial system's reliance on short-term funding of long-term assets with potentially low market liquidity has been the main source of instability in this and previous financial crises. Brunnermeier, *Fundamental Principles* 40. Northern Rock and other casualties in the GFC might well have survived with the same assets if their funding's average maturity had been longer. Ibid. xii.

36 Silos are business lines, legal entities, or geographical units operated in isolation from one another, with limited information shared across the firm and, in some cases, competition between silos. Basel Committee on Banking Supervision, 'Corporate governance principles for banks' (8 July 2015) 30.

37 Stephen Bainbridge, 'Caremark and enterprise risk management' (March 2009), 34 *Journal of Corporation Law* 967, 971 [Bainbridge, ERM].

38 See § 6.3.5.

and risk management and compliance processes. Many finance industry senior executives defensively opined that they could not be held responsible for not preparing for an event of the magnitude of the GFC. This defense rings hollow. Certain other conglomerates took effective action in the face of ominous signs without being able to precisely forecast the depth and severity of the oncoming crisis.[39]

For risk management, the challenge in assessing severe, highly improbable events is due to the fact that the outcomes associated with such risks are not normally distributed but tend to have fat tails.[40] Identifying and communicating to senior management the potential of extreme events requires quantifying the probability and magnitude of severe losses. In such instances, uncertainty in generating such a distribution poses a severe identification and communication challenge.[41]

A risk management function that has an independent, autonomous, and credible status in a firm with unalloyed access to the board can limit tail exposure preceding and during a market crisis.[42] However, the pre-crisis risk management function by and large lacked these attributes. In the pre-crisis corporate environment, communicating extreme risks to senior business executives was highly problematic. Moreover, this challenge was made even more daunting by compensation schemes with hidden, embedded tail risks[43] or by managers who assessed risks based on historical data and thus did not account for low-probability events that later turned out to be highly material. Finally, at the apex of the corporate governance system, board directors need to have the necessary competence to understand the significance of extreme, improbable events so that they can appropriately weigh them in formulating business strategy within the firm's risk appetite. Many boards of financial conglomerates prior to the GFC did not have this level of competence.

6.2.5.3 Principal-agent conflict as a contributing cause to risk management failure

The deeper problem underlying this poor business judgment is the principal-agent conflict that is endemic in financial institutions.[44] Establishing effective incentive compensation schemes and strong ICs has been a perennial conundrum in large financial conglomerates in which the principal-agent conflict plays an

---

39 See § 6.2.5.5, which summarizes the Senior Supervisors Group's 2008 report on poorly and better performing firms.

40 Bainbridge, ERM 971 (citing Linda Allen, Jacob Boudoukh, and Anthony Saunders, *Understanding Market, Credit, and Operational Risk: The Value at Risk Approach* (Blackwell: 2004) 25 [Allen, VaR]).

41 Bainbridge, ERM 971 (citing Allen, VaR 26).

42 Andrew Ellul and Vijay Yerramilli, 'Stronger risk controls, lower risk: evidence from U.S. bank holding companies' (October 2013), 68 *Journal of Finance* 1757, 1796.

43 Senior Supervisors Group, 'Observations on risk management practices during the recent market turbulence' (6 March 2008) 7, at <www.occ.treas.gov/publications/publications-by-type/other-publications-reports/pub-other-risk-mgt-practices-2008.pdf> [SSG, Observations]. See § 6.2.5.2.

44 See § 3.3.2. Also see § 4.2.2.1 regarding the incentive to optimize return on equity by limiting equity financing and incurring debt in its stead.

outsized role.[45] This conflict also was a reason risk management lacked resources, authority, and independence throughout the finance industry, deficiencies that the FRB has sought to remedy in its post-crisis macro-prudential guidance.

Compensation schemes incentivized both the senior and lower executive ranks to generate high returns with little downside risk. Their focus was on the asset side of the balance sheet. Boards of directors and senior management, facing increasingly heated competition in generating high earnings, decided to enter subprime MBS origination and securitization, in some cases just as the market was reaching its peak. CEOs would be punished by the stock market, and their compensation docked, if they did not actively seek market share in subprime assets. Compensated by short-term windows of equity performance, executives viewed high-yielding subprime asset exposure as a sure bet in generating high return on equity. In sum, excessive risk-taking can occur as competition erodes banks' franchise value.[46] In an effort to reduce the agency costs revealed by the crisis, post-crisis regulation and supervision has focused on correcting compensation schemes for senior executives.

Lower in the management ranks, pay-for-performance compensation incentivized traders to game internal performance metrics that measured risk-adjusted returns. Poorly designed risk controls did not require economic capital charges commensurate with the risk assumed by trading desks.[47] Quite simply, traders had incentives to assume hidden tail risks and were able to do so.[48] Firms use VaR[49] to compare traders across business lines and compensate them for their profits in relation to the risks they assume. A trader that apparently assumes less risk for a given amount of capital than other traders will be more highly compensated and granted higher position limits. Though well intentioned, the system led to perversely distorted incentives as traders sought out exposure that was not reflected in the horizon window on which VaR is based,[50] thus generating 'fake alpha'. In sum, VaR was not measuring risk properly. Firms invested in fat tail risk without fully realizing it.[51]

Post-crisis agency guidance is aimed at rectifying this principle-agent problem in the lower echelon through enhanced ICs and independent risk management

---

45 Rethinking Capital Regulation 2.

46 *Systemic Risk and Macroprudential Regulation* 329.

47 An example was UBS's practice of not charging capital corresponding to risks relating to CDOs and other investments with long tail risk. '[E]mployee incentivisation arrangements did not differentiate between return generated by skill in creating additional returns versus returns made from exploiting UBS's comparatively low cost of funding in what were essentially carry trades.... [T]he relatively high yield attributable to Subprime made this asset class an attractive long position for carry trades.' UBS AG, 'Shareholder report on UBS's write-downs' (18 April 2008) 42, at <http://maths-fi.com/ubs-shareholder-report.pdf>.

48 Rethinking Capital Regulation 9. Traders could count on their income spread exceeding the low hurdle rate that contributed to bonuses. Ibid.

49 § 3.7.2.3 discusses VaR in greater detail.

50 The data made the standard deviation component of the VaR artificially low.

51 Till Guldimann, 'The creator of VaR explains how large banks measure the risk of their own portfolios' (25 June 2018) *Odd Lots*, podcast with Joe Wiesenthal and Tracy Alloway, at <https://podcasts.apple.com/us/podcast/creator-var-explains-how-large-banks-measure-risk-their/id1056200 096?i=1000414564268>.

and compliance functions that enjoy a high level of credibility and authority in their organizations, in addition to compensation schemes that better align business strategy with longer-term, prudent risk-taking.

6.2.5.4 Risky capital structure

On the asset side, when the credit crisis gained steam in late summer 2007, many financial conglomerates had substantial holdings of subprime MBS-related assets. This strategy was contrary to the stated rationale of securitization, much lauded by regulators adhering to the market-based ethos, to off-load and spread risk into the capital markets.[52] When housing prices and then MBS valuations began to decline, firms had to write-down their assets by hundreds of billions of dollars.[53] Through August 2008, UBS had written down $43 billion; Citigroup, $56 billion; and Merrill Lynch, $45 billion.[54] The enormous impairment charges against a small amount of capital in turn created the ground for investor concern and the subsequent credit and liquidity crisis of Phase II. On the liability side, the financial conglomerates financed these long-term illiquid assets with short-term, low-cost debt. They sourced most of this debt with wholesale funding from the uninsured shadow-banking sector. Unlike deposits, the favored funding source of smaller banks, wholesale funding is more 'runnable, prone to evaporate in a crisis'.[55]

6.2.5.5 Senior Supervisors Group's assessment of risk management practices

The Senior Supervisors Group (SSG), whose members are financial market supervisors from several countries,[56] surveyed 11 global financial conglomerates[57] early in the crisis. Firms began reporting material write-downs with losses concentrated in US subprime mortgage-related credits, particularly in business lines in warehousing, structuring, and trading of subprime-backed CDOs.

The SSG divided the firms into better and more poorly performing institutions. The better performing firms typically shared information effectively across business lines, had rigorous internal processes requiring critical business judgment in asset valuation, applied consistent valuations across the firm, did not rely exclusively on credit rating agencies (CRAs) but did independent credit analysis, aligned treasury functions closely with risk management practices, charged business lines for contingent liquidity exposures, and relied on a wide range of risk

---

52 Figure 1.1 at § 1.1.3.1 illustrates the securitization process.

53 Banks, including sophisticated investment banks, were some of the most active buyers of structured products. Markus Brunnermeier, 'Deciphering the liquidity and credit crunch 2007–2008' (Winter 2009), 23 *Journal of Economic Perspectives 77*, 80 [Deciphering the liquidity crunch].

54 Julia Werdigier, 'After $43 billion in write-downs, UBS to split main businesses', *New York Times* (12 August 2008).

55 Jeremy Kress, 'Solving banking's "too big to manage" problem' (7 March 2019), [forthcoming 104 *Minnesota Law Review* 2019], 17–18, at <https://ssrn.com/abstract=3348593>.

56 Representatives included banking and securities regulators from France, Germany, Switzerland, UK, and the US, represented by the FRB, FRBNY, SEC, and OCC. The SSG shares information on risk management, governance, and other issues involving financial conglomerates.

57 SSG, Observations.

measures to gain different perspectives on risk.[58] The more poorly performing firms were deficient in some or many of these areas. Table 6.1 summarizes the SSG's findings concerning risk management practices of the two groups in four areas.

6.2.5.6 Regulatory response relating to risks revealed in Phase I

Regulators, pursuant to Basel III/Dodd-Frank as well as under their discretionary authority, adopted a number of enhanced prudential approaches to address the deficiencies in risk management exhibited in Phase I in the run up to the GFC. These measures included increasingly enhanced expectations regarding corporate governance, risk management, and compliance specifically relating to the roles of the board of directors, senior management, and line management, and structural mandates such as board-level risk committees (Chapter 6). The FRB instituted Pillar II supervisory measures consisting of the LISCC program on liquidity management and capital planning and the CCAR and the DFAST stress testing programs (Chapter 7).

6.2.6 Phase II: liquidity and credit crisis

The financial conglomerates' poor risk management practices reflected in the severe mismatch of assets and liabilities and overdependence on subprime MBS-related assets to generate high returns were one of many factors that contributed to the liquidity and credit crisis of the GFC. Nevertheless, these practices share significant blame for the depth and severity of the crisis once it began in late summer 2007.

6.2.6.1 Starting point of liquidity and credit crisis

Incipient signs of a liquidity problem appeared in February 2007 with an increase in subprime mortgage defaults, reflected in the increase in CDS prices for subprime mortgages.[59] In June, Bear Stearns bailed out two MBS-related hedge funds, and in July, the ABCP market showed refinancing difficulties. As the series of events unfolded in 2007, their balance sheets exposed commercial and investment banks to a severe maturity mismatch through their off–balance sheet liquidity facilities backed by MBS-related assets and increased reliance on repo financing.[60]

---

58 David Viniar, Goldman Sachs' CFO during the GFC, observed that the firm reviewed its P&L position under VaR every day to make sure the P&L was consistent with its risk model forecasts. In December 2006, its mortgage business lost money ten days in a row. 'It wasn't a lot of money, but by the 10th day we thought we should sit down and talk about it.' Goldman Sachs reviewed every trading position of the firm. They examined VaR and other risk models. They talked about how the MBS market 'felt'. 'We decided to "get closer to home"'. Joe Nocera, 'Risk mismanagement', *NYT Magazine* (2 January 2009).

59 This was reflected in a decline in the ABX price index, which is based on CDS prices. Deciphering the liquidity crunch 82–83.

60 Deciphering the liquidity crunch 80. The structured investment vehicles (SIVs) that sold ABCP were subject to funding liquidity risk, whereby investors, mainly money market funds, would cease

Table 6.1 Risk management practices of better and more poorly performing firms in GFC

Best-practice risk management area	Better performing firms	Poorly performing firms
1. Effective firm-wide risk identification and analysis	• Shared quantitative/qualitative information effectively across firm • Thus, able to identify sources of significant risk early on, reducing exposures and hedging while still practical and not prohibitively expensive	• Business line and senior managers did not discuss firm's risks in light of evolving market conditions • Left business lines to act in isolation regarding business growth and hedging, in some cases increasing rather than mitigating risk exposure
2. Consistent firm-wide application of independent and rigorous valuation practices	• Rigorous internal processes requiring critical judgment and discipline in valuations of complex or potentially illiquid assets • Skeptical of CRAs' assessment of complex structured credit; developed inhouse expertise to conduct independent assessments • Once deciding on valuation, sought consistent use across firm	• Continued to price super-senior CDO tranches at or close to par despite observable deterioration in performance of underlying RMBS collateral and declining market liquidity • Management did not exercise sufficient discipline over valuation process • Relied sometimes too passively on credit risk from CRAs
3. Effective management of funding liquidity, capital, and balance sheet	• Aligned treasury functions closely with risk management practices, incorporating information from all business lines in global liquidity planning • Incentivized control over balance sheet growth by charging business lines for contingent liquidity exposures, reflecting liquidity cost in challenging market conditions	• Weaker controls over balance sheet growth • Treasury functions not closely aligned with risk management processes • Lacked complete access to information across all business lines • Did not properly consider risk of certain exposures or price appropriately for balance sheet use
4. Informative and responsive risk management reporting and practices	• Management information systems assessed risk positions with variety of tools and with several underlying assumptions • Management had more adaptive (not static) risk management processes and systems that could rapidly alter assumptions to reflect current market conditions • Relied on wide range of risk measures to gather more information and different perspectives on same exposures • Many able to integrate measures of market risk and counterparty risk positions across businesses	• More dependent on specific risk measures using outdated or inflexible assumptions • Lost sight of how risk was evolving or could change in the future • Some could not easily integrate market and counterparty risk positions across businesses, making it difficult to identify consolidated firm-wide sensitivities and concentrations

Source: Senior Supervisors Group, 'Observations on Risk Management Practices During the Recent Market Turbulence' (6 March 2008).

Most commentators mark 9 August 2007 as the starting point of the liquidity and credit crisis. BNP Paribas halted redemptions in three investment funds due to its inability to value their underlying structured investments. Beginning August 9, the critical interbank lending market became highly illiquid, with rapidly rising LIBOR rates.[61] In short order the ECB and Federal Reserve collectively injected over $100 billion of overnight credit into the interbank lending market. ABCP outstanding plunged by hundreds of billions of dollars in August and for the remainder of 2007.[62] In December, for reputational reasons Citigroup brought its SIV programs onto its balance sheet to avoid downgrades of the programs' creditworthiness, further eroding its capital.[63] In the repo market creditors demanded increasing haircuts in a run on that market, leading to a downward spiral of asset sales and further declines in the value of the collateral backing this debt.[64] Ultimately lenders ceased to roll over banks' repo debt due to concerns about the value and liquidity of the collateral backing these obligations.[65]

The crisis spread through contagious sentiment to other repo securitization asset classes as creditors began to doubt the value of underlying non-MBS related collateral. In December the FRB initiated the first of several unconventional liquidity facilities with the creation of the Term Auction Facility that provided depository institutions collateral-backed short-term loans.[66]

6.2.6.2 Escalation of the liquidity and credit crisis: bailouts of TBTF firms

The first non-bank bailout, of Bear Stearns, occurred in March 2008 when hedge funds withdrew short-term funds, causing a severe loss of liquidity. The FRB orchestrated a purchase of the company by JPMorgan Chase, with a loan

---

buying SIVs' ABCP that had funded SIVs' long-term assets. The bank sponsors of SIVs provided a liquidity facility to the SIVs that committed the banks to fund SIVs' long-term assets if necessary, in effect, bringing these assets back onto the banks' balance sheets.

61 In the interbank market, banks lend to each other at LIBOR on an unsecured basis with maturities ranging from overnight to three months.

62 SIV-backed ABCP fell by about $70 billion, or 80%, and new issue maturities shortened considerably as investors sought to hedge their risk. Daniel Covitz, Nellie Liang, and Gustavo Suarez, 'The evolution of a financial crisis: panic in the asset-backed commercial paper market', Finance and Economics Discussion Series, Federal Reserve Board (18 August 2009) 12–13.

63 Liz Moyer, 'Citigroup goes it alone to rescue SIVs', Forbes (13 December 2007).

64 The percentage of total bank assets financed by overnight repos had increased approximately twofold from 2000 to 2007, with a higher portion consisting of overnight funding, thus increasing liquidity risk. Brunnermeier, Deciphering the liquidity crunch 80.

65 Such collateral ceased to be 'informationally insensitive', causing investors to reduce their exposure. Slapped in the face 4. Insured bank deposits are truly 'informationally insensitive', meaning that depositors and counterparties need not worry about the value of the checks that depositors write due to FDIC insurance so that checks function as currency. The AAA-rated MBS and other collateral used in shadow banking served as 'insurance', making the short-term debt informationally insensitive. Ibid. 7–9.

66 This facility allowed banks to bid for loans anonymously backed by a wide range of collateral, including MBS. Deciphering the liquidity crunch 87. In March 2008 the FRB extended liquidity assistance to non-banks in launching the Term Securities Lending Facility, permitting investment banks to swap agency and other mortgage-related bonds for Treasury bonds, and the Primary Dealer Credit Facility, which provided overnight funding to investment banks. Ibid. 88.

guarantee of $30 billion of toxic assets. A major concern of the regulators concerned Bear Stearn's interconnectedness.[67] The crisis reached a crescendo in September 2008. The US government put the two GSEs, Fannie Mae and Freddie Mac, into conservatorship on September 7. Lehman Brothers filed for bankruptcy protection on September 15, and on September 16, again due to concerns on interconnectedness, the FRB injected $85 billion of equity into AIG.

The financial markets completely shut down in the weeks following the Lehman bankruptcy. The US Treasury provided an $80 billion guarantee for money market funds to avoid a shutdown of their market after a leading fund 'broke the buck', with its share price falling below $1. The Federal Reserve introduced a commercial paper funding facility after non-asset-backed securities (ABS) backed commercial paper suffered a dramatic decline in issuance. The stock market lost $8 trillion in market value. The government launched additional facilities to buy commercial paper, ABS, and GSE bonds.[68]

6.2.6.3 Both types of systemic risk occurred in GFC

As this narrative makes clear, a combination of the two models of systemic failure, a simultaneous shock and interconnectedness, occurred in the financial crisis of 2007–09.[69] The financial conglomerates were connected to one another in an opaque network involving thousands of derivatives and short-term debt transactions. Regulators, unable to decipher firms' balance sheets, intervened in hastily orchestrated bailouts. CCR, the risk of default of a trading counterparty on its obligation, paralyzed the debt markets.[70] Subprime mortgages, at the heart of the crisis, were too small in amount to cause a systemic event. This makes contagion a necessary element in spreading the panic to the credit markets generally.[71]

6.2.6.4 Regulatory response relating to risks revealed in Phase II

Dodd-Frank addresses potential future liquidity and credit crises through a comprehensive and multifaceted approach. The legislation seeks to reduce the likelihood of government bailouts of TBTF firms and prevent future bank runs. Policymakers' measures include enhanced expectations for corporate governance

---

67 According to testimony by FRB Chair Ben Bernanke, if the government had allowed Bear Stearns to fail, it would have led to a 'chaotic unwinding' of the bank's investments held by its counterparties. 'Bernanke Defends Bear Stearns Bailout', *CBS News* (3 April 2008).

68 Deciphering the liquidity crunch 90.

69 There is a continuing debate among academic commentators and policymakers on the primary causes of the financial crisis. Hal Scott has made a strong case that contagion, the first model described in § 6.2.1.2, was the root cause of the crisis, not interconnectedness. Scott defines contagion as run behavior in which fears of widespread financial collapse lead to withdrawal of funding from financial institutions. Hal Scott, *Connectedness and Contagion: Protecting the Financial System from Panics* (MIT Press: 2016) 5.

70 Viral Acharya and Matthew Richardson, 'Causes of the financial crisis' (2010), 21 *Critical Review* 209.

71 A useful analogy, suggested by Gorton, is an E. coli outbreak. An isolated outbreak in a small part of the food supply will lead a large portion of the population to avoid many other types of foods. As with E. coli, no investor knew where the risks were, leading to uncertainty concerning which counterparties would fail. Gary Gorton and Andrew Metrick, 'Haircuts' (November–December 2010), *Federal Reserve Bank of St. Louis Review* 507, 511.

and the control functions and FSOC as a systemic risk coordinator with SIFI designation authority (Chapter 6); liquidity regulation and more loss-absorbent capital that more closely reflects a firm's risk profile (Chapter 7); capital planning through CCAR and DFAST stress testing and LISCC capital planning oversight[72] (Chapter 7);[73] resolution plans, SPOE resolution with BHC capital structure requirements, and the OLA rules (Chapter 8).

6.2.7 Phase III: the Great Recession

The Great Recession, which officially began in December 2007 and ended in June 2009, was the worst economic downturn since the Great Depression. Recessions that are associated with systemic banking crises impose huge costs on an economy.[74] In the Great Recession, US GDP contracted by more than 4% and it took nearly four years for it to regain the prerecession GDP level.[75] According to the International Monetary Fund the recession became global in 2009, the fourth and deepest recession since World War II.[76] The panic in the GFC played a central role in the severity of the Great Recession.[77] According to Ben Bernanke, a leading scholar of the Great Depression and FRB chair during the GFC, the collapse of the financial system in the early 1930s was a major reason for the persistence of the Great Depression.[78]

Moreover, the factors most strongly associated with financial panics, the run on short-term funding and other forms of contagion such as occurred during the crisis in the securitization markets, are the best predictors of poor economic performance.[79] A strong link exists between the breakdown of financial intermediation and economic downturns:

> Financial instability occurs when problems (or concerns about potential problems) within institutions, markets, payments systems, or the financial system in general significantly impair the supply of credit intermediation services – so as to substantially impact the expected path of real economic activity.[80]

---

72 The CCAR and LISCC programs supplement Dodd-Frank's systemic risk regulation but were not mandated by it.

73 The GFC was a run on the shadow-banking sector. FSOC's designation authority is a key tool in Dodd-Frank's multiprong approach to systemic risk.

74 *This Time Is Different* 172. Such banking crises are typically an amplification mechanism of a previous shock. Ibid.

75 Diane Schanzenbach and others, 'Nine facts about the great recession and tools for fighting the next downturn' (May 2016), The Hamilton Project, Brookings Institution 1.

76 Bob Davis, 'What's a global recession?', *Wall Street Journal* (22 April 2009).

77 Ibid. 4.

78 *This Time Is Different* 146.

79 Real effects of disrupted credit 4.

80 Eric Rosengren, 'Defining financial stability, and some policy implications of applying the definition' (3 June 2011), Keynote remarks at the Stanford Finance Forum, Graduate School of Business, Stanford University, at <https://www.bostonfed.org/news-and-events/speeches/defining-finan cial-stability-and-some-policy-implications-of-applying-the-definition.aspx> (cited in Anil Kashyap, Dimitrios Tsomocos, and Alexandros Vardoulakis, 'Principles for macroprudential regulation' (April 2014), *Financial Stability Review* No. 18, 173, 174).

Exacerbating the effect of downturns associated with financial crises, in a recession, as bank asset quality deteriorates and bank capital declines, banks seek to preserve liquidity and capital by reducing lending, leading to less investment and consumption and further output declines.[81] Risk aversion also certainly plays a role. Financial crises raise intermediation costs and restrict credit, thereby restraining activity in the real sector and resulting ultimately in low growth and recession.[82]

An important lesson drawn by lawmakers and policymakers from the Great Recession was that banks need capital sufficient to continue their vital role in credit intermediation. Due to their enormous MBS-related write-downs, banks had to replenish their capital before they would be able to lend further. Such unprecedented balance sheet impairments later served as precedent for the Federal Reserve's severely adverse scenarios in its stress testing programs.

6.2.7.1 Regulatory response relating to risks revealed in Phase III

Dodd-Frank adopts measures involving enhanced expectations for corporate governance (Chapter 6): hard-wired capital ratios, capital planning through CCAR and DFAST stress testing, and LISCC capital planning oversight (Chapter 7). All these responses are designed to ensure that banks can absorb losses while still adequately serving as credit intermediaries.

6.2.8 Regulators' lessons from the GFC and their macro-prudential response

The GFC has had a profound impact on lawmakers, bank regulators, banks' systems of corporate governance, and financial economists and macroeconomists. The great majority of Dodd-Frank's provisions relate to systemic issues involving risk management, capital planning, liquidity management, avoiding financial institutions' disorderly failure, and TBTF more generally in some form or fashion.[83] They are animated by a desire to avoid future taxpayer-funded bailouts.

6.2.8.1 Pre-GFC focus on safety and soundness of individual banks

Policymakers realized that prudential regulation had been too preoccupied with the safety and soundness of individual banks by seeking to make regulatory capital move more closely in accord with banks' own calculation of economic capital.[84] In addition, firms' efforts to remain solvent in a crisis through asset sales, reducing loans to good credits, or requiring more collateral ultimately undermines

---

81 *This Time Is Different* 144.

82 Franklin Allen and Douglas Gale, 'Financial contagion' (2000), 108 *Journal of Political Economy* 1, 2. See Ben Bernanke and Mark Gertler, 'Agency Costs, Net Worth, and Business Fluctuations' (March 1989), 79 *American Economic Review* 14–31.

83 This statement is also true of Title X, which created the Consumer Financial Protection Bureau (CFPB). Predatory retail lending to millions of borrowers who could not afford their mortgage payments was a contributing systemic risk factor in the GFC.

84 Brunnermeier, *Fundamental Principles* 6.

the financial system's stability.[85] Before the GFC, prudential regulation largely ignored interconnections between financial institutions resulting in CCR. Another example of myopia was regulators' lack of awareness of systemic risks from the rapidly increasing reliance on securitization throughout the financial markets.[86]

6.2.8.2 Objective of new macro-prudential framework to internalize systemic risks

The new framework of macro-prudential bank regulation reflects regulators' understanding of the key risks revealed in the three phases outlined in this chapter[87] and a deeper understanding of the concepts of systemic risk and TBTF. The primary macro-prudential regulatory objective of Basel III/Dodd-Frank is to compel financial conglomerates to internalize the negative externalities that they impose on the financial system due to failures as both *going* and *gone* concerns. The former involves firms' excessive balance sheet shrinkage following a financial crisis and the latter, potential market instability from their failure and taxpayer-funded rescues. Where firms' practices do not lead them to internalize these costs, regulators seek to understand why, and to regulate and supervise them accordingly.[88]

6.2.8.3 Systemic risk coordinators in the US, UK, EU, and globally

The GFC brought home the importance of coordinating regulatory responses in modern financial crises, which invariably involve both banking and capital market instability, and the critical need for international coordination in light of the globally integrated financial system. In the US, the primary financial agency officials worked relatively well together in crafting *ad hoc* solutions in the rapidly escalating crisis. Coordination was much less successful in Europe, in both the GFC and the subsequent sovereign debt crisis. Authorities in the world's major financial markets realized that such coordination needed to be systematized and formalized.

Dodd-Frank created FSOC to coordinate systemic risk oversight and designate certain large financial conglomerates by supermajority vote as 'systemically important financial institutions' (SIFIs), a defined term in the statute.[89] FSOC has ten voting members, which include the heads of the major federal financial regulators and the Treasury Secretary, acting as chair. FSOC is charged with proactively detecting, and recommending measures to prevent, potential risks to the

---

85 Kenneth French and others, *The Squam Lake Report: Fixing the Financial System* (Princeton University Press: 2010) 135.

86 Ibid. 136.

87 Phase I (§ 6.2.5); Phase II (§ 6.2.6); Phase III (§ 6.2.7).

88 Samuel Hanson, Anil Kashyap, and Jeremy Stein, 'A macroprudential approach to financial regulation' (Winter 2011), 25 *Journal of Economic Perspectives* 3, 5.

89 Dodd-Frank also authorizes FSOC to designate 'financial market utilities' (FMUs), such as the Chicago Mercantile Exchange, Inc., as SIFIs, of which there are eight. FMUs undertake clearance and settlement of cash, securities, and derivatives transactions. Several FMUs are central counterparties that clear trades in their specialized markets.

stability of the US financial system.[90] Financial institutions FSOC designates as SIFIs are subject to FRB supervision and EPS, Dodd-Frank's prudential regulatory requirements for financial conglomerates. FSOC's global counterpart, the FSB, monitors and makes recommendations regarding systemic risk globally and coordinates national authorities and standard-setting organizations with the aim of strengthening and maintaining the stability of the international financial markets.

FSOC is one of the primary mechanisms for regulating TBTF. It is also one of the only devices under Dodd-Frank for regulating the shadow-banking system. FSOC's interagency coordinating role is especially important in light of the US's highly fragmented, institutional supervisory structure. However, FSOC's record in regulating non-bank SIFIs is less than stellar. It designated four non-bank financial conglomerates as SIFIs, but none of these remains so designated.[91] BHCs with $250 billion in assets are automatically SIFIs under Dodd-Frank.

Globally, coordination among regulators to mitigate systemic risk is also not well institutionalized. In the UK the BoE oversees regulation and supervision of systemic risk, but a legally separate body is not charged with this task. The BoE's FPC, with representatives from the BoE, PRA, and FCA, external members, and a Treasury observer, oversees systemic risk issues. In the EU, the European Systemic Risk Board (ESRB), established in 2010, is responsible for the macro-prudential oversight of the EU's financial system with a view to preventing or mitigating systemic risks to financial stability. However, its recommendations are non-binding.

6.2.8.4 Political and organizational challenges involving systemic risk oversight

The experience of FSOC in designating non-bank financial institutions, and subsequently rescinding, all of the non-bank SIFI designations, and the lack of a separate legal entity in the UK, albeit under the BoE's aegis, responsible for systemic risk, and the ESRB's lack of regulatory authority, underscores the challenges facing supra-agency bodies tasked with systemic risk oversight. It is difficult to design an effective supervisory structure accountable for macro-prudential policy. Several factors may contribute to this, including the lack of experience in identifying and measuring systemic risk, specifying goals for macro-prudential policy, or understanding the transmission mechanism of systemic risk.[92]

---

90 Dodd-Frank also created the Office of Financial Research to assist FSOC in assessing emerging systemic risk.

91 FSOC designated American International Group, Inc., General Electric Capital Corporation, Inc., Prudential Financial, Inc., and MetLife, Inc. as SIFIs. However, a federal district court rescinded MetLife's SIFI designation in March 2016. FSOC rescinded GE's designation in June 2016, AIG's in September 2017, and Prudential's in October 2018.

92 Ed Balls and Anna Stansbury, 'Twenty years on: is there still a case for Bank of England independence?' (1 May 2017), VOX CEPR Policy Portal. See 6.2.1.2, which discusses the lack of a unified concept of systemic risk.

6.3 Risk management and compliance expectations for large BHCs

The GFC is widely viewed as a failure not only of financial regulation but also of private-sector risk management and compliance. The BHCs' fragile capital structure, exacerbated by the conglomerates' complex corporate operations,[93] played a key role in these governance failures. By the time the crisis in Phase II began in late summer 2007 it was too late for most financial conglomerates to take preventive measures. These firms were unable to resist the competitive market dynamics. However, certain firms, such as Goldman Sachs, drew in their horns before it was too late, and other firms, such as JPMorgan Chase, had strategically decided not to strive for high market share in subprime assets in the first place.[94]

In response, Dodd-Frank mandates several risk management and compliance requirements for the largest BHCs and FSOC-designated SIFIs and somewhat less rigorous requirements for other large BHCs. The implementing rules are in Regulation YY.[95] In a series of regulatory policy letters and releases that supplement or revise pre-GFC guidance under this regulation, the FRB has spelled out its internal governance expectations for financial conglomerates. Collectively, the FRB guidance serves as a foundation for the post-crisis regulatory program concerning corporate governance. More generally, policymakers seek to establish a forward-looking set of regulatory expectations. Rather than correcting specific risk management failures of the past, the agencies have formulated a broader corporate governance reform designed to enhance conglomerates' ability to detect, and take effective measures to reduce, exposure to new, yet unidentifiable, emerging systemic risks.

A key theme that runs throughout this guidance is the crucial necessity for large BHCs to ensure that business strategies do not exceed the capability of business line management and of the risk management function to effectively contain and control the risks arising from each business line charged with executing its strategy. Risk tolerance must reflect the capacity of the risk management infrastructure.

Most recently, the FRB issued two sets of proposed guidance which this section discusses in detail, one on boards of directors in 2017 and the other on business management and the control functions in 2018. This guidance is based on a comprehensive review of large BHCs' corporate governance practices. The guidance sets forth highly explicit regulatory expectations for these components of BHCs' corporate governance. This guidance is part of the FRB's broader initiative to develop a supervisory rating system for LFIs.[96]

---

93 See § 1.3.3.

94 JPMorgan generally ceased its subprime mortgage origination in fall 2006. From July 2007 through the second quarter of 2008, JPMorgan incurred only $5 billion in losses on high-risk CDOs and leveraged loans, compared with $33 billion at Citigroup and $26 billion at Merrill Lynch. Shawn Tully, 'How J.P. Morgan steered clear of the credit crunch', *Fortune* (2 September 2008).

95 12 CFR Part 252.

96 Large Financial Institution Rating System; Regulations K and LL, 82 Federal Register 39049 (17 August 2017). The LFI initiative would apply generally to depository institutions with $50 billion

6.3.1 FRB guidance on large BHCs' board effectiveness

The FRB published proposed guidance in August 2017 on the effectiveness of boards of directors of BHCs and savings and loan holding companies with total consolidated assets of at least $50 billion, a threshold likely to increase to $250 billion, and non-bank designated SIFIs.[97]

The FRB views an effective board of directors as central to maintaining the safety and soundness and continued resiliency[98] of a firm's consolidated operations. The key thrust of the guidance is to distinguish between the roles of a board and of senior management by focusing on boards' 'core responsibilities' as a key means of enhancing financial stability. The FRB listed five core responsibilities of a board:

(1) Set clear, aligned, and consistent direction for the firm's strategy and types and levels of risk, or 'risk tolerance'.[99]
(2) Actively manage information flow and board discussions.
(3) Hold senior management accountable.
(4) Support the independence and stature of risk management, compliance, and internal audit.
(5) Maintain a capable board composition and governance structure.[100]

The practical objective of the guidance is to ensure that boards maintain their oversight role by not becoming enmeshed in the chore of implementing their own approved strategy and risk management directives. This implementation is the function of senior management.[101]

6.3.1.1 Business strategy clearly aligned with risk tolerance
The primary focus of and priority in the 2017 guidance on effective boards is to ensure that a board's business strategy and risk tolerance are 'clear and aligned'

---

or more in total consolidated assets, a figure likely to be raised to $250 billion to harmonize with the 2018 amendment to Dodd-Frank.

97 Proposed Guidance on Supervisory Expectation for Boards of Directors, 82 Federal Register 37219 (9 August 2017) [FR, Board of Directors Guidance]. In finalizing the guidance, the FRB will likely modify the $50 billion threshold, since Congress in June 2018 enacted amendments to Dodd-Frank's EPS regulation from $50 billion to $250 billion in consolidated total assets but granted discretion to the FRB in regulating BHCs with total consolidated assets of at least $100 billion.

98 The guidance defines 'resiliency' as maintaining effective governance and controls, including effective capital and liquidity governance and planning processes and sufficient capital and liquidity, to provide for the firm's continuity, and promote compliance with laws and regulations, including those related to consumer protection, through a range of conditions. Ibid 37224.

99 This book considers 'risk tolerance' and 'risk appetite' to have an equivalent meaning.

100 FR, Board of Directors Guidance 37220.

101 A leading legal practitioner in corporate governance has stressed the same dividing line between the board and senior management. According to Martin Lipton, boards cannot be involved in day-to-day management. Instead, through their oversight role, directors should satisfy themselves that senior executives and risk managers have designed and implemented risk management P&Ps that are consistent with the firm's strategy and risk appetite. The board should be aware of the type and magnitude of the company's principal risks and ensure that the CEO and the senior executives are fully engaged in risk management. Martin Lipton, 'Risk Management and the Board of Directors' (20 March 2018), Harvard Law School Forum on Corporate Governance and Financial Regulation, at <https://corpgov.law.harvard.edu/2018/03/20/risk-management-and-the-board-of-directors-5/>.

with one another and that business strategy includes a long-term perspective on risks and rewards consistent with the capacity of a firm's risk management framework. Put another way, a firm's business initiatives should not outrun its capacities to manage the risks created by these firms. For example, if a firm expands into a new line of business the board should consider the increased level of risk and the need to enhance control requirements to ensure that the risk management infrastructure can adequately incorporate the new business line.

The board should ensure that its risk tolerance is sufficiently detailed so that senior management can identify strategic objectives, create effective management structures, implement plans and budgets for each business line, and establish effective control functions. When clearly stated, risk tolerance will enable the CRO to set firm-wide risk limits, in the aggregate (by concentration and risk type) and on a granular basis. P&Ps that formalize these processes would promote alignment of business strategy with risk management. A firm's business strategy and risk tolerance are aligned when they are 'consistent, developed, considered, and approved together'. A board should approve 'significant policies, plans, and programs',[102] such as liquidity risk management, if consistent with business strategy, risk tolerance, and risk management. To this end, significant policies, plans, and programs should contain sufficient clarity and allocation of responsibilities to allow a board to oversee senior management's implementation.

6.3.1.2 Information flow
The FRB found in its review that boards are overwhelmed by the quantity and complexity of the information they receive. Its guidance seeks to remedy this weakness.[103] A board actively manages information flow and deliberations so that it can make sound, well-informed decisions. The guidance states that effective boards direct senior management to provide timely and accurate information with an appropriate level of detail and context. Directors should take an active role in setting board meeting agendas so that content, organizations, and time allocation allows the board to discuss strategy trade-offs. If needed, directors can seek information outside routine board meetings. The BCBS 239 guidance on risk data aggregation and risk reporting dovetails with the FRB guidance on information flow.[104]

6.3.1.3 Accountability of senior management
The FRB guidance identifies several attributes of effective boards vis-à-vis senior management. Broadly, boards should hold senior management accountable

---

102 'Significant policies, plans, and programs', in effect a defined term, consist of a capital plan, recovery and resolution plans, an audit plan, enterprise-wide risk management policies, liquidity risk management policies, compliance risk management programs, and incentive compensation and performance management programs. FR, Board of Directors Guidance 37225.

103 In separate, related guidance, the FRB also revised its policy to provide MRIAs and MRAs to senior management rather than to directors in the first instance. See § 2.7.1.1 for a discussion of MRIAs and MRAs.

104 § 6.3.5.1.

for implementing strategy and risk tolerance and maintaining a sound control framework. The guidance specifies a number of actions and activities by a board that can promote these objectives.

First, boards should evaluate senior management's performance and compensation. Second, boards must 'actively engage' with senior management. This entails ensuring sufficient time to hold frank discussions and debate on management presentations, encouraging diverse points of view, and considering how senior management's assessments and recommendations support board-approved strategies and risk tolerance. Third, effective boards translate robust and active inquiry into drivers, indicators, and trends related to current and emerging risks.[105] Fourth, boards should inquire into senior management's adherence to board strategy and risk tolerance, material and persistent deficiencies in the control functions, compensation programs that encourage 'prudent' risk-taking, and practices that emphasize regulatory compliance. Fifth, an effective board sets clear financial and non-financial performance objectives for the CEO, CRO, CAE, and other senior management that are aligned with the approved strategy and risk tolerance.[106]

6.3.1.4 Support of independence and stature of control functions

Effective boards support the independence and stature of the control functions through active engagement on their audit and risk committees. They promote this goal by inquiring into material or persistent breaches of risk appetite and risk limits, timely remediation, and the appropriateness of the annual internal audit plan.

The FRB guidance indicates several ways in which boards can support such independence and stature. Boards should communicate directly with the CRO on material risk management issues; review its risk budget, staffing, and systems; give it direct, unrestricted access to the risk committee; ensure its inclusion on senior management committees; and ensure that risk tolerance and strategy align with risk management capacity after considering the risk management framework in relation to the firm's risk profile, size, and complexity. The FRB gives similar guidance with respect to internal audit.[107]

6.3.1.5 Maintain capable board composition and governance structure

Boards should have a composition, governance structure, and set of practices relative to the firm's size, complexity, operations, and risk profile that ensure it can govern the firm effectively. To this end, the composition of the board should have the appropriate diversity of skills, knowledge, experience, and perspectives that enable it to perform its oversight role.[108]

---

105 Independent directors should be empowered to serve as a check on senior management. As examples the FRB points to a lead independent director with authority to set board meeting agendas or call meetings without the CEO and board chair.

106 FR, Board of Directors Guidance 37225.

107 Ibid. 37225–37226. See § 3.7.1, which describes the key elements in a risk management framework.

108 FR, Board of Directors Guidance 37226.

6.3.2 FRB guidance on senior and business line management of large BHCs

The FRB issued proposed guidance in January 2018[109] on a board's role and responsibilities vis-à-vis senior management and the control functions that dovetails with its 2017 guidance on board effectiveness. The 2018 guidance presents its expectations for both senior management[110] and line management[111] and for the risk management and internal audit functions.

6.3.2.1 Senior management

Senior management has responsibility for managing the firm's day-to-day operations, ensuring safety and soundness, and compliance with regulations and internal P&Ps. Key responsibilities include overseeing the activities of the firm's business lines[112] and the firm's independent risk management (IRM) function and system of ICs. Senior management is responsible for implementing the board-approved business strategy and risk tolerance. In this connection, it should maintain and implement an effective risk management framework and ensure that the firm appropriately manages risk consistent with its strategy and risk tolerance. Senior management also ensures a smooth firm-wide flow of information. In these day-to-day roles, it should base its decisions on a full understanding of the firm's risks and activities.[113]

6.3.2.2 Business line management

The FRB's expectations for business line management's risk management responsibilities and business decision making are to operationalize senior management's directives. Line managers set business and risk objectives for each business line in alignment with firm-wide strategy and risk tolerance. Line managers need to manage information flow upward effectively by explaining how they manage risks consistently with the firm's risk tolerance so that senior managers can act effectively regarding business strategy and risks. In addition, line managers should identify and manage risks stemming from business line activities and

---

109 Proposed Supervisory Guidance, 83 Federal Register 1351 (11 January 2018) [FR, Proposed Guidance on Business Management and Control Functions]. The guidance applies to domestic BHCs with at least $50 billion of total consolidated assets, the combined US operations of FBOs with combined US assets of at least $50 billion, and SIFI-designated non-banking firms. It also applies to savings and loans at the same threshold. FBOs are required to create intermediate BHCs and US risk committees in order to fulfill the FRB's corporate governance requirements.

110 These individuals are defined as the core group of individuals directly accountable to the board of directors for the sound and prudent daily management of the firm. Ibid. 1353.

111 These individuals are defined as the core group of individuals responsible for the prudent day-to-day management of the business line and who report directly to senior management. Ibid. 1353–1354.

112 A 'business line' is a defined unit or function of a financial institution, including associated operations and support, that provides related products or services to meet firm's business needs and of its customers, such as corporate treasury.

113 FR, Proposed Guidance on Business Management and Control Functions 1371. These include staying on top of key risk drivers and trends and material limit breaches; assessing the impact of the firm's activities and risk positions on the firm's capital, liquidity, and overall risk profile; and maintaining robust MIS. Ibid.

changes in external conditions. Managers should understand how risks of their individual business lines affect their business line in the aggregate.[114]

The FRB emphasizes the importance of clearly delineated roles and responsibilities to ensure that the business units act within the approved risk tolerance and within risk limits established by the IRM. Internal controls should demarcate the respective roles relating to business strategy and risk management. P&Ps should clearly define management's authority and align behavior with performance incentives. In addition, managers should ensure that their business lines ensure accountability for operating within internal policies and guidelines and regulations.[115]

Consultation with senior managers on limit exceptions should result in well-informed decisions on whether to accept or reduce risk exposure. Line managers also are responsible for testing controls to ensure that they are managing risks effectively and for remedying deficiencies. As the first line of defense, line managers are responsible for ensuring that controls prevent, detect, and remediate risk management and compliance failures.[116]

6.3.3 FRB guidance on risk management and other control functions

The FRB devotes considerable space to the 'IRM' function,[117] illustrating its increasingly high regulatory expectations regarding risk management. The FRB's proposed guidance builds on Regulation YY, which mandates risk management's independence and appointment of CROs. Even in the context of other recent guidance, IRM guidance is quite prescriptive[118] compared to that for other corporate governance roles. Chapter 3 provides a basic understanding of corporate governance and the principles and elements of risk management that is useful in understanding this FRB guidance. This section also covers the compliance risk function, the CRO, the CAE, and ICs, all of which support or otherwise promote the IRM function.

6.3.3.1 Overall objective of the IRM

The overall objective of IRM is to provide an objective, critical assessment of risks and ensure that a firm's business strategies remain aligned with its stated risk tolerance.[119] The FRB guidance covers three areas of IRM's remit: risk tolerance and limits; risk identification, measurement, and assessment; and risk reporting.

---

114 Ibid. 1358.

115 Ibid. 1359.

116 Ibid. 1358.

117 The FRB's defined term for risk management is 'independent risk management'. This book uses the term risk management while discussing the attributes that contribute to its independence. It assumes this defined term does not alter the FRB's overall substantive guidance on this topic.

118 Nevertheless, the FRB states that except for CRO and CAE roles, the guidance does not 'purport to prescribe in detail the governance structure for a firm's IRM and controls'. FR, Proposed Guidance on Business Management and Control Functions 1359.

119 Ibid.

6.3.3.2 IRM: risk tolerance and limits[120]

IRM should evaluate whether the firm's risk tolerance appropriately captures the firm's material risks and confirm that the risk tolerance is consistent with the capacity of the risk management framework. This specifically involves assessment whether the firm has sufficient resources and infrastructure. Notably, the FRB states that IRM should separately evaluate the firm's risk tolerance, which the board presumably has already approved,[121] to ensure it appropriately captures material risks and aligns with the firm's strategy and corresponding business activities. IRM should additionally evaluate the risk tolerance to determine whether it:

- addresses risks under normal and stressed conditions and considers changes in the risk environment;
- includes risks associated with the firm's revenue generation and other aspects of risks inherent to the business, such as compliance, IT, and cybersecurity;
- incorporates realistic risk and reward assumptions that, for example, do not overestimate expected returns from business activities or underestimate risks associated with business activities; and
- guides the firm's risk-taking and risk mitigation activities.

IRM should also determine that enterprise-wide risk limits are consistent with the firm's risk tolerance for the firm's full set of risks. In addition, it should ensure assignment of clear, relevant, and current limits to specific risk types, business lines, legal entities, jurisdictions, geographical areas, concentrations, and products or activities that correspond to the firm's risk profile.[122] Quantitative risk limits can relate to earnings, assets, liabilities, capital, or liquidity, among other areas. Qualitative limits can relate to other areas such as constraining business in a specified country.

The FRB states that, where possible, risk limits should:

- consider the range of possible external conditions;
- consider firm-wide aggregation and interaction of risks;
- be consistent with the firm's financial and non-financial resources; and
- reinforce compliance with regulation and consistency with supervisory expectations.

IRM monitoring should be ongoing. Thus, IRM should update risk limits, particularly when the firm's risk tolerance is updated, its risk profile changes, or

---

120 This guidance is found at ibid. 1360–1361.

121 Several groups in the firm, including IRM, provide input and advice to the board in the approval process for the risk tolerance.

122 The guidance gives several examples, including single counterparty credit exposures and funding concentrations. FR, Proposed Guidance on Business Management and Control Functions 1361.

external conditions change. In addition, IRM should identify significant trends in risk levels to evaluate whether risk-taking and risk management practices are consistent with the firm's strategic objectives.

6.3.3.3 IRM: risk identification, measurement, and assessment[123]

IRM should identify and measure current and emerging risks within and across business lines, and by legal entity or jurisdiction, as necessary. If quantitative risk assessment is difficult, IRM should do so qualitatively. Risk identification and assessment should be ongoing to reflect changes in exposures, business activities, the broader operating environment, and regulatory expectations.

IRM should identify risk types[124] and establish minimum identification and measurement standards to ensure consistency across risk types. Standards should be dynamic, inclusive, and comprehensive. IRM should obtain access to information about all risk-related exposures and seek input across the firm in risk identification while not relying on business line information exclusively. In addition, it should aggregate risks across the entire firm and assess them relative to the firm's risk tolerance and assess the likely and potential impact of material or critical concentrations of risks. Furthermore, it should assess risks and risk drivers within and across business lines and risk types.

IRM should analyze any assumptions related to risk identification, including information gaps, uncertainties, and limitations in risk assessments for senior management or the board, as appropriate. An example are new products or business lines. In such a case, IRM should acknowledge areas of insufficient information that limit a complete risk assessment and provide a plan to obtain the necessary information.

6.3.3.4 IRM: risk reporting[125]

IRM should provide the board and senior management risk reports accurately, concisely, and in a timely manner, conveying material risk data and assessments and covering current and emerging risks and adherence to risk limits and the firm's ongoing strategic, capital, and liquidity planning processes. Reports should enable prompt escalation and remediation and support or influence strategic decision making. Such reporting should cover aggregate risks within and across business lines.

6.3.3.5 CRO[126]

The CRO's role is to guide IRM to establish and monitor compliance with enterprise-wide risk limits, identify and aggregate the firm's risks, assess the firm's risk positions relative to the parameters of the firm's risk tolerance, and provide relevant risk information to senior management and the board. The CRO

---

123 Ibid.

124 These include credit, market, operational, liquidity, interest rate, legal, compliance, and related risks (such AML/BSA).

125 FR, Proposed Guidance on Business Management and Control Functions 1361–1362.

126 Ibid. 1359–1360.

should escalate issues to senior management and the board when firm-wide, risk-specific, or business line activities do not align with the firm's overall risk tolerance. An example is if risk management capacity is insufficient to manage risks of a new product line.

The FRB stresses the importance of the independence, authority, and stature of the CRO. The CRO must report directly to the board's risk committee and the CEO in order to promote the IRM's stature[127] and independence and must submit quarterly reports to the risk committee. The CRO should inform the board if his or her stature, independence, and authority are insufficient to provide independent assessments of the firm's risk management framework. Also, the CRO should be included in key decisions relating to strategic planning and other areas. To ensure independence from the business lines, the CRO should establish clearly defined roles, responsibilities, and reporting lines. The CRO should also assess whether IRM has appropriate staffing, sufficient authority to identify and escalate material risk management and control deficiencies, and challenge business managers when warranted.

6.3.3.6 Chief audit executive[128]

The internal audit function conducts independent assessments of the effectiveness of a firm's IC system and risk management framework. The board should appoint a CAE who has sufficient capability, experience, independence, and stature to manage the internal audit function's responsibilities and the authority to oversee all internal audit activities. The CAE should report findings and audit-related issues to the board's audit committee and senior management.

6.3.3.7 Internal controls[129]

The FRB sets forth two principles governing ICs. First, a firm should identify its IC system and demonstrate that it is commensurate with the firm's size, operations, activities, risk profile, strategy, and risk tolerance and is consistent with all applicable regulation. Business line management, among other parties, is responsible for developing and maintaining an effective system of ICs. A firm should integrate control activities into daily functions of all relevant personnel. The FRB guidance lists several categories of ICs.[130]

---

127 The guidance defines stature, among other things, as the ability and authority to influence decisions and effect change throughout a firm. Ibid. 1359 n. 43.

128 Ibid. 1360.

129 Ibid. 1362.

130 The guidance specifies the following categories:

- P&Ps that set expectations relating to the firm's business activities and support functions.
- P&Ps that establish levels of authority, responsibility, and accountability for overseeing and executing the firm's activities and standards for prudent risk-taking behaviors.
- Clear assignment of roles and responsibilities and appropriate separation of duties.
- Physical controls for restricting access to tangible assets.
- Approvals and dual authorizations for key decisions, transactions, and execution of processes.
- Verifications of transaction details and periodic reconciliations, such as those comparing cash flows to account records and statements.

Second, a firm should regularly evaluate and test the ICs' effectiveness using a risk-based approach, and monitor their functioning to identify and timely communicate deficiencies. Thus, a firm should have mechanisms to test ICs and identify and escalate issues concerning deficiencies. Typically, testing is periodic and monitoring is ongoing. A firm should establish management information systems (MIS) that track IC weaknesses and escalate serious matters to all appropriate parties, including the board.

6.3.4 Board risk committee requirements for large BHCs[131]

Dodd-Frank originally required publicly traded BHCs with at least $10 billion and less than $50 billion in total consolidated assets to have risk committees and an enterprise-wide risk management framework, with more stringent requirements for BHCs at the $50 billion threshold. The Bipartisan Banking Act in 2018 continued to require FRB rules for $50 billion BHCs and *reserved* authority for it to require risk committees for BHCs with at least $10 billion in total consolidated assets. The FRB stated that BHCs in the latter category do not need to comply with the risk committee requirements until it has issued a revised rule. This section thus summarizes the rule provisions applicable to BHCs with $50 billion in total consolidated assets

6.3.4.1 Risk committees of BHCs with $50 billion or more in total consolidated assets

BHCs must maintain a risk committee that approves and periodically reviews the risk management policies of its global operations and oversees the operation of its global risk management framework. Such a framework must correspond to the firm's size, risk profile, and complexity and, at a minimum, include the following components:[132]

- *Policies and procedures.* P&Ps are required for risk management governance, procedures, and infrastructure for global operations.
- *Processes and systems.* These facilitate implementing and monitoring compliance with the aforesaid P&Ps.[133]
- *Risk committee's responsibility.* The committee must include liquidity risk management as per the liquidity rule's specifications.[134]

- Access controls, change management controls, data entry controls, and related controls.
- Escalation procedures with a system of checks and balances in situations allowing for managerial or employee discretion.Ibid.

131 This section covers only requirements for US BHCs. Separate requirements apply for FBOs.
132 12 CFR § 252.33.
133 Such 'processes and systems' must identify and report risks and risk management deficiencies, establish managerial and employee responsibility for risk management, ensure independence of the risk management function, and integrate risk management and associated controls with management goals and compensation structures for global operations. 12 CFR § 252.33(a)(2)(i)–(ii).
134 The BHC's board, among other things, must annually approve an acceptable level of liquidity risk and at least semi-annually determine if the BHC is operating within its liquidity risk tolerance.

- *Corporate governance requirements.* The committee must be an independent board committee with sole, exclusive responsibility for IRM policies for global operations and oversight of the global risk management framework, report directly to the BHC's board, and receive and review quarterly reports from the BHC CRO. The committee must have a board-approved formal, written charter, and quarterly meetings with fully documented proceedings.
- *Member requirements.* At least one member must have experience in identifying, assessing, and managing risk exposures of large, complex firms. The chair must be an independent director.[135]

6.3.5 Regulatory expectations for risk data aggregation and risk reporting

The BCBS has issued guidelines concerning risk data aggregation and risk reporting for large banking organizations that the US banking agencies have yet to implement. Nevertheless, these guidelines form an important source of regulatory expectations for internationally active banking firms. US regulatory expectations for BHCs and intermediate holding companies (IHCs) of FBOs[136] regarding stress testing and living wills are consistent with these BCBS principles. This section covers the most important aspects of these guidelines.

6.3.5.1 BCBS 239

The BCBS issued 14 principles, known as BCBS 239, on data aggregation and risk reporting in 2013. It noted that a key lesson of the GFC was the inability of management of large, complex financial institutions to obtain timely, material information on the risk exposures throughout their firms.[137] Timothy Geithner had flagged a warning in a similar vein in 2005.[138] Shortcomings in data aggregation likely materially contributed to risk management deficiencies highlighted in this chapter during Phase I that preceded the crisis.[139] Leading up to and during

---

The rule provides in granular detail the parameters of required liquidity risk management pertaining to contingency planning and event management, risk limits, testing, and types of acceptable collateral for counterparties. 12 CFR § 252.34.

135 UK and EU regulators focus more on the composition of the risk committee as a whole. The EBA requires members with 'appropriate knowledge, skills, and experience concerning risk management and control practices'. Steve Marlin, 'Bank risk committees: desperately seeking risk managers', *Risk.net* (27 June 2018). Members' skill set can include an understanding of non-financial risks such as geopolitical, reputational, and cyber risk. Ibid.

136 Foreign banking organizations are required to form IHCs in order to operate in the US.

137 Basel Committee on Banking Supervision, 'Principles for effective risk data aggregation and risk reporting' 1 (January 2013) [BCBS, Risk data aggregation].

138 Timothy Geithner, FRBNY president at the time, stated that most firms faced considerable challenges in aggregating exposures across the firm, capturing exposure concentrations in credit and other risks, and conducting stress tests and scenario analysis on a fully integrated bases to gauge exposures generated across an increasingly diverse array of activities. Timothy Geithner, 'Risk management challenges in the US financial system', Speech before the Global Association of Risk Professionals (28 February 2006), at <www.bis.org/review/r060303a.pdf>.

139 § 6.2.5.

the GFC many banks lacked the ability to aggregate risk exposures and identify concentration quickly and accurately at the BHC level, across business lines, and between legally separate entities. This significantly undermined their ability to conduct risk management, with systemic risk ramifications.[140]

BCBS 239's ultimate objective is to ensure that banks have a strong governance framework, risk data architecture, and IT infrastructure.[141] 'Risk data aggregation' involves defining, gathering, and processing risk data according to a bank's risk reporting requirements to enable it to measure its performance against its risk appetite.[142] In this regard, IT systems are of paramount importance to achieve compliance with BCBS 239. Banks need IT and data aggregation capabilities to support firm-wide management of risks.

Aggregated risk reporting is a key need for regulators to identify emerging systemic risks. Improving banks' risk data aggregation capabilities also improves resolvability, such as finding merger partners, often an eleventh-hour but preferable solution to insolvency during a market crisis. National resolution authorities should have access to this information for G-SIBS.[143] The FSB has launched several initiatives to improve data aggregation and reporting for regulatory purposes.[144]

6.3.5.2 Progress in compliance with regulatory expectations under BCBS 239

Progress in BCBS 239 compliance has been uneven. The BCBS noted in a 2017 assessment that most banks had made, at best, marginal progress in implementation of BCBS 239, with only three of the 30 G-SIBs achieving full compliance.[145] In the US, the CCAR and DFAST stress testing, which are data intensive exercises, and living will programs have led the large BHCs to devote considerable resources to enhancements in data governance and reporting, which should bring US banking organizations closer to BCBS 239 expectations. A core CCAR requirement includes ICs to ensure reliable data and information systems. However, as the 2018 CCAR results show, progress has not been smooth.[146]

---

140 BCBS, Risk data aggregation 1.

141 Ibid. 6. A banking group's structure should not hinder consolidated data risk aggregation at any level. Ibid. 7.

142 Ibid. 1–2.

143 Ibid. 1. Moreover, such capability results in efficiency gains, reduced probability of losses, enhanced strategic decision making, and ultimately increased profitability. Ibid.

144 These include a Legal Entity Identifier system and a common data template for G-SIFIs to address key information gaps identified during the GFC, such as OTC bilateral exposures and exposures to countries, sectors, and instruments. Ibid. 2.

145 Basel Committee on Banking Supervision, 'Progress in adopting the principles for effective risk data aggregation and risk reporting' (21 June 2018) 4.

146 The FRB objected to a foreign bank's capital plan due, in part, to material weaknesses in data capabilities and controls. Federal Reserve Board, 'Comprehensive Capital Analysis and Review 2018: Assessment Framework and Results' (June 2018) 24. More generally, certain firms fell short of regulatory expectations in data and IT infrastructure. Ibid. 3.

6.3.6 Supervisory regime for LISCC firms and other large, complex BHCs

The FRB established the LISCC in 2010 to coordinate supervisory oversight of SIFIs. LISCC firms are the largest BHCs and FSOC-designated non-banks.[147] There were 12 LISCC firms as of 9 November 2018. To put this number in perspective, 35 BHCs participated in the CCAR 2018 program. As necessary, the LISCC takes action to increase the financial and operational resiliency of SIFIs in order to reduce the potential of their material financial distress or failure. To achieve these objectives, the LISCC develops both micro- and macro-prudential views of LISCC firms, using multidisciplinary input from the Federal Reserve Banks. This input includes feedback from supervisors, economists, payments system experts, and market analysts; information from horizontal examinations, stress testing, and scenario analysis; and increased collection and use of consistently and timely reported firm-specific data.[148]

6.3.6.1 CCAR, CLAR, and SRP components of LISCC program

The Federal Reserve has four priority areas in supervising LISCC firms: capital adequacy and capital planning; liquidity sufficiency and resiliency; corporate governance; and recovery and resolution planning. The LISCC operating committee oversees the execution of the three horizontal exercises involving LISCC firms and directs resources toward these priorities: the CCAR, the Comprehensive Liquidity Analysis and Review (CLAR), and the Supervisory Assessment of Recovery and Resolution Preparedness (SRP). Chapter 7 discusses the CCAR program in detail.[149] The CLAR is the Federal Reserve's annual, horizontal, forward-looking program to evaluate LISCC firms' liquidity position and liquidity risk management practices. The SRP is the Federal Reserve's annual horizontal review of LISCC firms' progress in removing impediments to orderly resolution. This SRP review is an additional layer of oversight over the 'living will' program.

6.4 Conclusion

Global regulators have developed a comprehensive program that tackles systemic risk on multiple fronts. This chapter has focused on the lessons learned in Phase I that preceded the GFC regarding the deficiencies in risk management and corporate governance practices that contributed to the ensuing liquidity and credit crisis. Those firms that performed relatively well had reduced their exposure to subprime mortgage assets or limited their entry into that market in the first instance.

---

147 FRB, 'SR 12–17: Consolidated Supervision Framework for Large Financial Institutions' (17 December 2012). The Federal Reserve designates LISCC BHCs based on size, interconnectedness, lack of available substitutes for services they provide, and cross-border activities. As of December 31, 2018, there were no non-bank financial institutions designated by FSOC as SIFIs.

148 Federal Reserve Board, 'SR 15–7: Governance Structure of the LISCC Supervisory Program' (17 April 2015) 2.

149 § 7.4.2.

The SSG identified certain governance processes and risk controls of these better performing firms. The guidance on boards, management, and risk management subsequently issued by the FRB and BCBS largely mirror these firms' risk management practices. These firms' internal governance mechanisms ensured that information relating to problems on the ground level moved promptly and effectively across business lines and up to the senior management. They generated asset valuations using a variety of internal and external sources and applied these valuations consistently across the firm. They imposed economic capital charges on business lines, reflecting a genuine attempt to incorporate the underlying fat-tail risks of a given banking or trading book exposure into their risk management framework and within their risk appetite. These internal processes allowed these firms not only to gather critically relevant information on a firm-wide basis but to act promptly to change strategic direction before risks became an existential threat to their franchise.

CHAPTER 7

The capital solution to systemic risk

Risk management and compliance implications

7.1 Introductory overview

The banking agencies have two primary objectives in macro-prudential capital regulation and supervision. First, they want to ensure that banks will continue lending in an economic downturn in order to reduce the severity of a recession. Second, capital regulation should ensure that banks can absorb losses that creditors or ultimately taxpayers would otherwise incur. These two objectives apply to all banks, but special regulatory focus is on the largest BHCs under Dodd-Frank's EPS rules given their outsized role as credit intermediaries.[1] The top ten BHCs hold 44% of commercial banks' total consolidated domestic assets.[2] Given their systemic importance, these firms thus justifiably incur higher capital charges and more comprehensive and intensive oversight than their smaller peers.

The GFC and Great Recession offered policymakers key lessons that inform their approach to these two regulatory objectives. On the first point, the Great Recession underscored the need for additional capital to maintain banks as going concerns to continue credit intermediation. Regulators designed CCAR and DFAST stress testing for large BHCs so that they could continue in this role even in highly adverse economic conditions. On the second point, the inadequacy of capital (and, by definition, high leverage) played a large role in the liquidity and credit crisis of the GFC that resulted in chaotic bailouts by panicked policymakers.[3] A key component of the macro-prudential tool kit is the requirement of additional capital for the large banks as gone concerns to avoid taxpayer bailouts.[4] Another component of the capital solution to systemic risk is liquidity regulation. Although liquid short-term assets are not equity capital, they do comprise a key element in bank's capital structure and are thus treated in this chapter.

---

1 The Economic Growth, Regulatory Relief, and Consumer Protection Act of 2018, Pub. L. No. 115–174 (2018) (Bipartisan Banking Act) generally raised the consolidated total assets threshold from $50 billion to $250 billion. The EPS rules govern stress testing, risk committees, liquidity requirements, and living wills, among other regulation. Regulation YY, 12 CFR Part 252.

2 As of June 2018, the ten largest BHCs, by domestic assets in the US, held $7.47 billion in domestic assets, or 44% of all commercial banks' total consolidated domestic assets ($16.84 billion). Federal Reserve Board, Total Assets, All Commercial Banks, at <https://fred.stlouisfed.org/series/TLAACBW027SBOG>; Federal Reserve Board, Large Commercial Banks, Federal Reserve Statistical Release at <www.federalreserve.gov/releases/lbr/current/>.

3 § 6.2.6.

4 Chapter 8 discusses Basel III/Dodd-Frank's structural solutions to systemic risk.

The chapter proceeds as follows. It first discusses Pillar I's RWA capital buffers, leverage ratios, and liquidity regulation applicable to advanced approaches banks and G-SIBs.[5] In each case the chapter covers the associated risk management and compliance requirements. It then turns to the Pillar II supervisory stress testing regime under DFAST and CCAR, which require a robust corporate governance and risk management infrastructure and related internal controls (ICs) and compliance P&Ps. With respect to the stress testing, it pays particular attention to the FRB's expectations for MRM.

7.2 Additional capital requirements for systemically important BHCs

Dodd-Frank imposes separate Pillar I macro-prudential capital charges. These include the countercyclical capital buffer (CCyB), the G-SIB surcharge, and supplemental and enhanced leverage ratio requirements. The agencies' EPS rules implement these requirements.

7.2.1 CCyB

Advanced approaches BHCs are required to have a 'CCyB'[6] ranging from 0% to 2.5% of RWA above the 8% RWA floor.[7] The agencies argue that cyclical adjustments produce smaller financial stability benefits and higher costs for smaller banking organizations. The countercyclical buffer must be comprised solely of CET1.[8] The agencies have discretion to increase the buffer based on a range of factors indicating increase in systemic risk, including country-specific exposure, credit conditions, GDP, a variety of asset prices, funding spreads, credit condition surveys, and indices based on CDS spreads.

7.2.1.1 Rationales for CCyB
In crafting the buffer, regulators point to two reasons. First, increases in capital during an expansionary phase can increase the resilience of the banking system to declines in asset prices and resulting losses when credit conditions weaken. The larger capital buffer absorbs abnormal losses following excessive credit growth. This helps banks continue to access funding in the capital markets, meet debt obligations, and continue to serve as credit intermediaries. Second, increasing capital in a boom phase may limit excessive credit unsupported by fundamentals.[9]

---

5 Chapter 4 covered advanced approaches banks' capital requirements for credit, market, and operational risk.

6 12 CFR § 217.11(b).

7 Advanced approaches banks have at least $250 billion in total consolidated assets or foreign exposures of at least $10 billion. Only the largest internationally active BHCs are qualified as advanced approaches banks. For the 2018 CCAR, 18 US-based BHCs were advanced approaches BHCs. See §§ 4.3.6–4.3.7 for a discussion of advanced approaches bank capital regulation.

8 § 4.3.4 describes the capital numerator component of risk-based capital ratio requirements.

9 Basel Committee on Banking Supervision, 'Basel III: A global regulatory framework for more resilient banks and banking systems' (1 June 2011) 5.

7.2.1.2 Application of capital buffer globally

Thus far, the US agencies have not imposed a CCyB on BHCs. Only a handful of Basel Committee member jurisdictions have done so.[10] This fact is perplexing in the context of a strong economy in 2018 and an economy that has steadily grown since the GFC, raising doubt about the effectiveness of this discretionary approach.[11] It can be conjectured that powerful political constraints limit agency discretion to increase the buffer in 'good times'. Regulators must give a one-year advanced warning before the buffer can be imposed. A decision to decrease the buffer is effective immediately.

7.2.2 G-SIB surcharge

Basel III/Dodd-Frank imposes a capital charge[12] on G-SIBs, a subset of advanced approaches BHCs, ranging in five buckets from 1% to 3.5% of RWA composed of CET1 capital.[13] The purpose of the surcharge is to compel G-SIBs to internalize their 'systemic footprint'.[14] The rationale is that the largest, most systemically important BHCs should hold additional capital to increase their resiliency in light of the greater threat they pose to financial stability and internalize the costs their failure would otherwise impose on society.

The charge is a function of a G-SIB's individual characteristics related to its size and complexity. The FRB designed the surcharge with a formula that establishes the amount of additional capital necessary so that the expected systemic costs of the failure of a G-SIB are equal to those of a reference non-GSIB BHC that is on the cusp of qualifying as a G-SIB. Calculation of the G-SIB surcharge is based on a 'systemic risk score'. In the calculations the G-SIB's additional capital is a function of its PD.[15]

---

10 These jurisdictions are Hong Kong (1.875%), Sweden (2%), and the UK (.50%). BIS, 'Countercyclical capital buffer (CCyB)' (13 February 2018), at <www.bis.org/bcbs/ccyb/>.

11 With respect to countercyclical regulation, several economists argue that in balancing discretion and rules, the more that regulatory action may provoke opposition from major interest groups the more their application should be based on pre-set, pre-announced rules. Countercyclical armory should be couched in presumptive, rules-based terms. Markus Brunnermeier and others, *The Fundamental Principles of Financial Regulation* (Princeton University Press: June 2009) 57 [Brunnermeier, *Fundamental Principles*].

12 12 CFR Part 217, Subpart H. The FSB annually publishes a list of G-SIBs. In 2018 these numbered 29. Of these G-SIBs, eight are US-based. Financial Stability Board, '2018 list of global systemically important banks (G-SIBs)' (16 November 2018), at <www.fsb.org/wp-content/uploads/P161118-1.pdf>.

13 No global G-SIB is in the 3.5% bucket. JPMorgan Chase is the only one in the 2.5% bucket.

14 A financial institution's 'systemic footprint' is another name for the externalities that it imposes on the financial system. See 12 CFR § 217.400 et seq. Quantifying this cost is challenging to say the least. The FRB has used five criteria in assessing this cost: size, interconnectedness, complexity, cross-jurisdictional activity, and substitutability of the firm's services. Regulatory Capital Rules: Implementation of Risk-Based Capital Surcharges for Global Systemically Important Bank Holding Companies, 80 Federal Register 49082, 49108 (Appendix) (14 August 2015).

15 The G-SIB formula equalizes the expected loss (EL) from a G-SIB's failure to the EL of the reference BHC, such that the EL (G-SIB) = the EL (reference BHC). The amount of the capital surcharge is equal to the amount required to lower the PD of the G-SIB so that the G-SIB's EL equals that of the reference BHC. Ibid. 49108–49116.

7.2.3 Supplementary leverage ratios and enhanced SLRs

An important innovation in post-crisis capital regulation is the introduction of a leverage ratio. There are three categories of leverage ratios. A 4% leverage ratio composed of tier 1 capital, of which 3% must be CET1, applies to all banking organizations for total on–balance sheet assets only.[16] A 3% (tier 1 capital) SLR applies to advanced approaches banks.[17] A 2% (tier 1 capital) leverage buffer under an 'enhanced supplementary leverage ratio' (eSLR) in addition to the SLR applies to US G-SIBs.[18] The two SLRs apply to both on– and off–balance sheet exposures.

G-SIBs thus must maintain a total eSLR of more than 5%, the sum of the 3% requirement and 2% buffer. They must maintain the 2% buffer to avoid limitations on capital distributions and certain discretionary bonus payments to executive officers. In addition, the G-SIBs' bank subsidiaries must maintain an SLR of 6% to be considered 'well capitalized' under the PCA framework.[19] In April 2018 the FRB and OCC jointly proposed revisions to the G-SIB add-on capital charge that would affect the eSLR.[20]

7.2.3.1 Risk management and compliance: SLR and eSLR

The SLR and eSLR capital requirements require valuation of off–balance sheet assets,[21] thus calling for compliance P&Ps and ICs specific to such requirements. However, these processes already should be in place for advanced approaches banks.

7.3 Liquidity regulation

A key lesson of the GFC was the critical need for financial institutions to have sufficient highly liquid assets to withstand stressful periods in the financial markets in order to manage the risks of their asset-liability maturity mismatch. Prior to the GFC, regulators only exercised supervisory oversight over banks' ALM

---

16 12 CFR § 217.10(a)(4), (b)(4). The Bipartisan Banking Act created a leverage ratio for eligible community banks with less than $10 billion in total consolidated assets. § 4.3.8.1 covers the 4% leverage ratio.

17 12 CFR § 217.10(a)(5), (c)(4).

18 12 CFR § 217.11(d). As of this book's writing, US regulators were considering revisions to the SLR rule that would replace the fixed leverage standard with a standard tied to a particular G-SIB's risk-based capital surcharge, which is based on the firm's individual characteristics. 'Regulatory Capital Rules: Regulatory Capital, Enhanced Supplementary Leverage Ratio Standards', 83 Federal Register 17317 (19 April 2018) [FR, Regulatory Capital Rules].

19 § 5.5 discusses the PCA program.

20 The proposed rule would revise the eSLR for US G-SIBs from the 2% buffer to 50% of the G-SIB capital surcharge to 'retain a meaningful calibration of the [eSLR] standards while not discouraging firms from participating in low-risk activities'. At the BHC level, the 2% buffer would equal one half of the firm's capital surcharge. The rule would similarly revise the current 6% requirement for subsidiaries of G-SIBs that are regulated by the FRB and OCC. FR, Regulatory Capital Rules 17317–17327.

21 The rule imposes specific requirements relating to such valuation. Advanced approaches banks and G-SIBs must use the potential future exposure method of valuation.

of this aspect of liquidity transformation.[22] Liquidity is one of the six CAMELs rating components. But no Pillar I rules directly regulated the size or composition of banks' liquid assets.

The maturity mismatch is an unavoidable element of the banking business model. To maximize NII, banks must balance the need for low-yielding highly liquid assets such as cash and US Treasury securities to cover deposit withdrawals against the business logic of making substantial investments in high-yielding, often illiquid assets such as loans. Banks make this determination in the context of their risk-return optimization analysis, which is conditioned by the federal implicit and explicit backstops, including the right to access the Federal Reserve's discount window for liquidity reasons.

Policymakers now view liquidity regulation as a core component of systemic risk regulation.[23] They want to avoid in the future such unprecedented emergency actions by the Federal Reserve and Treasury Department that occurred in Phase II of the GFC. The central bank flooded the market with liquidity and stepped into the role as intermediary in maturity transformation through innovative liquidity facilities for the entire financial system.[24]

However, Dodd-Frank's liquidity rule imposes hard-wired constraints on the short-term assets and liabilities mix that banks seek to optimize in determining their capital structure. This introduces yet one more source of tension between the regulatory framework and banks' business model. Analogous to the potential gap between economic and regulatory capital, the new liquidity ratios potentially create a conflict between what banks consider advisable in their ALM strategy and Dodd-Frank's liquidity requirements. This tension creates a risk factor that should be considered in designing risk controls and compliance P&Ps. It also explains the industry's successful effort to garner an amendment to the liquidity rule to include municipal securities, typically a significant portion of banks' existing portfolios, as qualifying liquid assets.[25]

7.3.1 Liquidity regulation's twofold approach

Basel III/Dodd-Frank adopts a twofold approach: a 30-day liquidity coverage ratio (LCR) for 'short-term resilience of a bank's liquidity risk profile' and a net stable funding ratio (NSFR) to ensure longer term liquidity. While the

---

22 See § 1.2.2.4 for a discussion of banks' ALM program.

23 As the BCBS notes, liquidity risk management is of 'paramount importance because a liquidity shortfall at a single institution can have system-wide repercussions'. BCBS, Principles for sound liquidity risk management and supervision' 1 (25 September 2008) [BCBS, Principles for sound liquidity risk management].

24 The Federal Reserve provided several liquidity facilities to the non-bank sector, exchanging short-term, high-quality assets such as Treasury securities for MBS and other assets that became illiquid after the Lehman bankruptcy filing. See § 6.2.6.1.

25 Municipal securities, issued by numerous governmental units throughout the country, are generally illiquid and are exempt from the SEC's registration requirements for public companies. Nonetheless, they now count as level 2B HQLA. 12 CFR § 50.20(c)(3). See § 7.3.1.2

liquidity ratio requirements differ from capital adequacy regulation in regulating the asset side of the balance sheet, both types of regulation place constraints on a bank's capital structure. The BCBS noted that liquidity regulation was necessary to correct a market failure in ALM management since private incentives to limit excessive reliance on unstable funding of core, often illiquid, assets are weak.[26] It noted that many banks viewed severe and prolonged liquidity disruptions as implausible and thus did not conduct stress tests as part of their ALM.[27]

7.3.1.1 Liquidity coverage ratio

The LCR under Dodd-Frank applies to BHCs with at least $250 billion in total consolidated assets or more than $10 billion in on–balance sheet foreign exposure.[28] It is designed to ensure that a bank has sufficient liquidity to withstand a short-term stress in the financial markets. By the end of the period, presumably either management has taken corrective action, or the authorities resolve the bank in an orderly manner while the central bank acts as a lender of last resort.[29] If the situation is still unresolved, the NSFR is designed to provide liquidity for an extended period of time.

7.3.1.2 Structure of the LCR[30]

The numerator of the LCR is a buffer of unencumbered 'high-quality liquid assets'[31] (HQLA) that can be converted into cash at little or no loss of value in private markets to meet liquidity needs over a 30-day period under a stress scenario. The rule specifies three categories of assets, with the topmost tier consisting of the most liquid assets with haircuts at progressively higher percentages applied in the two lower tiers.[32] The denominator is stress tested by both firm-specific and system-wide shocks to determine the net cash outflows. The rule requires the LCR to be equal to or greater than 100%. If a bank experiences actual financial distress, banks may use their stock of HQLA, with the expectation that the LCR will fall below 100%.[33]

---

26 Basel Committee on Banking Supervision, 'Basel III: the liquidity coverage ratio and liquidity risk monitoring tools' (7 January 2013) 1 [BCBS, Liquidity coverage ratio].

27 BCBS, Principles for sound liquidity risk management 1–2.

28 The rule also applies to consolidated depository subsidiaries with at least $10 billion in total assets. A modified version applies to certain S&L holding companies with at least $50 billion in consolidated total assets.

29 BCBS, Liquidity coverage ratio 4.

30 This summary is based on 12 CFR Part 249.

31 Such assets consist of central bank reserves and government and corporate debt that can be converted easily and quickly into cash.

32 Level 1 assets consist of reserves held at Federal Reserve Banks and Treasury securities and securities backed by the full faith and credit of the US, with no restrictions. Level 2A (15% haircut) and Level 2B assets (50% haircut) are capped at 40% of a bank's HQLAs. The inflows are capped at 70% of outflows.

33 The ratio is defined as LCR = HQLA/total net liquidity outflows (defined as the bank's projected cash flows minus projected cash inflows over 30 days) ≥ 100%.

The BCBS has stressed that the LCR rule establishes a minimum level of liquidity for internationally active banks and that banks are expected to meet the standard as well as adhere to principles for sound liquidity management.[34]

7.3.1.3 Proposed net stable funding ratio

The NSFR, which is still in the proposal stage,[35] is designed to ensure that banks have a sustainable funding structure that will reduce the likelihood that disruptions to their regular sources of funding will erode their liquidity position in a way that would increase the risk of their failure and potentially lead to broader systemic stress.[36] As rationale for the rule, regulators point to the extended period of erosion of funding structures in the GFC, beginning in summer 2007 when problems surfaced in the subprime mortgage market.

Mandating high-quality liquidity for an extended period is problematic if banks are to continue their role in credit extension. Requiring HQLA for longer than 30 days is expensive. The NSFR would require that banking institutions maintain a sound funding structure over one year in an extended firm-specific stress scenario. The NSFR's proposed structure is similar to the LCR's. A bank's available amount of stable funding must equal or exceed 100%.[37]

7.3.2 *Liquidity regulation risk management and compliance*

The LCR adds a layer of complexity on top of an already complex daily risk management exercise under banks' existing ALM program. Moreover, the liquidity rules insert themselves into, and place significant constraints on, a business model in which banks seek to maximize their NII.[38] The incentive to maximize NII can lead to compliance deficiencies without strong risk management controls and their related compliance P&Ps.

The BCBS has provided guidance on the risk management and supervision of liquidity and funding risk. Key principles for a bank's risk management include[39] establishing a 'liquidity risk tolerance' appropriate for its business strategy (Principle 2); incorporating liquidity costs, benefits, and risks in internal

---

34 BCBS, Liquidity coverage ratio 2. The BCBS has also observed that many banks most exposed to liquidity risk in the GFC did not have an adequate framework that accounted satisfactorily for liquidity risks posed by individual products and business lines and that incentives were misaligned with their overall risk tolerance. BCBS, Principles for sound liquidity risk management 1.

35 The Trump administration has halted its implementation so that it can be reassessed and calibrated. See Department of the Treasury, 'A financial system that creates economic opportunities: banks and credit unions' 13 (June 2017) [Treasury Department, report on bank regulation]. It also has not been implemented elsewhere. In the EU, the EBA monitors NSFR compliance with the current Basel III standards.

36 Basel Committee on Banking Supervision, 'Basel III: the net stable funding ratio' (31 October 2014) 1.

37 The NSFR is defined as the amount of available stable funding relative to the amount of required stable funding. Ibid. 2.

38 This is one of the reasons why the industry has pushed back on the rollout of the NSFR. See Treasury Department, report on bank regulation 13.

39 BCBS, Principles for sound liquidity risk management 2–3.

pricing, performance measurement, and new product approval for all significant business activities (Principle 4); establishing a sound process to identify, measure, monitor, and control liquidity risk (Principle 5); conducting regular stress tests for a variety of short-term and protracted scenarios (Principle 10); and establishing a formal contingency funding plan (Principle 11).

7.4 Pillar II stress testing programs

The stress testing programs are the cornerstone of Pillar II bank capital regulation and supervision for the large BHCs. The current stress testing regime evolved from previous experience with stress testing, most notably the Federal Reserve's highly effective stress test, the Supervisory Capital Assessment Program (SCAP), in spring 2009.[40] Stress testing's overall objectives are to ensure banks have sufficient loss-absorbing capital in a severe economic downturn to continue lending and to avoid insolvency. The tests are also forward looking. Banks make projections of losses and asset valuations based on scenarios and shocks that reflect evolving economic conditions such as the impact of the US 2017 tax cut and emerging threats such as cybersecurity incidents.[41]

7.4.1 Overview of CCAR and DFAST

BHCs, depending on their size, must comply with one or two sets of stress test programs, the DFAST and the CCAR program. Both DFAST and CCAR are applied at the consolidated, BHC level. This integrated, firm-wide approach reflects the regulators' concern that risks that can interfere with regulatory objectives are not isolated in a BHC's bank subsidiaries. All three banking agencies run, and have issued rules for, the DFAST program, still one more example of the inefficiencies of the US's fragmented institutional supervisory structure.

The key distinction between DFAST and CCAR is that unlike CCAR, DFAST is not a capital-planning exercise by banks. The primary agency under DFAST cannot make a binary decision to allow or reject a BHC's ability to execute its capital plan, although a poor performance may result in an unfavorable supervisory decision to require more capital.

---

40 The Federal Reserve created SCAP to stress test BHCs with over $100 billion in total assets, 19 US BHCs in all. It specified an adverse scenario and calculated loss and revenue estimates for each BHC using its own model and detailed portfolio information provided by each BHC. It ran SCAP on a trading book and banking book level, with expected losses arising from each unique bank portfolio gauged against minimum required capital ratios. The 19 banks needed only $185 billion of additional capital. SCAP was highly successful in its objective of restoring confidence in the country's largest banks and helped to ensure that stress testing would become a core programmatic requirement for the large BHCs. William Dudley, 'U.S. experience with bank stress tests', Remarks at the Group of 30 plenary meeting, Bern, Switzerland (28 May 2011), at <www.newyorkfed.org/newsevents/speeches/2011/dud110627>.

41 Greg Gelzinis, 'The Fed's proposed stress testing changes are a mixed bag', Center for American Progress (20 March 2018). This article provides a good analysis of the FRB's proposals to refine and increase transparency in the CCAR testing program.

7.4.2 CCAR

CCAR,[42] a program developed and run only by the Federal Reserve but not mandated by Dodd-Frank, assesses the capital adequacy and planning of large US financial institutions under quantitative and qualitative assessment criteria. It requires 'large and non-complex firms'[43] with at least $100 billion in total consolidated assets to submit capital plans and demonstrate an ability to meet minimum regulatory capital requirements as part of CCAR's quantitative exercise. These firms are not subject to the qualitative component.[44] The Federal Reserve's expectations increase as the size and complexity of the firms increase. LISCC firms and other large and complex firms[45] are subject to both the quantitative and qualitative components. The Federal Reserve can object to their capital plans on the basis of either assessment. It is expected that the FRB will amend its CCAR rules to be generally consistent with the Bipartisan Banking Act, which made substantial amendments to Dodd-Frank's provisions governing DFAST.

In the *qualitative* component, LISCC and other large and complex firms are required to create and run their own models and scenarios that correspond to their risk profile. This component does not apply to large and non-complex firms. In the *quantitative* component, also called a supervisory test, the Federal Reserve conducts an independent supervisory assessment of a BHC using its own internally developed model. In effect, this component serves as a quantitative benchmark for assessing the BHC's own modeling output and capital levels under the three baseline, adverse, and severely adverse scenarios. These firms need to pass *both* CCAR's qualitative and quantitative components in order to avoid rejection and carry out their capital plan. If the Federal Reserve objects to a firm's capital plan, it can only make capital distributions that the Federal Reserve has not objected to in writing and must resubmit their plans after 'substantial remediation' of the deficiencies that led to the objection.

BHCs are fully committed to passing the CCAR exercise and make substantial investments to do so. Rejection of a capital plan has dire consequences. The inability to issue stock dividends and make buybacks and other capital distributions has a direct, negative impact on a BHC's stock price and executive compensation on which it is based. BHCs are required to publish the test results. In addition, the FRB publishes results for each BHC and the test outcomes.[46]

---

42 The FRB issued a capital plan rule to govern CCAR. 12 CFR § 225.8 et seq.

43 These are BHCs or US IHCs of FBOs that (1) have average total consolidated assets of $50 billion or more, but less than $250 billion; (2) have average total non-bank assets of less than $75 billion; and (3) are not US global systemically important banks.

44 The qualitative and quantitative components are discussed in detail in § 7.4.2.1 and § 7.4.2.2, respectively.

45 These are non-LISCC BHCs and IHCs with $250 billion or more in total consolidated assets or average total non-bank assets of $75 billion or more. See Federal Reserve Board, 'Comprehensive capital analysis and review 2018: assessment framework and results' (June 2018) 1.

46 These disclosures are intended in part to exert market discipline on BHC management in accord with Pillar III.

7.4.2.1 CCAR's qualitative component

The core element of CCAR's qualitative component and CCAR as a whole is the Federal Reserve's assessment of the robustness of a BHC's corporate governance framework, risk management and compliance systems, ICs, and the BHC's ability to accurately capture its own risk profile and effectively translate this internal evaluation into a capital plan appropriate to this risk profile. Within this context, the Federal Reserve's focal point is the firm's MRM program.[47] Effective MRM will reflect effective risk management, internal audit, and compliance within a robust corporate governance system. Modeling assumptions must accurately capture the unique existing and emerging risks of the BHC's multiple bank and non-bank business lines. It is for this reason that CCAR is an intensive, collaborative, integrated risk management exercise. It is a very costly, in labor and time commitments.

CCAR's emphasis is on the BHC's *own ability* in company-run tests to do capital planning in determining how much it can prudently pay out in capital distributions. In the words of William Dudley in 2011, then-president of the Federal Reserve Board of New York (FRBNY), if only supervisory tests were run, 'we would be in the position of a parent who shows his child how to solve each problem in her homework – and never discovers whether the child can do the work on her own or not'.[48] The FRB walks a fine line in the level of transparency in its CCAR guidance. It wants to ensure CCAR is genuinely a *learning* exercise rather than an opportunity for firms to *model to* regulatory expectations.[49]

7.4.2.2 CCAR's quantitative component

Under the quantitative component, the Federal Reserve assesses whether firms have sufficient capital to continue operating and lending to creditworthy households and businesses throughout times of economic and financial market stress, even after making all planned capital distributions. The supervisory stress models used in the quantitative component are highly resource intensive 'bottom-up' models that the Federal Reserve developed using detailed industry data, including loan level data for the loan book, which are then applied to each bank's portfolio. The objective is to improve banks' ability to understand and measure risks and supervisors' ability to understand the firm's risks and the risks in the banking system as a whole.[50]

---

47 Federal Reserve Board and Office of Comptroller of the Currency, 'SR 11–7: Model Risk Management', Attachment (4 April 2011) [SR 11–7, MRM]. § 7.5 covers MRM under CCAR.

48 William Dudley, 'U.S. experience with bank stress tests', Remarks at the Group of 30 plenary meeting, Bern, Switzerland (28 May 2011), at <www.newyorkfed.org/newsevents/speeches/2011/dud110627> [Dudley, SCAP].

49 Nellie Liang, a former Fed official who played a key role in creating the stress test process after the GFC, cautioned that disclosing too much information to banks could turn the tests into an ineffective 'take-home exam'. Alan Rappeport and Binyamin Appelbaum, 'A tale of two Washingtons awaits Wall Street banks', *New York Times* (9 November 2018).

50 Franklin Allen et al (eds.), 'Enhancing prudential standards in financial institutions' (3 December 2014) 13–14.

7.4.3 DFAST

DFAST[51] requires BHCs with at least $250 billion in total consolidated assets and all G-SIBs to undergo supervisory stress tests annually and undertake company-run stress tests[52] periodically,[53] using its baseline and severely adverse scenarios for both.[54] BHCs with at least $100 billion in total consolidated assets but less than $250 billion no longer are required to undertake company-run stress tests but must undergo supervisory stress tests on a periodic basis. BHCs that do not meet the $100 billion threshold are exempt from DFAST. These thresholds reflect changes made by the Bipartisan Banking Act to Dodd-Frank and have various transition periods before they become effective.

DFAST's company-run stress tests differ in kind from the BHC's modeling in the CCAR qualitative component, but to some extent serve the same objectives.[55] DFAST incorporates a bank's capital plan based on recent dividend levels and does not incorporate share buy-backs.

7.4.4 Risk management and compliance expectations under CCAR and DFAST

Both the CCAR and DFAST exercises involve substantial risk management and compliance expectations. However, by far the greatest expectations are those under CCAR's qualitative component. CCAR requires a huge undertaking in IT infrastructure and staffing for the banks in data governance, MRM, and associated ICs. The Federal Reserve calculates its own projections of a firm's balance sheet, RWAs, net income, and resulting regulatory capital ratios under its scenarios using data on firms' financial conditions and risk characteristics provided by the firms and a set of models developed or selected by the Federal Reserve.

The FRB's overriding expectation under both stress testing programs is that BHCs have capital sufficient to withstand a 'severely adverse' operating environment and continue to be able to lend to households and businesses, maintain operations and ready access to funding, and meet obligations to creditors and counterparties.[56]

---

51 Dodd-Frank, Section 165(i)(1)-(2). The FRB's DFAST rules are at 12 CFR 252.41 et seq.

52 Supervisory stress tests are based on models and assumptions developed by the Federal Reserve rather than models the banks have themselves developed.

53 Dodd-Frank, as amended by the Bipartisan Banking Act, does not define 'periodic' but leaves the frequency of testing to the FRB's determination.

54 The Bipartisan Banking Act raised the threshold from $50 billion to $250 billion. The regulatory thresholds discussed in this section also apply to savings and loan holding companies and savings associations unless otherwise indicated. The Bipartisan Banking Act also eliminated the middle, 'adverse', scenario.

55 The results of the company-run stress tests help the agencies to assess whether the BHCs have robust, forward-looking capital planning processes that account for their unique risks and have sufficient capital to continue operations throughout economic downturns and during financial turmoil. See 'FDIC: Annual Stress Test', 77 Federal Register 62417, 62420 (15 October 2012).

56 Federal Reserve Board, 'Dodd-Frank Act stress test 2018: supervisory stress test methodology and results' (June 2018) iii.

7.4.4.1 Internal modeling runs under qualitative CCAR component

CCAR requires BHCs to develop their own models to run the three FRB-provided scenarios over a nine-quarter period – a baseline, adverse, and severely adverse macro scenario – employing 28 variables, including unemployment rates, asset prices, interest rates, GDP, inflation, and foreign exchange rates.[57] BHCs must also conduct model runs using scenarios they have created that are tailored to their own risks and exposures. The forecasted projection of revenues, asset losses, and liabilities must include data across all lines of business and contain details to the lowest level of account balances created and fully reconciled and consistent across other regulatory metrics and internal management reports.

7.4.4.2 Mandatory elements of a CCAR capital plan

The FRB in its capital plan rule[58] specifies four elements of a capital plan that BHCs must submit. First, the BHC must provide an assessment of the expected sources and uses of capital over the planning horizon that reflects the firm's size, complexity, risk profile, and scope of operations, assuming both expected and stressful conditions.[59] These estimates are based on scenarios provided by the Federal Reserve and at least one BHC stress scenario. The firm must discuss how it will maintain minimum regulatory capital ratios under expected conditions and the required stressed scenarios and the results of the stress tests required by law or regulation. It must explain how the capital plan takes these results into account. It must also describe all planned capital actions by the firm over the planning horizon.

Second, the firm must provide a detailed description of its process for assessing capital adequacy. Third, it must provide its capital policy. The capital policy is the capital plan approved by the BHC's board, whose approval must occur prior to submission of the plan to the Federal Reserve. Fourth, it must discuss any expected changes to its business plan that are likely to have a material impact on its capital adequacy or liquidity.

7.4.4.3 Typical reasons for rejection of capital plans

The FRB's qualitative assessment criteria emphasize six areas in capital planning: governance, risk management, ICs, capital policies, scenario design, and projection methodologies.[60] Capital plan rejections typically involve multiple

---

57 In addition, BHCs with large trading positions must apply a global market shock provided by the FRB, and BHCs with substantial trading or processing operations must apply a scenario including the default of a large counterparty.

58 12 CFR § 225.8.

59 The assessment must include, among other things, estimates of projected revenues, losses, reserves, and pro forma capital levels, including minimum regulatory capital ratios (e.g., eSLR) over the planning horizon under baseline conditions and under a range of stressed scenarios.

60 Federal Reserve Board, 'Comprehensive capital analysis and review 2016: assessment framework and results' (June 2016) 15.

THE CAPITAL SOLUTION TO SYSTEMIC RISK

deficiencies in one or more of these areas.[61] Reasons for a qualitative objection vary widely. The following are some of the most common grounds:

- There are material unresolved supervisory issues.
- The assumptions and analyses underlying the capital plan are not reasonable or appropriate.
- The BHC's methodologies for reviewing the robustness of its capital planning process are not reasonable or appropriate.
- The CCAR results indicate that the BHC's capital planning process or proposed capital distributions would be an unsafe or unsound practice or would violate a law, regulation, board order, directive, or any condition imposed by, or written agreement with, the Federal Reserve.

7.5 Model risk management under CCAR

Regulatory guidance on MRM is a logical adjunct to CCAR's intensive modeling and risk management exercise. MRM is an industry-wide issue that has relevance well beyond stress testing. The GFC likely would have been much less severe if models used by investment banks, depository institutions, CRAs, and insurance companies had accurately captured financial and economic risks and had been used appropriately. Modeling errors led to misguided decisions by boards of directors and senior management.[62] This section highlights the main points of the FRB's key MRM guidance, SR 11–7.[63]

7.5.1 Background and context

Although SR 11–7 is directed to banks in fulfilling their stress testing obligations, it also has general lessons for all financial institutions' use of models. As the OCC had observed earlier in 2000, all models are prone to error, and thus require procedural checks, by independent parties, to continually identify and eliminate errors. Regulators' expect an ongoing, continuous MRM process to lead to constant improvement in banks' modeling. SR 11–7 requires multiple lines of defense to filter out errors, with model validators challenging developers' models, internal audit assessing overall MRM governance, and ultimately, regulators reviewing the quality of the MRM framework. The FRB has a strong focus on MRM because banks use models to forecast CCAR and DFAST capital positions and are generally relying increasingly on models for managing their various

---

61 Federal Reserve Board, 'Comprehensive capital assessment and review 2018: assessment framework and results' (June 2018) 25.

62 See generally Sisi Liang and Joseph Breeden, 'Keys to success in model risk management for CCAR & DFAST', Prescient Models LLC (2013), at <https://prescientmodels.com/articles/Best-Practices-in-Model-Risk-Management.pdf>.

63 Federal Reserve Board, Supervisory guidance on model risk management: SR 11–7 (4 April 2011) [SR 11-7].

business lines. The potential for losses caused by model errors is an important risk management concern in the banking industry.

7.5.1.1 Capsule summary of SR 11–7

The SR 11–7 guidance breaks MRM into three components.

(1) *Model development and documentation.* Model developers should begin with a clear statement of purpose so that model development aligns with intended use. Developers should document a model's design, theory, and logic and ensure that components work as intended. They should rigorously assess data quality and relevance. Testing is critical in model development to determine that the model is working as intended.[64]

(2) *Model validation.* Validation consists of processes and activities designed to verify that models are performing as expected, in line with their design objectives and business uses. Effective validation helps ensure that models are sound and identifies potential limitations, assumptions, and possible impact. Validation requires a certain degree of independence, performed by people not responsible for development or use.[65]

(3) *Governance, policies, and controls.* Even if model development, implementation, use, and validation are satisfactory, a weak governance function will reduce MRM's effectiveness. A strong governance framework provides explicit support and structure to risk management functions. Governance policies define relevant MRM activities, implementation, resource allocation, and monitoring of compliance with P&Ps. Policies should require maintenance of detailed documentation of all aspects of the MRM framework, including an inventory of models in use, results of the modeling and validation processes, and model issues and their resolution.[66]

7.5.2 Applying principles of MRM

Model risk management is a vast subject. This section identifies some of the key aspects of the discipline.

7.5.2.1 Sources of model risk and role of MRM governance

According to SR 11–7, there are two sources of model risk: bad models and good models used badly.[67] First, a model may have fundamental design errors, such as faulty assumptions, and produce inaccurate outputs in view of the design objective and intended business uses. Second, a model may be used incorrectly

---

64 Ibid. 5–8.
65 Ibid. 9–16.
66 Ibid. 16–21.
67 I owe this crisply apt phrase to Lisheng Su.

or inappropriately or there may be a misunderstanding about the limitations and weaknesses in the model.

MRM under CCAR is fundamentally a corporate governance and risk management exercise. It is one of the most challenging missions for BHCs since all business lines and control groups of the BHC must act in coordination to produce the capital plan analysis required by CCAR under a tight timeline. Soundly designed CCAR models successfully incorporate all relevant material risks. A CCAR BHC typically has hundreds of models subject to MRM under SR 11–7. Regulators expect BHCs to establish model risk committees that approve and oversee models, model development, and model validation, and include senior officials from several groups across the BHC. Other committees include a model risk assessment committee that prioritizes models in risk management and committees to interpret regulators' feedback, in CCAR and other examinations.

7.5.2.2 What is a CCAR model?

A critical threshold question addressed by SR 11–7 is: what is a model?[68] This decision has important implications for risk management's design of ICs and therewith compliance with regulatory expectations. In CCAR, BHCs must give the FRB a detailed inventory of models the BHC uses for capital projections. Given the guidance's broad definition of model, determining what is a model is not straightforward. A bank risks non-compliance with the guidance's requirements for validation, among other things, if bank examiners determine that a one-page Excel worksheet is a model that was erroneously excluded from the CCAR model inventory. Such a mistake involves poorly designed ICs. Responsibility for designating such ICs lies with the governance, policies, and controls group of the BHC and, more indirectly, the internal audit group.

There are a large number of CCAR-specific models. A short list includes loss estimation/revenue and balance sheet projection modeling; RWA projections; ALLL projections; and operational, market, and counterparty risk models. Models that project expected loss on the balance sheet are themselves broken down into PD, LGD, and EAD models. SR 11–7 also notes the increasing importance in the banking industry of models that facilitate business decisions, specifically pointing to the potential for financial losses from relying on models, poor business and strategic decision making, or damage to a bank's reputation.[69]

7.5.2.3 Role of model errors, mistakes, and faulty assumptions in GFC

Mistakes in use of models can involve a wide variety of errors, some of which can have catastrophic consequences. There are many examples of the two categories of model risks summarized in SR 11–7, such as errors in data, assumptions, methodology, model parameters, and estimates, and errors in using the models,

---

68 According to SR 11-7, '[T]he term model refers to a quantitative method, system, or approach that applies statistical, economic, financial, or mathematical theories, techniques, and assumptions to process input data into quantitative estimates.' SR 11-7 3. Further, a model consists of an information input component, a processing component, and a reporting component. Ibid.

69 Ibid. 1.

which in many ways contributed to the GFC. Culpable parties included banks, underwriters, government-sponsored enterprises, the CRAs, and institutional investors.[70] Additionally, a fatal modeling error concerning MBS-related assets that had proliferated throughout the industry contributed significantly to the systemic risk in the GFC.[71]

Faulty assumptions are a key source of model risk because of the large number of external macroeconomic factors and how they interact with a BHC's idiosyncratic risks. These factors are difficult to predict but are integral to developing stress test models for CCAR. For example, choosing an inappropriate macroeconomic stress for calculating LGD in bank-run stress tests can materially impact a BHC's aggregate model output and thus its top-level capital calculation that determines its compliance with capital requirements. The LGD variable, which is highly sensitive to economic cycles, is a key input in many of the models that contribute to this aggregate output.[72]

7.6 Conclusion

Basel III/Dodd-Frank's capital solution to systemic risk under Pillar I relies on a combination of the existing but enhanced RWA framework and a new framework consisting of leverage ratios and liquidity regulation to increase the loss-absorbency of the largest banks' regulatory capital. The stress testing programs governing the large BHCs are the centerpiece of the Pillar II macro-prudential supervisory regime. Those banking firms that have enterprise-wide risk management practices are best placed to incorporate the agencies' heightened and continuously increasing expectations for advanced approaches banks and G-SIBs.

The EPS' and stress testing programs' considerable risk management and compliance obligations had placed smaller, but still large, BHCs at a competitive disadvantage. Rectifying this was an important impetus for the Bipartisan Banking Act of 2018. That legislation, the first major deregulatory initiative since Dodd-Frank was enacted, relieved a significant segment of the banking industry from the most rigorous obligations in two respects. First, it increased the EPS asset size threshold from $50 billion to $250 billion in total consolidated assets, with some level of to-be-determined regulation for banks at $100 billion and above.

---

70 See W. Scott Frame, Kristopher Gerardi, and Paul Willen 'The failure of supervisory stress testing: Fannie Mae, Freddie Mac, and OFHEO', Federal Reserve Bank of Atlanta, Working Papers Series, 2015–3 (March 2015).

71 An analyst at JPMorgan Chase developed a formula based on the Gaussian copula to price credit risks in CDOs backed by subprime mortgages. RMS-backed CDOs are notoriously difficult to price. The formula purportedly allowed banks to gauge the risk of default of multiple securities at once using CDS prices and assumed the correlation between the securities was constant. The use of the short CDS pricing history that captured rising housing prices but not the risk of declining housing prices and an assumption of stable correlation both proved fatally flawed as the credit crisis deepened. See Susan Lee, 'Formula from hell', Forbes (9 May 2009).

72 Federal Reserve Board, 'Capital planning at large bank holding companies: supervisory expectations and range of current practice' (August 2013) 23.

This change removes from Dodd-Frank's most rigorous provisions an estimated 25 of the 38 largest US and foreign banking institutions with US operations holding in aggregate $3.5 trillion in assets.[73] Second, the legislation seeks to constrain supervisory discretion, highly criticized by the industry, in differentiating among firms by specifying criteria that the agencies must apply in imposing EPS rules to banks that fall within the $100 billion to $250 billion total assets bucket.[74] The implications of the Dodd-Frank amendments for financial stability remain to be seen until the next financial crisis.

---

73 Greg Gelzinis and Joe Valenti, 'Fact sheet: the Senate's bipartisan Dodd-Frank rollback bill' (28 February 2018), Center for American Progress.
74 These criteria are capital structure, riskiness, complexity, financial activities, and size.

CHAPTER 8

The structural solution to systemic risk

Risk management and compliance implications

8.1 Introductory overview

Following the GFC, the national authorities with resident financial conglomerates sought to address TBTF through various structural reforms. In the US, Dodd-Frank's structural solution to systemic risk consists of two basic approaches. The first approach is an *ex post* design for an orderly wind down of a failing financial conglomerate through an enhanced parent company capital structure, a new liquidation mechanism, and resolution plans (living wills). This approach enjoys a relative consensus among global policymakers. The second approach regulates firms *ex ante* as going concerns by requiring a change in corporate structure or scope of permitted business designed to reduce the potential negative impact of risky activities on these firms' depository subsidiaries and other entities providing vital financial services. Unlike the first approach, global consensus does not prevail concerning the type of this structural reform. Two versions exist: prohibiting these risky activities (US) or permitting them but walling them off from conventional commercial banking (UK). The EU failed to introduce an *ex ante* structural version due in part to industry resistance.

The risk management and compliance implications of the *ex post* orderly wind down approach are considerable. The 'single point of entry' (SPOE) concept at the holding company level requires capital raising from investors that may be 'bailed in'. Drawing up living wills demands resource-intensive engagement across business lines and the control functions, particularly in the US, where the onus for drafting wills is placed entirely on the private sector. The implications of the *ex ante* approach depend on the version at issue. The Volcker rule, the US version, imposes far-reaching, highly prescriptive regulatory requirements that call for a comprehensive risk management and compliance infrastructure and robust IC environment, with daily monitoring and recordkeeping. The UK firewall approach makes fewer demands on risk management and compliance once the investment is made in corporate restructuring.

The chapter proceeds as follows. It first discusses the *ex post* approach to preventing costly and hastily orchestrated government bailouts of financial conglomerates, consisting of SPOE regulation, the US's Orderly Liquidation Authority (OLA), and living wills. The chapter then turns to the *ex ante* approach. It discusses the Volcker rule in considerable detail not only because of its importance in financial regulation but also for its broader insights concerning US regulatory and supervisory policy. Finally, it discusses the UK's ringfencing approach. Both *ex ante* regulatory approaches seek to achieve the same prudential objective, the safety and soundness of the banking system.

8.2 *Ex post* approach: SPOE, OLA, and resolution plans

Dodd-Frank adopted three major components in *ex post* structural regulation: SPOE, OLA, and living wills. These three components form a relatively coherent regulatory framework for tackling TBTF. The US's living wills regulation appears to place generally more substantial demands on firms' risk management and compliance systems than similar regulation in other jurisdictions. Compounding the challenges of the *ex post* approach, management is asked to plan its own firm's demise. Though forward looking, such planning is foreign to their fundamental role in plotting a growth-oriented business strategy. In contrast, Dodd-Frank's OLA provisions and other jurisdictions' approach to insolvency of financial conglomerates do not require specific risk management and compliance investment or processes.

8.2.1 SPOE and TLAC

The SPOE concept is globally the most prominent among the various strategies for winding down troubled financial conglomerates. Several key national authorities have endorsed the SPOE approach to TBTF. In the US, SPOE prepares conglomerates for the OLA process should it be chosen to avoid the 'poor choice' of bailouts or disorderly bankruptcy.[1] SPOE is structured to stabilize the financial system by maintaining the financial and operational viability of a holding company's operating subsidiaries, thereby enabling them to continue to provide vital services to the financial markets. The SPOE[2] strategy relies on winding down and liquidating a failing systemically important financial conglomerate at its parent holding company level, financed by both regulatory capital and specified forms of long-term, loss-absorbing parent-level debt, termed 'total loss-absorbing capital' (TLAC), in compliance with mandated ratios. This wind down would occur either via the OLA or in bankruptcy court.

8.2.1.1 Mechanics of the SPOE process envisioned by FRB and FDIC
The SPOE proposal provides the legal and operational framework for resolving financial conglomerates through the OLA. Subject to certain conditions, the

---

1 Resolution of Systemically Important Financial Institutions: The Single Point of Entry Strategy (18 December 2013), 78 Federal Register 76614, 17615 [FDIC, SPOE Strategy]. The release does not propose a rule but sets forth the strategy involving the SPOE approach and requested comment. This section is based on the SPOE release.

2 There is also a 'multiple-point-of-entry' (MPOE) strategy in which multiple entities enter into separate resolution procedures in different regions. In the SPOE concept only the G-SIB's top-tier holding company enters resolution.

FDIC would wind down any financial institution[3] whose failure threatens the stability of the financial system. The success of an SPOE-orchestrated wind down depends on a preexisting BHC structure. While the BHC is nearly universal in the US, this is not the case in the EU, which would call for more costly corporate restructuring.

The FDIC would be appointed receiver of only the top-tier holding company of the conglomerate (HoldCo) and would organize a new parent bridge financial company (Bridge FinCo) into which it would transfer the HoldCo's assets, including loans to subsidiaries. It would remove and replace culpable senior management. The FDIC would arrange Bridge FinCo's issuance of new debt and equity securities in exchange for creditors' written-down, transferred claims in the HoldCo, thus capitalizing Bridge FinCo and ensuring its financial viability. Senior unsecured and subordinated debt would not generally be transferred to the Bridge FinCo.[4] Eventually, the FDIC would terminate Bridge FinCo when it no longer posed systemic risk and could be resolved in bankruptcy, either reorganized or liquidated.[5]

Thus, HoldCo's shareholders and creditors, rather than taxpayers, would incur the losses caused by its failure. This arrangement is designed to satisfy Dodd-Frank's mandate that failing financial conglomerates are liquidated with losses imposed on their shareholders and creditors and that market discipline replaces moral hazard in generating stakeholder incentives.[6]

8.2.1.2 Total Loss-Absorbing Capacity and Long-Term Debt

The SPOE strategy relies on a sufficient amount of equity and unsecured debt to absorb losses and adequately recapitalize and insulate the operating subsidiaries. The FRB addressed this component in the TLAC rule,[7] which applies to G-SIBs. The TLAC rule specifies the minimum requirements for the capital structure of G-SIBs' parent holding companies.[8] G-SIBs must maintain TLAC equal to the greater of 18% of RWA and 7.5% of total leverage exposure[9] plus capital conservation buffers above the leverage and RWA components.[10] TLAC is intended to enhance a firm's resiliency and resolvability since preexisting equity is likely

---

3 Title II of Dodd-Frank provides that the FDIC has the power to undertake the orderly liquidation of a financial conglomerate placed in receivership. 12 USC § 5390(a). Title I governs resolution plans.

4 Claims relating to these positions would remain against HoldCo, to be repaid, likely at a loss, from Holdco's receivership estate. FDIC, SPOE Strategy 76618.

5 FDIC, SPOE Strategy 76623.

6 This is not entirely the case. There is a contingent government backstop, an 'Orderly Liquidation Fund', provided for in the OLA law in case funds are not sufficient to provide liquidity for Bridge FinCo. The government would assess the industry to recoup any payments.

7 External Long-term Debt Requirement, External Total Loss-absorbing Capacity Requirement and Buffer, 12 CFR § 252.60 et seq., Subpart G.

8 TLAC is the sum of the G-SIB's tier 1 capital it has issued and eligible LTD.

9 Total leverage exposure includes both on– and off–balance sheet assets of advanced approaches banks.

10 The rule adds a 2% leverage-based buffer and an RWA buffer equal to 2.5% plus the applicable G-SIB and countercyclical buffers. As the buffers decline below these levels, increasing restrictions apply to capital distributions and discretionary bonuses.

to be substantially depleted near the point of insolvency. The G-SIB must hold external LTD, generally unsecured plain vanilla debt and subject to certain maturity requirements, of the greater of 6% plus the surcharge required under the G-SIB capital rule and 4.5% of total leverage exposure. To promote quick and orderly resolution, the G-SIB cannot issue debt that is subject to complex, conditional terms.[11]

Market awareness of the G-SIB's capital structure is a key component of the SPOE framework. G-SIBs must publicly disclose that their unsecured debt would absorb losses ahead of other liabilities. Separate TLAC and LTD requirements apply to the top-tier US IHCs of FBOs.[12]

8.2.1.3 Global acceptance of SPOE approach

The FSB, whose membership includes the world's leading central bank and finance officials, endorsed the SPOE concept for resolving large financial conglomerates. It supports a TLAC but not an LTD requirement. The FSB set forth 12 key attributes for resolution regimes of systemically important financial institutions to ensure their resolvability. The objective mirrors that of Dodd-Frank in seeking to ensure that national authorities can resolve systemically important financial conglomerates in an orderly manner without taxpayer exposure to loss from solvency support, while maintaining continuity of their vital economic functions.[13] Separately, the UK, German, and Swiss national authorities have embraced the SPOE strategy as a primary resolution mechanism.

The SPOE concept may make international resolution more feasible by allowing cross-border operating subsidiaries to continue as ongoing concerns. The SPOE concept potentially addresses concern that foreign authorities would ring-fence their domestic operating subsidiaries to shield them from market turmoil elsewhere, thus imperiling the orderly wind down of the parent G-SIB. International cooperation and adoption of SPOE is essential since G-SIBs typically have hundreds if not thousands of foreign subsidiaries.

8.2.1.4 SPOE and TLAC risk management and compliance implications

In the US the risk management and compliance costs involving the SPOE concept and TLAC requirements are not significant, beyond the need to ensure compliance with TLAC's required capital and debt ratios. Direct costs generally would arise from issuing additional equity and debt and the ICs and P&Ps necessary to ensure compliance with these ratios. In addition, firms must undertake due diligence to ensure compliance with the 'clean holding company requirements'

---

11 These 'clean holding company requirements', among other things, prohibit debt whose contractual terms, complexity, and short-term funding could impede an orderly resolution.

12 The rule applies to US-based FBOs subject to the FRB enhanced prudential standards and controlled by a foreign G-SIB. The amount of required TLAC and LTD depends on whether the relevant resolution regime is based on an MPOE or SPOE approach.

13 Financial Stability Board, 'Key attributes of effective resolution regimes for financial institutions' (15 October 2014) 37 [FSB, Key attributes]. The G20 subsequently endorsed the FSB's 12 attributes.

involving holding company debt. However, the perennial tension between regulatory capital (and, in this case, debt) and what a company considers necessary in its risk-return assessment poses a challenge. As elsewhere noted, the costs of externally imposed equity issuance from management's perspective can be significant.

Restructuring costs and reconfiguration of risk management and compliance systems will be more significant outside the US and UK. Many banking groups do not use BHC structures and among those that do, many parent holding companies do not issue significant amounts of plain vanilla debt. US management typically issues LTD at the parent company level. Holding company-issued debt, which is structurally subordinated to subsidiary debt, would also have higher risk premiums, making the SPOE concept an expensive undertaking.[14]

8.2.2 OLA

The OLA[15] would be expected to employ a structure that the G-SIBs[16] will have put in place, capitalized pursuant to the TLAC rules, with a resolution blueprint detailed in their living wills. The OLA provisions involve an administrative resolution process based on the existing Federal Deposit Insurance Act resolution regime for insured banks.

8.2.2.1 Procedures for triggering OLA

The OLA's elaborate procedure for triggering its effectiveness is colloquially known as the 'three keys turning'. Two-thirds of the FRB's governors and FDIC's board of directors must make recommendations to the Secretary of Treasury that (1) the financially troubled firm is in default or in danger of default, (2) use of insolvency laws to resolve the entity would have 'serious adverse effects on financial stability' in the US, and (3) the effect on creditors is appropriate due to dangers to financial stability if resolution occurs in bankruptcy. If both the FRB and FDIC recommends instituting the OLA, the Treasury Secretary would consult with the President for a final determination. If all these conditions are satisfied, a 24-hour judicial review process would begin.[17] With no court intervention, FDIC would be appointed the firm's receiver.

Critics argue that the OLA is a cumbersome process for determining FDIC receivership if resorted to in the midst of market turmoil and point to the FDIC's limited experience in resolving financial conglomerates.[18]

---

14 Bob Penn, 'Single point of entry resolution: a milestone for regulators: a millstone for banks?', Allen & Overy (5 December 2014), at <www.allenovery.com/publications/en-gb/lrrfs/uk/Pages/Single-point-of-entry-resolution.aspx>.

15 Dodd-Frank, Title II, Section 201 et seq.

16 However, OLA resolution could potentially involve other troubled financial conglomerates in addition to G-SIBs.

17 A court hearing would only occur if, among other things, the firm's board objects to appointment of the FDIC.

18 Most of FDIC receiverships have involved banking institutions that do not approach the size of the financial conglomerates. David Skeel, *The New Financial Deal* (Wiley: 2011) 124.

8.2.3 Resolution plans ('living wills')

Resolution plans are more advanced in the US and UK than in the EU. The FRB and FDIC oversees the living will program in accordance with the US's institutional supervisory framework.[19] The UK follows a twin-peaks structure in its approach to living wills as it does in other bank regulatory matters.

8.2.3.1 Resolution plans: US

Dodd-Frank's first choice in tackling TBTF is an orderly wind down through a firm's own prepared resolution plans under the Bankruptcy Code.[20] The OLA serves as the primary backstop if bankruptcy is not feasible. Congress preferred the bankruptcy process whose end result is privately negotiated to a government-operated resolution if it does not cause financial instability. To that end, Dodd-Frank[21] requires large BHCs to draw up their own blueprint for their possible demise through the bankruptcy process, without governmental support.[22]

The US living will process, which involves capital and liquidity planning, is similar to that of the CCAR and CLAR programs in its requirement to conduct a firm-wide assessment of internal governance issues. Firms must annually submit plans, in this case jointly to the FDIC and FRB. Like CCAR, the process is iterative between the firm and regulator, as both parties seek to improve effective bankruptcy pre-planning. The living will requirement applies to BHCs with at least $250 billion in assets,[23] G-SIBs, and FSOC-designated SIFIs.

The Federal Reserve and FDIC may jointly determine that a resolution plan is not credible or would not facilitate an orderly resolution of the company under the Bankruptcy Code. A 'not credible' finding is only possible if both agencies agree. If a plan indicates a firm is not resolvable in bankruptcy, the agencies may jointly impose more stringent capital, leverage, or liquidity requirements on the company or its subsidiaries. In addition, the agencies may restrict a firm's growth, activities, or operations, but can also break up a financial conglomerate if it repeatedly fails to provide a credible resolution plan. A negative outcome in CCAR, prohibition of capital distributions, is less existential in its consequences.

Regulators, as in CCAR, appear to deliberately avoid full transparency in conveying their regulatory expectations regarding living wills. They do not issue clear directions on how firms can avoid rejection of resolution plans. Whether deliberate or not, this can be an effective supervisory strategy as it keeps banks 'on their toes' by compelling bank management to spare no lack of attention or

---

19 In practice, the living wills supervisory structure is institutional but in theory it is twin-peaks. The requirement applies to FSOC-designated non-bank SIFIs of which there are currently none.

20 Dodd-Frank Section 165(d) requires the largest BHCs and FSOC-designated SIFIs to prepare a resolution plan for a 'rapid and orderly resolution in the event of material financial distress or failure'. The FDIC and FRB issued a final rule pursuant to this mandate. 76 Federal Register 67323 (1 November 2011).

21 Section 165(d).

22 The FDIC and FRB rule is at 12 CFR Part 381.

23 The amendment to Dodd-Frank in June 2018 raised the threshold from $50 billion to $250 billion. The FRB retains authority to require resolution plans for BHCs with at least $100 billion in assets.

cost in an effort to prove that they can wind down a financial conglomerate in an orderly manner.[24]

8.2.3.2 Resource intensive process of 'knowing your structure' for US resolution plans

Analogous to CCAR, where the senior management must have a firm grip on managing its firm-wide risk profile for capital planning purposes, senior management in charge of drawing up resolution plans should 'know their structure'. This is much more involved than it sounds at first glance. They must fully know and understand the legal, organizational, and operational structure of their firm. Financial conglomerates typically do not have integrated legal structures. Critical business lines operate across legal entities and jurisdictions, and funding is often dispersed among affiliates.[25] These features significantly complicate the design of feasible resolution plans.

Guidance in 2018 highlighted six areas relating to a plan's credibility as a resolution mechanism:

(1) *Capital*. A firm's ability to provide sufficient capital to material entities without creditor intervention to continue critical operations.

(2) *Liquidity*. Ability to reliably estimate and meet liquidity needs prior to and in resolution.

(3) *Governance mechanisms*. A 'playbook' for boards and senior management with triggers identifying the onset of financial stress events, allowing time to prepare for resolution.

(4) *Legal entity rationalization and separability*. Firms' legal structure facilitates orderly resolution with criteria supporting a preferred resolution strategy and its integration into daily decision making.

(5) *Operational*. Capabilities to carry out the preferred resolution strategy.

(6) *Derivatives and trading activities*. Derivatives and trading activities can be stabilized and de-risked during resolution without causing significant market disruption.[26]

Living wills involve significant resource commitments. First, perhaps more so than in the CCAR process, virtually all of a firm's operational units must allocate time and consume resources to produce the report submitted to the agencies that comprehensively addresses the areas just listed. Second, faced with their firm's potential forced restructuring, board and senior management need to reconfigure

---

24 Peter Eavis, 'How regulators mess with bankers' minds, and why that's good', *New York Times* (14 April 2016). One senior agency official said that they try not to make the exercise so clear that the banks treat it just like any other compliance exercise. Ibid.

25 European Banking Authority, 'Final report: guidelines on internal governance under directive 2013/36/EU' (26 September 2017) 29.

26 Resolution Planning Guidance for Eight Large, Complex U.S. Banking Organizations, 83 Federal Register 32856, 32857–32858 (16 July 2018). A firm's resolution strategy calls for parent company recapitalization and liquidity support for material subsidiaries prior to a bankruptcy filing. Ibid. 32857 n. 4.

operations and their legal structure, eliminate certain businesses, and otherwise take potentially costly business decisions that do not promote the business strategy and risk appetite that a board has established.[27]

8.2.3.3 Resolution regimes and living wills in the UK

In the UK, the BoE is the resolution authority for a variety of financial institutions, including all banks, building societies, and some investment firms. It is the BoE's responsibility to draw up resolution plans for individual firms, UK groups, and UK subsidiaries of groups outside the European Economic Area.[28] The plans follow three strategies: bail-in, partial transfer, or insolvency. To this end, firms must submit 'resolution packs' that contain information on financial, legal, operational structures and the critical functions the firms provide.[29] The PRA or the FCA, for investment firms regulated solely by the FCA, in consultation with the BoE, decide whether a bank should enter the resolution process and what the process should be.

8.2.3.4 Resolution regimes and living wills in the EU

The EU suffers from national political pressures and different legacies in a variety of supervisory cultures that limit its ability to reach consensus on a uniform resolution regime. For this and other reasons, a EU resolution regime is still in its infancy compared to that of the US.[30] Nevertheless, the EU's policy approach resembles that of Dodd-Frank.

The EU issued the Bank Recovery and Resolution Directive[31] (BRRD) in 2014 whose objective is to ensure orderly resolution of failing banks without disrupting the financial system or real economy by maintaining continuity of a bank's critical functions while minimizing taxpayer losses.[32] It requires banks to formulate recovery plans according to uniform standards. The Single Resolution Mechanism (SRM)[33] provides a framework for bank resolution that consists of the Single Resolution Board, responsible for resolving large banks, and National Resolution Authorities of the member states, responsible for resolving other failing banks in their jurisdictions. These bodies undertake bank resolution when they determine that a failing bank cannot go through normal insolvency proceedings without harming the public interest and causing financial instability.

---

27 This resource-intensive and time-consuming corporate restructuring includes, among other things, rationalizing the corporate structure in the number of entities, establishing a clean holding company so that the parent does not operate critical operational services, and ensuring access to shared services during resolution. PwC, 'Resolution: single point of entry strategy ascends' (July 2015) 5.

28 The European Economic Area includes non-EU members which enjoy the benefits of the EU's single market.

29 Bank of England, 'The Bank of England's approach to resolution' (October 2017) 27.

30 J. Crabb, 'PRIMER: a comparison of EU and US bank resolution regimes' (3 April 2018) *International Financial Law Review*.

31 European Commission, Bank recovery and resolution – Directive 2014/59/EU (2014).

32 Single Resolution Board, Resolution Q&A, at <https://srb.europa.eu/en/content/resolution-qa>.

33 Ibid. The SRM is structured like, and complements, the SSM, which is the framework for prudential bank supervision in the EU. See § 2.5 for a discussion of the SSM.

In addition, the FSB in 2011 established uniform standards for financial institution resolution, subsequently endorsed by the G20. These 'key attributes" primary focus are the G-SIBs. The BRRD has applied the key attributes in the EU context by endeavoring to create a harmonized framework for bank resolution. Among the primary resolution tools under the key attributes are bail-in, business sales, bridge institution financing, and asset separation, with government support only as a last resort.[34]

8.2.3.5 Resolution plans' risk management and compliance issues

Two features of US living will regulation pose challenges for a firm's ability to deliver a 'credible' plan to the regulators. First, a bank's board and senior management think strategically as a going concern but must draft a will for a gone concern. The living will process involves extensive review by legal, accounting, and financial professionals and corporate restructuring experts whose services do not contribute revenue or even reduce future costs other than minimize the compliance risk of a plan's rejection. Second, the plan must ensure that each material entity – particularly each banking subsidiary – has sufficient capital, liquidity, and other resources to act on a stand-alone basis, requiring a potentially costly restructuring of operations. This requirement conflicts with the standard business strategy of creating synergies through centralized cross-affiliate services.

8.3 *Ex ante* approach: reducing the impact of risky activities

Of Dodd-Frank's many structural approaches to systemic risk, by far, the Volcker rule has been the most notable. It is also the most controversial. Lawmakers and regulators globally have endorsed some type of *ex ante* restriction on risky, presumably non-bank activities, although many have not succeeded in implementing this policy. Of these, the US's Volcker rule and UK's Vickers' ringfencing structure, two contrasting approaches, are the most significant. This section discusses both approaches but devotes most attention to the Volcker rule and its risk management and compliance requirements.

8.3.1 *Eliminating risky activities and businesses: the Volcker rule*

Commentators and practitioners have called the Volcker rule out for having the most draconian and detailed compliance requirements of all of Dodd-Frank's regulations.[35] The rule's complexity arises from its definitional layers and its many exceptions to the proprietary trading prohibition. It requires considerable investment in a risk control and compliance infrastructure in order to demonstrate genuine market-making, the major exception to its prohibition on proprietary

---

34 FSB, Key attributes 6–11.

35 The rule as proposed received over 18,000 comments, of which more than 600 were 'unique' rather than form letters. Prohibitions and Restrictions on Proprietary Trading and Certain Interests in, and Relationships With, Hedge Funds and Private Equity Funds, 79 Federal Register 5535, 5539 (31 January 2014). The rule is located at 12 CFR Part 248.

trading. The rule has become the poster child for critics who call Dodd-Frank the full employment act for lawyers and compliance professionals.

8.3.1.1 Overview of regulatory structure

The Volcker rule prohibits what its authors consider to be two major activities in the banking industry that put FDIC-insured deposits at risk. It prohibits a financial institution affiliated with one or more 'banking entities'[36] from (1) engaging in proprietary trading and (2) from acquiring or retaining an ownership interest in or sponsoring a hedge fund or private equity fund. The rule then exempts from these prohibitions market making, underwriting, and risk-mitigating hedging activities. The rule potentially has sweeping global application.[37] The rule that the five agencies[38] issued under Section 619 of Dodd-Frank has a primarily prescriptive, rules-based design that includes prudential safeguards that preserve for the agencies a significant degree of supervisory discretion that heightens compliance risk. Paul Volcker himself was disappointed with the outcome. He noted that one must make a trade-off between the two approaches but endorsed a principles-based approach.[39]

Contrary to some reports, the Volcker rule does *not* reinstate Glass-Steagall, the 1934 statute that had separated commercial and investment banking and that Gramm-Leach repealed in 1999, introducing the FHC structure.[40] The rule's remit is limited in tackling only two segments of the non-banking activities that BHCs were progressively allowed to enter over the past four decades.

Many critics of the Volcker rule attack its ban on proprietary trading as incoherent and misguided. For these opponents, the benefits of the Volcker rule in particular and other structural solutions in general are illusory. Addressing risky activities through capital adequacy and liquidity regulation would be much more effective.[41] Recent deregulatory initiatives address this criticism while keeping

---

36 A 'banking entity' is defined as (1) any insured depository institution; (2) any company that controls an insured depository institution; (3) any FBO; and (4) any affiliate of the foregoing. Section 13(h)(1), 12 U.S.C. § 1851.

37 This is due to the breadth of the 'banking entity' definition, which includes any foreign company subject to the International Banking Act of 1978 and their affiliates. Sullivan & Cromwell, 'Volcker Rule' (27 January 2014) 1.

38 The FRB, OCC, FDIC, SEC, and CFTC.

39 Volcker called the principles-based approach 'trust-but-verify'. Paul Volcker, 'Commentary on the restrictions on proprietary trading by insured depository institutions' (2012) 4–5, at <https://online.wsj.com/public/resources/documents/Volcker_Rule_Essay_2-13-12.pdf> [Volcker, Commentary]. The phrase aptly sums up the revision to the pre-crisis market-based regulatory philosophy.

40 The FHC structure allows BHCs to conduct investment banking and other non-banking activities, generally within separate subsidiaries. § 1.3.2.3 discusses the repeal of Glass-Steagall and the FHC requirements. Unlike some of its foreign counterparts, the Volcker rule relies on 'total separation' of certain risky activities from banking institutions rather than ringfencing these activities in a separately capitalized affiliate. It is debatable how complete this separation is.

41 See Randall Guynn and Patrick Kenadjian, 'Structural solutions: blinded by Volcker, Vickers, Liikanen, Glass Steagall and narrow banking', Davis Polk & Wardwell LLP (19 March 2015), at <www.davispolk.com/files/52559206_1.pdf>. The attempt to substantially eliminate proprietary trading has been particularly controversial among financial economists. Matthew Richardson generally agrees with the Volcker rule's approach to limiting risky trading and investments but puts forward a quantitatively structured safe harbor for market making. See Matthew Richardson, 'Why

the rule intact. The 2018 amendment to Dodd-Frank[42] exempts banking entities with $10 billion or less in total assets and total trading assets and liabilities of 5% of total assets.[43] In 2018 the three banking and two capital markets agencies proposed amendments due to concerns that the Volcker rule is overly complex and should be tailored to reduce compliance costs and clarify application of its provisions.[44]

8.3.1.2 Rule's restriction of activities to 'core' banking activities

The major assumption underlying the Volcker rule is that restricting banking to 'core' activities such as deposit-taking and credit extension would reduce systemic risk. Paul Volcker articulated this assumption in a strong counter-position to the industry's vociferous opposition on the rule's restrictions:

> [T]he comfort for creditors and others inherent in the ability of institutions engaged in proprietary trading to resort to the Federal "safety net" can only tend to encourage greater leverage and risk-taking. Commercial bank proprietary trading is thus at odds with the basic objectives of financial reforms: to reduce excessive risk, to reinforce prudential supervision, and to assure the continuity of essential services.[45]

In a related argument, Volcker said that eliminating proprietary trading would help to reduce the risk-taking culture that had come to characterize the banking industry.[46]

What are 'core' banking activities that would exclude proprietary trading? The question of what is the 'business of banking' has been a perennial topic for bank regulators and industry commentators since the inception of federal deposit insurance in 1934. Congress and the banking agencies progressively dismantled Glass-Steagall's wall separating commercial and investment banking, culminating in its repeal in 1999. Nevertheless, the debate concerning what activities are

---

the Volcker rule is a useful tool for managing systemic risk' (February 2012), at <www.sec.gov/comments/s7-41-11/s74111-316.pdf>. Charles Calomiris, on the other hand, argues that the rule risks the 'destruction' of US global universal banks, and that guess work about what is or is not 'core' in banking has often been wrong. See Charles Calomiris, 'The uncertain dangers of the Volcker rule', American Enterprise Institute (22 July 2013).

42 The Economic Growth, Regulatory Relief, and Consumer Protection Act of 2018, Pub. L. No. 115–174 (2018) (Bipartisan Banking Act).

43 Section 203 of the Bipartisan Banking Act created this exemption to ensure that the rule and other systemic risk regulations do not cover community banks.

44 Following the tailored approach that characterizes much of the Trump administration's financial regulatory reform, the agencies propose to divide up banking entities into three tiers with larger entities holding significant trading assets subject to the greater compliance requirements. Proposed Revisions to Prohibitions and Restrictions on Proprietary Trading and Certain Interests in, and Relationships With, Hedge Funds and Private Equity Funds, 83 Federal Register 33432, 33440 (17 July 2018).

45 Volcker, Commentary 1.

46 '[T]his kind of trading affects the culture of the whole institution ... you've got some highly paid people taking this kind of risk and speculating ... [and traditionally conservative people elsewhere in the bank] want to be better paid too and ... to take some more risk'. John Light, 'The Volcker Rule: An Essential Reader' (10 December 2013) (quoting from an interview with Bill Moyers), at <https://billmoyers.com/2013/12/10/the-volcker-rule-an-essential-reader/>.

proper incidents to banking reemerged in the wake of the GFC, as the extent of banks' expansion into a broad array of market activities became apparent.

Opponents of the Volcker rule argue that the rule's prohibitions do not advance the goal of financial stability by safeguarding the government safety net that supports its banking arm. They point out that, on a relative basis, capital markets activities, including proprietary trading, did not result in significant losses in the financial crisis. Instead, it was long-term holdings of subprime MBS-related assets such as CDOs that caused financial conglomerates to approach insolvency. In actual fact it was lending – unambiguously a 'core' banking activity – following deficient or fraudulent underwriting that planted the seeds of the crisis.[47] Proponents of the rule argue that the risks that emerge in any future financial crisis cannot be predicted, and that proprietary trading is undeniably a risky activity subject to market volatility and conflicts of interest. The recurrent multibillion-dollar rogue trading losses such as occurred in the JPMorgan London Whale trading scandal in 2012 are exhibits to their brief.

8.3.1.3 Volcker rule's proprietary trading prohibition

Section 619 of Dodd-Frank mandates the five agencies to issue rules with a broad brush. The intent of the rule is to eliminate, or drastically reduce, proprietary trading and sponsorship and ownership of certain investment funds, two activities of BHCs deemed by Dodd-Frank to be systemically risky. Section 619 defines proprietary trading as engaging as a principal for the firm's 'trading account', which it in turn defines, among other things, as an account used principally for the purpose of selling in the near term or otherwise with the intent to resell in order to profit from short-term price movements. The *purpose* and *intent* phrases in Section 619 place a heavy evidentiary burden on firms to disprove violation.[48] The rule excludes transactions, among others, that are lending activities, such as a repo transaction, which is in substance a collateralized short-term loan.[49]

8.3.1.4 Volcker rule's prudential backstop

The rule imports a prudential mechanism through its catchall anti-evasion provisions that allows the agencies to enforce safety and soundness concerns even if a banking entity is in technical compliance. A banking entity cannot use an exemption from the prohibition on proprietary trading if its activity results in a 'material conflict of interest, material exposure to high-risk assets or high-risk trading strategies, or … a threat to the safety and soundness of the banking entity or to the financial stability of the United States'[50]. The same provision exists for

---

47 See the discussion at § 6.2.5.4.

48 The provisions exempt the following activities from this prohibition: (1) trading in US government, agency, and municipal obligations; (2) underwriting and market making-related activities; (3) risk-mitigating hedging activities; (4) trading on behalf of customers; (5) trading for the general account of insurance companies; and (6) foreign trading by non-US banking entities. 12 CFR § 248.4–248.6.

49 12 CFR § 248.3(b)(1). Trading accounts are also subject to a risk-based capital ratio under Dodd-Frank's market risk capital rule and accounts for which the banking entity is a swap dealer.

50 12 USC § 1851(d)(2)(A)(ii).

exempted fund investments. The prudential backstop complicates risk management and compliance because firms cannot assume supervisors will not challenge
trading under the market-making exception even if they satisfy the rule's various
prescriptive requirements.

8.3.2 Volcker compliance requirements

The rule's fulsome compliance requirements are intriguing because nowhere does
Dodd-Frank's Section 619 specifically *require* banking organizations to establish
a full-blown, dedicated compliance program to fulfill regulatory expectations.
Instead, under the prudential backstop provision, captioned 'Anti-evasion', the
statute cryptically states: 'The [appropriate agency] shall issue regulations, as
part of the rulemaking ... regarding internal controls and recordkeeping, in order
to insure compliance with this section'.[51]

8.3.2.1 Structure and rationale of Volcker compliance requirements
Complementing its compliance mandates, the rule requires substantial documentation requirements to ensure an internal auditing trail and effective regulatory
oversight. The rule's architecture is built squarely on the negative assumption
that the industry will seek to evade the rule, through regulatory arbitrage or otherwise. The rule has a sliding scale of compliance requirements that become
increasingly rigorous as firm size and thus systemic risk concerns increase, as
shown in Table 8.1.

8.3.2.2 Compliance issues in market-making exception
While highly prescriptive, the market-making exception avoids a bright-line
approach urged by the industry, instead adopting a flexible approach based on
an analysis of the overall 'financial exposure' and 'market-maker inventory' of a
'trading desk'. The trading desk serves as the fulcrum for the rule's compliance
system as a whole. Compliance officers and risk managers will not grasp the
intricacies of the rule without understanding the full import of these definitions.

The quantitative metrics implied by 'financial exposure' and 'market-maker
inventory' call for an extensive IT infrastructure. The rule permits market-making
by a given trading desk if the trading desk meets six tests. The two most significant tests require the trading desk to ensure that its 'market-maker inventory' is
designed not to exceed the 'reasonably expected near term demand' of customers, clients, and counterparties, referred to as RENTD, and that the banking entity
maintains an appropriate internal compliance program, including 'risk limits' on
the trading desk's market-maker inventory and financial exposure.[52] In sum, the

---

51 12 USC § 1851(e)(1).

52 The other four tests are (1) the trading desk 'routinely stands ready' and is 'willing and available' to trade certain instruments; (2) if a risk limit is exceeded, the trading desk promptly takes action
to again become compliant with the limits; (3) the banking entity's compensation requirements are
not designed to reward or incentivize prohibited proprietary trading; and (4) the banking entity is
appropriately licensed or registered to engage in the market-making activity. 12 CFR § 248.4(b)(2).

Table 8.1 Compliance programs for Volcker banking entities

	Exempt (Bipartisan Banking Act)	Standard program	Enhanced program
Eligibility	< $10 billion in total assets and total trading assets and liabilities ≤ 5% of total assets	≥ $10 billion < $50 billion in total assets	≥ $50 billion in total assets
Compliance requirements	N/A	Six-point compliance program;* documentation	Six-point compliance program;* CEO attestation; more detailed documentation on position limits; additional requirements⁺
Reporting requirements	N/A	No metrics reporting	Highly detailed metrics reporting

* Policies and procedures, controls, governance, independent testing, training, and recordkeeping.
⁺ Document authorizing types of clients, customers, and counterparties; mapping of each trading desk to a managing entity; risk management documentation; liquidity management plan and monitoring; policies for monitoring and prohibiting conflicts of interest.

structure of the market-making exception opens up a trading desk's calculations and determinations to several avenues of post-hoc supervisory challenge.

8.3.2.3 Corporate governance and compliance requirements

The enhanced compliance program requirements[53] mandate significant internal P&Ps and ICs. The rule requires banking entities to establish and enforce a governance and risk management framework to prevent violations by making senior managers down to business-line trading desks accountable for enforcing compliance and clearly delineating reporting lines. It mandates managers to provide a detailed description of the MIS for Volcker rule compliance, including titles, qualifications, and locations of managers and each person's specific responsibilities. The rule further mandates that compensation schemes not incentivize proprietary trading and create a risk-reward system that encourages excessive risk-taking. The CEO of the banking entity must attest annually in writing to the agencies that the firm has processes to establish, maintain, enforce, review, test, and modify the compliance program reasonably designed to achieve Volcker rule compliance.[54]

8.3.2.4 Volcker rule's risk management and IC requirements[55]

(1) *Written policies and procedures.* The rule requires a banking entity to provide a comprehensive description of its risk management program.

---

53 Enhanced Minimum Standards for Compliance Programs,12 CFR Appendix B to Part 248.
54 Ibid. II.a.6. CEO attestation.
55 Ibid. II.a.2. Description of risks and risk management processes.

The description must include, at a minimum, the supervisory and risk management structure governing all trading activities and the process for developing, documenting, testing, approving, and reviewing all models used for valuing, identifying, and monitoring the risks of trading activity and related positions. The rule requires robust MRM. The program document must describe the periodic, independent testing of the models' reliability and accuracy; developing, documenting, testing, approving, and reviewing each trading desk's limits; and purchasing or selling a security in accordance with the firm's liquidity management plan.

The document must also cover the management review process, including escalation procedures, for approving any temporary exceptions or permanent adjustments to trading desk limits on activities, positions, strategies, or risks. In addition, it must cover the role of the internal audit, risk management, compliance, and other relevant units for conducting independent testing of trading and hedging activities, techniques, and strategies.

(2) *Implementation and enforcement of ICs.* The banking entity must implement and enforce ICs for each trading desk that are reasonably designed to ensure Volcker rule compliance. Risk limits must be based on probabilistic and non-probabilistic measures of potential loss (e.g., VaR and notional exposure, respectively) and be measured under normal and stressed market conditions.

At a minimum, these ICs must enable trading desks to monitor, establish, and enforce limits on the financial instruments, including the types and exposures that the trading desk may trade and the types and levels of risks that the trading desk may take. The ICs must also do the same for the types of hedging instruments and strategies used and amount of risk effectively hedged.

(3) *Review, back-testing, and remediation.* The rule requires the banking entity to analyze and measure each trading desk's trading activity to ensure its consistency with the compliance program. Trading desk management must test and review models that identify, measure, and limit risk to ensure that trading activities do not understate risk and exposure or allow proprietary trading. The firm must also undertake periodic and independent back-testing, with remediation, limits, strategies, and hedging, as needed, to contain risk and ensure compliance. The rule imposes several reportable quantitative measurement requirements.[56]

---

56 At a minimum, these include (1) ICs and written P&Ps designed to ensure the accuracy and integrity of such measurements; (2) ongoing, timely monitoring and review of such measurements; (3) numerical thresholds and heightened review of trading activity not consistent with those thresholds to ensure compliance; and (4) immediate review and compliance investigations of the trading desk's activities, escalation to line of business senior management, timely notification to the relevant agency, appropriate remedial action, and documentation of the investigation findings and remedial

8.3.3 UK's ringfencing of risky activities and businesses

The UK's ringfencing reform requires UK banks with over £25 billion of retail deposits to separate their core retail banking services from their investment and international banking activities. It became effective on 1 January 2019.[57] 'Ringfencing' is the separation of a business line into an affiliate, separately capitalized, and independent of the parent holding companies' other businesses.[58]

8.3.3.1 Rationales for ringfencing

According to John Vickers, who chaired the Independent Commission on Banking (ICB) whose report resulted in the ringfencing regulation, ringfencing provides three advantages. First, separation between traditional retail banking and investment banking can provide an 'internal firebreak' and independent loss-absorbency for retail banking. Second, *ex ante* separation helps crisis management and resolution. Third, curtailing the implicit taxpayer guarantee and requiring higher loss absorbency improves *ex ante* discipline in risk-taking.[59] In drawing the line between retail and investment banking, the ICB identified prohibited activities, among other things, as underwriting, derivatives (other than hedging retail risks), and lending to other kinds of financial institutions.[60] The UK ringfencing requirement is thus broader in scope than the Volcker rule in defining 'non-core' banking activities.

8.3.3.2 Compliance implications of UK ringfencing requirements

Risk management and compliance implications of UK ringfencing are considerable but differ markedly in nature from those facing US banking institutions seeking to comply with the Volcker rule. Any major corporate restructuring is costly, requiring extensive legal analysis, accounting, and corporate governance changes. Firms will have to adopt new legal structures and establish complex restructuring programs. UK banking groups must conduct compliance due diligence to ensure that the structure of their businesses is consistent with structural

---

action taken when the investigation indicates a reasonable likelihood that the trading desk has violated the Volcker rule. 12 CFR Appendix B to Part 248, II.a.5.

57 Bank of England, 'Implementing structural reform', at <www.bankofengland.co.uk/prudential-regulation/key-initiatives/structural-reform> [BoE, Implementing structural reform]. The European Commission, after considering ringfencing, decided against adopting it. Huw Jones, 'EU scraps its answer to U.S. Volcker rule for banks', *Reuters* (24 October 2017).

58 Dodd-Frank originally included a firewall protection that walled off derivatives trading operations from depository institutions. The Lincoln 'swaps push-out' provision prohibited federal assistance, including through FDIC guarantees, to swaps operations, effectively forcing banks to either 'push out' a wide variety of swaps activities into a separately capitalized non-bank affiliate or cease such activities. The provision proved extremely unpopular with banks, which lobbied vigorously for its repeal ever since its enactment because of the costs of separately capitalizing swaps activities, and the high margins available since counterparties demanded less collateral from FDIC-insured entities. Congress narrowed the provision's scope of application in December 2014. Dodd-Frank, Section 716(b)–(f), 15 USC § 8305(b)–(f).

59 John Vickers, 'Banking reform in Britain and Europe', Paper presented at Rethinking Macro Policy II: First Steps and Early Lessons Conference (16–17 April 2013) 3. Vickers includes several caveats that structural reform is not a straightforward regulatory solution to systemic risk. Ibid. 2–3.

60 BoE, Implementing Structural Reform.

reform requirements and obtain authorizations and approvals from the BoE.[61] However, once firms complete their ringfencing restructuring, it would appear that ongoing compliance is substantially less than under the Volcker rule.

8.4 Conclusion

The financial crisis made TBTF global policymakers' central concern. This concern translated into several innovative structural approaches in macro-prudential regulation. These involve either ringfencing or prohibiting the activities of firms deemed too risky by policymakers or requiring extensive pre-planning and, in some cases, restructuring to limit the impact of their failure on the financial system. Some of the structural approaches to systemic risk make substantial resource demands on firms due to the need to revamp risk management and compliance systems, comprehensively assess and sometimes restructure firm-wide corporate structures and operations, and submit detailed information and reports to supervisors. The Volcker rule requires extensive *Volckerization* of firms' risk management and compliance systems. A number of firms have exited business lines due to the high compliance costs and compliance risk the rule entails, though some firms have still managed occasional outsized returns.[62]

The Volcker rule holds lessons regarding the US's fragmented supervisory structure. Five agencies drafted the rule and, among these agencies, the banking and capital markets agencies had potentially conflicting regulatory objectives. This factor also will likely extend the rulemaking period significantly for any Volcker rule amendments.

---

61 Ibid.

62 A Goldman Sachs high-yield bond trader made over $100 million in trading profits in 2016 by buying bonds ahead of a rally. 'How one Goldman Sachs trader made more than $100 million', *Wall Street Journal* (19 October 2016).

CHAPTER 9

The role of risk management and compliance in consumer protection regulation

9.1 Introductory overview

A vast network of statutory and regulatory law governs banks' interaction with the consumers of their products and services. This is not surprising, given that the vast majority of the US population interacts with the banking system on a daily basis in order to meet basic financial needs. Consumer protection regulation of financial services can be grouped into four main areas: laws governing credit extension; depository services; unfair, deceptive or abusive acts or practices (UDAAPs); and privacy and consumer information. These laws, in turn, adopt distinct regulatory approaches, each of which has risk management and compliance implications: regulation of disclosure, terms and conditions, and business conduct.

Of the three primary objectives of financial regulation, fair and transparent business conduct is the primary focus in consumer protection law. Business conduct failures vis-à-vis consumers are of two types: retail conduct affecting consumers directly and market conduct failure affecting them indirectly from market-wide retail or wholesale failures.[1] Thus, wrongful conduct in providing financial services may also implicate the other two primary regulatory objectives, financial stability and safety and soundness of individual banks.[2] Predatory lending to subprime mortgage customers throughout the US in the first half of the 2000s had systemic implications in the GFC. Many of the enormous fines assessed against banks globally since the crisis, estimated by one account to total $321 billion through 2016,[3] involved wrongful conduct. In response, US lawmakers created a new federal agency, the CFPB, solely devoted to protection of consumers of financial services.

---

1 Basel Committee on Banking Supervision, 'Guidance on the application of the core principles for effective banking supervision to the regulation and supervision of institutions relevant to financial inclusion' (September 2016) 6 [BCBS, Financial inclusion].

2 According to the EBA, recent developments in financial services have shown that wrongful conduct of firms toward their customers not only can cause significant consumer harm but also undermine market confidence, financial stability, and the integrity of the financial system. European Banking Authority, 'Guidelines on product oversight and governance arrangements for retail banking products' (15 July 2015) 3, at <https://eba.europa.eu/documents/10180/1141044/EBA-GL-2015-18+Guide lines+on+product+oversight+and+governance.pdf/d84c9682-4f0b-493a-af45-acbb79c75bfa>.

3 Boston Consulting Group, 'Global risk 2017: staying the course in banking' (March 2017) 4–5, at <http://image-src.bcg.com/BCG_COM/BCG-Staying-the-Course-in-Banking-Mar-2017_tcm9-146794.pdf>.

This chapter first provides an overview of the unique risks that banks must address in providing services to consumers. It then discusses firms' risk-return optimization relating to consumer compliance costs and risk. It next turns to the concepts of inherent risk and residual risk and the attributes of an effective compliance management system, or CMS, that mitigate inherent risk. Having established this foundation, it discusses the four primary areas of consumer protection regulation and the interface of state consumer protection law with federal law.

9.2 Overview of compliance risk in financial consumer services

The preeminent concern in financial consumer protection is wrongful conduct that harms consumers, officially denoted as 'conduct risk'.[4] The FSB in 2013 identified business conduct as a new risk category in bank regulation.[5] The economics of consumer harm are straightforward. Fraudulent or negligent conduct that negatively impacts retail consumers causes small costs to consumers individually who thus have little incentive to seek redress, but the profits and incentives for such conduct can be quite high for financial institutions and their employees. These customers also suffer from a significant informational disadvantage. This market dynamic creates a high level of compliance risk that regulators have sought to mitigate in a variety of ways. It also has implications for firms' risk-return optimization analysis. Chapter 3's framework for assessing COIs for retail customers is relevant in this regard.[6] After reviewing the sources of compliance risk, this section discusses firms' assessment of risk-return optimization relating to consumer protection regulation.

9.2.1 Factors creating unique compliance risks in banking consumer protection

A number of factors relating to the consumer protection laws create a high degree of compliance risk[7] for banking institutions.

---

4 Conduct risk concerns the manner in which a firm, its management, and its lines of business employees' activities approach their customers, compensation arrangements, and mitigation of COIs. See § 3.2.1.3 concerning agency costs and § 3.3.2 on managing conflicts of interest.

5 According to the FSB:

One of the key lessons from the crisis was that reputational risk was severely underestimated; hence, there is more focus on business conduct and the suitability of products, e.g., the type of products sold and to whom they are sold. As the crisis showed, consumer products such as residential mortgage loans could become a source of financial instability.

Financial Stability Board, 'Thematic review on risk governance: peer review report' (12 February 2013) 18, at www.fsb.org/wp-content/uploads/r_130212.pdf>.

6 § 3.3.2.

7 'Compliance risk' is the risk of legal or regulatory sanctions, material financial loss, or loss to reputation a bank may suffer as a result of its failure to comply with laws, regulations, rules, related SRO standards, and codes of conduct applicable to its banking activities. Basel Committee on Banking Supervision, 'Compliance and the compliance function in banks' (April 2005) 7.

9.2.1.1 Voluminous and detailed rules combined with conglomerates' diverse business lines and geography

The rules issued under many consumer protection statutes are highly detailed and prescriptive, creating significant compliance risk due to inadequate training or due to the incentives motivating front-office employees that may conflict with consumer protection obligations. Compounding the risk of non-compliance is the extension of services into different geographical regions, with their own unique challenges and local law requirements. Thus, a centralized approach to compliance can be a crucial means of managing consumer protection compliance risk.[8] Moreover, the agencies expect banks to adopt a risk-based approach in tackling the myriad risks arising from their financial products and services through their risk management and compliance systems.

9.2.1.2 Constant change of consumer protection laws

Financial consumer protection laws and regulations are subject to constant change. Congress frequently amends the consumer protection statutes, followed by implementing rules by the agencies. It is for this reason that a key focus in agency supervisory guidance is the capability of a bank's consumer protection compliance system to promptly incorporate change in law. This is the objective of the 'change management process'.[9] A comprehensive training system should ensure that the large numbers of customer-facing bank employees are conversant with the intricacies of the most recent consumer protection rules.

9.2.1.3 High level of competition in consumer services

The consumer financial services industry is fiercely competitive, not only in the commercial banking space but in the newly encroaching FinTech space as well. To compete, banks are continuously developing new products and services, often highly complex, with hidden COIs. These COIs and complexity introduce the compliance risk that these innovations do not comply with consumer protection laws' existing prohibitions, restrictions, and exceptions.

9.2.1.4 High risk of reputational harm

Reputational harm, a component of compliance risk, is particularly elevated in the provision of financial consumer services. A high-profile problem is almost certainly to entail congressional hearings and investor and consumer scrutiny. In this competitive space, other firms quickly attract disgruntled customers. The subprime mortgage crisis that began in 2007 is a case study of reputational harm.

---

8 The Wells Fargo account opening scandal disclosed in 2016 is a prime example of the flaws in a decentralized compliance model, particularly for a G-SIB. One of the key findings in the firm's internal investigation was the need to centralize risk management and compliance and upstream awareness of compliance risk involving depository services and all other areas of compliance regulation. 'Independent directors of the board of Wells Fargo & Company: sales practices investigation report', Shearman & Sterling (10 April 2017) 8, at <www08.wellsfargomedia.com/assets/pdf/about/investor-relations/presentations/2017/board-report.pdf>.

9 A change management system identifies rule changes, considers their impact, and assigns responsibility for modifying the risk management and compliance system. See § 9.3.3.3.

Intermediaries loaned millions of retail borrowers mortgages whose terms they did not understand, and whose repayment became virtually impossible either in a rising interest rate environment or by virtue of the eventual decline in housing prices. As with the macro risks of the GFC in general, the high costs from mis-selling of mortgage products and reputational damage this caused financial firms were not foreseen.

9.2.2 Firms' assessment of compliance cost and compliance risk

All of the enumerated sources of compliance risk collectively create significant risks in banks' provision of consumer services. Banking institutions, with varying levels of formality, engage in a risk-return optimization calculus in assessing the risk-return trade-off in existing business strategies and in considering new products and services. A bank will often exit a consumer business because of the high level of risk and cost of compliance with the governing laws and regulations. For example, a board and its senior management may avoid certain high-yielding but high-risk areas such as home equity lending or subprime lending whose level of compliance risk would exceed their risk appetite.[10]

9.3 Constructing a risk management and compliance consumer protection infrastructure

Understanding how the banking agencies approach compliance risk is essential in establishing an effective risk management and compliance system. The agencies expect banks to establish a formal risk management and compliance system based on an in-depth and ongoing assessment of the unique compliance risks that their consumer services model creates. Supervisors' examination of firms' approach to consumer protection can be divided broadly into three areas: (1) identifying the inherent risks in consumer products and services, (2) evaluating the risk controls that will mitigate these risks, and (3) measuring the residual risk remaining after accounting for these controls and determining whether it is acceptable.[11] This three-prong approach fits firmly within an existing risk management framework: identify risks; assess the risks; and decide to either tolerate, mitigate, or eliminate the risks.[12]

9.3.1 Identification of inherent risk

Supervisors first undertake a formal assessment of risk of consumer harm (ARCH) in identifying and assessing the *inherent risk* of a bank's products and services. The ARCH process determines the scope of the examination of a bank.

---

10 § 3.5.2 discusses banks' risk-return optimization within a risk management framework.

11 Dorothy Stefanyszyn and Joe Detchemendy, 'Managing compliance risk through consumer compliance risk assessments', *Consumer Compliance Outlook* (4th Quarter 2014), at <https://consumercomplianceoutlook.org/2014/fourth-quarter/managing-compliance-risk-through-consumer-compliance-risk-assessments/> [FRB, Risk assessments].

12 See § 3.7.1.

9.3.1.1 Relationship between inherent risk and consumer harm

The agencies employ the concepts of *consumer harm* and *inherent risk* in their supervision of compliance with the consumer protection statutes. The concepts are closely linked. Consumer harm is 'an actual or potential injury or loss to a consumer, and whether such injury or loss is economically quantifiable', such as an overcharge, or is a non-quantifiable loss, such as when a bank unfairly denies a consumer credit.[13] Inherent risk is the compliance risk associated with product and service offerings and practices that could directly or indirectly result in significant consumer harm or non-compliance with consumer protection rules and regulations, before accounting for risk management, compliance, and other governance controls.[14]

Inherent risk may be prevalent in a new loan product, a change to deposit account terms, or a third-party relationship.[15] In cases of violations of law or regulations, banks must remediate and remove underlying incentives to engage in harmful practices. Regulators' ARCH examination process in identifying, addressing, and preventing consumer harm helps to achieve the objective of promoting public confidence in the financial system.[16]

9.3.1.2 Factors contributing to inherent risk

The level of inherent risk is a function of institutional, environmental, and legal and regulatory factors:

(1) *Institutional factors.* These include a firm's organizational structure, business model and strategies, the structure of risk management, and supervisory history. Also important are changes in business activity, product complexity, growth, vendor management, product volume, and historical trends. Specific items that determine the level of inherent risk include complex products, decentralized operations, or third-party relationships.[17]

(2) *Environmental factors.* These include local business conditions, competition, and demographics. For example, banks operating in a rural market may have a lower level of risk than institutions in larger markets that exhibit greater diversity of income, ethnicity, and business competition.[18]

(3) *Legal and regulatory factors.* Such factors include the complexity of the regulations that apply to an institution's business activities, changes in regulation, and the consumer compliance scrutiny that arise from these factors.[19]

---

13 Compliance Examination Manual, FDIC, II-2.1 (March 2017) [FDIC Exam Manual]. Consumer harm may be caused by a financial institution's violation of a federal consumer protection law or regulation, a disregard for supervisory guidance, or a wrongful act by a financial institution or a third party. Ibid.

14 Ibid.

15 Ibid.

16 Ibid.

17 FRB, Risk assessment.

18 Ibid.

19 Ibid.

9.3.2 Assessment of a bank's risk controls to address inherent risks

The second step in supervisors' assessment of compliance risk involves an eval-uation of the adequacy of a bank's risk controls in reducing inherent risk. These involve the management systems and whether they effectively monitor and con-trol the inherent risks arising from the institution's business activities. In evaluat-ing mitigating controls and processes, bank examiners consider the effectiveness of the 'four pillars' of a sound consumer compliance management program: (1) the level of board and senior management oversight; (2) the adequacy of policies, procedures, and staff training; (3) the adequacy of risk monitoring and MIS; and (4) the adequacy of ICs.[20]

9.3.2.1 Managing inherent risk: CMS

Regulators require banking institutions to develop and maintain a CMS that is integrated into the overall risk management strategy of the institution to manage and mitigate inherent risk.

A CMS enables a banking institution to learn about its compliance responsi-bilities and ensure that employees understand these responsibilities; to ensure that requirements are incorporated into business processes; to review operations to ensure responsibilities are carried out and requirements are met; and to take corrective action and update materials as necessary.

9.3.2.2 Regulatory expectations of a CMS

The agencies have formalized their regulatory expectations regarding controlling inherent risk of consumer harm through guidance on a firm's CMS.[21] A robust CMS addresses the need for an enterprise-wide approach to controlling risks fol-lowing the GFC as they relate to consumer protection.

A CMS generally has four interdependent components: board and management oversight, a compliance program, an effective system for responding to con-sumer complaints, and a compliance audit function.[22] Following their maxim that 'no one size fits all', the agencies' examination manuals take a principles-based approach in setting forth the basic requisites for a sound CMS. However, the fact that the agencies *require* banks to design and implement a CMS can be a rationale for enforcement actions.

---

20 Ibid.

21 The CEO must take the lead in developing a strong CMS and building a culture of consumer protection. This responsibility cannot be left to the CCO. KPMG, 'Compliance management systems: consumer protection transforming risk management' (2013) 2, at <https://advisory.kpmg.us/content/dam/advisory/en/pdfs/nss-consumer-finance-reg-pov.pdf>.

22 Consumer Financial Protection Bureau, 'CFPB Supervision and Examination Manual', Com-pliance Management Review (1 October 2012) 2 [CFPB Exam Manual]. An effective compliance audit program addresses all products and services of the bank, all aspects of relevant operations, and all departments and branch locations. Office of the Comptroller of the Currency, 'Comptroller's Handbook: Compliance Management System' (17 May 2012) 4 [OCC, CMS].

A CMS formulizes reporting lines for compliance responsibilities, communicates those responsibilities to employees, and incorporates responsibilities for meeting legal requirements and internal policies into business processes. A CMS also requires review of operations to ensure that management carries out responsibilities, meets legal requirements, takes corrective action, and updates tools and systems, as necessary.[23]

An important component is the 'change management process', a set of procedures designed to ensure that a bank uses standardized methods and procedures for efficient and prompt handling of all changes related to evolving business strategies and regulatory changes.[24] This became particularly important with the enactment of Dodd-Frank and the avalanche of rules that followed. A change management process enables management to detect new or amended rules and regulations, evaluate these rules, and understand how the new requirements affect a bank's processes. Management can then make the appropriate modifications to its compliance controls. A similar process should also apply to changes in bank processes and practices and in developing new products and services.[25] Firms create inherent risk by continuously assessing and modifying their product and service offerings and operations in order to be profitable in a dynamic market environment.[26]

9.3.2.4 Consumer complaint system

Of a CMS's four components,[27] a consumer complaint response program plays a unique role. A bank should be prepared to handle consumer complaints promptly. Procedures should specify how to handle them and the process of using complaint data and individual cases to drive adjustments to business practices and the remediation of P&Ps for receiving, escalating, and resolving consumer complaints and inquiries. A consumer complaint response protocol should permit recording of complaints, with prompt resolution, and the use of complaints in modifying compliance training and monitoring.[28]

9.3.2.5 Corporate governance issues relating to a CMS

The agencies stress that the board of directors is ultimately responsible for establishing an effective CMS. To facilitate this objective, they expect a CMS to be

---

23 FDIC Exam Manual II-3.1.

24 Allison Burns, 'Managing change effectively', Consumer Affairs Update, Federal Reserve Bank of Minneapolis (14 March 2016), at <www.minneapolisfed.org/publications/banking-in-the-ninth/managing-change-effectively>.

25 The relevant components are identifying changes, creating action items, establishing accountable parties, tracking due dates, and evaluating the effectiveness of changes following implementation. Ibid.

26 FDIC Exam Manual II-3.1.

27 These are board and management oversight, a compliance program, a consumer complaint system, and a compliance audit function. CFPB Exam Manual 2.

28 CFPB Exam Manual 10–11.

incorporated within a bank's overall corporate compliance framework and culture.[29] The bank must appoint a compliance officer or compliance committee to be responsible for implementing and monitoring the CMS. As for regulators, examination objectives include determining the quality and effectiveness of board and senior management supervision and administration of the CMS; the adequacy of the compliance program and audit function; management's degree of reliance on the CMS; the level of compliance, reputation, and transaction risk; and Community Reinvestment Act (CRA) ratings.[30]

9.3.3 Residual risk exposure

A supervisor's third step in assessing a firm's management of compliance risk concerns residual risk. Residual risk is the risk exposure that remains after identifying the level of inherent risk and factoring in the strength of the mitigating factors to control that risk.[31] In their supervisory role, examiners assess the residual risk for each of a bank's material products and aggregate these risks to capture the residual risk for the institution as a whole. For their part, a bank's board and management should have accurately measured their firm's residual risk. If the exposure is not within the firm's risk appetite, they are expected to implement additional controls or revise their business strategy.

9.3.3.1 Regulators' assessment of residual risk exposure

With the CMS in place, examiners can identify the residual risk exposure. For example, a bank might introduce a new overdraft program with no due diligence, no monitoring or auditing, but with numerous customer inquiries. This is a high risk product with no effective CMS elements to mitigate inherent risk. Since a higher level of residual risk remains, the examiner must review the program and undertake transaction testing during an examination.[32] More generally, firms should apply a CMS to the entire product and service life cycle to gauge residual risk. This would include product development, design, customer service, and marketing practices, among other things.[33]

9.3.3.2 Examiners' risk-based approach to CMS

In their examination of a bank's CMS, supervisors have found a risk-based approach a practical necessity given the enormous volume of consumer laws and

---

29 'Institution management and staff should have a clear understanding that compliance is important to the [b]oard and senior management, and that they are expected to incorporate compliance in their daily operations'. FDIC Exam Manual II.3–1.

30 OCC, CMS 5. CRA ratings are designed to encourage banks to satisfy the credit needs of the communities in which they operate. Unlike other consumer protection laws, the CRA does not explicitly limit banking practices, but does so implicitly. A bank cannot undertake a merger if it has an unsatisfactory CRA rating. CRA, 12 U.S.C. 2901, Pub. L. No. 95–128, 91 Stat. 1147 (1977).

31 FDIC Exam Manual II-2.3.

32 Ibid.

33 Office of the Comptroller of the Currency, Comptroller's Handbook, Consumer Compliance (CC): Compliance Management Systems (June 2018) 31.

regulations and variety of banks' products and services. Thus, the FDIC focuses on areas of higher risk of consumer harm rather than uncovering technical issues in reviewing a CMS. To do this, examiners analyze a bank's CMS history, previous supervisory actions and deficiencies that have not been addressed, its current products and services, its markets, and third-party relationships. In turn, the agencies expect the CMS to be risk-based as well and integrated into banks' overall risk management framework. This also facilitates the examination process.[34]

9.4 The primary areas of consumer protection law and risk management and compliance implications

This section begins with a summary of the jurisdiction of the CFPB. It then summarizes the three regulatory approaches that characterize consumer financial protection laws. It next provides an overview of the laws and regulations governing credit extension; depository services; prohibition of UDAAPs; and privacy and consumer information. It provides a capsule summary of state consumer protection law in financial services and its relationship to federal law.

9.4.1 Consumer Financial Protection Bureau

Dodd-Frank created the CFPB, the first federal agency dedicated solely to consumer protection in financial services. The CFPB's remit is to implement and enforce federal consumer protection law to ensure that consumers have access to markets for consumer financial products and services and that these markets are fair and transparent. The agency occupies an unusual position in the hierarchy of federal financial agencies. It resides in the FRB, is self-funded through FRB earnings, and has a single director rather than a group of commissioners.[35] Through its appointment of a newCFPB director, the Trump administration has substantially reduced its enforcement and rulemaking actions.

Congress transferred rulemaking authority for many consumer protection laws from the banking agencies and other financial regulators to the CFPB. The primary banking regulators retain supervisory and examination authority for depository institutions with $10 billion or less in assets. They share such authority with the CFPB over firms with over $10 billion in assets.[36] Dodd-Frank granted the CFPB authority to enforce numerous financial services statutes, but

---

34 FDIC Exam Manual II-2.1–2.2.

35 The decision making and governance structure of the CFTC and SEC have several institutional constraints not present in the case of the CFPB. They must obtain annual funding from Congress. They also have a five-member commission of which no more than three may be from the same party as the President, who appoints the commissioners. These commissioners take enforcement and regulatory actions by majority vote.

36 In a political compromise that helped to ensure enactment of Dodd-Frank, Congress gave no direct supervisory or examination authority to the CFPB over the members of the Independent Community Bankers' Association, the vast majority of whose assets were below $10 billion. Robert Kaiser, *Act of Congress: How America's Essential Institution Works and How It Doesn't* (Vintage: 2014) 161.

the agency has relied upon its authority to prosecute UDAAPs more than any other authority.[37]

9.4.2 Three regulatory approaches in consumer protection law

Regulators have developed three approaches to regulating conduct risk in financial services. First, one of the most fundamental aspects of consumer financial services is the enormous informational advantage that the providers of these services have vis-à-vis retail consumers. This asymmetry is particularly worrisome when COIs are present, incentivizing intermediaries to exploit their advantage. Disclosure to investors and other consumers is generally US policymakers' and regulators' first choice for mitigating conduct risk.[38] Nevertheless, accessible and readily understood disclosure of the risks involving financial products is particularly challenging. The products, even plain vanilla bonds, are often too complex for the average investor to readily comprehend. Furthermore, the risks they pose are often not evident until several years after a transaction has closed.

In many cases, bank regulators have intervened with two additional, more aggressive forms of regulation due to the intractability of intermediaries' COIs vis-à-vis their customers.[39] These consist of direct regulation of the conduct of financial intermediaries (conduct regulation) and exclusion of disadvantageous terms and conditions or inclusion of provisions that are favorable to customers (terms-and-conditions regulation).[40] A consumer financial protection law often employs all three forms of regulation. This section indicates which regulatory approach a law appears to employ, as necessary.

9.4.2.1 Risk management and compliance implications of the three regulatory approaches

Each of the regulatory approaches has risk management and compliance implications. For all three, a firm's CMS, particularly its change management process,[41] should ensure that ICs and P&Ps are updated to reflect the latest changes in regulatory requirements.

Of the three approaches, disclosure and terms-and-conditions regulation appear to be the more straightforward for firms to implement in a CMS. A primary task is

---

37 Anand Raman, 'CFPB defines "unfair," "deceptive" and "abusive" practices through enforcement activity', Skadden's 2015 Insights – Financial Regulation (January 2015).

38 The first federal legislation in the area of credit extension, the Consumer Credit Protection Act of 1968, was disclosure-oriented and was the foundation for subsequent consumer protection banking law. Pub. L. No. 90–321, 82 Stat. 146 (1968).

39 The SEC, with the most experience with COIs of all federal financial regulators, relies primarily on disclosure regulation to ensure investors can make an informed decision. However, it also requires investment advisers and companies under Rule 206(4)-7 to design P&Ps to mitigate COIs. 17 CFR Parts 270 and 275.

40 Dodd-Frank's requirements under Regulation Z in the definition of 'qualified mortgages' illustrate both regulatory approaches. Regulation Z regulates conduct by requiring lenders to assess borrowers' ability to repay and uses terms and conditions by prohibiting high-risk terms such as balloon loans. 12 CFR § 1026.43(e).

41 See § 9.3.2.3.

to ensure that disclosures and contracts are compliant with the latest rules. P&Ps can ensure that the products sold to customers contain the correct disclosures, thus reducing the amount of staff training necessary for compliance. Automated software can embed ICs in the process of extending loans and opening deposit accounts. The effectiveness of disclosure and terms-and-conditions regulation in achieving their regulatory objective in particular cases is a separate issue.[42]

Conduct regulation is the more challenging area of compliance. Training, corporate culture, including 'tone at the top', compensation schemes, among other things, all play a role in minimizing conduct risk where rules regulate conduct.

9.4.3 The lending laws

The extension of credit to retail customers is one of the most highly regulated areas of financial consumer protection law. Consumer credit can be broadly defined as credit provided primarily to individuals for personal, family, or household purposes. Consumer credit includes mortgage loans, auto loans, credit cards, and unsecured personal loans.

9.4.3.1 Anti-discrimination lending laws

(1) *Equal Credit Opportunity Act* (ECOA). ECOA prohibits discrimination in any aspect of a credit transaction. It applies to any extension of credit, including extensions of credit to small businesses, corporations, partnerships, and trusts.[43] ECOA is expansive in scope. It applies to all elements of a credit agreement, including promotion, underwriting, servicing, debt collection, and termination of a credit relationship. *ECOA is primarily business conduct regulation.*

(2) *Fair Housing Act* (FHA). FHA prohibits discrimination in 'residential real-estate related transactions', including, among other types of transactions, making loans to buy, build, repair, or improve a dwelling; purchasing real estate loans; selling, brokering, or appraising residential real estate; or selling or renting a dwelling. FHA prohibits discrimination based on several factors.[44] *FHA is primarily a business conduct law.*

The procedures for ECOA and FHA emphasize racial and national origin discrimination in residential transactions, but the key principles apply generally to non-residential transactions.[45]

---

42 For an analysis of disclosure regulation, see Omri Ben-Shahar and Carl Schneider, *More Than You Wanted to Know: The Failure of Mandated Disclosure* (Princeton University Press: 2014).

43 The ECOA prohibits discrimination based on race or color, religion, national origin, sex, marital status, age, the applicant's receipt of income derived from any public assistance program, or the applicant's exercise, in good faith, of any right under the Consumer Credit Protection Act, 15 USC § 1691 et seq. The CFPB administers the ECOA under Regulation B, 12 CFR Part 1002.

44 The Department of Housing and Urban Development's (HUD) regulations implementing FHA are at 24 CFR Part 100. HUD, not the CFPB, administers it.

45 FDIC Exam Manual IV – 1.8.

9.4.3.2 Other lending laws

Several other lending laws provide a variety of protections for specific types of credit extension. This subsection also includes the Consumer Credit Protection Act (CCPA), which regulates debt collection practices.

(1) *Homeowners Protection Act of 1998* (HPA). This law addresses perceived difficulties homeowners experience in canceling private mortgage insurance (PMI) coverage. The HPA establishes provisions for the cancellation and termination of PMI, sets forth disclosure and notification requirements, and requires the return of unearned premiums. *HPA is primarily business conduct and disclosure regulation.*

(2) *Home Mortgage Disclosure Act* (HMDA). The HMDA[46] requires lenders to gather and report to the FFIEC a Loan Application Register that provides a substantial amount of data on mortgage applications that financial institutions receive and the mortgage loans that they originate or purchases. The objective is to determine if financial institutions are serving their communities' needs and to identify potential discrimination.[47]

(3) *Real Estate Settlement Procedures Act* (RESPA). RESPA has four primary functions: (1) to disclose the costs of real estate settlement services; (2) to eliminate kickbacks and referral fees; (3) to regulate servicing and escrow accounts; and (4) to establish the qualified written request for borrowers to resolve loan servicing issues.[48] Lenders must give borrowers a good faith estimate of settlement costs. Mortgage loan originators (MLOs) must register with the Nationwide Mortgage Licensing System and Registry, a database for state licensing of MLOs. *RESPA involves all three regulatory approaches.*

(4) *Secure and Fair Enforcement for Mortgage Licensing Act* (SAFE Act). States must license and register MLOs who are not employed by agency-regulated institutions. The SAFE Act also requires federal banking agencies to jointly establish and maintain a federal registration system for individual employees of regulated institutions who engage in residential mortgage loan origination.[49] *The SAFE Act is a form of conduct regulation that governs the front-end loan origination sector through entry requirements.*

(5) *Consumer Leasing Act* (CLA). CLA requires certain disclosures about consumer leases, including whether or not a lease relates to a motor vehicle.[50] *CLA is a disclosure statute.*

---

46 12 USC § 4901 et seq.

47 12 USC § 2801 et seq. Regulation C implements the HMDA, administered by the CFPB. 12 CFR Part 1003.

48 12 USC § 2601 et seq. The CFPB administers Regulation X under this law. 12 CFR Part 1024.

49 CFPB administers the SAFE Act. 12 CFR Part 1008.

50 Consumer Leasing Act, 15 USC § 1667. The CLA applies to lessors of personal property. CFPB administers the CLA. 12 CFR Part 1013.

(6) *Consumer Credit Protection Act* (CCPA). Administered by the FTC, CCPA protects consumers against abusive practices by financial institutions and other firms that undertake debt collection from consumer borrowers. Among other things, the law defines consumers' rights vis-à-vis debt collectors and establishes debt collection guidelines. Lenders must also disclose APRs and make full disclosure of loan terms and a loan's potential costs. *CCPA involves all three regulatory approaches.*

9.4.3.3 The Truth in Lending Act

The Truth in Lending Act[51] (TILA), which has broad scope of application, is one of the most important of the lending laws. TILA applies to all persons who originate loans, including mortgage brokers and their employees, as well as bank mortgage loan officers. Loans can be highly complex transactions. TILA's purpose is to promote consumers' informed use of credit by requiring disclosure of its terms and cost.

TILA seeks to ensure full disclosure of a loan's terms in a uniform format so that consumers can compare competing products and make a rational decision whether to incur the debt. Loan disclosure regulation is intended to rectify the enormous informational and bargaining advantage that the lender enjoys vis-à-vis retail borrowers. But Congress, in enacting TILA, faced a significant challenge: the average American's low level of financial literacy.

TILA also protects retail borrowers against inaccurate and unfair credit billing and credit card practices by giving them rescission rights, imposing rate caps and minimum standards on certain loans secured by dwellings, placing limits on home equity lines of credit and certain closed-end home mortgages, and defining and prohibiting unfair or deceptive mortgage lending practices.[52] *TILA employs all three regulatory approaches.*

9.4.3.4 Risk management and compliance implications of TILA's prescriptive ruleset

The risk management and compliance implications of TILA are evident in its implementing rule, Regulation Z.[53] The regulation is a good example of the level of prescriptive detail generally contained in consumer protection regulation. Regulation Z defines two dozen key financial terms such as 'open-end credit', 'security interest', and 'finance charge'. Merely determining the amount of a finance charge can present a significant technical challenge. The rule defines a finance charge as any charge payable directly or indirectly by the consumer and imposed directly or indirectly by the creditor as a condition of or incident to the extension of credit.

Bank personnel involved in consumer lending decisions must understand how Regulation Z operates in actual practice in order to ensure legally compliant

---

51 Truth in Lending Act, 15 USC § 1601 et seq. Regulation Z is at 12 CFR § 226.
52 FDIC Exam Manual V-1.4.
53 12 CFR Part 1026. Originally under the FRB's jurisdiction, the CFPB now administers Regulation Z.

disclosure. In addition, to the extent disclosure requirements are not correctly incorporated in P&Ps, compliance deficiencies may become systematic. Turning again to 'finance charge', the bank officer will follow a lengthy decision tree in determining whether Regulation Z applies to a given charge, what types of disclosure are necessary, and the timing of such disclosures. One of the most complex requirements is to determine if a specific charge must be included in the disclosed finance charge. For example, charges by settlement or closing agents are finance charges if the bank requires the service that results in the charge and such charge is not otherwise excluded pursuant to a 'finance charge tolerances' chart.[54] For a 'closed-end credit' secured by real property, banks must make an integrated disclosure that combines TILA disclosure with disclosures required by RESPA whose purpose is to eliminate certain unnecessary fees that increase settlement costs.[55]

9.4.4 Depository services laws

Like the lending laws, the laws governing depository services involve a core line of the banking business. The following are the among the most important laws governing depository services.

(1) *Electronic Fund Transfer Act* (EFTA). This law establishes the rights and obligations of consumers, retail businesses, and financial institutions relating to automated teller machine (ATM) transfers, point-of-sale terminal transfers in stores, telephone bill-payment services, remittance transfers, and pre-authorized transfers from or to a consumer's account (e.g., direct deposit and Social Security payments).[56] Regulation E, the implementing rule, limits consumers' liability for unauthorized use of a consumer's debit card or ATM card and requires federal institutions to provide certain disclosures to consumers prior to issuing an access device. The law establishes the liability of card holders or card issuers for lost or stolen cards. *The EFTA involves all three types of regulation.*

(2) *Truth in Savings Act* (TISA).[57] TISA requires certain disclosures at account opening, in account statements, and in advertising, and mandates pre-notification of changes in terms. It also has interest rate and annual percentage yield (APY) disclosure requirements. The law's objective is to give consumers the means to make informed decisions about deposit accounts. Its mandated disclosures enable consumers to do comparison shopping through disclosure of fees, APYs, and interest

54 FDIC Exam Manual V-1.7–1.8. For credit card accounts under an 'open-end' credit plan, creditors must adopt reasonable procedures to ensure that the bank mails or delivers periodic statements at least 21 days prior to the due date disclosed in the periodic statement to customers.

55 Ibid. V-1.15.

56 15 USC § 1693 et seq. Regulation E implements the EFTA. 12 CFR Part 1005.

57 Office of the Comptroller of the Currency, Comptroller's Handbook – Depository Services (August 2010) 71–107 [OCC Handbook – Depository Services]. Regulation DD implements TISA. 12 CFR Part 1030.

rates. It specifies how balances and APYs are calculated. *TISA is primarily a disclosure statute.*

(3) *Expedited Funds Availability Act* (EFA Act).[58] The EFA Act specifies time periods within which a bank must make deposited funds available for withdrawal. It requires certain disclosures on hold periods of deposits. It ensures speedy collection and return of unpaid checks. *The EFA Act is both disclosure and business conduct regulation.*

9.4.5 Prohibition of UDAAPs

Both the Federal Trade Commission (FTC) and the CFPB share authority under a complicated arrangement to regulate unfair and deceptive acts or practices (UDAPs).[59] Dodd-Frank strengthened the UDAPs law by making it unlawful for any provider of consumer financial products or services to engage in any UDAAPs and granted the CFPB authority to regulate and enforce this enhanced provision.

Congress likely added the authority to regulate and prosecute 'abusive acts or practices' as a catchall anti-fraud provision given the predatory lending practices that had preceded the GFC.[60] The CFPB's authority regarding this provision has been controversial. Industry proponents argue that the authority is overbroad when combined with the CFPB's atypical structure as an independent agency with a single director. Proponents argue that the additional authority provides needed flexibility in addressing the fast-paced innovations in the financial markets.

9.4.5.1 FTC's regulation and enforcement of UDAPs law

The FTC retains authority to regulate and prosecute UDAPs. Under FTC and judicial precedent, an *unfair* act or practice has three components. The act or practice (1) has caused, or is likely to cause, substantial consumer injury, (2) which cannot be reasonably avoided, and (3) is not outweighed by consumer or competitive benefits. An act or practice is also *deceptive* according to a three-part test: (1) the representation, omission, or practice misleads or is likely to mislead the consumer; (2) is considered from the perspective of a reasonable consumer; and (3) is material. Unlike many other consumer protection laws, UDAPs law also applies to non-consumers and businesses.

The banking agencies have authority to enforce UDAPs law. Technological advances and changes in banks' organizational structure have enabled banks to structure financial products in increasingly complex ways and to market such products with increasingly sophisticated methods. The pace and complexity of

---

58 12 USC § 4002. See OCC Handbook – Depository Services 49–69. Regulation CC implements the EFA Act. 12 CFR Part 229.

59 Section 5 of the Federal Trade Commission Act, 15 USC §45(a).

60 Dodd-Frank defined 'abusive', among other things, as 'an act that materially interferes with the ability of a consumer to understand a term or condition of a consumer financial product or service; or takes an unreasonable advantage of a lack of understanding on the part of the consumer of the material risks, costs, or conditions of the product or service'. Section 1031(d), 12 USC § 5531(d).

these advances increase the potential for consumer harm, warranting increased scrutiny by the banking agencies.[61]

9.4.5.2 UDAAPs risk management and compliance

UDAAPs law's expansive scope under the nebulous 'abusive acts or practices' standard complicates firms' analysis of compliance risk and costs. For example, under the CFPB's supervisory authority to prosecute UDAAPs, examiners can review any products or services that can increase the difficulty of consumers' understanding of the overall costs or risks of the product or service. This provides authority to CFPB to address disclosures and practices related to consumer financial products, including deposits.

The CFPB has been transparent regarding its examination objectives. These are to assess the effectiveness of the regulated entity's compliance and risk management systems, including ICs and P&Ps, in avoiding UDAAPs and for identifying acts or practices that materially increase the risk of subjecting consumers to UDAAPs. The CFPB's documentation review includes a financial institution's training materials; lists of products and services, including fee structure, disclosures, notices, agreements, and account statements; P&Ps for servicing and collections; board minutes and management committees; compensation arrangements; and new product development.[62]

9.4.6 Laws regulating privacy and consumer information

Privacy laws that apply to banks include the following statutes.

(1) *Gramm-Leach-Bliley Act.*[63] Gramm-Leach, whose privacy provisions the CFPB administers,[64] is one of most important financial consumer privacy laws. It restricts a financial institution's right to disseminate 'personally identifiable, non-public financial information' that it collects from individuals. It requires financial institutions to develop security and confidentiality P&Ps. Gramm-Leach also prohibits disclosure of credit, deposit, or transaction accounts to a non-affiliated party for marketing purposes. Financial institutions must notify their customers about their information-sharing practices and inform them of their right to opt out of information sharing. Gramm-Leach also regulates commercial recipients of consumer financial information through restrictions on the use and disclosure of such information. *Gramm-Leach is both disclosure and business conduct regulation.*

(2) *Children's Online Privacy Protection Act* (COPPA).[65] COPPA's primary goal is to ensure parents have control over the information

---

61 FDIC Exam Manual VII-1.1.
62 Examination Handbook: CFPB Consumer Laws and Regulations – UDAAP, CFPB (2011) 1–2.
63 FDIC Exam Manual VIII-1.1–1.31.
64 Regulation P, 12 CFR Part 1016.
65 15 USC § 6501 et seq. The FTC administers the rule under this law. 16 CFR Part 312. See FDIC Exam Manual VIII-2.1.

collected online from their children who are under 13. COPPA applies to operators of commercial websites and online services (including mobile apps) that collect, use, or disclose personal information from children. It also applies to operators of general audience websites or online services where such operators have actual knowledge that they are collecting, using, or disclosing personal information from children under 13. Among other things, operators must post clear and comprehensive online privacy policies, obtain verifiable parental consent before collecting information from children, and provide parents access to collected information with a right to its deletion. *COPPA is primarily disclosure and business conduct regulation.*

(3) *Right to Financial Privacy Act* (RFPA).[66] Administered by the FTC, REPA generally restricts the government's obtaining of consumer financial records from financial institutions without consent. *REPA is business conduct regulation.*

(4) *Fair Credit Reporting Act* (FCRA).[67] The FCRA's objective is to ensure the privacy, accuracy, and fairness of information, including credit information, that consumer reporting agencies obtain from consumers by regulating the collection, dissemination, and use of this information. The FTC administers the FCRA in conjunction with the Fair Debt Collection Practices Act, which regulates third-party debt collectors. *The FCRA is disclosure and business conduct regulation.*

9.4.7 State financial consumer protection laws

The US is a 'dual banking system' under which banks can choose either to obtain a charter from a state banking authority or from the OCC and become a national bank. The chartering authority has regulatory and supervisory authority over the chartered company. State consumer financial law historically has played an important role in financial consumer protection. Until the late 1960s, state law offered the only protection for consumers of financial services. The dual banking system raises the issue of federal preemption of state financial consumer protection laws.

9.4.7.1 Dodd-Frank's modification of state preemption law
Dodd-Frank changed preemption law in certain important ways.[68] The relevant issue is generally whether state laws prevent or interfere with a national bank's

---

66 12 USC § 3401 et seq. FDIC Exam Manual VIII-3.1–3.2.

67 12 USC § 1681 et seq. FDIC Exam Manual VIII-6.1–6.43.

68 With respect to national banks and federal thrifts, state consumer financial laws are preempted only if (1) they discriminate against national banks; (2) a given law 'prevents or significantly interferes with the exercise by the national bank of its powers'; or (3) the state law is preempted by another federal law. State laws rarely discriminate against national banks. Karl Belgum, 'Dodd-Frank Act alters preemption rules for national banks and federal thrifts', Nixon Peabody (28 July 2010), at <www.nixonpeabody.com/en/ideas/articles/2010/07/28/dodd-frank-act-alters-preemption-rules-for-national-banks-and-federal-thrifts> [Belgum, Dodd-Frank alters preemption].

powers.[69] Dodd-Frank allows greater scrutiny of national banks and thrifts by states and local authorities. Moreover, Dodd-Frank provides that state attorneys general are authorized to enforce regulations issued by the CFPB,[70] which should benefit consumers. Although Dodd-Frank preempts state consumer protection laws for national banks under certain circumstances, it also ensures that state laws that provide greater protection than federal law are not preempted.[71]

9.4.7.2 Federal preemption and non-preemption of certain state laws

Federal law preempts, to some degree, state laws regulating interest rates, account fees, account charges, ATM fees, deposit account charges, and truth-in-lending and truth-in-savings laws. However, state laws are generally not preempted relating to contracts, torts, criminal law, debt collection rights, and property acquisition and transfer.[72] By and large, state laws regulate interest rates that banks can charge for consumer and commercial loans. These laws are also generally enforced at the state level.[73]

Moreover, every state has a UDAP law, which have somewhat vague and subjective standards that potentially reach many types of bank products and services, including marketing and advertising, product design, mortgage and consumer lending, security, and deposit taking.[74]

9.4.7.3 New York State consumer protection law

New York, the home to many financial conglomerates and other financial institutions, occupies a large presence in financial consumer protection. The remit of the Financial Frauds & Consumer Protection Division, part of the New York State Department of Financial Services, is to protect and educate consumers and combat financial fraud. A Consumer Examinations Unit performs consumer compliance and fair lending, among other examinations. The mission of the Banking Department's Consumer Services Division is to ensure that regulated institutions abide by the consumer protection, fair lending, and community reinvestment requirements of the New York State Banking Law and regulations.

New York's Truth in Savings law applies to deposits below $100,000 accepted from a US resident depositor in a New York branch.[75] If a state has a shorter hold for a certain category of checks than is provided for under federal law governing expedited funds availability, the state requirement will supersede the federal provision if the state law was effective on or before 1 September 1989.

---

69 Ibid.

70 Section 1042(a)(2)(B), 12 U.S.C. § 5552(a)(2)(B).

71 Belgum, Dodd-Frank alters preemption.

72 'Issue Brief: Federal Preemption and Oversight in Banking', Office of Legislative Research (7 September 2017), at <www.cga.ct.gov/2017/rpt/pdf/2017-R-0018.pdf>.

73 Federally chartered, national banks are permitted to charge an interest rate on a loan that is the greater of: the rate allowed by the state in which the bank is located or 1% above the discount rate on 90-day commercial paper in effect in the bank's Federal Reserve district. 12 USC § 85.

74 Ibid.

75 Truth in Savings, 3 NY CCR Part 13.

9.4.7.4 Importance of compliance with state consumer protection law

In sum, compliance implications of state law are not straightforward. Dodd-Frank preserves enforcement powers of state attorneys general to bring civil actions against national banks and federal savings banks to enforce applicable law.[76] Thus, banks should ensure that their compliance systems incorporate state consumer law and its regulations in addition to applicable federal laws.

9.5 Conclusion

Wrongful conduct in financial retail services can cause significant harm to consumers due to their informational disadvantage and the incentives of financial institutions to exploit this and other weaknesses. This dynamic creates a high level of compliance risk. Several other factors contribute to compliance risk in the provision of consumer financial services: detailed, constantly changing rules under numerous statutes, highly competitive markets, and a high potential of reputational harm. To address compliance risk, regulators expect banks to establish a CMS that is well integrated within a formalized risk management and compliance infrastructure. Boards and senior management are expected to engage actively in managing compliance risk through the firm's CMS. The high level of compliance risk involved in providing consumer services compels boards and senior management to carefully weigh whether to make the investment necessary to manage this risk or to downgrade or even terminate an existing business line or business initiative.

---

76 12 USC § 25b(i)(1).

CHAPTER 10

The role of risk management and compliance in the payments system

AML/CFT regulation

10.1 Introductory overview

Regulation of money laundering and financing of terrorism (AML/CFT) is globally one of the costliest and most resource-intensive sources of risk management and compliance obligations. These costs are not only due to the personnel and systems necessary to satisfy these obligations, but also because of the significant fines that regulators levy on banks for AML/CFT deficiencies. Moreover, the criminalization of this area of financial regulation since 1986 has significantly exacerbated banks' compliance risk. AML/CFT regulation shares the prescriptive regulatory design characteristic of consumer protection laws covered in Chapter 9. Nevertheless, regulators stress the need for firms to adopt a risk-based approach. As with bank regulation generally, there is a surprising amount of international consensus regarding banks' AML/CFT obligations.

Liability under AML/CFT law primarily arises from negligent or wrongful business conduct of employees tasked with identifying and reporting suspicious activities of their customers. Significant conflicts exist in AML/CFT regulation that can impede compliance. However, these differ in kind from those existing in consumer services and other client-facing business lines. A fundamental conflict exists between banks' core business model of funding long-term assets through low-cost deposits, on the one hand, and their obligation to review all account openings and activity with a view to potentially curtailing or even ceasing to provide highly profitable depository and other payment services, on the other. This tension exists at all levels of management overseeing these business lines. In short, the conflict is between firms' business strategy and regulatory mandates. As will be clear, AML/CFT violations also involve issues of banks' safety and soundness.[1] The banking agencies expect AML/CFT risk management and compliance to be brought within an integrated, firm-wide risk-based control structure, with the board of directors ultimately accountable.

The chapter proceeds as follows. It first provides an overview of money laundering (ML) and financing of terrorism (FT) and the challenges these pose both

---

1 AML/CFT regulation does not fit neatly within the threefold set of primary regulatory objectives. Arguably, the primary objective is criminal law enforcement against money laundering and terrorist financing.

for regulators and for banking institutions. It then turns to the regulatory framework and expectations for AML/CFT risk management and compliance, which center around 'KYC', recordkeeping, and reporting to the federal government, particularly the key role played by suspicious activity monitoring and customer due diligence. The chapter closes with a discussion of banks' AML/CFT risk-return optimization analysis and a case study illustrating the factors at play.

10.2 Challenges of ML and FT for risk management and compliance

The seriousness of the criminal activities that underlie ML and FT easily explain the intense regulatory focus reflected in AML/CFT law. These include drug trafficking, prostitution, tax evasion, and the funding of terrorist organizations, among other things. AML/CFT law regulates both bank and non-bank financial institutions as potential conduits for accepting funds originating in or related to criminal activities. Banks play the predominant role in allowing, unwittingly, but sometimes with willful ignorance or intent, entry of these funds into the financial system.

10.2.1 Banks' two roles in the payments system

Banks play a critical, twofold role in the US payments system, which allows institutions and individuals to safeguard cash or cash equivalents and to transfer and settle monetary transactions for a wide variety of purposes.[2] First, banks help to ensure a healthy market economy by operating the payments system in a smooth and efficient manner. For this reason, the FRB exercises prudential supervisory oversight over the banks' operation of the payments system. More broadly, the payments system is part of the US 'financial market infrastructure' (FMI), consisting of the payments, clearing, settlement, and recording systems for cash deposits, securities and derivatives transactions, and other financial transactions. Dodd-Frank created a regulatory framework for the FMI due to the systemic risk that it entails.

Second, the government mandates that banks take affirmative steps to monitor and halt the use of the payments system for ML and terrorist financing, the subject of this chapter.

10.2.1.1 Definition of ML and FT

Money laundering is defined as the movement of illicit cash or cash equivalent proceeds into, out of, or through US or US financial institutions in an attempt to disguise proceeds of illegal activity in a way that they appear to come from legitimate sources or activities.[3] Money laundering occurs in three stages:

---

2 The prime example of a bank's handling of a payments service is the deposit by a customer of funds in an account held with her bank, either for the depositors' future cash liquidity needs or for the transfer to a third party's bank account in payment for goods or services. A bank may also create a deposit of proceeds of a loan to a customer.

3 Money Laundering and Related Crimes, 31 USC § 5340(2).

(1) placement, where illegally obtained funds are introduced into the financial system; (2) layering, which are transactions designed to disguise the audit trail; and (3) integration, where funds return to the launderer in what appear to be legitimate transactions. A typical example of placement is 'smurfing', the parceling out of a large amount of cash in small deposit transactions below reportable transaction thresholds.

In contrast to ML, FT refers to funds that do not necessarily originate in illegal operations but which finance, intentionally or unintentionally, terrorists and terrorist activities. It is primarily the *purpose* of depositing the funds rather than the underlying *source* of the funds that is illicit. National authorities publish lists of proscribed sources, which include state and non-state actors.

However, the outcome of both ML and FT is essentially the same, the placement of funds into the financial system related to some criminal activity. ML and FT have different risk attributes but are generally regulated in the same manner.

10.2.1.2 AML/CFT's 'four pillars' of compliance

The US agencies expect banking firms' AML/CFT risk management and compliance program to include the following formal minimum requirements, known as the 'four pillars' of compliance: (1) a system of ICs to ensure ongoing compliance; (2) independent testing of AML/CFT compliance; (3) designation of an individual or individuals responsible for managing compliance (an AML/CFT compliance officer); and (4) training for appropriate personnel.[4]

10.2.2 *Regulatory and compliance challenges relating to AML/CFT*

At the entry point of ML or FT funds into the payments system, banks are uniquely situated to monitor, report on, and stop the deposit of such funds. The government has enlisted banks in their law enforcement efforts because banks have the capability of reducing the predicate criminal activity, both by cutting off the ability of criminals to reap the fruits of their crime and by helping law enforcement authorities to identify the individuals responsible for the crime. More importantly, with regard to the regulatory and compliance risk of banks, Congress has imposed harsh criminal liability on banks and bank employees for, among other things, aiding and abetting violations of ML law. The challenges in AML/CFT compliance are several.

10.2.2.1 Fluid nature of payments system complicates compliance

Banks' compliance challenges in satisfying AML/CFT regulatory expectations arise from the speed of deposit transactions, their enormous transaction volume, the variety of devices used to disguise the source and purpose of the funds' entrance into the system, the interface of financial conglomerates with the global

---

4 Federal Financial Institutions Examinations Council, Bank Secrecy Act/Anti-Money Laundering Examination Manual – BSA/AML Compliance Program – Overview (2014) 28–33.

payments system, and the inherent anonymity of the system that make it especially difficult to monitor. The New York Clearinghouse succinctly describes the compliance challenge facing banks as follows:

> The volume of payments, the speed at which payments must move, and the indistinguishability of payments combine to make it virtually impossible to identify and intercept payments unless the originator, the recipient, or both are identified as problematic in advance and are clearly identified in the transmittal information. Once a person is able to inject funds into the payment system that are the product of a criminal act or are intended to finance a criminal act, it is highly difficult, and in many cases impossible, to identify those funds as they move from bank to bank. Similarly, the scope necessary for an effective payment system requires broad availability and thereby greatly limits the feasibility of blanket exclusions based on geography or origin.[5]

Thus, once the cash is on the 'other side' of the teller's counter in the banking payments network, it has entered the formal economy and de facto has become less risky for those involved in the illicit activity.[6]

10.2.2.2 Twofold AML/CFT regulatory paradox

Two paradoxes, one involving banks' business model and the other the regulatory regime, complicate national authorities' AML/CFT regulation and banks' risk management and compliance efforts.

First, banks are asked to monitor, report on, and potentially halt depository and other payments services for their customers, yet depository services are a core part of their business model that involves funding of long-term assets at low cost. AML/CFT regulation holds a unique place in the panoply of banking law, prudential regulation, and compliance expectations. An AML/CFT compliance system does not, by itself, directly bolster the financial health of a bank, enhance the quality of its services to customers, or help to safeguard the FDIC insurance fund. The regulatory objective of AML/CFT law is largely external to the safety and soundness concerns of traditional banking regulation. The ML and FT funds that enter the payments system become fungible with all of a bank's other deposits, contributing to its revenue, and do not necessarily undermine its efficient functioning or raise other prudential issues. However, the associated compliance risk, if realized, may eventually result in reputational damage and substantial monetary penalties.

Second, AML/CFT regulation occurs on a national level to address a problem that is fundamentally an international, cross-border activity. ML and FT often involve transactions with high-risk, foreign correspondent banks. This introduces an inherent contradiction into the AML/CFT regulatory framework. While foreign correspondent banking relationships reflect the global interbank market, global

---

5 'Guidelines for counter money laundering policies and procedures in correspondent banking' (March 2002), The New York Clearing House Association L.L.C. 1, at <http://216.55.97.163/wp-content/themes/bcb/download.php?file=http://216.55.97.163/wp-content/themes/bcb/bdf/law/usa/Procedures_in_Correpond_Banking.pdf>.

6 Jesse Morgan, 'Dirty names, dangerous money: alleged unilateralism in U.S. policy on money laundering' (2003) 21 Berkeley Journal of International Law 771, 777.

markets continue to be regulated by national authorities. Nevertheless, the global standard-setting by the international Financial Action Task Force (FATF), analogous to the role of the BCBS, to formulate a globally consistent regulatory approach to ML and FT goes far in resolving this paradox.[7] National regulators from most of the world's financial centers belong to FATF and generally incorporate the FATF's list of high-risk countries into their national standards. Moreover, The BCBS looks to the FATF guidelines in drafting its AML/CFT compliance guidance.

10.2.2.3 Technical challenges in AML/CFT compliance

In addition to the tensions between banks' business model and regulatory obligations, compliance with AML/CFT law is highly problematic due to the constant evolution of devices employed by criminals in evading controls, once put in place. This attribute reflects the fast-changing nature of the financial markets. The prototypical ML used to be a large cash deposit in a depository institution. Since then, transmission of ML and FT funds into the banking system has grown increasingly sophisticated. Launderers are constantly inventing new ways to commit financial crimes and launder their funds, using innovative products and services such as mobile banking and even engaging in cryptocurrency transactions. If they receive the funds, banks are held accountable all the same. In sum, technological innovation has enabled money launderers to establish convoluted and intricate, yet flexible and adaptive, laundering strategies. Regulators recognize that they cannot keep up with this evolution. They therefore expect banks' risk management and compliance program to be flexible, adaptable, and risk-based, and therefore mandate periodic updates.[8]

10.3 Regulatory framework and expectations for AML/CFT programs

Over several decades Congress and the agencies have created a comprehensive AML/CFT regulatory framework and have mandated highly prescriptive risk management and compliance requirements for banks and other financial institutions. On a general level, AML/CFT banking regulation takes a two-prong approach to addressing the entry of ML and FT cash into the financial system.

First, banks are responsible to 'know their customer' and should thus vet a potential relationship prior to engaging in business with that customer. Second, banks should continuously monitor all accounts for 'suspicious activity'. Even if the customer initially passes muster, that customer may later become corrupt or be used by criminals to facilitate deposits and other transactions involving ML and TF. As in consumer protection and other bank regulation, the agencies adopt a risk-based approach based on a reasonableness standard.[9] Given the enormous

---

7 Ibid. 778.

8 Kris Hinterseer, *Criminal Finance: The Political Economy of Money Laundering in a Comparative Legal Context* (Kluwer Law International: 1989) 24.

9 Both at the international and national level regulators expect firms to adopt a risk-based approach in their risk management and compliance systems. See Financial Action Task Force, 'Guidance for a risk-based approach: the banking sector' (October 2014).

number of payment transactions, no bank could scrutinize every customer and his account with the same intensity.

10.3.1 Evolution of statutory and regulatory framework

Congress has unrelentingly campaigned against ML and FT. Since the enactment of the Currency and Foreign Transactions Reporting Act of 1970, commonly known as the Bank Secrecy Act (BSA), which initiated regulation of ML, Congress has passed 13 separate legislative acts that have progressively enhanced the government's powers under the BSA.[10]

10.3.1.1 Evolution of AML/CFT law

The BSA was at first only a recordkeeping and reporting law, requiring banks to help identify the source, volume, and movement of currency deposited in financial institutions, among other things. A 1986 amendment imposed criminal liability on individuals and their institutions for knowingly assisting in laundering money or structuring transactions to avoid reporting them and imposed affirmative compliance obligations on banks to establish and maintain procedures reasonably designed to ensure and monitor compliance with the recordkeeping and reporting requirements. In passing this law, Congress expressed frustration over the banking industry's lack of compliance and regulators' forbearance over the previous 16 years.[11] Due to this frustration, Congress required agencies to issue rules mandating compliance procedures and issue cease and desist orders to address non-compliance.[12]

In 1988, concerned that deficient recordkeeping was not being adequately addressed, Congress authorized a civil money penalty of $10,000 per day for willful or gross negligence in recordkeeping.[13] In 1992, Congress strengthened sanctions for BSA violations and enhanced the role of the Treasury Department. In 1996, regulators developed the Suspicious Activity Report (SAR), which banks must file when they detect a known or suspected criminal violation of the BSA.[14]

10.3.1.2 Role of September 11 in AML/CFT law

The September 11 terrorist attacks, which led to enactment of the Patriot Act,[15] marked a watershed in the evolution of AML/CFT obligations. Title III of the

---

10 The BSA is at 31 USC § 5311 et seq. This book uses 'AML/CFT' to mean anti-terrorism financing and AML law and is intended to be generally synonymous with the 'BSA/AML' acronym widely used by regulators and the industry.

11 '[A] major law enforcement tool has been rendered a virtual nullity by an industry that didn't seem to care and by a regulatory structure that proved to be ineffective.' 'History of the Bank Secrecy Act' (16 October 2016) American Banking Association Appendix C: C11 [History of BSA].

12 Ibid. C11.

13 Ibid. C16.

14 Federal Financial Institutions Examination Council, Bank Secrecy Act/Anti-Money Laundering Examination Manual (2014) 3 [FFIEC BSA/AML Exam Manual]. The 1986 and 1992 amendments were, respectively, the Money Laundering Control Act of 1986, Pub. L. No. 99–570, 100 Stat. 3207 (1986), and the 1992 Annunzio-Wylie Anti-Money Laundering Act, Pub. L. No. 102–550, 106 Stat. 4044 (1992).

15 Uniting and Strengthening America by Providing Appropriate Tools Required to Intercept and Obstruct Terrorism Act of 2001, Pub. L. No. 107–56, 115 Stat. 272 (2001).

statute criminalized FT; strengthened customer identification procedures; prohibited financial institutions from engaging in business with foreign shell banks; required financial institutions to have due diligence procedures and, in some cases, enhanced due diligence procedures for foreign correspondent and private banking accounts; increased criminal penalties; and required regulators to consider a bank's compliance record when reviewing a bank's M&A transactions.[16]

More generally, the Patriot Act changed law enforcement agencies' retrospective approach toward ML and FT to a prospective approach, with enforcement efforts now focused on preventing and deterring ML and FT in the first instance. Banks' risk exposure and regulatory and compliance obligations have increased accordingly.

10.3.1.3 OFAC

As part of its AML/CFT compliance program, a bank must also ensure that it will not violate regulations of the Office of Foreign Assets Control (OFAC), part of the Treasury Department. OFAC administers economic and trade sanctions against targeted individuals, countries, regimes, and terrorists, among others engaged in terrorism and other criminal activity affecting national interests. OFAC regulations require, among other things, blocking of assets and accounts of these entities and individuals located in the US or held by US persons.[17] OFAC was formally established in 1950 after China entered the Korean War.[18]

10.3.2 AML/CFT reporting and recordkeeping requirements

The BSA requires banks to create and keep records on potential criminal activity involving funds transfers and payments. Although effective compliance is not directly tied to safety and soundness, violation of these statutes and the rules issued under them can have severe repercussions for banking institutions that may raise this prudential concern. As a general rule, recordkeeping violations under banking regulation do not result in hefty fines and criminal sanctions, but they can under AML/CFT law.

10.3.2.1 Role of CTRs and SARs

The BSA and the regulations issued under it require banks to file several reports, but two of these play a key role in compliance and law enforcement: CTRs[19] and SARs.[20] The Financial Crimes Enforcement Network (FinCEN), an arm of the Treasury Department, administers most of the reports required to be filed and sent

---

16 FFIEC BSA/AML Exam Manual 4.

17 Ibid. 142–143. Banks must ensure that they have a current 'specially designated nationals and blocked persons list' of individuals and companies owned or controlled by, or acting for or on behalf of, targeted countries, and individuals, groups, and entities designated under programs that are not country-specific. Ibid.

18 President Truman declared a national emergency, blocking access to Chinese and North Korean assets subject to US jurisdiction.

19 31 CFR § 1010.310.

20 31 CFR § 1010.320.

to the government. Banks must file CTRs for transactions in excess of $10,000 but authorities can aggregate multiple transactions to reach this threshold if the bank has knowledge that they are by or on behalf of the same person. A CTR identifies the persons conducting the transaction and must include documentation used to establish such persons' identity.

Banks must file SARs when they detect certain known or suspected violations of federal law or suspicious transactions related to a ML or FT activity or a violation of the BSA. As defined, a 'suspicious activity' has no business purpose or apparent lawful purpose. An eligible SAR transaction includes deposits, withdrawals, account transfers, currency exchanges, lending, securities transactions, and ATM transactions, among other things. SAR filings are required in the case of activity that indicates potential violations of the BSA or other law, or is otherwise suspicious, and the transaction involves $5,000 or more. The government has found SARs to be highly useful in launching major ML and terrorist financing investigations. A statistical analysis of a SARs database enables FinCEN to identify and track emerging trends in criminal financial activity.

Compliance requirements arise specifically regarding the due diligence regarding CTRs and SARs to ensure that they are accurate, timely, and reasonably include the universe of potential transactions the reports are designed to capture. SAR compliance is particularly challenging due to the myriad ways that suspicious activity can arise and the need to identify beneficial ownership, requiring experience and judgment on the part of the employee tasked with identifying such activity.

10.3.2.2 Law enforcement and banking agencies' enforcement efforts focus on SARs

Of the two forms, CTRs and SARs, FinCEN and other law enforcement agencies place heavier emphasis on banks' obligation not only to file SARs but also on their ability to accurately identify the parties involved through a risk-based compliance program. SAR filings are the linchpin of the BSA reporting system.

For both SAR and CTR forms, frequent, consistent, or recurring delay in filing, a low percentage of filings compared to peers' filings, or a significant number of filings with errors or data omissions, are an examination red flag pointing to systematic compliance problems. Agencies are to take supervisory action 'if failure to file SARs shows a systematic breakdown in policies, procedures, and processes to identify and research suspicious activity'.[21]

More generally, the following deficiencies are common instances that can lead to cease and desist orders and fines for less than adequate compliance with the BSA. Failure to:

- adequately identify and report large cash transactions in a timely manner;
- report 'suspicious activities' in SARs, such as deposit layering of cash transactions;

---

21 FFIEC BSA/AML Exam Manual 42.

- reasonably identify and verify customer identity; and
- maintain adequate documentation of financial transactions, such as the purchase or sale of monetary instruments and originating or receiving wire transfers.[22]

10.3.3 Customer identification and monitoring compliance requirements

The agencies consider comprehensive customer due diligence (CDD) policies, procedures, and processes for all of a bank's customers to be the cornerstone of risk-based AML/CFT compliance programs. CDD should enable the bank to predict with relative certainty the types of transactions a given customer is likely to undertake. In short, the bank initially verifies the customer's identity, assesses the risks in transacting with that customer, and undertakes enhanced CDD for high-risk customers.[23] The FDIC highlights the purposes of a CDD program:

> The goal of a CDD program is to develop and maintain an awareness of the unique financial details of the institution's customers and the ability to relatively predict the type and frequency of transactions in which its customers are likely to engage. In doing so, institutions can better identify, research, and report suspicious activity as required by BSA regulations. Although not required by statute or regulation, an effective CDD program provides the critical framework that enables the institution to comply with regulatory requirements.[24]

10.3.3.1 'Know your customer' requirements

'Know your customer' (KYC) is one of the key means for preventing and detecting ML and FT, whose main goal is to obscure the true ownership and control of the ML and FT funds by keeping the identity of the other party hidden. KYC translates into substantial requirements for gathering information and fact-checking about the identity of clients when they open an account.[25]

The BSA requires a banking organization to develop and implement a written, board-approved customer identification program (CIP) appropriate for its size, which allows a bank, among other things, to verify a customer's true identity and define the process used to do so, maintain records generated during the collection and verification process, and check the customer's name against specified targeted entities and individuals. The purpose of the CIP is to enable a bank to form a reasonable belief that it knows the true identity of each of its customers. The CIP must contain risk-based procedures for verifying the identity of the customer within a reasonable time after account opening. The bank must verify sufficient information to form a reasonable belief as to the customer's true identity.[26]

---

22 FDIC, Risk Management Manual (April 2005) 8.1–8.33 [FDIC Risk Management Manual].

23 FFIEC BSA/AML Exam Manual 63.

24 FDIC Risk Management Manual 8.1–8.17.

25 Daniel Becker and others (eds.), 'Know your customer: designing an effective anti-money laundering plan' (2002), American Corporate Counsel Association/Global Corporate Counsel Association (2002) 8.

26 FFIEC BSA/AML Exam Manual 47.

10.3.3.2 Beneficial ownership rule

In 2018 a 'beneficial ownership' rule[27] issued by FinCEN became effective. It requires banks and other financial institutions to identify and verify the identity of an individual or individuals who own legal entity customers. The legal entity customer must identify its ultimate beneficial owner or owners and not 'nominees' or 'straw men'. Banks must establish and maintain written procedures that are reasonably designed to identify and verify the beneficial owners of legal entity customers at the time a new account is opened. The information elicited under the rule is relevant for identifying suspicious activity and whether the owner is an OFAC-sanctioned person.[28]

10.3.3.3 Risks involving bank foreign correspondent accounts

The agencies' examinations focus particularly on a bank's foreign correspondent accounts. Congress considers foreign correspondent accounts to be 'gateways into the US financial system'.[29] Banks must establish a due diligence program in order to detect and report any *known or suspected* ML activity conducted using correspondent accounts at the bank in the US for foreign financial institutions.[30]

Such a program must include (1) determining whether each such foreign correspondent account is subject to enhanced customer due diligence, (2) assessing the ML risks presented by each such foreign correspondent account, and (3) applying risk-based procedures and controls to each such foreign correspondent account reasonably designed to detect and report known or suspected ML activity. The program must include a periodic review of the correspondent account activity sufficient to determine consistency with information obtained about the type, purpose, and anticipated activity of the account. Banks must review correspondent certifications for reasonableness and accuracy and request the foreign bank to verify or correct information the correspondent suspects is not correct. They must close the account if they do not receive the necessary or corrected information.[31]

10.3.4 BCBS guidelines on AML/CFT safety and soundness, best practices, and risk management

The BCBS has published guidelines on AML/CFT programs.[32] Significantly, its purpose was to support implementation of FATF standards by national authorities.

---

27 31 CFR § 1010.230 et seq.

28 The FFIEC provides a detailed description of the compliance requirements of the rule. See FFIEC BSA/AML Examination Manual, Beneficial Ownership Requirements for Legal Entity Customers – Overview (5 May 2018). The rule is considered a 'fifth pillar' of compliance.

29 Federal Financial Institutions Examination Council, Foreign Correspondent Account Recordkeeping, Reporting, and Due Diligence – Overview, at <https://bsaaml.ffiec.gov/manual/RegulatoryRequirements/10>.

30 Ibid.

31 Ibid.

32 Basel Committee on Banking Supervision, 'Sound Risk Management of Risks Relating to Money Laundering and Financing of Terrorism' (February 2016) [BCBS, Sound Risk Management – ML and FT].

It is a high-level summary that reflects the consensus among policymakers regarding the inherent risks of ML and FT and the essential components of AML/CFT risk management and compliance programs. The following subsections summarize the BCBS's key points.

10.3.4.1 BCBS's prudential safety and soundness concerns

Banks should include ML and FT risks within their overall risk management system. The BCBS links 'sound ML/FT risk management' to the overall safety and soundness of banks and of the banking system. In particular, the BCBS links deficiencies in ML and FT risk management to reputational, operational, compliance, and concentration risks. Enforcement actions result in direct and indirect costs incurred by banks due to lack of diligence in applying appropriate risk management P&Ps and ICs. In addition to incurring fines and sanctions, any of the risks could result in significant financial costs to banks (e.g., through the termination of wholesale funding and facilities, claims against the bank, investigation costs, asset seizures and freezes, and loan losses) as well as the diversion of limited and valuable management time and operational resources to resolve problems.[33]

10.3.4.2 BCBS best practices

The BCBS guidelines also include specific measures banks should take. A bank should develop a thorough understanding of the inherent ML and FT risks existing in its customer base, products, delivery channels and services offered (including products under development or to be launched), and the jurisdictions within which it or its customers do business.[34] A bank's monitoring system should be able to provide accurate information for senior management relating to key items, including changes in the transactional profile of customers. Enhanced due diligence may be warranted for an individual planning to maintain a large account balance and conduct regular cross-border wire transfers or for an individual who is a 'politically exposed person' (PEP).[35] Enhanced due diligence, such as senior management approval, is required for foreign PEPs and decisions to do business with higher-risk customers.[36]

10.3.4.3 'Consolidated risk management'

The BCBS further emphasized the importance of 'consolidated risk management'. Such a process coordinates and applies P&Ps on a firm-wide basis in order to implement a consistent and comprehensive baseline for managing a bank's

---

33 Ibid. 2.

34 Ibid. 4.

35 The FATF defines a PEP as an individual who is or has been entrusted with a prominent public function. Due to their position and influence, many PEPs are in positions that potentially can be abused for the purpose of committing money laundering and related predicate offences, including corruption, bribery, and terrorist financing. Financial Action Task Force, 'FATF Guidance: Politically Exposed Persons (Recommendations 12 and 22)' (June 2013) 3.

36 BCBS, Sound Risk Management – ML and FT 7.

risks across its international operations. The BCBS noted that implementing such firm-wide AML/CFT procedures is more challenging than many other risk management processes due to privacy considerations. Some jurisdictions restrict banks' ability to transmit customer names and balances across national borders. In addition, banks should coordinate information sharing by requiring subsidiaries and branches to proactively provide the head office with information concerning higher-risk customers and activities relevant to the global AML/CFT standards. Group-wide standards should describe the process for banks to follow in all locations to identify, monitor, and investigate unusual circumstances and to report suspicious activity.[37]

10.4 The AML/CFT compliance cost calculus

This final section discusses the dynamics of the tension between a bank's revenue-generating strategies and AML/CFT obligations.

10.4.1 Compliance costs and compliance risks involving AML/CFT regulation

Financial institutions must assess how much to invest in a risk management and compliance program to reduce inherent compliance risk to an acceptable level of residual risk. It is perhaps in the AML/CFT programs that banks face the greatest challenge in making the necessary risk-return analysis. There are two reasons why this may be the case.

First, attracting deposits is critical to a bank's business model, which relies on low-cost short-term funding.[38] Banks that grow their deposit base have financing available to increase their lending capacity and undertake other profitable business activities. Moreover, the more non- or low-interest bearing deposits a bank has, the greater its NII-based revenue. In addition, deposit accounts generate fee revenue from account maintenance and other payments services. Thus, increasing deposits has a threefold positive impact on banks' revenue generation: increased lending, NII, and fee income. However, AML/CFT laws require banks to reject depositor accounts under certain circumstances, thus reducing the ability to generate revenue in these three areas.[39]

Second, the cost side of the ledger involving AML/CFT programs can be substantial. An effective program imposes high overhead costs due to the extensive sets of controls, dedicated compliance staff, training, auditing and testing, IT infrastructure, and other related changes in corporate governance systems

---

37 Ibid. 15.

38 § 1.2.2.1.

39 This discussion of the revenue side of account services assumes the services banks provide are legitimate. Undoubtedly, as many prosecutions show, some financial institutions, attracted by high profits from the demand for secrecy, may not comply with AML/CFT law due to willful blindness or criminal intent. Taxation, regulation (creating an incentive to evade it), and prohibition (i.e., of criminal activity) explain much of the demand for secret services involving money. Ingo Walter, *The Secret Money Market* (Harper Collins: 1990) 14–17. Walter presents an economist's analysis of the market for money laundering services and other forms of 'secret money'.

THE PAYMENTS SYSTEM: AML/CFT REGULATION

required to oversee some of the largest business lines of any bank. Furthermore, the costs for non-compliance in the form of liability arising from civil and criminal prosecutions can be enormous. Separately, such potential liability and the *ad hoc* nature of criminal prosecutorial decision making increase the amount and variability of compliance risk in the risk-return equation. All of these factors create the incentive to invest in AML/CFT programs and to 'de-risk' by exiting high-risk correspondent relationships.[40] The government's law enforcement objectives have made AML/CFT law one of the most punitive of all bank regulatory areas.

In sum, firms face a challenging risk-return cost optimization calculus in determining how to balance the revenue and cost sides of their operations.

10.4.1.1 Variability of the compliance risk variable: the case of DPAs

Civil and criminal prosecutors enjoy significant authority under AML/CFT law to investigate and prosecute financial institutions. The DOJ has extensively used DPAs, frequently with a substantial fine and other monetary penalties attached.[41] The DOJ entered into a DPA with BNP Paribas, imposing an $8.9 billion fine for OFAC violations.[42] Another notable example is the DPA entered into by HSBC in which HSBC paid $1.9 billion in forfeitures and civil penalties to bank regulators and agreed to remedy a host of AML/CFT deficiencies. These consent agreements with high fines, that appear to be determined in an *ad hoc* manner, introduce considerable variability into compliance risk. Commentators have criticized the DOJ's use of DPAs since it only prosecutes the business organization and not any of its individual executives whose incentive is to settle rather than litigate, often at high cost to shareholders, and who may have engaged in the underlying criminal misconduct.

10.5 Conclusion

Broadly speaking, two challenges confront banks in establishing cost-effective AML/CFT compliance programs. At first glance, compared to regulatory expectations in other areas of bank regulation, AML/CFT expectations appear to have an unusual amount of clarity that would ordinarily imply low variability in compliance risk and ability to accurately estimate compliance costs. The intense focus of Congress, the Treasury Department, law enforcement agencies, and financial regulators has resulted in guidance and enforcement precedents that provide an actionable set of regulatory expectations. SARs and CTRs are highly formalized documents. Simplistically, it is a matter of filing accurate, complete, and timely reports with the federal government.

---

40 See, e.g., Bukola Adisa, 'AML de-risking: an effective method of plugging AML control failures?', Association of Certified Anti-Money Laundering Specialists (August 2014).

41 § 2.2.5.1, 5 Enforcement powers and their use, and §§ 3.6.2.4–3.6.2.5 describe DPAs and NPAs as a prosecutorial enforcement tool.

42 DOJ, 'BNP Paribas Agrees to Plead Guilty and to Pay $8.9 Billion for Illegally Processing Financial Transactions for Countries Subject to U.S. Economic Sanctions', Press Release (30 June 2014). BNP also violated AML/CFT law.

In fact, the matter is far more complex, particularly for the conglomerates. The 'KYC', 'CIP', and monitoring for suspicious activity mandated by law are a risk-based compliance mandate that must capture the appropriate level of material risk presented by a bank's unique risk profile and business strategy. Centralized enterprise-level risk management is essential for financial conglomerates operating in dozens of countries with competitive service offerings. Moreover, these programs require a highly specialized background of the employees who operate them and the senior management who oversee them, adding considerable cost in scaling up a new or existing business line to meet regulatory expectations.

The other challenge in effective AML/CFT compliance is satisfactorily resolving, at the board level, the unusually sharp tension between the revenue-generating potential of depository and other payment services and effective compliance with AML/CFT law. Board-level decision making and an unequivocal 'tone at the top' take on special meaning in this compliance area. The recurring and often brazen deficiencies revealed in enforcement actions and DOJ prosecutions center around insufficient resource allocation coupled with aggressive initiatives to expand highly profitable correspondent banking relationships. This is the reason why regulators view board and senior management commitment to provide resources commensurate with a firm's risk appetite to be so critical.

CHAPTER 11

The future of bank regulation, risk management, and compliance

11.1 Introductory overview

More than ever before, banking agencies rely on banks' internal governance systems and control functions to manage the risks of their evolving business model. This is not likely to change for two major reasons. First, banking business strategies will become more complex as banks adapt to the digital services revolution and launch new business initiatives in a highly competitive marketplace. This will require more sophisticated risk controls on an enterprise-wide level. Second, the GFC introduced systemic risk as a permanent policy concern into global bank regulation. Both of these factors augur for an increased reliance on the capability and capacity of banks, through their core governance mechanisms, to effectively identify, assess, and manage 'unknown' risks facing their firms and the banking sector generally.

The two deregulatory trends highlighted throughout this book do not undercut this thesis. Policymakers are positioned to continue tailoring existing regulation, thus reducing obligations for smaller firms, and incrementally easing substantive requirements applicable to all firms. Tailoring is a ready-made deregulatory approach, easy to communicate and effectuate on a bipartisanship basis, in lieu of the far more complex, lengthy process of fundamentally altering or eliminating substantive requirements. Nevertheless, the Bipartisan Banking Act[1] and the recent rule proposals to implement it will significantly reduce regulation and thus risk management and compliance obligations for many large banking organizations.

This short chapter follows the mode of analysis adopted in this book as a whole. It first outlines the likely medium- and long-term evolution of the banking business model. What will its key risks be and the likely regulatory response? Market forces will not replace the fundamental role of banks in liquidity transformation. Nevertheless, the greatest potential threat to this model is long-term, in the form of distributed ledger technology (DLT). An important development will be increased capabilities of banks in data aggregation and reporting and in regulators' ability to monitor risk through RegTech. Finally, the chapter argues that the current nature and scope of deregulation is not likely to change and that the Basel III/Dodd-Frank framework will largely continue intact.

---

1 The Economic Growth, Regulatory Relief, and Consumer Protection Act of 2018, Pub. L. No. 115–174 (2018).

11.2 The future banking business model

In both the medium- and long-term, the key risks in banking relate to banks' core role in liquidity transformation, as it has in all previous times of the industry's transformation. Banks adapted their intermediation function to the rise of securitization by assuming several intermediary roles in the origination process. Likewise, banks are adopting FinTech in order to compete effectively with non-bank financial firms in intermediating credit and payments services. However, DLT poses a more serious, long-term challenge to the banks' role of liquidity transformation.

11.2.1 Impact of post-crisis regulation on banks' profitability and industry structure

Before turning to FinTech, it is important to describe the current state of the post-crisis business model. All bank regulation involves a trade-off between the economy-wide costs associated with compliance and regulatory capital that can place constraints on lending, on the one hand, and ensuring safety and soundness of banks and stability of the financial system, on the other. Dodd-Frank moved this balance decidedly toward the latter end of the spectrum.

Dodd-Frank, in the US, and Basel III, as implemented by other national authorities, through a combination of enhanced capital regulation, liquidity regulation, and the stress testing and living will programs, have compelled firms to make their corporate structures less complex, their business lines less risky, and, in some cases, their balance sheets smaller in size. Some firms that were the largest on the eve of the crisis have reduced complex corporate structures and eliminated or reduced capital markets activities. Post-crisis regulation, which led to significantly higher capital and liquid assets on banks' balance sheets, is a primary contributor to the considerable decline in banks' capital markets activities as well as a decline in return on equity. Customer deposit funding has increased, while businesses have tended to redirect strategy towards less complex and less capital-intensive business lines, including retail banking and, in some cases, wealth management.[2]

As for complexity, Warren Buffet, who famously eschews complex investments, took a sizable position in the largest US banking firm, JPMorgan, in November 2018. A good indicator of size is membership in the list of G-SIBs. Royal Bank of Scotland, at £2.4 trillion in assets the largest bank globally before the GFC, has fallen off this list.[3] More generally, as a percentage of GDP, total consolidated assets of the ten largest global banks before the crisis are considerably lower.[4] There is also some evidence of erosion of banks' franchise value due partly to the new regulatory requirements.[5]

---

2 Committee on the Global Financial System, 'Structural changes in banking after the crisis', Bank for International Settlements (January 2018) 14.

3 Stephen Morris and Nicholas Megaw, 'RBS drops off list of world's most important banks', *Financial Times* (16 November 2018).

4 Yalman Onaran, 'Can we survive the next financial crisis?', *Bloomberg* (10 September 2018).

5 According to one study, based on the market value of equity, banks are no less levered than before the crisis. The market's discount reflects a lower expected stream of future profits, in turn,

11.2.2 Banks' medium-term advantages and weaknesses vis-à-vis FinTech

FinTech presents both advantages and risks to banks in the medium term. 'Fin-Tech' is broadly defined here to include all manner of products and services involving digital technology: peer-to-peer payment, DLT, long-term innovations in 'big data' management, quantum computing, among many other initiatives. DLT promises 'immutability, immediacy, and transparency'.[6] It only allows transaction parties to 'append', not 'amend' or 'delete', a transaction record. Ideally, eliminating intermediaries can significantly reduce both closing times and transaction costs. Each party has the same copy, or ledger, of the transaction history.

In all these cases, banks will certainly continue their economic role in credit intermediation and payments services. However, FinTech competition in the payments space is driving and will continue to drive changes in the banking business model that underlies the payments function. In the medium term, non-bank Fin-Tech competition is unlikely to fundamentally challenge the banking franchise.

11.2.2.1 Advantages in the medium-term

Banks enjoy several advantages in the FinTech race. First, banks' privileged status under the federal safety umbrella will continue to provide leverage to the banking industry in attracting and retaining short-term creditors. Deposits, which are guaranteed, are a source of stable, short-term funding.[7] Regulators will not expand the safety net to non-bank financial services without support from the banking sector.

Second, banks have the financial resources to enter the FinTech marketplace and compete effectively against non-banking institutions. Several large banking firms have made multiple FinTech acquisitions[8] or are developing FinTech platforms through organic growth. A premier example is Goldman Sachs' Marcus, its successful no-fee retail banking arm. Third, banks enjoy the advantage, through their core role in operating the international payments system, of integrating Fin-Tech payments services firmly into their existing business lines.

11.2.2.2 Weaknesses in the medium term

Nevertheless, thus far banks have not been highly successful in realizing the potential market for digital payments services. Twenty-four banking firms, representing about half of all US deposits, joined Zelle, which is owned by a consortium of banks launched in 2017. Banks' legacy infrastructures have hampered their ability to compete via Zelle with their smaller non-bank

---

reflecting, a 'dramatic decline' in banks' franchise value. Natasha Sarin and Lawrence Summers, 'Understanding bank risk through market measures' (Fall 2016), Brookings Papers on Economic Activity 57, at <www.brookings.edu/wp-content/uploads/2017/02/sarintextfall16bpea.pdf>.

6 Cliff Moyce, 'How blockchain can revolutionize regulatory compliance', Corporate Compliance Insights (10 August 2016) [Moyce, How blockchain can revolutionize].

7 Only depository institutions are legally empowered to accept deposits.

8 Olaf Storbeck, 'Deutsche Bank takes minority stake in payments fintech ModoPayments', *Financial Times* (24 August 2018).

competitors. Most Zelle transactions occur between customers at the same bank, evidence that banks have not yet been successful in significantly expanding their reach to a new customer base in the FinTech space.[9] Depository Trust & Clearing Corporation abandoned its blockchain pilot project to clear and settle repurchase agreements due to fewer than expected efficiency gains by its clients.[10]

Several non-bank firms have bypassed the banking system by creating digital payments systems that do not involve cash or physical cards. Digital payments are likely to amount to $5 trillion globally by 2020.[11] Non-bank financial institutions enable retail customers to store value or engage directly with one another. This presents a competitive threat to banks as fewer payment interactions will result in fewer and less engaged customers. Convenient, efficient payment services are critical in the race to keep customers in the banks' fold for other services, including deposit accounts. The most recent development potentially posing the greatest threat to banks' dominance in payments systems is Facebook's Libra project. The new digital currency platform would gain immediate traction from Facebook's enormous existing user base. International and US policymakers' reaction to the initiative has been prompt and highly negative, promising a long development process should the initiative go forward. Congress, the administration, and regulators have raised concerns involving national security, ML, and monetary policy.[12]

11.2.3 FinTech's long-term advantages and threats

Longer-term developments point to a riskier, more uncertain future for the banking industry. As in the medium term, banks have abundant financial resources to compete with non-banks. However, in the longer term, the evolution of DLT poses a more fundamental threat to the banking sector.

11.2.3.1 Advantages of banks vis-à-vis FinTech

The large BHCs have the financial firepower to make the risky investments in long-term, moonshot projects that may yield a competitive advantage in providing banking services. JPMorgan has invested in quantum computing, whose returns – if they occur – are in the distant future but could radically transform the approach to uncertainty in the financial markets. The new technology, which

9 Christina Rexrode and Peter Rudegeair, 'Nobody says 'zelle me'': banks struggle to catch up to Venmo', *Wall Street Journal* (31 July 2018).

10 Anatol Antonovici, 'DTCC, BNP Paribas, SIX Group shelve blockchain pilots', *Cryptovest* (28 March 2018).

11 Stefan Dab and others, 'How banks can thrive as digital payments grow', Boston Consulting Group (21 December 2017), at <www.bcg.com/publications/2017/banks-thrive-digital-payments-grow.aspx>.

12 Dave Michaels, Kate Davidson, and Sam Schechner, 'Facebook confronts bipartisan resistance to cryptocurrency plans', *Wall Street Journal* (16 July 2019). The company's plans for Libra cannot be disentangled from the existing controversy surrounding its digital advertising business model and misuse of customer data. Ibid.

involves probabilistic analysis, may allow banks to build better, more accurate non-linear models of these markets.[13]

11.2.3.2 Threat of DLT

Two factors make DLT a significant competitive threat to banks in the longer term. First, DLT could radically alter the competitive terrain by eliminating intermediaries providing payments and other financial services. DLT could facilitate trading of OTC financial assets, a market in which banks generate significant revenue. It could also replace banks in the clearing and settlements industry in which banks now play a central role.

Second, banks are ideologically resistant to developing DLT to its fullest potential. Blockchain was invented in 2009 in the midst of the GFC with the explicit objective of bypassing financial intermediaries in the first instance. Moreover, DLT's inherent transparency is in direct conflict with banks' strategic need to keep many transaction details secret. Banks appear to have the more limited objective of employing DLT for its potential efficiency gains.[14] The increased competition from FinTech and regulatory obligations have forced banks to look to shared database technology to increase speed and reduce costs by automating back-office operations through DLT systems across the banking sector.[15]

Nevertheless, DLT's proponents must overcome several technical hurdles before financial institutions can adopt DLT on a broad scale. These include scalability as greater use can slow down the system through data replication; interoperability; speed of execution; and issues with transparency in the financial markets.[16] Speed is an issue because of the cryptographic element, which requires large computer resources. The performance gap between VISA and other payment services for now remains 'unbridged'.[17]

11.3 Future regulatory trends and risk management and compliance implications

This final section discusses the regulatory, risk management, and compliance implications of FinTech and its impact on the banking business model. The risks presented by FinTech involve prudential safety and soundness issues due to franchise risk. It then discusses the two trends in bank regulation noted throughout the book – deregulatory tailoring and incremental lightening of substantive regulatory obligations. These trends will continue to exercise significant influence on risk management and compliance but are not expected to derail the decades-old

---

13 Richard Waters and John Thornhill, 'Quantum computing: the power to think outside the box', *Financial Times* (3 September 2018).

14 Kadhim Shubber, 'Banks find blockchain hard to put into practice', *Financial Times* (12 September 2016).

15 Ibid.

16 Tanzeel Akhtar, 'Moody's: Threat of Blockchain and Cryptocurrencies Is Distant but Inevitable', *Bitcoin Magazine* (24 October 2017). The technology's transparency threatens financial firms' exploitation of their informational advantage as intermediaries.

17 Moyce, How blockchain can revolutionize.

trend toward corporate governance cooptation. In addition, absent another crisis, fundamental reform of the US financial institutional supervisory structure is highly unlikely.

11.3.1 Regulatory and risk management implications of FinTech

The primary regulatory implication of FinTech is the long-term risk posed to banks' role in credit intermediation. This threat is to the bank franchise and ultimately could be existential in nature.

The existing prudential regulatory framework is sufficiently flexible to address the risk posed by the competitive, long-term threat of FinTech's DLT technology. Ultimately, however, the staying power of the financial conglomerates can be partly attributed to the perennial concern of Congress to protect the banking sector given its central role in the economy. Congress and the agencies would act to preserve depository institutions' intermediation role due to their primacy as agents of liquidity transformation and payments services. This was the case in the 1980s when Congress moved to deregulate the banking sector in order to enable banks to compete with the emerging threat on both the asset and liability sides of liquidity transformation.[18]

11.3.2 Benefits of RegTech for risk management and compliance

'RegTech' is the use of new technologies to solve regulatory and compliance requirements more effectively and efficiently.[19] DLT's immutability underpins its value as compliance 'proof-of-process'.[20] Regulators could have 'read-only' access, enabling them to have a proactive role, intervening as necessary, reducing regulatory reporting time and costs. Regulators would benefit from a shared and trustworthy DLT record chain without the need to collect, store, reconcile, and aggregate data themselves. Not duplicating firms' data aggregation would be an enormous saving of regulatory costs. For their part, financial institutions would benefit by using the same platform for execution and for storing information and regulatory reporting.[21]

11.3.2.1 AML/CFT regulation

In AML/CFT regulation, DLT could create an audit trail in real time allowing supervisors to trace all stages of onboarding users of financial services. 'Know your customer' rules requiring validation, confirmation, and verification could be collapsed into a single auditable record. Moreover, 'smart contracts', which

---

18 See 1.3.2, which details legislative deregulation that permitted banks to compete with non-bank financial institutions.

19 Institute of International Finance, 'Regtech in financial services: solutions for compliance and reporting' (22 March 2016) [IIF, RegTech].

20 Moyce, How blockchain can revolutionize.

21 Chami Akmeemana and others, 'Using blockchain to solve regulatory and compliance requirements', *Medium* (23 January 2017).

create triggers and alerts when a transaction step is accomplished or fails, provides real-time monitoring by internal compliance. Beneficial ownership could have a single repository, or 'market-wide utility'. Nevertheless, cross-border privacy restrictions are an obstacle to initiating such a platform.[22]

11.3.2.2 Data aggregation and reporting

Many regulations issued since the financial crisis require risk data reporting on both a granular and aggregate level, an area in which RegTech could make significant contributions. The new technology could enable supervisors in real time to detect buildup of risk in both individual firms and in the financial system as a whole. The FSB envisions, and Dodd-Frank requires, that SIFIs provide detailed reports on counterparty exposures. Data aggregation is relevant for advanced approaches banks in compliance with capital rules.[23] Liquidity risk compliance requires frequent, granular reporting for clearing positions, aggregation of counterparty names, and application of mandated assumptions and haircuts to determine regulatory compliance.[24]

In these other instances, RegTech will help to ensure that data management for business purposes and regulatory compliance will be better aligned. The business model of managing large amounts of data will bolster compliance with the standards of BCBS 239.[25]

11.3.3 Path-dependency of current US and global regulatory framework

The uppermost concern in post-GFC macro-prudential regulation is reduction of systemic risk through a bevy of reforms that regulate financial institutions on both an *ex ante* and *ex post* basis. This fundamental thrust of regulatory reform will unlikely change given the momentous, historical nature of the GFC. Also, because these features in Dodd-Frank's regulatory architecture are generally congruent with the BCBS precepts, they can be considered relatively permanent. BCBS standard setting is a consensus-driven process that is unlikely to move dramatically from its current approach to capital and structural regulation. Moreover, regulatory cooptation of financial institutions' corporate governance reflects a long-term evolution in financial regulation

11.3.3.1 Continuing obsolescence of US supervisory structure

The institutional structure of US financial regulation is here to stay, absent a financial crisis that clearly reveals the risks posed by leaving significant gaps in regulation of non-bank financial institutions. Even without a crisis, certain deficiencies of the regulatory toolbox have already become evident. FSOC was a key tool in Dodd-Frank to regulate systemic risk in the shadow-banking sector.

---

22 Moyce, 'How blockchain can revolutionize'.
23 Regulation of interest rate risk in the banking book requires a large set of aggregated data. IIF, RegTech 7.
24 Ibid.
25 See § 6.3.5.

FSOC's designation of SIFIs has become a dead letter, reflecting the poorly conceived SIFI designation process and FSOC's politicized governance structure.[26] The US's entrenched institutional supervisory structure is a further roadblock to resolving regulatory gaps. Effective systemic risk regulation that would place authority in a single supervisory body would invade too many financial regulatory turfs.[27]

Additionally, several policymakers have argued that the next crisis will likely be in the shadow-banking sector involving capital market activities. Resistance by asset managers had stymied FSOC regulation even under the Obama administration. A top former FRB policymaker considers potential curtailment of short-term wholesale funding on which banks rely heavily and the potential for rapid redemptions from investment funds could result in rapidly declining asset prices due to fire sales.[28] Like the financial conglomerates before the GFC, the fund management industry is highly concentrated.[29] Nearly half of the $70 trillion of globally managed assets offer investors redemption on short notice.[30] The macroeconomic risk is that abrupt changes in asset allocation would severely decrease credit extension to key economic areas.[31]

11.3.3.2 International framework
The international bank regulatory framework is highly resistant to change. It is globally centralized in the BCBS's standard setting process. The BCBS appears to be genetically programmed to continue refining its risk-based approach in assessing the creditworthiness of bank portfolios. Moreover, despite the recent breakdown of several international agreements at US initiative, it is expected that US policymakers will continue to adhere to international norms as enunciated by the FSB and BCBS. The financial markets are not as trade-related as the commodities and manufactured goods markets. Randal Quarles, the FRB vice chairman for supervision, became the new chair of the FSB, which oversees the BCBS, signifying the US's continued global leadership in financial regulation in stark contrast to other policy areas.

11.3.4 Prospective evolution of US regulation will not fundamentally alter risk management and compliance

The banking agencies under the Trump administration have adopted an attractive three-point mantra – 'simplicity, transparency, and efficiency', a phrase that it has used in a wide array of non-financial sectors. These three amorphous precepts can

---

26 None of the four non-bank SIFIs retain FSOC's SIFI designation.

27 §§ 6.2.8.3–6.2.8.4.

28 Katy Burne, 'Tarullo says shadow banking risks could reappear', *Wall Street Journal* (21 October 2016).

29 The top ten firms account for about one-fifth of assets under management. Mark Carney, 'The future of financial reform', 2014 Monetary Authority of Singapore Lecture (17 November 2014) 11.

30 Ibid. 10.

31 Ibid. 11.

be collapsed into two operating principles that underlie current financial dereg-ulation: tailoring and transparency. First, regulatory 'tailoring' involves making regulation more efficient by limiting it on a risk-based principle to the largest, most complex firms and by reducing the complexity of existing regulation by simplifying obligations rather than eliminating them. The approach can elimi-nate as well as reduce substantive obligations of the smaller but still large firms. Second, greater transparency means clarifying regulatory expectations. The most obvious examples are in stress testing and living wills.[32]

Both tailoring and transparency have obvious positive implications for risk management and compliance. Using the book's analysis in Chapter 2, tailor-ing and greater transparency can result in greater clarity in regulatory guidance and less compliance risk, two variables that firms assess in carrying out risk-return optimization.

11.3.4.1 Regulatory tailoring

'Tailoring', which at bottom is a risk-based approach to regulation, is not new in financial regulation. It is also international in scope. As it has evolved, its application has deepened. It is a rare bipartisan solution in a partisan environ-ment to refining Basel III/Dodd-Frank's fulsome set of financial regulations. The proposed amendments to the Volcker rule, whose compliance requirements are already risk-based according to asset size, would simplify its compliance require-ments for all banking entities. In addition, BCBS, in its Fundamental Review of Trading Book,[33] has moved toward the standardized approach, reducing reliance on the internal ratings and modeling for advanced approaches banks. Advanced approaches capital regulation involves highly sophisticated, costly risk manage-ment and compliance systems.

The three main banking agencies in December 2018 proposed to form four tiers of banking organizations that would reduce capital and liquidity require-ments through further tailoring that would focus regulatory attention on the larg-est banking firms.[34] It and other tailoring deregulation will significantly reduce regulatory compliance requirements for mid-sized and large regional institutions. Regulatory requirements would vary according to four standards for banking firms: Category I for G-SIBs, Category II for non-G-SIB firms with $700 billion in assets or $75 billion in cross-jurisdictional activity, Categories III and IV for firms with $100 billion to $250 billion in assets based on four 'risk-based indica-tors' designed to align the standards with a firm's risk profile.[35]

---

32 See § 8.2.3 (living wills) and § 7.4 (stress testing).

33 See § 4.3.7.5.

34 'Proposed Changes to Applicability Thresholds for Regulatory Capital and Liquidity Require-ments', 83 Federal Register 66024 (21 December 2018).

35 The four standards, applicable to four categories of banking organizations, would be based on size, cross-jurisdictional activity, weighted short-term wholesale funding, and off–balance sheet exposure, and non-bank assets. Ibid. 66026.

11.3.4.2 Greater transparency

The Department of Treasury report on banking regulation would subject the FRB's stress testing and capital planning to the notice and comment process.[36] Further, the qualitative component of stress testing,[37] criticized by the industry as opaque, arbitrary, and overly subjective, would no longer be the sole reason for rejecting a bank's capital plan.[38] Furthermore, the agencies have stated they will not take enforcement action based on supervisory guidance and that their practice is to seek public comment on guidance.[39]

11.4 Conclusion

Banks' core function of liquidity transformation will be under threat in the long term as DLT evolves into an effective business model for non-bank financial services. Nevertheless, market forces will not replace banks, which play several essential economic roles. Moreover, the technology emerging from DLT will benefit both regulators and private industry, including the banking sector. Specifically, this will involve enhanced capabilities of banks in data aggregation and reporting and in regulators' increased ability to monitor banks' risks through RegTech. Despite these dramatic changes, the current regulatory framework governing the banking industry is not likely to fundamentally change.

---

36 Department of the Treasury, 'A Financial System That Creates Economic Opportunities: Banks and Credit Unions' (June 2017) 12 [Treasury Report: Banks].

37 See 7.4.2.1.

38 Treasury Report: Banks 12.

39 FRB, FDIC, OCC, 'Interagency Statement Clarifying the Role of Supervisory Guidance' (12 September 2018) 1.

REFERENCES

Note: Statutes, regulations, agency guidance, and international standards are listed separately in the Table of Legal Sources. Certain official publications, including officials' speeches, are not considered official guidance and are listed here as References.

Abrams, R. and Taylor, M., 'Issues in the unification of financial sector supervision' (1 December 2000), IMF Working Paper WP/00/213.

Acharya, V. and Richardson, M., 'Causes of the financial crisis' (2010), 21 *Critical Review* 198.

Adam, S., Ho, Y., and Sam, C., 'How the 1MDB scandal led to Goldman's first criminal charges', *Bloomberg* (21 December 2018).

Adisa, B., 'AML de-risking: an effective method of plugging AML control failures?', Association of Certified Anti-Money Laundering Specialists (August 2014).

Adoboli, K., 'How to stop finance companies succumbing to cultural failure', *Financial Times* (12 March 2017).

Adrian, T. and Shin, H., 'The changing nature of financial intermediation and the financial crisis of 2007–09' (April 2010), FRBNY Staff Report No. 439.

Afonso, G., Santos, J., and Traina, J., 'Do "too-big-to-fail" banks take on more risk?' (December 2014), *FRBNY Economic Policy Review*.

Akhtar, T., 'Moody's: threat of blockchain and cryptocurrencies is distant but inevitable', *Bitcoin Magazine* (24 October 2017).

Akmeemana, C. and others, 'Using blockchain to solve regulatory and compliance requirements', *Medium* (23 January 2017).

Allen, F. and Gale, D., 'Financial contagion' (2000), 108(1) *Journal of Political Economy* 1.

Allen, F. and others, 'Enhancing prudential standards in financial institutions' (3 December 2014), Federal Reserve Bank of Philadelphia.

Allen, L., Boudoukh, J., and Saunders, A., *Understanding Market, Credit, and Operational Risk: The Value at Risk Approach* (Blackwell: 2004).

Antonovici, A., 'DTCC, BNP Paribas, SIX Group shelve blockchain pilots', *Cryptovest* (28 March 2018).

'Appendix C: History of the Bank Secrecy Act' (16 October 2016), American Banking Association, at <www.aba.com/Compliance/Documents/BSA-AppendixC.pdf>.

Association for Financial Markets in Europe, 'Impact of Regulation on Banks' Capital Markets Activities: An ex-post assessment' (April 2018).

Avraham, D., Selvaggi, P., and Vickery, J., 'A structural view of U.S. bank holding companies' (July 2012), *FRBNY Economic Policy Review*.

Baer, J., 'How one Goldman Sachs trader made more than $100 Million', *Wall Street Journal* (19 October 2016).

Baer, M., 'Governing corporate compliance' (2016), 50 *Boston College Law Review* 949.

Baily, M., Elliott, D., and Swagel, P., 'The big bank theory: breaking down the breakup arguments' (31 October 2014), Brookings Institution, Economic Policy Program.

Bainbridge, S., 'Caremark and enterprise risk management' (March 2009) 34 *Journal of Corporation Law* 967.

_____, *Corporate Governance After the Financial Crisis* (OUP: 2012).

_____, *Corporation Law and Economics* (Foundation Press: 2002).

Balls, E. and Stansbury, A., 'Twenty years on: is there still a case for Bank of England independence?' (1 May 2017), VOX CEPR Policy Portal.

Bank for International Settlements, 'History of the Basel Committee' (April 2018), at <www.bis.org/bcbs/history.htm>.

_____, *64th Annual Report* (1994).

Basel Committee on Banking Supervision, 'Basel Committee finalises capital treatment for bilateral counterparty credit risk' (1 June 2011), Press Release, at <www.bis.org/press/p110601.pdf>.

Baxter, L., 'Administrative and judicial review of prompt corrective action decisions by the federal banking regulators' (1993), 7 *Administrative Law Journal* 505.

Becker, D. and others, 'Know your customer: designing an effective anti-money laundering plan' (2002), American Corporate Counsel Association/Global Corporate Counsel Association (2002).

Belgum, K., 'Dodd-Frank Act alters preemption rules for national banks and federal thrifts', Nixon Peabody (28 July 2010), at <www.nixonpeabody.com/en/ideas/articles/2010/07/28/dodd-frank-act-alters-preemption-rules-for-national-banks-and-federal-thrifts>.

Ben-Shahar, O. and Schneider, C., *More Than You Wanted to Know: The Failure of Mandated Disclosure* (Princeton University Press: 2014).

Berger, A., Herring, R., and Szegö, G., 'The role of capital in financial institutions' (1995), 19 *Journal of Banking & Finance* 393.

'Bernanke Defends Bear Stearns Bailout', *CBS News* (3 April 2008).

Bernanke, B. and Gertler, M., 'Agency costs, net worth, and business fluctuations' (March 1989) 79 *American Economic Review* 14.

_____, 'The real effects of disrupted credit: evidence from the global financial crisis' (13 September 2018), Brookings Papers on Economic Activity, Brookings Institution.

Black, J., 'The rise, fall and fate of principles based regulation' (2010), LSE Law, Society and Economy Working Papers 17/2010.

Boston Consulting Group, 'Global risk 2017: staying the course in banking' (March 2017), at <http://image-src.bcg.com/BCG_COM/BCG-Staying-the-Course-in-Banking-Mar-2017_tcm9-146794.pdf>.

Boughey, S., 'The three lines of defense – a Sisyphean labor?', *Risk.net* (31 October 2017).

Boylan, M., 'Overview of federal bank enforcement actions', *Venable LLP* (15 February 2012), at <www.venable.com/insights/publications/2012/02/overview-of-federal-bank-enforcement-actions>.

Brunnermeier, M., 'Deciphering the liquidity and credit crunch 2007–2008' (Winter 2009) 23 *Journal of Economic Perspectives* 77.

_____, M. and others, *The Fundamental Principles of Financial Regulation* (Princeton University Press: 2009).

Burne, K., 'Tarullo says shadow banking risks could reappear', *Wall Street Journal* (21 October 2016).

Burns, A., 'Managing change effectively' (14 March 2016), Consumer Affairs Update, Federal Reserve Bank of Minneapolis, at <www.minneapolisfed.org/publications/banking-in-the-ninth/managing-change-effectively>.

Calomiris, C., 'The uncertain dangers of the Volcker rule', American Enterprise Institute (22 July 2013).

Carnell, R., 'A partial antidote to perverse incentives: the FDICIA Improvement Act of 1991' (1993), 12 *Annual Review of Banking Law* 317.

Carnell, R., Macey, J., and Miller, G., *Law of Financial Institutions* (Wolters Kluwer: 2013).

Carney, M., 'The future of financial reform', 2014 Monetary Authority of Singapore Lecture (17 November 2014).

Cecchetti, S. and Schoenholtz, K., 'Primers', *Money, Banking, and Financial Markets*, at <www.moneyandbanking.com/primers/>.

_____, 'Conflicts of Interest in Finance' (12 January 2015), *Money, Banking, and Financial Markets*, at <www.moneyandbanking.com/commentary/2015/1/12/conflicts-of-interest-in-finance>.

Cetorelli, N., McAndrews, J., and Traina, J., 'Evolution in bank complexity' (December 2014), *FBRNY Economic Policy Review*.

Cetorelli, N., Mandel, B., and Mollineaux, L., 'The evolution of banks and financial intermediation: framing the analysis' (July 2012), *FRBNY Economic Policy Review*.

Charette, R., 'Chapter 15: Enterprise risk management – supplemental material' 2, in P. Simon, *The Next Wave of Technologies: Opportunities in Chaos* (Wiley: 2010).

Choudhry, M., *The Principles of Banking* (Wiley: 2012).

Coates, J., 'The Volcker rule as structural law: implications for cost-benefit analysis and administrative law' (2015), 10(4) *Capital Markets Law Journal* 447.

Coleman, T., *A Practical Guide to Risk Management* (Research Foundation of CFA Institute: 8 July 2011).

Collison, D. and others, 'Shareholder primacy in UK corporate law', Certified Accountants Educational Trust (2011).

Committee of Sponsoring Organizations of the Treadway Commission, 'Enterprise Risk Management – An Integrated Framework: Executive Summary' (September 2004).

_____, 'Enterprise Risk Management: Understanding and Communicating Risk Appetite' (January 2012).

_____, 'Internal Control – Integrated Framework' (1992).

Committee on the Global Financial System, 'Structural changes in banking after the crisis', Bank for International Settlements (January 2018).

Copeland, A., 'Evolution and heterogeneity among larger bank holding companies: 1994 to 2010' (July 2012), *FRBNY Economic Policy Review*.

Coppola, F., 'Deutsche Bank: a sinking ship?', *Forbes* (2016).

Covitz, D., Liang, N., and Suarez, G., 'The evolution of a financial crisis: panic in the asset-backed commercial paper market', Finance and Economics Discussion Series, Federal Reserve Board (18 August 2009).

Crabb, J., 'PRIMER: a comparison of EU and US bank resolution regimes' (20 November 2018), *International Financial Law Review*.

Crouhy, M. and Galai, D., *The Essentials of Risk Management* (McGraw-Hill Education: 2014).

Cunningham, L., 'A prescription to retire the rhetoric of "principles-based systems" in corporate law, securities regulation and accounting' (2007), 60 *Vanderbilt Law Review* 1411.

Dab, S. and others, 'How banks can thrive as digital payments grow', Boston Consulting Group (21 December 2017), at <www.bcg.com/publications/2017/banks-thrive-digital-payments-grow.aspx>.

Davis, B., 'What's a global recession?', *Wall Street Journal* (22 April 2009).

Department of Justice, 'BNP Paribas agrees to plead guilty and to pay $8.9 billion for illegally processing financial transactions for countries subject to U.S. economic sanctions' (30 June 2014), Press Release.

_____, 'Deputy Attorney General Rod Rosenstein delivers remarks to the New York City Bar White Collar Crime Institute' (9 May 2018), Press Release.

Department of the Treasury, 'Blueprint for a modernized financial regulatory structure' (March 2008).

_____, 'A financial system that creates economic opportunities: banks and credit unions' (June 2017).

di Florio, C., 'Conflicts of interest and risk governance', Speech before National Society of Compliance Professionals (22 October 2012), at <www.sec.gov/news/speech/2012-spch103112cvdhtm>.

Drucker, P., 'Managing for business effectiveness' (May 1963), *Harvard Business Review*, at <https://hbr.org/1963/05/managing-for-business-effectiveness>.

Dudley, W., 'Opening remarks at reforming culture and behavior in the financial services industry: expanding the dialogue' (20 October 2016), at <www.newyorkfed.org/newsevents/speeches/2016/dud161020>.

_____, 'U.S. experience with bank stress tests', Remarks at the Group of 30 plenary meeting, Bern, Switzerland (28 May 2011), at <www.newyorkfed.org/newsevents/speeches/2011/dud110627>.

Duffie, D., 'Prone to fail: the pre-crisis financial system' (8 December 2018) Hoover Institution, Economics Working Paper No. 18120.

Eavis, P., 'How regulators mess with bankers' minds, and why that's good', *New York Times* (14 April 2016).

Edwards, F. and Mishkin, F., 'The decline of traditional banking: implications for financial stability and regulatory policy'(July 1995), *FRBNY Economic Policy Review*.

Ellul, A. and Yerramilli, V., 'Stronger risk controls, lower risk: evidence from U.S. bank holding companies' (October 2013), 68 *Journal of Finance* 1757.

Ethics Resource Center, *The Federal Sentencing Guidelines for Organizations at Twenty Years* (2012), Ethics Resource Center's Independent Advisory Group.

European Central Bank, 'What is a deposit guarantee scheme?' (11 April 2018), at <www.ecb.europa.eu/explainers/tell-me-more/html/deposit_guarantee.en.html>.

European Council and Council of the European Union, 'Single supervisory mechanism', at <www.consilium.europa.eu/en/policies/banking-union/single-supervisory-mechanism/>.

Farrell, L., 'Making "three lines of defense" work: coordination, cooperation, and communication, for a start', *Banking Exchange* (11 June 2015).

'Final Market Risk Capital Rule', Practical Law, Article No. 8–522–3223 (16 November 2012).

'Financial Institution Risk Management Issues' (January 2014), Advisen Insurance Intelligence, White Paper.

Financial Services Authority, 'The Turner Review: a regulatory response to the global banking crisis' (March 2009).

Financial Stability Board, 'Thematic review on risk governance: peer review report' (12 February 2013), at <www.fsb.org/wp-content/uploads/r_130212.pdf>.

Finch, G., 'World's biggest banks fined $321 billion since financial crisis', *Bloomberg* (1 March 2017).

Foerster, J. and Onaran, Y., 'Deutsche Bank to settle U.S. mortgage probe for $7.2 billion', *Bloomberg* (23 December 2016).

Ford, C., 'Principles-based securities regulation in the wake of the global financial crisis' (July 2010), 55 *McGill Law Journal* 257.

Frame, W., Gerardi, K., and Willen, P., 'The failure of supervisory stress testing: Fannie Mae, Freddie Mac, and OFHEO', Federal Reserve Bank of Atlanta, Working Papers Series, 2015-3 (March 2015).

Frantz, P. and Instefjord, N., 'Rules vs principles based financial regulation' (25 November 2014), at <https://ssrn.com/abstract=2561370>.

Freixas, X., Laeven, L., and Peydró, J., *Systemic Risk, Crises, and Macroprudential Regulation* (MIT Press: 2015).

French, K. and others, *The Squam Lake Report: Fixing the Financial System* (Princeton University Press: 2010).

Furfine, C., 'Interbank exposures: quantifying the risk of contagion' (2003), 35 *Journal of Money, Credit, and Banking* 111.

Geithner, T., 'Risk management challenges in the US financial system' (28 February 2006), Speech before the Global Association of Risk Professionals, at <www.bis.org/review/r060303a.pdf>.

_____, *Stress Test: Reflections on Financial Crises* (Broadway Books: 2014).

Gelzinis, G. and Valenti, J., 'Fact sheet: the Senate's bipartisan Dodd-Frank rollback bill' (28 February 2018), Center for American Progress, at <www.americanprogress.org/issues/economy/reports/2018/02/28/447264/fact-sheet-senates-bipartisan-dodd-frank-rollback-bill/>.

_____, 'The Fed's proposed stress testing changes are a mixed bag', Center for American Progress (20 March 2018).

Goodhart, C. and others, *Financial Regulation: Why, How, and Where Now?* (Routledge: 1998).

Goodhart, C., 'The organizational structure of banking supervision' (February 2002), 31(2) *Economic Notes: Review of Banking, Finance and Monetary Economics* 1.

Gorton, G. and Metrick, A., 'Haircuts' (November–December 2010), *Federal Reserve Bank of St. Louis Review* 507.

Gorton, G., 'Slapped in the face by the invisible hand: banking and the panic of 2007' (9 May 2009), at <https://papers.ssrn.com/sol3/papers.cfm?abstract_id=1401882>.

Griffith, S., 'Corporate governance in an era of compliance' (2016), 57 *William & Mary Law Review* 2075.

'Guidelines for counter money laundering policies and procedures in correspondent banking' (March 2002), The New York Clearing House Association L.L.C., at <http://216.55.97.163/wp-content/themes/bcb/download.php?file=http://216.55.97.163/wp-content/themes/bcb/bdf/law/usa/Procedures_in_Correpond_Banking.pdf>.

'Guiding principles for anti-money laundering policies and procedures in correspondent banking' (February 2016), The Clearing House, at <www.theclearinghouse.org/-/media/new/tch/documents/payment-systems/chips-tch-aml-correspondent-banking-guiding-principles-2016.pdf>.

Guldimann, T., 'The creator of VaR explains how large banks measure the risk of their own portfolios' (25 June 2018), *Odd Lots*, podcast with Joe Wiesenthal and Tracy Alloway, at <https://podcasts.apple.com/us/podcast/creator-var-explains-how-large-banks-measure-risk-their/id1056200096?i=1000414564268>.

Guynn, R. and Kenadjian, P., 'Structural solutions: blinded by Volcker, Vickers, Liikanen, Glass Steagall and narrow banking', Davis Polk & Wardwell LLP (19 March 2015), at <www.davispolk.com/files/52559206_1.pdf>.

REFERENCES

Haldane, A., 'The dog and the frisbee', Speech given at Federal Reserve Bank of Kansas City's 36th Economic Policy Symposium, 'The Changing Policy Landscape' (31 August 2012).

_____, 'Capital Discipline' (9 January 2011), Speech to American Economic Association, at <www.bis.org/review/r110325a.pdf>.

Hamilton, R., 'Failure of Continental Illinois' (22 November 2013), Federal Reserve Bank of Richmond, at <www.federalreservehistory.org/essays/failure_of_continental_illinois>.

Heineman, B., 'Too big to manage: JP Morgan and the mega banks', *Harvard Business Review* (3 October 2013), at <https://hbr.org/2013/10/too-big-to-manage-jp-morgan-and-the-mega-banks>.

Hinkel, T., 'CAMELS ratings and financial regulatory reform: the (m)anagement element' (12 August 2010), *Safe Systems Newsletter*.

Hinterseer, K., *Criminal Finance: The Political Economy of Money Laundering in a Comparative Legal Context* (Kluwer Law International: 1989).

Independent Directors of the Board of Wells Fargo & Company: Sales Practices Investigation Report', Shearman & Sterling (10 April 2017), at <https://www08.wellsfargomedia.com/assets/pdf/about/investor-relations/presentations/2017/board-report.pdf>.

Institute of Internal Auditors, 'IIA position paper: the three lines of defense in effective risk management and control' (January 2013).

_____, 'Leveraging COSO across the three lines of defense' (July 2015).

_____, 'Attribute standards 1100 – independence and objectivity' (2017).

Institute of International Finance, 'Regtech in financial services: solutions for compliance and reporting' (22 March 2016).

Institute of Risk Management, 'A risk management standard' (2002), at <www.theirm.org/media/886059/ARMS_2002_IRM.pdf>.

International Organization for Standardization, 'International standard 31000: risk management – principles and guidelines' (2009).

'Issue brief: federal preemption and oversight in banking', Office of Legislative Research (7 September 2017), at <www.cga.ct.gov/2017/rpt/pdf/2017-R-0018.pdf>.

Jackson, H., 'The expanding obligations of financial holding companies' (1994), 107 *Harvard Law Review* 507.

Jones, H., 'Basel eases capital hit from new trading book rules for banks', *Reuters* (14 January 2019).

_____, 'EU scraps its answer to U.S. Volcker rule for banks', *Reuters* (24 October 2017).

Jorion, P., 'Risk management lessons from the credit crisis' (2009), at <https://merage.uci.edu/~jorion/papers/RiskMgtCreditCrisis.pdf>.

Kaiser, R., *Act of Congress: How America's Essential Institution Works and How It Doesn't* (Vintage: 2014).

Kaplan, R. and Mikes, A., 'Risk management – the revealing hand' (Winter 2016), 28 *Journal of Applied Corporate Finance* 8.

Kashyap, A., Rajan, R., and Stein, J., 'Rethinking capital regulation' (12 March 2008), 2008 Economic Symposium, 'Maintaining Stability in a Changing Financial System', Federal Reserve Bank of Kansas City.

Kashyap, A., Tsomocos, D., and Vardoulakis, A., 'Principles for macroprudential regulation' (April 2014), *Financial Stability Review* No. 18, 173.

Kaufman G. and others, *Perspectives on Safe & Sound Banking: Past, Present, and Future* (MIT Press: 1986).

Kaufman, G., 'Too big to fail in banking: what does it mean?' (2014), 13 *Journal of Financial Stability* 214.

Kohn, D., 'Commentary: has financial development made the world riskier?' (2005), Federal Reserve Bank of Kansas City.

Korobkin, R., 'Behavioral analysis and legal form: rules vs. standards revisited' (2000), 79 *Oregon Law Review* 23.

KPMG, 'Compliance management systems: consumer protection transforming risk management' (2013), at <https://advisory.kpmg.us/content/dam/advisory/en/pdfs/nss-consumer-finance-reg-pov.pdf>.

Kress, J., 'Solving banking's "too big to manage" problem' (7 March 2019), [forthcoming 104 *Minnesota Law Review* 2019], 17–18, at <https://ssrn.com/abstract=3348593>.

Lee, S., 'Formula from hell', *Forbes* (9 May 2009).

Lehman Brothers 2007 Annual Report.

Liang, S. and Breeden, J., 'Keys to success in model risk management for CCAR & DFAST', Prescient Models LLC (2013), at <https://prescientmodels.com/articles/Best-Practices-in-Model-Risk-Management.pdf>.

Light, J., 'The Volcker rule: an essential reader' (10 December 2013), Moyers & Company (quoting from an interview with Bill Moyers), at <https://billmoyers.com/2013/12/10/the-volcker-rule-an-essential-reader/>.

Linsmeier, T. and Pearson, N., 'Risk measurement: an introduction to value at risk' (July 1996), Working paper 96-04, available at SSRN: <https://ssrn.com/abstract=7875>.

Lipton, M., 'Risk management and the board of directors' (20 March 2018), Harvard Law School Forum on Corporate Governance and Financial Regulation, at <https://corpgov.law.harvard.edu/2018/03/20/risk-management-and-the-board-of-directors-5/>.

Llewellyn, D., 'Institutional structure of financial regulation and supervision: the basic issues', Paper presented at World Bank seminar: Aligning Supervisory Structures with Country Needs (6–7 June 2006).

_____, 'The economic rationale for financial regulation' (April 1999), FSA Occasional Papers Series 1.

Macey, J. and O'Hara, M., 'Bank corporate governance: a proposal for the post-crisis world' (August 2016), *FRBNY Economic Policy Review*.

_____, 'The corporate governance of banks' (April 2003), *FRBNY Economic Policy Review*.

Macey, J., 'The business of banking: before and after Gramm-Leach-Bliley' (2000), 25 *Journal of Corporation Law* 691.

_____, 'The demise of the reputational model in capital markets: the problem of the "last period parasites"' (2010), 60 *Syracuse Law Review* 427.

Marlin, S., 'Fed's risk proposal puts banks on the defensive: new supervisory guidance will make business heads responsible for risk management', *Risk.net* (2 April 2018).

_____, 'Bank risk committees: desperately seeking risk managers', *Risk.net* (27 June 2018).

Masters, B., 'FSA to give way to "twin peaks" system', *Financial Times* (1 April 2013).

Mauboussin, M. and Rappaport, A., 'Reclaiming the idea of shareholder value' (1 July 2016), *Harvard Business Review*, at <https://hbr.org/2016/07/reclaiming-the-idea-of-shareholder-value>.

Merriam Webster Dictionary, at <https://www.merriam-webster.com/dictionary>.

Michaels, D., Davidson, A., and Schechner, S., 'Facebook confronts bipartisan resistance to cryptocurrency plans', *Wall Street Journal* (16 July 2019).

Migueis, M., 'Is operational risk regulation forward-looking and sensitive to current risks?' (21 May 2018), FEDS Notes, at <https://doi.org/10.17016/2380-7172.2198>.

Miller, G., 'An economic analysis of effective compliance programs' (December 2014), New York University Law and Economics Working Papers 396.

———, 'Banking's cultural revolution', Compliance and Enforcement, New York University (8 June 2016), at <https://wp.nyu.edu/compliance_enforcement/2016/06/08/bankings-cultural-revolution/>.

Mishkin, F., 'Prudential supervision: why is it important and what are the issues?' (September 2000), 28 NBER Working Papers No. 7926.

———, *The Economics of Money, Banking, and Financial Markets* 298 (Pearson, 10th ed.: 2013).

Morgan, J., 'Dirty names, dangerous money: alleged unilateralism in U.S. policy on money laundering' (2003), 21 *Berkeley Journal of International Law* 771.

Morris, S. and Megaw, N., 'RBS drops off list of world's most important banks', *Financial Times* (16 November 2018).

Moyce, C., 'How blockchain can revolutionize regulatory compliance', Corporate Compliance Insights (10 August 2016).

Moyer, L., 'Citigroup goes it alone to rescue SIVs', *Forbes* (13 December 2007).

Nazareth, A., 'Remarks before the SIFMA compliance and legal conference' (26 March 2007), at <www.sec.gov/news/speech/2007/spch032607aln.htm>.

Nocco, B. and Stulz, R., 'Enterprise risk management: theory and practice' (Fall 2006), 18(4) *Journal of Applied Corporate Finance*.

Nocera, J., 'Risk mismanagement', *New York Times Magazine* (2 January 2009).

Nouy, D., 'Gaming the rules or ruling the game? – how to deal with regulatory arbitrage' (15 September 2017), European Central Bank, Speech at 33rd SUERF Colloquium, Helsinki.

O'Reilly, C. and Matussek, K., 'Siemens to pay $1.6 billion to settle bribery cases', *Washington Post* (16 December 2008).

Omarova, S., 'One step forward, two steps back?' 137–165, in Huang, R. and Schoenmaker, D. (eds.), *Institutional Structure of Financial Regulation* (Routledge: 2015).

Onaran, Y., 'Can we survive the next financial crisis?', *Bloomberg* (10 September 2018).

Pan, E., 'The duty to monitor under Delaware law: from Caremark to Citigroup', The Conference Board (February 2010).

Penn, B., 'Single point of entry resolution: a milestone for regulators: a millstone for banks?', Allen & Overy (5 December 2014), at <www.allenovery.com/publications/en-gb/lrrfs/uk/Pages/Single-point-of-entry-resolution.aspx>.

PwC, 'A closer look: US Basel III regulatory capital regime and market risk final rule' (July 2012).

———, 'Resolution: single point of entry strategy ascends' (July 2015).

Rajan, R., 'Has financial development made the world riskier?' (2005), Federal Reserve Bank of Kansas City.

Raman, A., 'CFPB defines "unfair," "deceptive" and "abusive" practices through enforcement activity', Skadden's 2015 Insights – Financial Regulation (January 2015), at <www.skadden.com/insights/publications/2015/01/cfpb-defines-unfair-deceptive-and-abusive-practice>.

Rappeport, A. and Appelbaum, B., 'A tale of two Washingtons awaits Wall Street banks', *New York Times* (9 November 2018).

Reinhart, C. and Rogoff, K., *This Time Is Different: Eight Centuries of Financial Folly* (Princeton University Press: 2009).

Rexrode, C. and Rudegeair, P., 'Nobody says 'zelle me': banks struggle to catch up to Venmo', *Wall Street Journal* (31 July 2018).

Richardson, M., 'Why the Volcker rule is a useful tool for managing systemic risk' (February 2012), at <www.sec.gov/comments/s7-41-11/s74111-316.pdf>.

Riewe, J., 'Conflicts, conflicts everywhere – remarks to the IA watch 17th annual IA compliance conference: the full 360 view' (26 February 2015), at <www.sec.gov/news/speech/conflicts-everywhere-full-360-view.html>.

Rosengren, E., 'Defining financial stability, and some policy implications of applying the definition' (3 June 2011), Keynote remarks at the Stanford Finance Forum, Graduate School of Business, Stanford University, at <https://www.bostonfed.org/news-and-events/speeches/defining-financial-stability-and-some-policy-implications-of-applying-the-definition.aspx >.

Rubin, G., 'U.S. markets regulator considers buyouts, extension of hiring freeze', *Wall Street Journal* (8 May 2018).

Ryan, D., 'Board governance: higher expectations, but better practices?', PwC (January 2016).

Salmon, F., 'The biggest weakness of Basel III', *Reuters* (15 September 2010).

Salz, A. and Collins, R., 'Salz review: an independent review of Barclays' business practices' (Barclays PLC: April 2013).

Sarin, N. and Summers, L., 'Understanding bank risk through market measures' (Fall 2016), Brookings Papers on Economic Activity 57, at <www.brookings.edu/wp-content/uploads/2017/02/sarintextfall16bpea.pdf>.

Schanzenbach, D. and others, 'Nine facts about the great recession and tools for fighting the next downturn' (May 2016), The Hamilton Project, Brookings Institution.

Schnabel, I., 'Europe's banking union lacks the key element of deposit insurance', *Financial Times* (28 August 2018).

Scott, H., *Connectedness and Contagion: Protecting the Financial System from Panics* (MIT Press: 2016).

Secrist, A-J, 'The link between risk management and compliance', *Lexology* (30 October 2013).

Securities Industry and Financial Markets Association, *The Evolving Role of Compliance* (March 2013).

Senior Supervisors Group, 'Observations on risk management practices during the recent market turbulence' (6 March 2008), at <www.occ.treas.gov/publications/publications-by-type/other-publications-reports/pub-other-risk-mgt-practices-2008.pdf>.

Shearman & Sterling, 'Basel III framework: US/EU comparison' (17 September 2013), Client Publication.

Shubber, K., 'Banks find blockchain hard to put into practice', *Financial Times* (12 September 2016).

Silver-Greenberg, J. and Protess, B., 'Bank regulators under scrutiny in JPMorgan loss', *New York Times* (25 May 2012).

Single Resolution Board, Resolution Q&A, at https://srb.europa.eu/en/content/resolution-qa (2018).

Skeel, D., *The New Financial Deal* (Wiley: 2010).

Soltes, E., 'Evaluating the effectiveness of corporate compliance programs: establishing a model for prosecutors, courts, and firms' (Summer 2018), *Journal of Law & Business* 965.

Stefanyszyn, D. and Detchemendy, J., 'Managing compliance risk through consumer compliance risk assessments', *Consumer Compliance Outlook* (Fourth Quarter 2014), at

<https://consumercomplianceoutlook.org/2014/fourth-quarter/managing-compliance-risk-through-consumer-compliance-risk-assessments/>.

Stevenson, R., 'G.A.O. puts cost of S.&L. bailout at half a trillion dollars', *New York Times* (13 July 1996).

Storbeck, O., 'Deutsche Bank takes minority stake in payments fintech ModoPayments', *Financial Times* (24 August 2018).

Sullivan & Cromwell, 'Volcker rule' (27 January 2014), at <www.sullcrom.com/siteFiles/Publications/SC_Publication_Volcker_Rule.pdf>.

Sum, K., 'The factors influencing the EU banking regulatory framework: impediments for the new regulations' in K. Sum, *Post-Crisis Banking Regulation in the European Union* (Springer: 12 October 2016).

Tarullo, D., *Banking on Basel: The Future of International Financial Regulation* (Peterson Institute: 2008).

_____, 'The evolution of capital regulation' (9 November 2011), Clearing House Business Meeting and Conference, at <www.federalreserve.gov/newsevents/speech/files/tarullo20111109a.pdf>.

Taylor, M., 'Regulatory reform after the financial crisis: twin peaks revisited', in Huang, R. and Schoenmaker, D. (eds.), *Institutional Structure of Financial Regulation* (Routledge: 2015).

Tooze, A., *Crashed: How a Decade of Financial Crises Changed the World* (Viking: 2018).

Townsend, A., 'Hector Sants says bankers should be 'very frightened' by the FSA', *The Telegraph* (12 March 2009).

Tully, S., 'How J.P. Morgan steered clear of the credit crunch', *Fortune* (2 September 2008).

UBS AG, 'Shareholder report on UBS's write-downs' (18 April 2008), at <http://maths-fi.com/ubs-shareholder-report.pdf>.

VanHoose, D., 'Systemic risks and macroprudential bank regulation: a critical appraisal' (April 2011), Networks Financial Institute, Indiana University, 2011-PB-04.

Vickers, J., 'Banking reform in Britain and Europe', Paper presented at Rethinking Macro Policy II: First Steps and Early Lessons Conference (16–17 April 2013), at <www.imf.org/external/np/seminars/eng/2013/macro2/pdf/jv2.pdf>.

Volcker, P., 'Commentary on the restrictions on proprietary trading by insured depository institutions' (13 February 2012), at <https://online.wsj.com/public/resources/documents/Volcker_Rule_Essay_2-13-12.pdf>.

Walker, R., 'Board oversight of a compliance program: the implications of *Stone v. Ritter*', at <www.corporatecompliance.org/Portals/1/731_1_stone-v-ritter_walker.pdf>.

Wallinson, P., 'Fad or reform: can principles-based regulation work in the United States?' (June 2007), American Enterprise Institute.

Walter, I., 'Conflicts of interest and market discipline among financial services firms' (August 2004), 22(4) *European Management Journal* 362.

_____, *The Secret Money Market: Inside the Dark World of Tax Evasion, Financial Fraud, Insider Trading, Money Laundering, and Capital Flight* (Harpcr Collins: 1990).

Waters, R. and Thornhill, J., 'Quantum computing: the power to think outside the box', *Financial Times* (3 September 2018).

Werdigier, J., 'After $43 billion in write-downs, UBS to split main businesses', *New York Times* (12 August 2008).

Wolcott, R., 'Time to merge risk management and compliance?', *Reuters* (5 April 2012).

INDEX

3LOD (three lines of defense): BCBS adoption 80; BUCOs (business line compliance officers) 82; business management, criticism by 82; control functions' lack of expertise 82–83; first-line 81–82; generally 80–83; internal audit's strong independence 83; MRM (model risk management) 82; risk management and compliance 81–82; second line 82; skewed risk-taking 81; third line 82–83

accounting leverage: defined 113
advanced internal ratings-based approach *see* credit risk capital rule, advanced approaches banks
adverse selection: causes skewed risks and rewards 26; created by safety net 142; created by TBTF 26–27; defined 23n30; facing banks 23–24; facing government 24 *Table 1.1*, 26; mitigation through chartering 139
A-IRB (advanced internal ratings-based approach) *see* credit risk capital rule, advanced approaches banks
ALM (asset liability management): ALM committee 22; risk management remit 22
American International Group *see* American International Group (AIG)
American International Group (AIG): FSOC designation and rescission 178n91; regulatory arbitrage 44n27
AML/CFT compliance program: banks' business model, paradox 252, 260–261; BCBS guidance 258–260; beneficial ownership rule 258; CDD (customer due diligence) 12, 62, 250, 257–258; CIP (customer identification program) 257; compliance risk-return optimization 260–261; consolidated

risk management 259–260; DPAs (deferred prosecution agreements) 261; enhanced customer due diligence 257–259; financial conglomerates 261; foreign correspondent accounts 258; 'four pillars' 251; KYC ('know your customer') 12, 62 *Table 2.2*, 253, 257, 268; PEP (politically exposed person) 259, 259n35; RegTech benefits 268–269; technical challenges 253
AML/CFT law and regulation: beneficial ownership rule 258; CTRs (currency transaction reports) 255–256; FATF (Financial Action Task Force) 253, 258; FinCEN (Financial Crimes Enforcement Network) 255–256, 258; foreign correspondent banks 255; foreign shell banks 255; KYC ('know your customer') 12, 62 *Table 2.2*, 253, 257, 268; law's evolution 254–255; liability 249, 251; OFAC (Office of Foreign Assets Control) 255, 255n17, 258, 261; Patriot Act 254–255; predicate crimes 250–251; private banking accounts 255; regulatory framework, general 253–260; regulatory paradox 252–253; reporting and recordkeeping 255–256; risk-based approach 253n9; SAR (Suspicious Activity Report) 254–257; suspicious activity, defined 256; suspicious activity monitoring 253–254
asset liability management *see* ALM (asset liability management)
audit committee 73

bail-in 11, 211, 218–219
bailouts 15, 26–27, 138, 163–165, 173–174, 176, 193, 211–212
bank compliance function: banking expertise 84; close relations with

FFIEC (Federal Financial Institutions Examination Council): creation 53–54, 152; HMDA reports provided to 240; uniform rating system, rationale 54

FHA (Fair Housing Act) 239, 239n44

FHCs (financial holding companies): activities 220n40; creation and regulation 32–33, 220; nearly all BHCs use 51; qualification 51n61; *see also* Gramm-Leach (Gramm-Leach-Bliley Financial Services Modernization Act in 1999)

fiduciary duty: agent's 69; board's duty of care 71; board's duty of loyalty 71; board's generally 71; conflicting duties of bank and BHC boards 74–75; high standard of liability 88–90; *see also* compliance obligations, state law and federal prosecution

Financial Action Task Force *see* FATF (Financial Action Task Force)

Financial Conduct Authority *see* FCA (Financial Conduct Authority)

financial conglomerates: emergence 28–36; entry into non-banking 29, 31, 32; FHC legal structure 220n40; FinTech space, competition in 265; increase in complexity 33–34; increasing concentration 35; restriction by Volcker rule 220; securitization, role in 29–31

financial crises: banking crises, a subset 160–161; banking panics 166; deep recessions, associated with 175–176; fire sales, a cause of 166; Great Recession 175–176; *see also* banking crises; shadow banks

Financial Policy Committee *see* FPC (Financial Policy Committee)

Financial Services Authority *see* FSA (Financial Services Authority)

financial stability objective *see* regulatory objectives, financial

Financial Stability Oversight Council *see* FSOC (Financial Stability Oversight Council)

financing of terrorism *see* FT (financing of terrorism)

FinCEN (Financial Crimes Enforcement Network) *see* AML/CFT law and regulation

FinTech: banks' adoption to compete with 264; competitive advantages and disadvantages 265–267; defined 265; DLT, long-term threat 267; Facebook's Libra initiative 266; financial conglomerate ownership 33; financial services competition 231; payments systems space 266; RegTech 268; regulatory implications 268

fire sales *see* financial crises

first line of defense, 3LOD: role 80–82; *see also* 3LOD (three lines of defense)

FOMC: role in monetary policy 17n8

foreign banking organizations *see* FBOs (foreign banking organizations)

foreign correspondent banking *see* AML/CFT compliance program; AML/CFT law and regulation

FPC (Financial Policy Committee): UK regulation, role in 54–55; systemic risk oversight 178

fractional reserve system: liquidity risk 20

franchise value: banks 15, 169, 264, 264–265n5; financial institutions generally 2, 75; of Wells Fargo 78

FRB (Federal Reserve Board): jurisdiction and powers 49–50; lender of last resort 16, 26, 115n13, 116, 142n8, 164, 198

Freddie Mac 29, 174; *see also* conservatorship, FDIC; Fannie Mae

FRTB (Fundamental Review of Trading Book): default risk charge 137; ES (expected shortfall) approach 137; IMA (internal modeling approach) 137; IRC (incremental risk charge) 137; non-modellable risk factors 137; overview and current status 134, 134n120, 137; *see also* market risk capital rule

FSA (Financial Services Authority): backlash against its principles-based approach 57; business conduct oversight favored over prudential 55; creation 45; loss of expertise, concern 55; market-based ethos 60–61; Parliament's cricism 55n79; prudential oversight, failure 45, 54; role in UK unitified supervisory structure 43–44; superagency prior to twin-peaks 54

FSB (Financial Stability Board): BCBS oversight 42n21; business conduct risk 230, 230n5; data aggregation and reporting initiatives 190, 269; four lines of defense 80n51; future viability 270; global systemic risk monitor 178; G-SIB list publisher 195n12; resolution

regulatory concern, gaming 131; risk
management and compliance 132; risk
mitigants 131–132
Orderly Liquidation Authority *see* OLA
(Orderly Resolution Authority)
originate-and-distribute model 29–31; *see
also* credit intermediation, securitization

path-dependent regulation: Dodd-Frank's
relative permanence 269; failure of
Treasury Department's twin-peaks
proposal 53; obstacle to twin-peaks
system 45
Patriot Act (Uniting and Strengthening
America by Providing Appropriate
Tools Required to Intercept and
Obstruct Terrorism Act of 2001) *see*
AML/CFT law and regulation
payments system: banks' operation of
18–19, 250, 250n2; disruption through
counterparty failure 163; FinTech
threat 266; monitoring, AML/CFT risk
251–252
PCA (Prompt Corrective Action)
program: capital restoration plans
157–158; FDIC inspector general
loss reports 157; five PCA categories
157–158, 157 *Table 5.1*; least-
cost resolution required 157; PCA
directives 157; predetermined actions
based on capitalization thresholds
156–157; risk-based insurance
premiums 157; safeguarding FDIC
insurance fund, objective 156; tripwire
approach 156
Phase I, deficient risk management:
agency costs, as factor 168;
compensation schemes, senior
management 169; heated competition,
MBS securitization 169; hidden tail
risk, lower ranks 169; risk management
practices (2008) 172 *Table 6.1*; risky
capital structure, composition 167,
170; siloed risk management 167; VaR
gaming 169; SSG survey 170–171, 172
Table 6.1
Phase II, liquidity and credit crisis: Bear
Stearns, hedge fund bailouts 171; Bear
Stearns bailout 173; BNP Paribas, fund
redemptions halted 173; generally 171,
173–175; GSE bailouts 174; Lehman
Brothers bankruptcy 174; repos,
increased haircuts 173; SIV sponsor

bailouts 173; stressed ABCP market
171; stressed interbank lending 173;
systemic risk causes, both evidenced
174; TBTF bailouts generally 173–174;
Term Auction Facility 173
Phase III, Great Recession 175–176;
deep recessions linked to banking
crises 175; financial panic factors
indicative of steep downturn 175;
Great Recession, global 175; impact
on credit intermediation 176; need for
going concern capital 176; regulatory
response 176
'piling on': DOJ's coordination to limit
piling on 49n48; multiple prosecutions
for same offense 48–49
Pillar I: defined 61n116, 111, 119
Pillar II: defined 61n116, 111, 119;
supervisory framework 141, 147, 152,
171, 194
Pillar III: defined 61n116, 111n2,
119; disclosure of risk management
practices 114; discourages risky bets
with disclosure 114; facilitates market
discipline 119, 201n46
populist antagonism: animus against
centralized power 31, 49, 57;
engendered by GFC 163
PRA (Prudential Regulation Authority):
created 2012 54; jurisdiction and
powers 54–55
primary regulator: defined 49–50
principal-agent relationship: agency
control mechanisms 72 *Figure 3.2*;
agency costs 70; agent's fiduciary duty
69; alignment of interests, function of
business organization 69; corporations,
pervasive in 69, 69 *Figure 3.1*, 70, 72
Figure 3.2; defined 69; effect of limited
liability versus partnership 69; *see also*
USSG (US Sentencing Guidelines)
principles- and rules-based regulation:
combined 5; generally 57–63, 62 *Table
2.2*, 111, 234; post-GFC criticism in
UK 60–61; post-GFC criticism in
US 61; rules' advantages for firms
59; rules' advantages for government
58; rules as 'roadmap for fraud' 59;
rules' drawbacks for firms 60; rules'
drawbacks for government 58–59;
Volcker rule 220
privacy law *see* consumer protection law
Prompt Corrective Action program *see*

structured investment vehicle *see* SIV
(structured investment vehicle)
superregulator *see* unified supervisory
structure
supervision: defined and explained 37, 40
Supervisory Assessment of Recovery
and Resolution Preparedness *see* SRP
(Supervisory Assessment of Recovery
and Resolution Preparedness)
supervisory structure: balkanized or
fragmented in US 4, 49, 52, 178, 200,
216, 268–270; clarity in regulatory
expectations 47; Dodd-Frank's
institutional approach 53; effectiveness
in overseeing financial conglomerates
47; enforcement powers and their use
48–49; EU's institutional approach
55; functional regulation 33, 37, 41,
43 *Table 2.1*, 44–45, 47, 51; impact
on risk-return optimization analysis
46–49; independence and accountability
elements 48; institutional (entity-based)
8, 41, 43 *Table 2.1*, 44–45, 47, 52;
potential for regulatory arbitrage 46;
supervisory resources 47–48; twin-peaks
(objectives-based) 41, 41n16, 43 *Table
2.1*, 45, 47, 51, 52–55, 216, 216n19;
twin-peaks, UK's conversion to 54–55;
unified (integrated) 41, 43 *Table 2.1*, 45
supplementary leverage ratio *see* SLR
(supplementary leverage ratio)
Suspicious Activity Report *see* AML/CFT
law and regulation
SVaR (stressed VaR) *see* market risk
capital rule
systemically important financial institution
see SIFI (systemically important
financial institution)
systemic risk: contagion, as cause
161–162; 'domino effect', synonymous
to interconnectedness 162;
interconnectedness, as cause 161–162;
two causes of 161–163; *see also* contagion

tail risk: board's difficulty in assessing
168; communicating to board,
challenges 168; compensation schemes
168; defined and described 168;
embedded tail risk 168
TBTF (too big to fail): bailouts, alteration
of creditor priorities 164; bailouts, anti-
competitive effects 164–165; bailouts,
resource misallocation 165; bailouts in

GFC 173–174; concentrated in financial
sector 164–165; concept analyzed
163–165; Dodd-Frank, internalization
of TBTF firms' risks 176–178; EU's
centralized oversight related to 2,
56–57; *ex post* structural regulation
212–217; failure of Continental Illinois
National Bank, origination of term 159;
GFC's contribution to TBTF debate
165; Lehman bankruptcy, inconsistent
approach 164; limits on exposure to
SIFIs 139; moral hazard, cause of 24
Table 1.1, 163–165; types of TBTF
resolution 164
third line of defense, 3LOD 81, 82–83;
see also 3LOD (three lines of defense)
three lines of defense *see* 3LOD (three
lines of defense)
three-peaks supervisory structure 41n16
TILA (Truth in Lending Act): generally
241–242; risk management and
compliance 241–242
TISA (Truth in Savings Act) 242–243
TLAC (Total Loss-Absorbing Capacity):
capital and debt requirements 213–214,
213n7; clean holding company
requirements 214, 214n11; risk
management and compliance 214–215;
rules-principles classification 62 *Table
2.2*, 213–215
tone at the top 84, 106, 239, 262; *see*
corporate culture
too big to fail *see* TBTF (too big to fail)
trading book *see* market risk capital rule
twin-peaks supervisory structure *see*
supervisory structure
two-tier board of directors *see* board of
directors
Type 1 and Type 2 COIs *see* COIs
(conflicts of interest), identification

UDAAPs law *see* consumer protection law
UK regulatory and supervisory structure
54–55
unified supervisory structure: failure in
UK 45, 54; *see also* superregulator;
supervisory structure
'unknown' risk: defined 100; role in risk
management 100; *see also* 'known' risk
US Sentencing Guidelines *see* USSG (US
Sentencing Guidelines)
USSG (US Sentencing Guidelines):
conditions for compliance 'credit' 92–93;

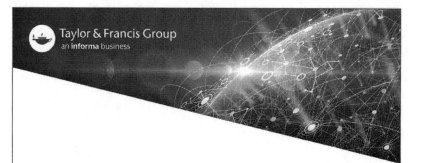